TRADITION IN AN UNTRAD

By the same author

Tradition in Transition (1987)
Traditional Alternatives (1988)

TRADITION
IN AN
UNTRADITIONAL
AGE

Essays on Modern Jewish Thought

JONATHAN SACKS

VALLENTINE, MITCHELL

First published in 1990 in Great Britain by
Vallentine, Mitchell & Co. Ltd
Gainsborough House, Gainsborough Road,
London E11 1RS

and in the United States of America by
Vallentine, Mitchell
c/o International Specialized Book Services, Inc.
5602 N.E. Hassalo Street, Portland, Oregon 97213

Copyright © 1990 Jonathan Sacks

British Library Cataloguing in Publication Data

Sacks, Jonathan
 Tradition in an untraditional age: essays on modern Jewish thought.
 1. Jewish thought
 I. Title
 181'.06

 ISBN 0-85303-239-4 (cased)
 ISBN 0-85303-240-8 (pbk)

Library of Congress Cataloging-in-Publication Data

  Tradition in an untraditional age : essays on modern Jewish thought / Jonathan Sacks.
      p.   cm.
   Includes bibliographical references.
   ISBN 0-85303-239-4 (cased)
   ISBN 0-85303-240-8 (pbk)
      1. Orthodox Judaism. 2. Judaism—20th century. I. Title
   II. Title: Modern Jewish thought.
   BM565.S22   1990
   296'.09'04—dc20   89-24960
                                                                    CIP

All rights reserved. No part of this publication may be reproduced in any form or by any means, electronic, mechanical, photocopying, recording or otherwise, without the prior permission of Vallentine, Mitchell and Company Limited.

Printed and bound in Great Britain by
BPCC Wheatons Ltd, Exeter

Dedicated to the memory of the late
Louis Mintz [1908-1987]
Yehudah Aryeh ben Yisrael Yitzchak
philanthropist, friend, and tireless fighter
for the cause of Jewish unity.
May his memory be a blessing.

CONTENTS

Acknowledgements ix
1. Introduction xi

RESPONSES TO MODERNITY

2. Samson Raphael Hirsch: Conditional Coexistence 3
3. Abraham Isaac Kook: The Dynamic of Sanctification 19
4. Joseph B. Soloveitchik: Conflict and Creation 35
5. Tradition as Resistance 57
6. Dilemmas of Modern Orthodoxy 81
7. An Agenda of Future Jewish Thought 107

TOPICS

8. The Holocaust in Jewish Theology 139
9. Jewish-Christian Dialogue: The Ethical Dimension 161
10. Wealth and Poverty: A Jewish Analysis 183
11. The Word 'Now': Reflections on the Psychology of Teshuvah 203
12. Alienation and Faith 219

THINKERS

13. Buber's Jewishness and Buber's Judaism 247
14. The Path of Return: A Preface to the Reading of Rosenzweig 259
15. Rabbi Joseph B. Soloveitchik: Halakhic Man 267
16. Rabbi Joseph B. Soloveitchik's Early Epistemology 287

Index 303

Acknowledgements

This volume gathers together a number of papers written over a period of some fifteen years on philosophical themes. The process of reading through these and other writings led me to reflect on the progress of Orthodox thought since emancipation. I decided to set out these reflections in a new presentation which forms the first section of the book, 'Responses to Modernity'. These chapters have not appeared in print before.

Because these essays are coextensive with my involvement with Jews' College, a number of thanks are in place. Rabbi Dr. Irving Jacobs and Rabbi Dr. Sidney Leperer have been friends and colleagues over the whole of that period and have created a lively atmosphere of academic debate. Frank Levine and more recently Simon Caplan and Simon Goulden have steered the College administratively with great distinction. Adele Lew and Marilyn Redstone have helped this and other projects in countless ways, but in particular through their work on *L'Eylah*, the journal we publish in conjunction with the Office of the Chief Rabbi. Editing *L'Eylah* has been one of my great pleasures over the past few years, not least because of the way we have worked together as a team. Ezra Kahn, senior librarian of the College, has supplied my voracious appetite for books needed for research.

My thanks, too, go to Rabbi Norman Lamm and Rabbi Maurice Unterman for encouraging me in the first instance to write; to Rabbi Ivan Binstock, Rabbi Fyvish Vogel and Mr. Bobby Hill for their helpful criticism over the years; and especially to the Chief Rabbi, Lord Jakobovits, President of Jews' College and Mr. Stanley Kalms, its Chairman, for their friendship, advice and help. Above all I am indebted to my predecessor and teacher, Rabbi Dr. Nachum Rabinovitch, currently head of Yeshivat Birkat Mosheh in Ma'aleh Adumim, who inspired all those who had the privilege of studying with him by his vast and courageous vision of the power and relevance of Torah.

The following chapters have appeared in print before. 'The Holocaust in Jewish Theology' was published as part of a booklet, *The Holocaust in History and Today*, by the Yad Vashem Charitable Trust, 1988. 'Jewish-Christian Dialogue: The Ethical Dimension' appeared in *L'Eylah* 26 (Autumn 1988), 13-20. 'Wealth and Poverty: A Jewish Analysis' was published as a pamphlet by the Social Affairs Unit, London, 1985. 'The Word "Now": Reflections on the Psychology of Teshuvah' appeared in *L'Eylah* 20 (Autumn 1985), 4-9. 'Alienation and Faith' was published in *Tradition* 13:4/14:1 (Spring-Summer 1973), 137-162. 'Buber's Jewishness and Buber's Judaism' was published in *European Judaism* 12:2 (Winter 1978), 14-19. 'The Path of Return' appeared in *European Judaism* 8:1 (Winter 1973), 3-7 and was reprinted in *European Judaism* 20:2 (Winter 1986), 18-22. 'Rabbi Joseph B. Soloveitchik: Halakhic Man' appeared in *L'Eylah* 19 (Spring 1985), 36-41. 'Rabbi Joseph B. Soloveitchik's Early Epistemology' was published in *Tradition* 23:3 (Spring 1988), 75-87. My thanks to those who have given their permission for these papers to be reprinted.

1
Introduction

'Know', said Rabbi Nachman of Bratslav, 'that a person walks in life on a very narrow bridge. The most important rule is not to be afraid.' Rabbi Nachman, one of the great masters of Chassidic thought, was deeply opposed to philosophy and philosophising, yet his aphorism perfectly describes the situation of the Jewish thinker in modern times.

Modernity for Jews in Europe meant the twin processes of enlightenment and emancipation, the one intellectual, the other social and political. Both threatened Jewish continuity in fundamental ways. Emancipation involved the integration of Jews into theoretically open societies. It spelled the end of the ghetto, symbol of the segregated and partially self-governing communities in which Jews had lived throughout the middle ages. Jews were invited to participate in predominantly non-Jewish and secular society and culture. For the first time in many centuries, a question that had not hitherto needed to be asked became urgent and invited a bewildering variety of answers: what is it to be a Jew?

Emancipation itself proceeded from and was accompanied by the intellectual revolution that was the Enlightenment. Some measure of what was in store for traditional Jewish belief had already been provided by Spinoza, excommunicated by the Amsterdam Jewish community in 1656. Fourteen years later he published his *Tractatus Theologico-Politicus*. In it he argued for a conception of God according to which revelation, miracles and Providence were impossible. The Torah was a secular and fallible history of the Jewish people. The commandments were a system of national legislation which had ceased to be binding since the collapse of Jewish national autonomy sixteen centuries earlier. Spinoza spoke in the name of rational enquiry, but it was clear that from enquiry conducted on these terms, no item of Jewish faith would survive.

Throughout the nineteenth century, as Jews encountered and internalised Western European culture, it became evident that they faced a language of thought into which Judaism could not be translated without being completely transformed. Kant defined ethics as a set of universal rules. What then became of the covenant of a singular people? He spoke of man as his own moral legislator. What then became of the authority of revelation? Hegelian history relegated Judaism to a slave morality. Nietzsche's polemics portrayed Judaism as the inversion of natural values. Darwin's biology called into question the Genesis account of creation. Wellhausen's biblical criticism attacked the literary unity of the Torah. Modernity was explosively subversive of all traditions. But the Jewish experience of it, combined as it was with the impact of emancipation, was particularly sudden, acute and overwhelming.

A clear choice presented itself: either radical accommodation to new modes of thought and social interaction, or radical segregation. From the first emerged a series of revolutionary new modes of Jewish existence: Liberal, Reform and Conservative Judaisms, Yiddish and Hebrew culturalism, Jewish socialism and secular Zionism. From the second came an intense revival of traditional Jewish life in the yeshivot and Chassidic circles of Eastern Europe. The former drew heavily on the intellectual assumptions of the nineteenth century; the latter fiercely resisted exposure to them. It seemed as if to embrace modernity was to abandon tradition; to preserve tradition was to reject modernity. There were some few thinkers who attempted to mediate between the two. But they walked, in Rabbi Nachman's phrase, across a very narrow bridge.

JEWISH PHILOSOPHY AND JEWISH THOUGHT

And yet that journey must be attempted repeatedly. For many Jews, perhaps most, have resisted the either/or of modernity. Whether in Israel or the diaspora they inhabit a secular world. But they continue to identify as Jews, and seek to understand that fact by reference to the biblical and rabbinic tradition. They stand on both sides of the divide. Only if there is a bridge between them can Jewish selfhood be made coherent in the modern world.

In such a situation, Jewish thought is not a luxury but a necessity. But what is 'Jewish thought', and how does it differ from that more ambitious phrase 'Jewish philosophy'? Jewish philosophy in the middle ages characteristically meant the confrontation between Judaism and philosophy. Both were relatively defined entities. 'Philosophy' meant one of the then available systems of conceptualising the world: Kalam or neo-Platonism or Aristotelianism. 'Judaism' meant that corpus of beliefs and practices embodied in the biblical and rabbinic literature. Neither term was problematic in itself. What was problematic, and formed the heart of the problem, was the relationship between the two. This was the question that animated the work of Saadia Gaon, Judah Halevi, Maimonides and others. A number of clear options were available: harmonisation, synthesis, or opposition. The agenda of Jewish philosophy was clear.

What was less clear was its relevance to the majority of Jews. For there were relatively few who had so made themselves at home in the high non-Jewish culture of their day that its tensions with Judaism became, for them, a matter of existential crisis. Maimonides prefaces his *Guide for the Perplexed* with the remark that it is intended for the person 'who has been trained to believe in the truth of our holy Law, who conscientiously fulfils his religious and moral duties, and at the same time has been successful in his philosophical studies.' [1] He is writing, in his day, for a cultural elite. The majority, he notes elsewhere in the *Guide*, 'believe traditionally in true principles of faith, and learn the practical worship of God, but are not trained in philosophical treatment of the principles of the Law.' [2] These were not the 'perplexed' for whom he wrote. Not having encountered philosophy in general, they experienced no tensions between it and their Jewish faith. As long as Jews remained exclusively within the Jewish intellectual world – which by and large in the middle ages they did – they felt no need of Jewish philosophy. It remained as a result an impressive but marginal achievement.

So the subject-matter of Jewish philosophy was straightforward, but its relevance to Jewish life was restricted to the few. Modernity has reversed this situation. For it is no longer the few, but the vast majority of Jews, who inhabit two cultures and who experience the tensions between them. In theory, Jewish philosophy should have become a central discipline of Jewish life. But at just this juncture, the terms that comprise it have lost their lucidity. For what is Judaism in the modern age? And what is philosophy? And what is the conceivable relationship between them?

No longer can a Jewish thinker philosophise on the basis of an agreed understanding of the central terms of Judaism: revelation, command, tradition, interpretation, covenant, exile and redemption. These terms have lost their traditional sense for liberal Jews on the one hand, secularists on the other. Even within Orthodoxy there are sharp differences of opinion between modernists and traditionalists, religious Zionists and those who deny religious significance to the state of Israel.

And if the reality designated by the word 'Judaism' has become fragmented, so has too the idea of secular culture. R. Soloveitchik, in his early but only recently published work *The Halakhic Mind* was one of the first to address this new reality.[3] In the twentieth century we have lost, he notes, the unified world of Newtonian, Galilean and Cartesian thought. The various disciplines that make up modern mathematics and science cannot themselves be organised into a single interconnecting view of the universe. The enterprise of philosophy has itself become problematic. Robert Bellah, in his recent study of contemporary American culture, notes that in the late twentieth century 'the world comes to us in pieces, in fragments, lacking any overall pattern'.[4] Soloveitchik called this 'cognitive pluralism' and it means that there is no longer a coherent and identifiable secular culture in relation to which Judaism might define its stance.

This is not to say that Jewish philosophy is impossible in the present intellectual climate. In 1980, to be sure, Menachem Kellner came to just this conclusion: there could be no contemporary Jewish philosophy, he argued, because 'Judaism no longer speaks with one voice.'[5] He was wrong, for soon afterward there appeared two of the most ambitious attempts this century to present a systematic account of the Jewish ideas of God and man, Michael Wyschogrod's *The Body of Faith* (1983)[6] and David Hartman's *A Living Covenant* (1985).[7] 'Religious experience is born in crisis', writes R. Soloveitchik,[8] and it is just when Jewish philosophy seems to be impossible that it appears.

What it does mean, though, is that something less ambitious than Jewish philosophy is both urgent and possible. That something is what we have called 'Jewish thought.' Jewish thought does not aim at embracing the whole of Jewish tradition and the whole of contemporary culture in a comprehensive engagement with one another. But it does aim at a coherent statement of what it means to be a Jew at this particular juncture of history and civilisation. It goes beyond the vague cluster of symbols, motifs and metaphors that constitute the public rhetoric of Jewishness and asks searching questions. What do these symbols mean? Are they compatible with one another and with traditional Jewish self-understanding? Which Jewish values are enhanced, and which endangered, by a particular intellectual environment? Which, if a choice must be made between conflicting values, stands closer to the heart of the Jewish enterprise? It is questions such as these that have become pressing and perplexing in the last two centuries. It is these that, if they do not beget fully-fledged philosophical systems, nonetheless give birth to a distinct and fascinating body of Jewish thought.

DIMENSIONS OF EXILE

Does it have some connecting theme? Though I have not touched on it explicitly in these essays, there is a *leitmotif* that runs through the whole range of Jewish thought since emancipation. It is the idea of *galut*, exile. It was this term, with its many dimensions of meaning, that more than any other had summed up the Jewish condition between the destruction of the Second Temple and the beginning of modernity. 'Because of our sins,' went the liturgical phrase, 'we were exiled from our land.' Exile meant the geographical dispersion of Jews throughout the world. It meant their political powerlessness, their lack of a sovereign state. It meant dislocation, for living outside Israel meant, in a profound sense, not being at home. It meant a kind of spiritual disorder. Outside Israel, argued Nachmanides, Jewish history lost its direct contact with Providence. In Jewish mystical thought exile was a cosmic catastrophe, a fracture between the transcendent and immanent aspects of God.

To live in a condition of *galut* is, virtually by definition, to live toward *ge'ulah*, redemption. Here too there was broad consensus on the core of meanings that the term implied. Redemption meant the messianic age. It meant that Jews would one day be gathered back from the ends of the earth to the land of Israel. There they would recover their autonomy. The kingdom of David would be restored. Israel would be ruled over by a messianic king who would fight the battles of the Lord, end Israel's subjection to the nations, establish the sovereignty of Torah, renew the covenant and rebuild the Temple. Beyond this, there were disagreements. Would the messianic age be natural or supernatural? Would it be accompanied by miracles, a new heaven and earth, or would nature pursue its normal course? What was the relationship between the messianic age and such concepts as 'the world to come' and the resurrection of the dead? How literally or metaphorically was one to understand the prophetic visions of the end of days? On such questions, argument was fierce but not divisive. One would, in the end, have to wait and see.

But between these two concepts, *galut* and *ge'ulah*, was an eloquent and echoing silence. How was the transition to be effected between the one and the other? This was the question that hovered over the whole of exilic Jewish history. Not accidentally was there no clear answer. For the messianic idea had been consistently the most explosive in Jewish history. According to the Talmud Yerushalmi, an identification of Bar Kochba with the messiah had led to a disastrous uprising against the Romans in the first century CE. Thereafter rabbinic thought was politically quietist. Redemption would come not through human means. It would come either at the time appointed by God, or through repentance and good deeds.

Messianic thought turned from the natural to the mystical, but it continued to erupt from time to time like a volcano. A series of false messiahs surfaced regularly throughout the middle ages, as Maimonides testifies in his *Epistle to Yemen*, wreaking havoc wherever they appeared. The most serious of these by far was Shabbetai Zevi in the seventeenth century, whose redemptive claims and subsequent apostasy traumatised Jewish communities throughout the world. The neutralisation of the messianic idea had been a constant necessity of Jewish thought, and it became all the more so in the eighteenth century in the wake of the Shabbatean heresy. Cultivating a sense of a-historical stasis – of patience and waiting – seemed necessary to Jewish self-preservation. But it left Jewish thought with few resources to handle, and a great many to oppose, the idea of historical change. For if the only significant terms to describe history are exile and redemption, then all change is messianic, and all messianism is premature.

It was this fact that was to become crucial in the nineteenth century. For emancipation *was* historical change. It meant the end, in social-structural terms, of the ways in which Jewish life had been organised since the days of the Babylonian Talmud. How, then, was this fact to be interpreted? Did it mean the end or the intensification of *galut*? Virtually all Jewish thought, revolutionary or traditional, since then has been an implicit answer to this question. Modern Jewish thought could be described as an extended midrash on, or a series of interpretations of, the idea of exile.

The two major breaks with tradition that have persisted to the present – Reform Judaism and secular Zionism – were both revolutionary transformations of the messianic idea. Radical Reform, which reached its heights in Germany in the 1840s and America in the 1880s, saw emancipation as messianic. Jews should abandon all thoughts of a return to Israel. Instead their mission lay in the diaspora, where through social integration they would be 'a light unto the nations', projecting a set of prophetic ethical ideals. The messianic age would be an era of tolerance and freedom for all mankind.

Secular Zionism, which reached mature expression in the closing decades of the century, took the opposite path. The rising tide of nationalism on the one hand, racial anti-semitism on the other, pointed toward a relocation of Jewish life from Europe to Israel. Exile had come to an end; it was no longer tenable. Instead Jews had to become active shapers of their own history. They should create a society in the land of their national past. There and there alone would they find redemption, variously conceived as safety from persecution, cultural renaissance, or a new society of equality, the dignity of labour and military pride. The messianic age would be the reconstitution of Jews as a people in their own land.

The same idea led, in other words, to a conception of Judaism as a religion without nationalism, and as a nationalism without a religion. But what the two had in common was their sense of nearing the end of *galut*. Jews were in sight, at last, of home. For Reform it was a home in a newly open diaspora. For secular Zionism it was a home in Israel. But each testified in its own way to the passion with which Jews sought an end to their long social, political and metaphysical homelessness and to what Gershom Scholem has called 'a life lived in deferment'.⁹ Necessarily, the defenders of tradition saw both as new variations on an old theme: a premature, destructive and heretical messianism. But they could not leave the matter there, without giving their own interpretation to the revolutionary change in the conditions of *galut*. Orthodoxy, as the defence of tradition in an untraditional age, grew to self-consciousness in the wake of these two confrontations, with Reform in Germany and Hungary, and with secular Zionism in Eastern Europe.

In the first section of the book, 'Responses to Modernity', I trace the history of this response through the four archetypal figures of R. Moses Sofer, R. Samson Raphael Hirsch, R. Abraham Kook and R. Joseph Soloveitchik. There have been other great figures in traditional Jewish thought in the last two centuries but these four more than any others set out the great alternatives. For Hirsch emancipation held out new possibilities for the Jewish mission in *galut*. For R. Kook, it did the opposite. *Galut* had run its course. Jewish life in the diaspora was atrophying beyond recovery. The future lay in Israel where a messianic process beckoned. But unlike the secular Zionists, R. Kook envisaged that Jewish national revival would be, inevitably, a religious revival also. R. Sofer, who preceded both, disagreed with both. Emancipation neither enhanced *galut* nor ended it. It deepened it. Judaism would survive only to the extent that Jews resisted its embrace. Living through a period of revolutionary change, Jews were commanded to reject all change.

The most striking feature of Jewish life in the last two decades has been the re-emergence of the views of R. Moses Sofer – represented by the yeshivah and Chassidic communities – as the most powerful voice in Orthodoxy, both in Israel and the diaspora. In the chapters 'Tradition as

Resistance' and 'Dilemmas of Modern Orthodoxy' I analyse some of the factors behind this phenomenon. Though it is one I respect and admire, in 'An Agenda of Future Jewish Thought' I argue against drawing from it unwarranted conclusions. The challenges to Judaism of an open society in the diaspora and a secular society in Israel remain as urgent as they were in the days of Hirsch and R. Kook. The bridges they built – *Torah im Derekh Eretz* and religious Zionism respectively – remain as narrow as ever and are in constant danger of being swept away. There is, I believe, no alternative but to keep rebuilding them. As Rabbi Nachman said: 'The most important rule is not to be afraid.'

RELIGIOUS FEAR

And yet fear afflicts the greatest. We recall the words in which the Torah describes Jacob, anticipating his meeting with Esau. 'Jacob was very afraid and distressed.' [10] Rabbinic interpretation caught the fateful dilemma that lay behind these words. '*He was very afraid*, that he might be killed. *He was distressed*, that he might have to kill.' [11] Jacob experienced physical fear that he might be overcome by Esau. But he experienced ethical fear also: that in overcoming Esau he might be forced to act like Esau. There are some victories that, in a spiritual sense, are a defeat.

For Esau read secular culture, and we have the dilemma that haunts the work of R. Joseph Soloveitchik. It is no accident that four of the essays in this book concern his work. It would be hard to find, in the history of Jewish thought, a figure who has brought inner conflict so near to the centre of his intellectual universe. 'Alienation and Faith', my first published essay on Jewish thought, written just before I became a student at Jews' College, reflects both my fascination and difficulty with this idea. It arose out of my first reading of his classic essay, 'The Lonely Man of Faith', surely one of the seminal documents of twentieth century Jewish religious thought. Though it is written in terms of the two biblical accounts of the creation of man, it could equally well have been written as a midrashic reconstruction of the thoughts of Jacob prior to his meeting with Esau. Jacob, 'covenantal man', is about to confront Esau, 'majestic' or secular man. He fears defeat, but more than defeat he fears victory. For in fighting Esau he will become like Esau. In conquering the secular world he will become secularised. What does Jacob do in such a situation?

The medieval commentator, Rashbam, suggested that Jacob tried to run away. 'The Lonely Man of Faith' ends with the same conclusion. 'When the hour of estrangement strikes, the ordeal of the man of faith begins and he starts his withdrawal from society . . . to his solitary hiding and his abode of loneliness.' He retreats from the encounter. To be sure, he returns to society in a prophetic role, but only to find 'triumph in defeat, hope in failure.' Such is the contemporary man of faith's 'exacting and sacrificial role.'[12]

I found almost sixteen years ago, as I still find today, those words to be among the most profound written about the Jewish condition in modernity, and at the same time the most despairing. Jewish thought must confront them constantly and constantly fight against them. For the biblical narrative simply does not say what R. Soloveitchik has it say. Elsewhere, in an essay entitled 'Catharsis',[13] he gives his own interpretation of Jacob's inner struggle, his great wrestling-match with an unnamed adversary in the loneliness of night. The reading is utterly characteristic. Jacob, at the point of victory, lets his opponent go. 'The Torah,' concludes R. Soloveitchik, 'wants man . . . to act heroically, and at the final moment, when it appears to him that victory is within reach, to stop short, turn around, and retreat.' But this is Kierkegaard, not Torah. The biblical Jacob does not retreat. He tells his opponent, 'I will not let you leave until you bless me.'[14] This sentence, crucial to the Jewish destiny, in reply to which the name Israel is first pronounced, is wholly absent from R. Soloveitchik's account.

In R. Soloveitchik's work, halakhic Judaism comes as close as it will ever get to the spiritual world of Kierkegaard: a religion of subjectivity, loneliness, paradox and conflict. In *The Halakhic Mind*, Judaism loses its ability to communicate with science and philosophy. In *Halakhic Man*,[15] halakhah becomes a theoretical world akin to modern mathematics, not a code of law that creates communities. The tragic hero of 'The Lonely Man of Faith' was already present in these works written twenty years before. Halakhic Man lives in the company of Hillel and R. Akiva, not in the real world of the contemporary Jewish community. He sees halakhah not as the discipline of resolving conflicts but as the celebration of conflicts to which, if there is a resolution at all, it lies in the mystical depths of the soul, not in the world of action, human relationship and society. This is not halakhah as the premodern Jew understood it.

It is not surprising that R. Soloveitchik's work, with its deep ambivalences, has given rise to two conflicting tendencies: one, a radicalism, evident in the work of such figures as Emanuel Rackman, David Hartman and Irving Greenberg, that pushes halakhic Judaism to its liberal limits and possibly beyond; the other, an ultra-conservatism that is deeply distrustful of contemporary culture. Both elements are present in his work, but the second is decisive. Implicit in my chapter 'An Agenda of Future Jewish Thought' is that R. Soloveitchik's work, unique though it is, is not an isolated statement in the history of Orthodoxy. It embodies a mood of premature despair that has been Orthodoxy's constant temptation in modern times. That despair leads directly to R. Moses Sofer's interpretation of history and to his strategy of disengagement from it. For R. Sofer, emancipation deepened the condition of *galut*. For R. Soloveitchik, secularisation has carried it into the Jewish soul.

Against this we must argue that premature despair is as much to be resisted as its opposite, premature messianism. Jewish thought must continue to wrestle with contemporary culture, the problems of diaspora and the project of a Jewish state, and with the Jewish people as a whole in its many shades of alienation. In this struggle it must say, 'I will not let you leave until you bless me.'

THE BRIDGE BETWEEN WORLDS

The other essays in this book are self-explanatory. One, 'Wealth and Poverty', attracted attention in the national press when it was first published. The *Times* and *Daily Telegraph* published articles praising it; the *Guardian* implicitly criticised it as a Jewish statement of the politics of the 'new right'. A careful reading will make it clear, however, that my concern was not to advocate a political position. It was instead to examine the nature of the interpretive and halakhic processes when biblical verses are applied to economic problems. It was a response to a certain kind of Christian politics – exemplified in David Sheppard's *Bias to the Poor*[16] – which assumed that a specific political programme could be extracted from the biblical text: in this case socialism. Christian interpretation of this kind – and this is true equally of Liberation Theology[17] – tends to treat the whole rabbinic tradition as non-existent. One contribution Jews can make to political debate in a pluralist society is to point out that rabbinic Judaism exists and that problems not identical with, but not totally dissimilar to, those faced today were constructively debated by the sages.

As to the relationship between Judaism and politics generally, I would suggest that neither halakhah nor aggadah dictate a particular political stance, but that they constitute a language of values and concerns within which policies can be argued and evaluated. That is what a living tradition is: not a series of answers but a framework of thought. To expect Judaism to provide a single, uncontestable answer to a question, say, of economic or social policy, is already to have yielded to a kind of fundamentalism, whether of the left or of the right. It is to ignore the entire tradition of argument which is rabbinic Judaism's singular and striking glory. There are many issues on which the halakhic system has already reached an authoritative consensus; but contemporary questions of economic and social policy are not among them. But to suggest, in the opposite direction, that Judaism has nothing of relevance to say to these questions is to have yielded to compartmentalisation. It is to have restricted Torah to the private domain, and to have conceded that Judaism has no part to play in the shaping of a pre-messianic society.

The bridge between these two positions, like every other bridge in contemporary Jewish thought, is very narrow. But the task of Jewish thought remains: to build a bridge between *galut* and *ge'ulah*, exile and redemption, the real and the ideal, a rope at a time and a plank at a time. Below are the deep waters of secularisation. Behind is the safety of never having attempted the journey. The way is narrow. The risks are great. But the challenge cannot be declined. For Judaism invites us to change, not accept, ourselves and the world. Rabbi Nachman's words remain true: 'The most important rule is not to be afraid.'

NOTES:

1. *Guide for the Perplexed*, introduction.
2. Ibid., 3, 51.
3. R. Joseph B. Soloveitchik, *The Halakhic Mind*, London: Seth Press, 1986.
4. Robert Bellah and others, *Habits of the Heart*, London: Hutchinson, 1988, 277.
5. Menachem Kellner, 'Is Contemporary Jewish Philosophy Possible? – No', in *Studies in Jewish Philosophy*, edited by Norbert Samuelson, Lanham, MD. University Press of America, 1987, 17-28.
6. Michael Wyschogrod, *The Body of Faith*, Minneapolis: Seabury Press, 1983.
7. David Hartman, *A Living Covenant*, New York: Free Press, 1985.
8. *The Halakhic Mind*, 3.
9. Gershom Scholem, *The Messianic Idea in Judaism*, New York: Schocken, 1971, 35.
10. Genesis 32:8.
11. *Tanchuma, Bereishit Rabbah* and Rashi ad loc.
12. R. Joseph B. Soloveitchik, 'The Lonely Man of Faith', *Tradition* 7:2 (Summer 1965), 5-67.
13. R. Joseph B. Soloveitchik, 'Catharsis', *Tradition* 17:2 (Spring 1978), 38-54.
14. Genesis 32:27.
15. R. Joseph B. Soloveitchik, *Halakhic Man*, translated by Lawrence Kaplan, Philadelphia: Jewish Publication Society of America, 1983.
16. David Sheppard, *Bias to the Poor*, London: Hodder and Stoughton, 1983.
17. For Jewish reflections on Liberation Theology, see Marc Ellis, *Toward a Jewish Theology of Liberation*, London: SCM, 1988; Dan Cohn-Sherbock, *On Earth as it is in Heaven*, New York: Orbis, 1987. Both of these studies, though, are severely handicapped, Ellis' by his indifference to the rabbinic tradition generally, Cohn-Sherbock's by his avoidance of the halakhic tradition specifically.

RESPONSES TO MODERNITY

2

Samson Raphael Hirsch: Conditional Co-Existence

Moses, confronted with his mission, asked "Who am I?" The modern Jew uses the same words but asks a different question. For Moses the doubt was about personal worthiness. For the modern Jew the doubt is about personal identity. Whatever else was fragile about pre-modern Jewish existence, religious self-definition was not. The Jew had his selfhood established by the community in which he lived, fleshed out by the norms of practice and belief in which he moved, confirmed by the Christian or Moslem culture by which he was surrounded. The pre-modern literature asks questions about faith and reason, history and destiny, mind and cosmos, but not about what it is to be a Jew.

Modernity thus forced upon Jews the question of identity, in particular in terms of their relationship to secular culture and citizenship. Orthodoxy, which maintained a sense of unbroken continuity with the Judaism of the Talmudic age and the Torah of Moses, was the least inclined of any of the Jewish responses of the nineteenth century, to see the need for redefinition. But no thinker could fail to see that the context of Jewish existence had radically changed, even if its content remained the same. Orthodoxy developed its own responses to modernity, and in this study we examine four of them: those of Samson Raphael Hirsch, Abraham Isaac Kook, Joseph B. Soloveitchik, and Moses Sofer. Seen schematically, as alternative models rather than as individuals set in unique social and historical circumstances, they map out the broad range of options available to Orthodoxy in an age unsympathetic to its commitments. Analysing their impact, we arrive at a paradoxical conclusion. But first, what were the problems they confronted?

SECULARISATION

First was the process which threatened to marginalise all religious systems: secularisation. By this is generally meant the transfer of territory, property and more generally, society's institutions and culture from ecclesiastic to lay power. Modernity is marked by the fact that religion ceases to dominate the way society organises itself, or the way individuals explain their decisions. Rational methods of scientific inquiry, the bureaucratic organisation of states and large organisations, the transformation of ethics from a code of duty to a system of producing beneficial results: all these effectively displace traditional systems of religious meaning. "Probably for the first time in history, the religious legitimations of the world have lost their plausibility not only for a few intellectuals and other marginal individuals but for broad masses of entire societies." [1]

Peter Berger, in his classic study of secularisation, notes that this does not constitute a terminal threat to organised religion. Contrary to the expectations of the more radical figures of the Enlightenment, religions have proved surprisingly tenacious in the modern world. What it does mean, however, is a relocation of the religious domain. Whereas the pre-modern individual found his religious meanings embedded in his vision of society and the cosmos, in a secular society:

> religion manifests itself in its peculiarly modern form, that is, as a legitimating complex voluntarily adopted by an uncoerced clientele. As such it is located in the private sphere of everyday social life and is marked by the very peculiar traits of this sphere in modern society. One of the essential traits is that of 'individualisation'. This means that privatised religion is a matter of the 'choice' or 'preference' of the individual or the nuclear family, *ipso facto* lacking in common, binding quality. Such private religiosity, however 'real' it may be to the individuals who adopt it, cannot any longer fulfil the classic task of religion, that of constructing a common world within which all of social life receives ultimate meaning binding on everyone.[2]

At first, this privatisation of religion – its metamorphosis from the political and coercive to the personal and freely chosen – was welcomed by Jews as providing the very basis for their equal entry into civil emancipation. This was the burden of Moses Mendelssohn's tract *Jerusalem* (1783), in which he argued against the right of the state, or indeed of religious institutions, to coerce the individual conscience. Judaism, for Mendelssohn, is rational, non-dogmatic, and since the destruction of the second Temple, essentially voluntary. As citizens, Jews share with others a set of beliefs and morals that are rational and universal. Their religious distinctiveness belongs to the private domain. His prescription for the modern Jew is: "Adapt yourselves to the morals and the constitution of the land to which you have been removed; but hold fast to the religion of your fathers too." [3]

Mendelssohn's Judaism, though formally a mere restatement of tradition in heavily Maimonidean terms, is a perfect example of Berger's thesis. In the world of the pre-modern Jew, Judaism was not a 'religion' in the sense of a private confession or a voluntarily adopted set of domestic rituals. It was the substance of an enveloping culture, the content of the traditional educational curriculum and the legislative norm of the self-governing *kehillah* (community). Mendelssohn, unaware of the magnitude of the change he was proposing, had transferred Judaism from the public to the private domain.

EMANCIPATION

The process of Emancipation, extending through Europe during the nineteenth century, brought about the changes Mendelssohn foresaw. Judaism's public domain was effectively dismantled. The autonomous powers of the *kehillah* were gradually abdicated. Traditional schools (*yeshivot*) were replaced, either by Jewish schools which were modelled on their non-Jewish counterparts, or by the public schools themselves to which Jewish parents sent their children to be socialised. Jews felt bound to master the language and adopt the clothes and manners of the wider society. There was internal and external pressure to abandon the marks of Jewish distinctiveness.[4]

This was not a neutral process, for Judaism in its classic

expressions was marked precisely by what Emancipation rules out *ab initio*: community, self-government by Jewish law, and a precise set of deliberately distinctive practices. It does not lend itself to privatisation. The promise of civil equality was at the same time a threat to Jewish continuity. It was, as Samuel Heilman has described it, "a new version of the age-old Christian efforts to convert Jews. Now instead of demanding conversion to Christianity, the Christians were demanding a Jewish conversion to secular citizenship." [5]

Some did indeed convert to Christianity. They were significant not so much by their numbers as by their visibility, for they included a number of highly prominent Jews, including some of Mendelssohn's own children, and David Drach, son-in-law of the Chief Rabbi of France. Reforming tendencies appeared in the religious life especially of German Jews, directed at reducing those elements of Jewish faith and practice that were seen as impeding the move towards Jewish integration: *kashrut*, for example, or the hope for a return to a Jewish homeland. These were given intellectual weight by the scholars of the 'Science of Judaism', who both spiritualised the Jewish vocation and distanced the Jewish past as history rather than living tradition.[6] Reform theologians such as Samuel Hirsch, Solomon Formstecher and Salomon Steinheim, contributed to an evolutionary view of Judaism as the progressive self-realisation of the spirit.[7] Against these powerful social and intellectual pressures, Jewish tradition seemed to offer little but the mores and superstitions of a benighted medieval past.

German Orthodoxy, however, had produced a series of distinguished rabbis who possessed both Talmudic depth and a secular education, and who were able to speak with the accents of modernity. They included Isaac Bernays, Jacob Ettlinger, Seligmann Baer Bamberger, Azriel Hildesheimer and David Zvi Hoffman.[8] The figure who left the most lasting impression, as the one who directly and systematically confronted the situation of Orthodoxy in an emancipated Europe, was Samson Raphael Hirsch (1808-1888).

HIRSCH'S VIEW OF EMANCIPATION

Hirsch [9] was born in Hamburg into a family which he

was later to describe as "enlightened-religious".[10] Some measure of the 'enlightenment' of his parents may be gauged by the fact that they sent him to be educated at the local non-Jewish grammar school, "in those days an extraordinary thing for pious Jewish parents to do".[11] The Hamburg of Hirsch's youth contained a striking role-model for a new kind of Orthodox leadership, Isaac Bernays (1792-1849), a student of the talmudist Abraham Bing and a graduate of Wurzburg University. No less a figure than Sigmund Freud described the impression Bernays made on his contemporaries: "This man educated us all . . . Religion was no longer treated as rigid dogma, it became an object of reflection for the satisfaction of cultivated artistic taste and of intensified logical efforts, and the teacher of Hamburg [Bernays] recommended it finally not because it happened to exist and had been declared holy, but because he was pleased by the deeper meaning which he found in it or which he projected into it." [12]

At the age of twenty Hirsch went to study under Jacob Ettlinger (1798-1871), another university-educated rabbi and a distinguished Talmud commentator and responsa writer, and from there to the University of Bonn where he became friendly with the man who was later to be the target of some of his most severe criticisms, the future Reform leader Abraham Geiger (1810-1874). In 1830 he succeeded Nathan Marcus Adler as rabbi of Oldenburg, Moravia, where he quickly established himself as a moderniser, in form if not in content. He wore the then-new rabbinical gown with white bands – a break with traditional rabbinic dress – preached in German, introduced a choir, and abolished the recitation of the Kol Nidre prayer on Yom Kippur.[13] It was there that he began his prolific writing career, and in 1836 published his *Nineteen Letters on Judaism*.

Its impact was immediate and dramatic. Orthodoxy had acquired a new voice. No longer was it on the defensive, resisting the new cultural conditions. Instead Hirsch had launched a counter-offensive. Here was an opportunity for the renewal of Judaism. "I bless emancipation," he wrote, quickly adding the proviso, "I bless it, if Israel does not regard emancipation as the goal of its vocation, but only as a new condition of its mission . . . We must become Jews, Jews in the true sense of the word, imbued with the spirit of the law, accepting it as the fountain of spiritual and ethical life. Then Judaism will gladly welcome emancipation as affording a greater opportunity for the fulfilment of its task, the realisation of a noble and ideal life." [14]

In retrospect it is difficult to capture the sense of revelation and revolution this conveyed at the time. Perhaps the most impressive testimony comes from the diary of the then nineteen year old Heinrich Graetz, later to become a great historian of the Science of Judaism school. "With avidity I devoured every word. Disloyal though I had been to the Talmud, this book reconciled me with it. I returned to it as to a mistress deemed faithless and proved true, and determined to use my utmost effort to pierce to its depths . . ." [15]

What, then, was the programme revealed in the *Nineteen Letters*? Part of the book's power lies in the directness with which Hirsch addressed the doubts of a young, half-assimilated generation, resentful of their Jewish heritage. It begins with the letter of a young man to his friend, a rabbi to whom he confesses his reservations. Judaism, he says, has brought nothing but misery to its adherents. The Torah is an impediment to the enjoyment of life. It isolates the Jew and thus creates suspicion and animosity on the part of others. It encourages submissiveness and discourages the arts and free thought. It neglects noble moral ideals in favour of insignificant details. [16]

To this comprehensive litany of objections, Hirsch replies in a sympathetic spirit. He concedes that the long exile has distorted Jewish existence. It "drove Israel away from a normal life, limited the free development of its noble character, and compelled many individuals to enter, for the sake of self-preservation, upon paths which they were too weak to refuse to enter." [17] There are those who practise the commandments as a mechanical habit, failing to understand their inner meaning. Jewish texts are taught without regard for the philosophy they embody. Reform therefore is called for, but a reform not of Jewish law but of Jewish education. Hirsch is pointed in his criticism of what he sees as the inauthenticity of those who would introduce substantive reform into Jewish law: "To take a standpoint somewhere outside of Judaism, to accept a conception derived from strangers, of the purposes of human life, and the object of liberty, and then to cut, curtail and obliterate the tenets and ordinances of Judaism – is that the Reform we need?" [18]

Hirsch sees in emancipation a significant opportunity to reconstruct Jewish education, and to renew the Jewish mission as a "people in the midst of the peoples" leading an exemplary life of obedience to the Divine will. He ethicises the commandments – taking strong objection to Maimonides' historical approach to the reasons for the commands [19] – seeing them as timeless embodiments of the values of justice, love and moral-spiritual education. Particularly striking is his interpretation of the *chukkim*, statutes, which some had seen as non-rational, and which Maimonides had tended to interpret as part of the Torah's struggle against idolatry.[20] Hirsch, by contrast, sees them as symbolising "Justice toward the earth, plants and animals" and towards one's own property and body.[21]

Emancipation therefore leads to conflict only if Jews internalise values antithetical to their mission, by wishing to assimilate, by interpreting Judaism through external categories (as he accused Mendelssohn of doing), or by adopting an autonomous ethic which sees man as the only judge of right and wrong. This last point is Hirsch's implicit criticism of Kantian ethics.[22] The pursuit of human ends is inevitably self-defeating and tends to unhappiness and corruption. Instead man must voluntarily submit to the will of God, but in so doing he will achieve a way of life which fulfils humanist ideals and will be universally recognised as such: "Picture every son of Israel a respected and influential priest of righteousness and love, disseminating among the nations not specific Judiasm – for proselytism is forbidden – but pure humanity." [23] This is the idyllic vision which allows Hirsch to find positive meaning in the Jewish entry into European society. By being an authentic Jew he will *ipso facto* be both a good citizen and an inspiring religious example.

CULTURAL CO-EXISTENCE

Hirsch was profoundly convinced of the compatibility between Judaism and secular culture. Science, properly understood, would reveal the Divine law operating in nature.[24] History, correctly studied, would deepen the sense of Jewish mission and Divine purpose.[25] This had been his own experience, and it was to provide the programme for his great educational experiment, the Jewish school which he opened in Frankfurt in 1853.

He invoked the rabbinic maxim, *Torah im Derekh Eretz*, in the sense attributed to it by Naftali Hartwig Wessely (1725-1805),[26] namely, the joint study and harmonisation of Jewish and secular disciplines. A secular education was needed, he argued, for three reasons: first, so that Jews would be capable of handling the challenges raised by their contacts with a wider society; second, as a necessary preparation for a career; third – and this he argued most passionately – it was in itself a religious duty, regardless of the exigencies of the moment.[27] Judaism encouraged a love of knowledge from whatever source. It contained a special blessing for the wise of the nations of the world.[28] That secular studies had not been part of the traditional curriculum was an aberration, not an ideal: "If in recent centuries German Jews remained more or less aloof from European civilisation the fault lay not in their religion but in the tyranny which confined them by force within the walls of their ghettoes and denied them intercourse with the outside world".[29]

It would be wrong, however, to regard *Torah im Derekh Eretz* as a form of synthesis. Despite Hirsch's unquenchable optimism about the compatibility of the two cultures, there were severe limits to the encounter. They did not meet on equal terms. Speaking of his Reform opponents he said: "For them, religion is valid only to the extent that it does not interfere with progress; for us, progress is valid only to the extent that it does not interfere with religion." [30] Although he believed that there would be no such conflict, he asserted: "We declare before heaven and earth that if our religion demanded that we should renounce what is called civilisation and progress we would obey unquestioningly, because our religion is for us truly religion, the word of God before which every other consideration has to give way." [31]

From this unshakeable base, Hirsch was able to mount effective critiques of the Science of Judaism,[32] the reformers of his day,[33] and an autonomous secular ethic.[34] In retrospect, these judgements have grown considerably in stature, and have been echoed a century later by those who in no way sympathise with Hirsch's Orthodoxy.[35] Precisely because his identity was so firmly rooted, he was able to maintain a clear-eyed critical perspective. But for the same reason, his stance towards modernity was in no way an open one. The Jew, he contended, "has to taste everything by the unimpeachable touchstone of his divine law; whatever does not stand this test for him does not exist." [36] In fact, "From the very beginning, God placed Judaism and with it its adherents in opposition to the age." [37] It was merely fortuitous – or rather, for Hirsch, the evolutionary effect of Jewish influence on civilisation – that the nineteenth century was one in which Jews could find themselves welcoming rather than doing battle with the surrounding culture.

Hirsch's *Torah im Derekh Eretz* was therefore not a synthesis nor a true dialogue,[38] but a guarded and relatively precarious form of co-existence, at any time capable of turning into a fierce opposition. Despite its appearance at the time as a revolutionary welcoming of modernity, in retrospect it seems far more like an energetic restatement of a highly guarded stance. The Jew must develop his own positive identity through an intense education in the Jewish sources. Self-understanding must proceed out of Judaism alone. The fault of Maimonides and Mendelssohn was that in their different ways they came to Judaism from the outside, through alien concepts and categories. The Jew who is thoroughly grounded in his own sources will possess norms and values which are invulnerable to criticism, for in the last analysis they are accepted not because they accord with the spirit of the time or the dictates of autonomous conscience but because they are the revealed will of God to which one must submit oneself uncritically.[39]

From this position of absolutely secure commitment, the modern Jew need neither be overly defensive towards secular culture, nor apologetic about Jewish tradition. The Jew would be able to accept all that is 'good and true' [40] in the civilisation around him, while being critical of its failings. He would be able to take an active role in the enterprises of society, not as an alternative mode of being, but rather as an extension of the Jewish mission to be exemplary citizens and living models of Divine peoplehood.

THE RELIGIOUS DOMAIN

Hirsch was explicit about how the Orthodox Jew could accept only part of modernity. He was less explicit about how modernity – as it presented itself in Germany – could accept only part of traditional Judaism. Hirsch's *Mensch-Jissroel* ('Man-Israel', his term for the combination of the worldly and religious roles),[41] at once faithful Jew and exemplary secular citizen, was not identical with the integrated Jew of pre-modernity. This is evident in the way Hirsch downplays certain motifs which were to re-emerge as central to other Orthodox philosophies.

Jewish nationalism takes a low profile in his teachings. The Jewish people is constituted by its religious laws rather than by any national aspirations. "This spiritual unity [conferred by Torah] . . . is the only communal bond we possess, or ever expect to possess, until that great day shall arrive when the Almighty shall see fit in His inscrutable wisdom to unite again His scattered servants in one land . . . For this future . . . we hope and pray, but actively to accelerate its coming is prohibited to us".[42] Exile is given a positive interpretation. It makes Israel realise that the nation-state is only a means, not an end. Indeed Israel had "accomplished its task better in exile than in the full possession of prosperity".[43] Not only did exile remove the temptation to identify religion with power and material welfare; it also scattered Israel among the nations, the better "to show themselves everywhere on earth as the glorious priests of God and pure humanity".[44] Thus "Dispersion opened a new, great and widespread field for the fulfilment of its mission".[45]

Nor did Hirsch lament the loss of judicial autonomy involved in the collapse of the old structures of the *kehillah*. The public domain is no longer parochially Jewish but universal: "We are ourselves fortunate enough to live in a time which we can regard as the dawn of a new era of justice in human affairs, in which the members of the Jewish people also will be invited to take an active part in all humane, social and political activities among the nations."[46] This provided the grounds for Mordecai Kaplan's[47] most trenchant critique of Hirsch's neo-Orthodoxy, that it "accepts with equanimity the elimination of the whole civil code of Jewish law, and is content to confine the scope of Jewish law to ritual observance".[48]

This judgement was more recently echoed by the historian Ismar Schorsch: "Like the spokesmen for reform, Hirsch dropped all demands for judicial autonomy and continuance of Jewish civil law. He insisted upon the wholly religious character of Judaism, reduced the significance of the periods of Jewish national independence, and divested the messianic concept of political overtones." [49] Endorsing Schorsch's remarks, the sociologist Charles Liebman notes that Hirsch tacitly accepted modern society's allocation of the place of religion at the margins of public life: "Areas which remained under the dictates of halakhah were those which nineteenth century German society viewed as falling within the prerogatives of religion." [50]

In short, the model Hirsch projected for the co-existence of Orthodoxy and modernity involved the recognition, tacit or explicit, of limits in both directions. On the one hand, there was to be no genuine encounter on equal terms. The faithful Jew had to accept as Divinely given certain truths and standards such that, if secular culture postulated alternatives, secularity had to be criticised and rejected. Judaism was to be expounded in the language of humanism – this was the great project of Hirsch's Bible commentary and his analysis of the commands in the *Nineteen Letters* and *Horeb* [51] – but it was not to be judged by humanist premisses. The communication was strictly one-directional.

On the other hand, Judaism itself was to be confined to 'religious' rather than 'national' motifs. There is no incipient political Zionism in Hirsch's writings – a fact that was to become more prominent in subsequent generations of Hirsch's followers [52] – nor is there a recognition that emancipation had enforced a contraction of Judaism's traditional domain. It was Hirsch's particular genius to see that such a 'religionised' Judaism need concede nothing to the substantive demands of Reform. Orthodoxy might need to change its clothes, its outer forms, but not its halakhic standards nor its code of beliefs. Orthodoxy could survive the 'ordeal of civility' [53] without compromising its inner essence. This, in retrospect, was no small achievement.

But the very tensions and limitations of this meeting with

modernity suggested that an alternative model was available, one which was driven by larger aspirations and a more expansive view of the relation between Torah and reality. It is to this model, provided by Abraham Isaac ha-Kohen Kook, that we now turn.

NOTES

1. Peter Berger, *The Sacred Canopy: Elements of a Sociological Theory of Religion*, New York: Doubleday, 1967, p. 125.
2. Ibid. pp. 132-3.
3. Moses Mendelssohn, *Jerusalem*, translated by Allan Arkush, University Press of New England, 1983, p. 133. See also Alexander Altmann, *Moses Mendelssohn: A Biographical Study*, University of Alabama Press, 1973.
4. See Jacob Katz, *Out of the Ghetto: The Social Background of Jewish Emancipation 1770-1870*, New York: Schocken Books, 1978; *Jewish Emancipation and Self-Emancipation*, Jewish Publication Society, 1986.
5. Samuel Heilman, 'The Many Faces of Orthodoxy', *Modern Judaism* 2:1 (February 1982), pp. 23-4.
6. I echo here the famous critical judgement of Gershom Scholem, *The Messianic Idea in Judaism*, pp. 304-313. This has been challenged by Eliezer Schweid, *Judaism and Mysticism according to Gershom Scholem*, Atlanta: Scholars Press, 1985, pp. 145-163.
7. Katz, *Jewish Emancipation and Self-Emancipation*, pp. 3-19.
8. See Heilman, op. cit.; Hermann Schwab, *The History of Orthodox Jewry in Germany*, London: The Mitre Press, 1950.
9. On Hirsch see Noah H. Rosenbloom, *Tradition in an Age of Reform: The Religious Philosophy of Samson Raphael Hirsch*, Philadelphia: Jewish Publication Society, 1976; Robert Liberles, *Religious Conflict in Social Context: The Resurgence of Orthodox Judaism in Frankfurt am Main, 1838-1877*, Westport: Greenwood Press, 1985; see also Dayan Dr. I Grunfeld, *Three Generations: The Influence of Samson Raphael Hirsch on Jewish Life and Thought*, London: Jewish Post Publications, 1958, and his Introduction to Samson Raphael Hirsch, *Judaism Eternal*, vol. 1, London: Soncino, 1959.
10. Rosenbloom, p. 44.
11. Grunfeld, *Judaism Eternal*, vol. 1, p. xxiii.
12. E. Freud (ed.), *Collected Letters of Sigmund Freud*, New York: 1960, pp. 17-22; quoted in Heilman, p. 37.
13. Rosenbloom, pp. 66-69.
14. Samson Raphael Hirsch, *The Nineteen Letters on Judaism*, prepared by Jacob Breuer, translated by Bernard Drachman, New York: Feldheim, 1960, pp. 109-111.
15. Cited in Rosenbloom, p. 71.
16. *Nineteen Letters*, pp. 23-6.
17. Ibid. p. 109.

18. Ibid. p. 114.
19. Ibid. pp. 117-126.
20. Maimonides, *Guide of the Perplexed*, III, 26, 29-32. Saadia had seen *chukkim* as non-rational, commanded to confer reward for obedience (Saadia Gaon, *The Book of Beliefs and Opinions*, III); but see Marvin Fox, 'On the Rational Commandments in Saadia's Philosophy: A reexamination', Marvin Fox (ed.) *Modern Jewish Ethics*, Columbus, Ohio State University Press, 1975, pp. 174-187.
21. *Nineteen Letters*, pp. 75, 78-79.
22. See Eliezer Schweid, 'Two Neo-Orthodox Responses to Secularization', *Immanuel* 19 (Winter 1984/5), pp. 107-117.
23. *Nineteen Letters*, p. 108.
24. *Judaism Eternal*, vol. I, p. 183; vol. II, pp. 253-9.
25. Ibid., vol. I, p. 208; vol. II, pp. 259-273.
26. Rosenbloom, pp. 46, 72.
27. It is clear that Hirsch himself did not intend his doctrine of *Torah im Derekh Eretz* as a mere *hora'at sha'ah* (temporary concession to the needs of the moment) as some of his latter-day interpreters have maintained. Hirsch specifically counters the view of those who "might sanction such a sacrifice [of time to secular study] as a necessary concession to the spirit of the age"; *Judaism Eternal*, vol. I, p. 203. The debate is surveyed in Grunfeld, *Three Generations*, pp. 111-133; Sir Immanuel Jakobovits, 'Torah im Derekh Eretz Today', *L'Eylah* 20 (New Year 5746), pp. 36-41.
28. *Judaism Eternal*, vol. I, 203-220.
29. Ibid., vol. II, p. 235.
30. Ibid., vol. II, p. 237.
31. Ibid., vol. II, p. 235.
32. Ibid., vol. II, p. 285.
33. Ibid., vol. II, pp. 213-244.
34. See Hirsch's *Commentary* to Genesis 2:9, 18:19.
35. Hirsch's criticism of the Science of Judaism was echoed by Ahad Haam, Chayyim Nachman Bialik and Gershom Scholem; see also Arthur A. Cohen, *The Natural and Supernatural Jew*, London: Vallentine Mitchell, 1967, pp. 50-51. His critique of Reform was tacitly acknowledged by the Reform movement itself, in the marked shift of positions from the Pittsburgh Platform of 1885 ("today we accept as binding only its [Judaism's] moral laws"), to the Columbus Platform of 1937 to the statement of Principles of the Central Conference of American Rabbis of 1976 (CCAR Yearbook, vol. LXXXVI), with its admission that "The past century has taught us that the claims made upon us may begin with our ethical obligations but they extend to many other aspects of Jewish living . . ." A post-holocaust critique of Kantian ethics is to be found in Emil Fackenheim, *To Mend the World*, New York: Schocken, 1982, pp. 266-273: "It is true that Kant's belief in humanity could at no time be verified. However, not until the advent of the Holocaust was this belief *refuted*."
36. *Judaism Eternal*, vol. II, p. 223.

37. Ibid., vol. II, p. 217.
38. See Norman Lamm, *Faith and Doubt*, New York: Ktav, 1971, pp. 69-81; Arthur A. Cohen, *The Natural and Supernatural Jew*, pp. 50-54.
39. Mordecai Kaplan was particularly critical of Hirsch's failure to engage in the kind of scholarly debate with critical attacks on Orthodoxy undertaken by David Zvi Hoffman and Isaac Halevy in relation to Biblical criticism and the history of the Oral Law, respectively (Mordecai Kaplan, *Judaism as a Civilization*, Jewish Publication Society of America, 1981, pp. 133-159). Hirsch's own conviction was that 'Jewish Science' should not be a response to external criticism, but rather an autonomous development, an attempt to "construct a science of Jewish ideas of nature and history, and, in the light of these truths which have been handed down by Judaism, to judge from the Jewish standpoint the events of the present, and the struggles and expectations of the peoples, along with the principles and views which guide them" (*Judaism Eternal*, vol. II, p. 285).
40. *Judaism Eternal*, vol. I, pp. 194, 207.
41. The concept is developed throughout the *Nineteen Letters*. See Rosenbloom, pp. 351-368.
42. *Nineteen Letters*, pp. 107-8.
43. Ibid., p. 64.
44. Ibid., p. 65.
45. Ibid., p. 63.
46. *Judaism Eternal*, vol. I, p. 210.
47. Kaplan, though he became the most radical theologian of the Conservative movement, advocating his own philosophy of "Reconstructionism", was originally an Orthodox rabbi, serving as assistant to the highly traditional Rabbi Moses Zebulum Margolies (Ramaz) in the Kehillat Yeshurun synagogue. The problem he raised, that of "compartmentalisation" between Jewish and secular spheres, had been anticipated in 1923 by Franz Rosenzweig in his essay, *The Builders*. Rosenzweig spoke of "Hirsch's orthodoxy" as "a rigid and narrow structure, unbeautiful despite its magnificence", and complained that it had created a division of life into Jewish and extra-Jewish spheres.See J. R. Marcus and A. J. Peck (eds.), *The American Rabbinate: A Century of Continuity and Change 1883-1983*, Hoboken: Ktav, 1985, pp. 32, 39, 80-1.
48. *Judaism as a Civilization*, p. 157.
49. Ismar Schorsch, *Jewish Reactions to German Anti-Semitism, 1870-1914*, Columbia University Press, 1972, p. 10.
50. Charles Liebman, 'Religion and the Chaos of Modernity', in Jacob Neusner (ed.), *Take Judaism, for Example*, University of Chicago Press, 1983, p. 157.
51. Samson Raphael Hirsch, *Horeb: A Philosophy of Jewish Laws and Observances*, translated by Dayan Dr. I Grunfeld, London: Soncino, 1972.
52. Hirsch's son-in-law and successor, Solomon Breuer (1850-1926), was a prominent member of the non-Zionist Agudas Yisroel. Solomon's son Isaac Breuer (1883-1946) became a leading theoretician of the

movement, strongly opposed to Zionism as an attempt to impose collective secularisation on the Jewish people.
53. The phrase is that of John Murray Cuddihy, *The Ordeal of Civility: Freud, Marx, Levi-Strauss and the Jewish Struggle with Modernity*, New York: Basic Books, 1974. See also George L. Mosse, 'Jewish Emancipation: Between *Bildung* and Respectability', in Jehuda Reinharz and Walter Schatzberg (eds.), *The Jewish Response to German Culture*, University Press of New England, 1985, pp. 1-16.

3
Abraham Isaac Kook: The Dynamic of Sanctification

The contraction of Judaism to a 'religious' domain ran counter to one fundamental thrust of Jewish law. Maimonides articulated what was clearly an assumption embedded in the halakhic system when he spoke of Jewish law in terms of the creation of a socio-political order. The function of the Law is the ordering of a community. Torah differs in this respect from secular legal systems only in its concern to inculcate in its adherents correct religious opinions. It shares with secular legislation the shaping of a polity and the abolition of injustice and oppression.[1] Jewish civil law is thus an essential part of Torah. Torah belongs to the public domain.

The longing for a return to Jewish sovereignty in the land of Israel had been a constant theme of medieval Jewish sentiment, reiterated daily in its liturgy, written into its self-definition as a people in *Galut* (exile, both physical and spiritual). It had flared into passion in the writings of the poet-philosopher Judah Halevi and the halakhist-exegete Nachmanides.[2] Emancipation posed two quite distinct, if interrelated, challenges to this longing.

The first was the need to establish the Jew as a loyal citizen of his country, a patriot who had no secret desire to leave and build a nation somewhere else. This led to the early Reformers' decision to exclude from their prayers all traditional expressions of the hope for a return to Zion. The American Reform declaration, in 1885, was typical in this respect: "We consider ourselves no longer a nation, but a religious community, and therefore expect neither a return to Palestine . . . nor the restoration of any of the laws concerning the Jewish state".[3]

The second was, as we have noted, the impoverishment of Jewish life itself, with the abandonment of *kehillah* self-government that had marked Diaspora existence since Talmudic times.[4] Specifically Jewish experience was now confined to a small and well-defended compartment of identity, culture and social interaction. Hirsch believed that on such a slender base a viable Jewish educational and congregational nexus could be constructed. But as Charles Liebman notes, the contraction ran counter to one of the basic premisses of pre-modern spirituality. "Traditional Judaism constituted a total way of life. Whereas it recognized distinctions between sacred and secular, holy and profane, it aspired to encompass under the rubric of its norms all activity in which a Jew was engaged. Nothing is foreign, irrelevant, or immaterial to Judaism." [5]

That Hirsch's ideal *Mensch-Jissroel* could translate modern culture into Jewish terms of reference could not conceal the fact that the culture itself had a dynamic wholly independent of Judaism. Nor could the neo-Orthodox deny what was palpably the case: that the majority of Jews preferred a less demanding synthesis of identities. Hirsch himself recognised the predominance of non-Orthodox voices in the communal structures of his day, and fought fiercely and successfully to lead his Frankfurt congregation to secession from the global Jewish organisation.[6] Neo-Orthodoxy was a minority of a minority, never consciously a programme for a collective Jewish renewal.

FORERUNNERS OF ZIONISM

The mid-nineteenth century thus provided the context for an alternative resolution to the conflicts between Judaism and modernity: a focussed effort to turn the age-old dream of a return to Zion into a practical programme. There Jewish life would be restored to its wholeness. There Jewish law would once again reoccupy the public domain. There too, in the collective national endeavour, the schisms between Orthodoxy and contemporary heterodoxies would be mended.

The first stirrings came from two rabbis retrospectively identified as forerunners of Zionism,[7] Yehudah Alkalai (1798-1878) and Zvi Hirsch Kalischer (1795-1874). Alkalai, who spent his boyhood in Jerusalem, was a mystic who was energised into proposing Jewish resettlement of the land by the spectre of renascent anti-semitism in, and the international Jewish response to, the Damascus Affair of 1840.[8] Citing traditional texts, he argued that messianic redemption – though it would be secured by Divine intervention – had to be prepared for by human endeavour and natural means: by a slow process of migration, the revival of Hebrew, and the establishment of a collective Jewish polity, an 'assembly of elders'. This would restore unity to a people whose current divisions were "an obstacle to the Redemption".[9]

Kalischer, who was born in Posen, halfway between the still undisturbed traditionalist communities of the East and the modernising Jewries of the West, took part in the polemics against Reform, in particular against its abandonment of references to the return to the Holy Land. His theories did not emerge fully fledged until the 1860s, when he began campaigning vigorously for the creation of agricultural settlements in Palestine. Like Alkalai, but even more forthrightly, he argued that it was a misreading of tradition to suppose that redemption was a matter of waiting passively and patiently for Heaven to act: "Cast aside the conventional view that the Messiah will suddenly sound a blast on the great trumpet and cause all the inhabitants of the earth to tremble. On the contrary, the Redemption will begin by awakening support among the philanthropists and by gaining the consent of the nations to the gathering of some of the scattered of Israel into the Holy Land." [10]

There is no doubt that these Orthodox figures, together with their socialist contemporary, Moses Hess (1812-1875), were influenced by the rise of European nationalism.[11] To some extent too they were prompted by the first signs of an incipient, ineradicable anti-semitism,[12] suggesting that the liberalisation of the modern world was not as benign as had been thought. But all three were moved by the prospect of a revival of the integrated world of tradition through such instrumentalities as the Hebrew language, agricultural labour, and the revival of national consciousness, none more so than Hess. The one-time colleague of Karl Marx and passionate admirer of Spinoza delivered, in *Rome and Jerusalem* (1862), the most incisive critique of Western Jewish assimilationism and of the spiritualising tendencies of Reform, which, he declared, had "sucked the last marrow out of Judaism and ... allowed nothing to remain of this sublime phenomenon of history but the shadow of a skeleton".[13]

Hess approached tradition from the outside, but his reading of the sources convinced him that Jews had, from the outset, "conceived their historic mission to be the sanctification not only of man's individual life but also his social life".[14] The religious tradition had lost its vitality only in the modern era, when emancipatory pressures had led Jews, for the first time, to be ashamed of their nationality.[15] "Only from the national rebirth will the religious genius of the Jews draw new powers, like that giant who touched the mother earth, and be again animated by the sacred spirit of the Prophets." [16]

The themes articulated by Hess receive their fullest expression from within the tradition in the work of Rav Abraham Isaac ha-Kohen Kook (1865-1935). In his thought – a rhapsodic blend of rabbinic, philosophical and poetic motifs, held together by a transfiguring mysticism – the idea of religious revival through national rebirth takes on a compelling utopian grandeur. All the facets of modernity, positive and negative, can be embraced and transmuted by the power of a newly released Jewish religious energy. But not in exile.

RAV KOOK: THE INTELLECTUAL BACKGROUND

Rav Kook [17] was born on the margins of modernity, in the small town of Grieve in Latvia. This was still part of the as yet unshaken hinterland of Eastern European Jewish life celebrated by A.J. Heschel in his prose-poem *The Earth is the Lord's*.[18] Early recognised as a Talmudic prodigy and an unusually rarified religious personality, he received a conventional rabbinic education, which eventually took him to the great yeshivah in Volozhyn, then presided over by Naftali Zvi Yehudah Berlin (*Netziv*, 1817-1893). Berlin was something of a paradox.[19] On the one hand he maintained a fierce resistance to secularisation, so much so that he eventually closed the yeshivah in 1892 rather than comply with the request of the Russian government that it introduce instruction in the Russian language. On the other, the yeshivah over which he presided was a cosmopolitan intellectual centre, attracting such figures as the poet Chaim Nachman Bialik (1873-1934) and the writer Micha Berdyczewski (1865-1921).

The dynamic of modernity took a different form in Eastern European Jewry than it had done in Germany. Ethnic, cultural, political and nationalist themes were prominent. Assimilation and religious reform did not present the direct threat that would have forced Orthodoxy into sharp philosophical self-definition. Berlin himself strongly opposed secessionist policies such as had been adopted by Hirsch in Germany and the followers of Moses Sofer in Hungary. Dividing the Jewish people into contending factions, he said, was "as painful as a dagger in the body of the nation".[20] He was sympathetic to the pre-Herzlian Chibbat Zion movement, and was one of its earliest members. The experience of Volozhyn and Rabbi Berlin was formative for Kook, and it provided him with a series of integrative themes that he was to make his own: unity, peoplehood, culture and Zion.

After serving as a rabbi in the Lithuanian towns of Zoimel and Boisk, he left Europe for Palestine in 1904, where he became chief rabbi of Jaffa. He was stranded in Europe at the outbreak of the First World War and spent some years in London as rabbi of the Machzikei Hadas congregation. When the war ended he returned to Palestine as its first Ashkenazi Chief Rabbi (1919), an office he held until his death sixteen years later.

Kook's thought is a kind of antithesis of that of Hirsch. The two men differed in education, background and temperament. Unlike Hirsch, who had received a dual education and knew Western culture from within, Rav Kook's intellectual upbringing was wholly bounded by tradition. He took an avid interest in the secular philosophies of his day, but his encounter with them took place at one remove, via their Hebrew-language interpreters and the literature of the Jewish enlightenment.[21]

Temperamentally, Kook was a mystic, subject to sudden moods of illumination which he strove vainly to capture in language.[22] He drew on the classic schemes of Jewish mysticism, and was particularly influenced by Lurianic Kabbalah and the thought of R. Judah Loew of Prague (*Maharal*, c.1525-1609). But the constructions he wove, out of densely textured quotations from the entire range of traditional Jewish literature of which he had a prodigious command, are wholly original. His biographer calls him "virtually the first literary mystic of Orthodox Judaism since post-biblical days".[23] His thoughts are unsystematic, held together by a unity of mood and theme rather than by analytic exploration, and were originally committed to notebooks in the form of extended aphorisms or meditations. Much of his writing was only edited and published after his death. He was also a halakhist of the first rank, best known for his legitimation of a device to exempt Jewish agriculture from restrictions of the sabbatical year,[24] and the author of several volumes of rabbinical responsa.[25]

EXILE AND DISHARMONY

Kook was conscious of living in revolutionary times. "Our generation", he wrote, "is extraordinary, a generation full of amazement, for which it would be hard to find a precedent in our entire history. It is comprised of opposites; light and darkness are intermingled." [26] Referring to the rabbinic statement about the messianic age, that "The Son of David will come only in a generation that is altogether righteous or altogether wicked",[27] Kook avers that the present generation is "both altogether wicked and altogether righteous." [28]

The paradox resolves itself in his thought in terms of the dual character of every movement in the life of the individual or society. What appears as evil or destructive is so only when considered in isolation. In the Divine economy it has its own constructive part to play in the orchestrated harmony which pulses through reality if we are attuned to it. Harmony and wholeness are, for him, the essence of the religious vision. Separation and division are the modes of alienation from the Divine.

These concepts permeate the whole of life. The individual Jew strives – though he may not know it – for harmony with himself, his people, his Torah and his land. The longing for one is a longing for the other. Wishing to be at one with oneself is wishing to be at one with Torah which is itself a wish to be united with the Jewish people and its holy land. Zionism is therefore central to Rav Kook's thought, in the most radical way. Nachmanides had maintained that the fulfilment of the commandments was metaphysically incomplete outside the land.[29] Judah Loew of Prague saw exile as an unnatural dislocation.[30] But for Kook, *Galut* is a systematic estrangement of the elements of Jewish life from one another, allowing for neither individual nor collective spiritual growth.

The disharmony can be traced back to the Babylonian exile, when for the first time a rift appeared between the religious and national spirit. Prophecy waned, and was replaced by the study of texts. Jewish nationalism, launched on an independent orbit, grew harsh and aggressive, a failing for which the second exile was a cure. In the course of the long dispersion there were periodic spiritual revivals, but "the nation itself is in a state of decadence in the diaspora".[31] Kook attributes a number of positive values to the period of exile, but it is clear that these are nearing their end. "Apart from the nourishment it receives from the life-giving dew of the holiness of Eretz Israel, Jewry in the Diaspora has no real foundation and lives only by the power of a vision and by the memory of our glory, i.e., by the past and the future. But there is a limit to the power of such a vision to carry the burden of life and to give direction to the career of a people – and this limit seems already to have been reached." [32]

Hence the extraordinary evaluation Kook gave of the various Jewish rebels against tradition, 'souls of chaos' as he called them.[33] Three elements comprise his judgement. First, Judaism itself had become narrowed and confined by its alienation from the "higher piety" of direct religious experience. Against this even atheism had a kind of integrity: it "arises as a pained outcry to liberate man from this narrow and alien pit . . . it is needed to purge away the aberrations that attached themselves to religious faith because of a deficiency in perception and in the divine service".[34] Second, the intellectual and moral upheavals were part of the revolutionary moment that preceded the messianic age, "The souls inspired by a destructive zeal reveal themselves especially at the end of days, before the great cataclysm that precedes the emergence of a new and more wondrous level of existence, when the old boundaries expand, just prior to the birth of a norm above the existing norms." [35] Above all, when rebellion took the form of secular Zionism, Kook recognised in it a genuine religious value, a desire to be joined to people and land which was part of the process of penitence:[36]

> The lower soul [nefesh] of the sinners in Israel in the generation preceding the coming of the Messiah, of

those who attach themselves in love to the things affecting the totality of Israel, the building of the land and the national revival, is more advanced than the *nefesh* of those faithful observers of Jewish law who do not evince as powerful an urge for the welfare of the nation and the building of the land. But the higher soul [*ruach*] is more advanced in the case of the pious observers of the Torah and the commandments.[37]

This remarkable statement is intelligible only in the light of Kook's belief that each represented a dialectical pole that would merge in a new synthesis. The secularists would endow the religious with a love of nation, while the religious would draw the secularists into their faith. Thus the various segments of the people – nationalist, socialist, religious – who existed in the Diaspora in a state of conflict would be caught up in the collective dynamic of a reborn Israel, each remedying the deficiencies of the other. Exile was fragmentation; redemption a reunification.

UNITY AND CONFLICT

At the heart of Kook's philosophy is a mystical affirmation breathtaking in its simplicity: "The Jewish outlook is the vision of the holiness of all existence".[38] Between the unifying vision of faith and the fragmentation of empirical reality is a tension between the individual and the universal. Each individual – object, person, nation, religion – is unique. At the same time each is part of an interlocking pattern whose "consummate harmony"[39] Kook constantly sought to expose.

The tragedy of human existence is that individuals do not understand themselves in terms of their place in the totality. Instead they understand the totality as a projection of themselves. Thus they take the fragment for the whole, and come into conflict with others who take another fragment as the whole. "All the defects of the world, the material and the spiritual, they all derive from the fact that every individual sees only the one aspect of existence that pleases him, and all other aspects that are uncomprehended by him seem to deserve purging from the world. And the thought leaves its imprint in individuals and groups, on generations and epochs, that whatever is outside one's own is destructive and disturbing. The result of this is a multiplication of conflict."[40]

The soul of the Torah is the mystical dimension in which conflicts are reconciled and the place of each element in the total scheme is revealed. No discipline, philosophy included, can penetrate to the heart of religion, since each embraces only a part of the whole. The individual who reaches beyond conceptual schemes to the sense of unity of creation is necessarily transformed as a moral being: "In the light of the mighty idea of the unity of existence there is eliminated the problem of self-love, which some have made into the source of all sin, and others as the source of all morality. There is only the love for all things, which is in truth an enlightened, nobler form of self-love."[41] Ultimately this love is completely universal, expressed in the reconciliation between Judaism and its 'brothers', Christianity and Islam,[42] and even in the messianic establishment of 'justice for animals'.[43] Kook speaks of the exalted individual who "rises toward wider horizons until he links himself with all existence, with all God's creatures, with all worlds, and he sings his song with all of them".[44]

Kook's is not a static mysticism. For this harmonic vision is both a Divine reality and a human *un*reality. Evil and conflict exist. Nonetheless, they are not natural states. All reality strives toward perfection. There is a perceptible moral evolution to increasingly universal visions: "Evolution sheds light on all the ways of God. All existence evolves and ascends . . . It ascends toward the heights of the absolute good."[45] In specifically religious terms, this forms the heart of Kook's account of *teshuvah* (penitence). Sin creates psychological dislocation and distress. The individual is conscious of acting out of harmony with the creation. Thus there is an analogy between sin and illness, between penitence and the desire for a cure. "Penitence is the healthiest feeling of a person. A healthy soul in a healthy body must necessarily bring about the great happiness afforded by penitence, and the soul experiences therein the greatest natural delight."[46]

TO SANCTIFY THE SECULAR

Kook was not a naive evolutionist. The conflict between

tradition and modernity, between the religious and the secularists of his day, was profound, and might continue if some synthesis could not be found between them. Kook believed that such a synthesis was not only available, but would occur. Nonetheless, he was acutely critical of the Orthodoxy of his day for failing to embrace it. "Orthodoxy in its present battle of negativism contents itself with illusions that are destroyed by life and reality, destroying those who entertain them together with them. We cannot find comfort in the fact that the element of our people that has yielded to heresy is even more vulnerable to destruction." [47]

He described the traditionalist group of the old Yishuv as being "absorbed in its quest for inner holiness, which thrusts aside whatever bears anything new in form, which excludes from its schools and yeshivot every foreign language, even the language of the government and country, and every secular study, even that which is most urgent for practical life".[48] He believed that rabbinical leadership had to be equipped with wider and deeper knowledge than it presently had as a result of its concentration of halakha. "The reaching out for worldly knowledge to the extent possible is a necessity. If every student of the Torah cannot be expected to master all branches of knowledge, he can be expected to attain familiarity with the general state of culture in the world and its impact on life, so that he may discern the spirit of his generation and thus be enabled to nurture it and improve it." [49]

But precisely here we encounter a critical ambivalence in his thought. On the one hand he envisaged a new kind of yeshivah. *Merkaz ha-Rav*, the yeshivah he established in Jerusalem, would, he hoped, be a model for this innovative curriculum. He was convinced that "the Torah cannot be confined to research of practical halakhah alone . . . Aggadah, exoteric and esoteric Midrash, works of research and study of Kabbalah, Mussar, philosophy, grammar, liturgy and poetry . . . these too are fundamentals of Torah".[50] The yeshivah would undertake the study of history, criticism, Jewish philosophy and poetry, establishing a new and genuine *Chokhmat Yisrael* (Science of Judaism). It would share the agenda but counteract the influence of the 'Science of Judaism' propounded by the

German-Jewish enlightenment, so that Jewish scholarship was no longer the exclusive preserve of "those who sought the destruction of Torah and faith".[51]

But this model, expansive though it is, does not embrace secular studies at all. Nonetheless Kook believed in a synthesis between secular and holy far more profound and thoroughgoing than that envisaged by Hirsch. "Each body of thought has its own logic and is tied to others by a systematic relatedness . . . It follows that there is no such thing as a vain or useless thought; there is nothing without its proper place; for all emanate from the same source in the divine wisdom . . . As man grows in the scale of perfection, he draws from all ideas, his own and those of others, their kernel of eternity, logic and good which derives from the source of wisdom."[52]

This suggested a radical transformation of the relationship between sacred and secular. Their relationship was one of form to substance. The sacred would be established on the secular foundations.[53] The secular has no independent existence, no ultimate reality. Secular disciplines describe that which is empirically available. The task of the holy is to animate each discipline by relating it to its source, and thence to the whole, thus endowing it with life and moral force.[54] Which institutional framework was to be the context of this sanctification of the secular, if not the yeshivah? Kook appears to have believed that it would occur naturally in such institutions of the renascent Jewish nation as the Hebrew University, at whose opening ceremony he delivered an address along these lines.[55]

APPROPRIATION

In fact, none of these developments happened. *Merkaz ha-Rav* did not establish the envisaged broad curriculum.[56] The schools founded by Rav Kook's followers resisted the introduction of secular studies. Under parental pressure they eventually included them but forbade humanist study and the integration of the secular and religious programmes.[57] The Hebrew University, and advanced academic study in Israel generally, have shown no signs of the anticipated synthesis.[58]

To understand why is to come to the heart of the problem of Rav Kook's relationship to modernity. It seems that Kook conceived of the religious domain as a kind of meta-discipline, unifying the elements of a diverse and warring culture by disclosing to each its proper limits and place within an overarching pattern. Thus located, they would co-exist in harmonic symbiosis. Kook was not, though he seems to have been taken to be,[59] tolerant towards secularity in the modern, pluralist sense of allowing it independent legitimacy and accepting it on its own self-definition. He did not seek a synthesis in which each side, the holy and the secular, would modify the other in equal measure. Nor did he seek the modest co-existence envisaged by Hirsch in which the holy accommodated carefully screened elements of secular culture, and engaged with it in joint civil projects. He sought instead the complete *absorption* of the secular into the holy, its appropriation by the higher wisdom. Kook spells this out, together with the meaning tolerance held for him, in an important passage:

> Every universal theory carries with it certainty to the extent of its universality, and together with its certainty, which rules out the possibility of doubt, there goes a refusal to share with others in any collaborative pluralism . . . Idolatry was tolerant, while the belief in the unity of God is intolerant; being universal and not particular, certain and not beset by doubt, it is singular and not particularistic. The principle of universality is not tolerant according to the superficial conception of tolerance, but in its very intolerance is contained the essential basis of tolerance . . . The basic thrust of its kind of tolerance is to find a place for every form of illumination, of life and of spiritual expression.[60]

The universality of Kook's vision is one in which each individual and school of thought accepts the place allocated to it in the global scheme. Tolerance involves accepting every phenomenon on the Torah's terms, not on terms autonomous to the phenomenon itself. But the very thrust of secularity, whether as academic discipline, political movement or social theory, is its *essential* autonomy, its insistence on its own internal criteria of evaluation. Kook's reluctance or refusal so to understand it marks him as a characteristically pre-modern thinker, one who demonstrated with unique brilliance and imaginative sympathy how much it was possible for a traditional perspective to embrace. What it did not embrace was the critical problem of modernity itself, the declared independence of the secular from religious legitimation. Kook could not conceive that the secular might itself mount a similar challenge to religion, seeking to absorb it within itself through such analyses as those of Marx, Durkheim and Freud. He could not entertain the thought that it was launched on an independent trajectory, whose result might be further divergence instead of his hoped-for convergence. Such propositions are antithetical to his system and have no conceivable place within it.

Kook therefore left the dynamics of history to fill the gap at the heart of his system. Torah *would* fill the whole of Jewish culture with light, as fringes on the corners of a garment reveal the sanctity of the garment in its totality.[61] The redemptive process would see a higher synthesis emerge, even if we could not as yet precisely specify the steps to be taken to bring it about. As such, his thought is utopian, a vision without a programme. This makes it no less inspiring, no less one of the great contributions of all time to the development of Jewish spirituality. But it was left to another thinker, Joseph B. Soloveitchik, to confront the irreducible tensions between tradition and modernity.

NOTES

1. Maimonides, *Guide of the Perplexed*, II: 40; see Gerald Blidstein, *Political Concepts in Maimonidean Halakha* [Hebrew], Bar Ilan University Press, 1983, pp. 40, 93-96.
2. For extensive treatments of the place of Zion in medieval Jewish thought, see Yitzhak Baer, *Galut*, New York: Schocken, 1947, and the essays by Shalom Rosenberg, Moshe Idel, Marc Saperstein and Michael Singer in Lawrence A. Hoffman (ed.), *The Land of Israel: Jewish Perspectives*, University of Notre Dame Press, 1986.
3. Pittsburgh Platform, 1885. See *Encyclopaedia Judaica*, Jerusalem: Keter, 1972, 14:26.
4. See L. Finkelstein, *Jewish Self-Government in the Middle Ages*, New York, 1924. For a global history of Jewish patterns of self-government, see Daniel J. Elazar and Stuart A. Cohen, *The Jewish Polity: Jewish Political Organization from Biblical Times to the Present*, Indiana University Press, 1985.

5. Charles Liebman, 'Religion and the Chaos of Modernity', in Jacob Neusner (ed.), *Take Judaism, for Example*, University of Chicago Press, 1983, p. 156.
6. See Robert Liberles, *Religious Conflict in Social Context: The Resurgence of Orthodox Judaism in Frankfurt am Main, 1838-1877*, Westport: Greenwood Press, 1985.
7. See Jacob Katz, *Jewish Emancipation and Self-Emancipation*, Jewish Publication Society, 1986, pp. 104-115.
8. Katz, pp. 93-4; Arthur Hertzberg, *The Zionist Idea*, New York: Atheneum, 1981, pp. 103-107.
9. Hertzberg, pp. 105-107.
10. Hertzberg, p. 111.
11. All three cite the contemporary parallels. See Katz, pp. 95-96.
12. This is particularly marked in Hess's work. Katz denies that antisemitism played a major role in the thinking of these precursors (*Jewish Emancipation and Self-Emancipation*, pp. 94-95, see also pp. 141-152). Certainly it did not play the part it was later to do – under the impact of the Russian pogroms of 1881 and the Dreyfus affair of 1895 – in the thought of Leo Pinsker and Theodor Herzl.
13. Moses Hess, *Rome and Jerusalem*, translated by Maurice J. Bloom, New York: Philosophical Library, 1958, pp. 49-50.
14. Ibid., p. 18.
15. Ibid., p. 74.
16. Ibid., p. 37.
17. On the life of Rav Kook, see Jacob B. Agus, *Banner of Jerusalem*, New York: Bloch, 1946, and Isidore Epstein, *Abraham Yizhak Hacohen Kook: His Life and Works*, London: Bachad, 1951. On his thought, see Zvi Yaron, *Mishnato shel ha-Rav Kook*, Jerusalem: World Zionist Organisation, 1974; Samuel H. Bergman, *Faith and Reason*, translated by Alfred Jospe, Washington: B'nai Brith, 1961, pp. 121-141; Natan Rotenstreich, *Jewish Philosophy in Modern Times*, Holt, Reinhart and Winston, 1968, pp. 219-238. Some of the writings of Rav Kook are available in English translation. See *Abraham Isaac Kook: The Lights of Penitence, The Moral Principles, Lights of Holiness, Essays, Letters and Poems*, translated by Ben Zion Bokser, London: SPCK, 1979; Alter B. Z. Metzger, *Rabbi Kook's Philosophy of Repentance* [a translation of *Orot ha-Teshuvah*], New York: Yeshivah University Press, 1968. Parts of *Chazon ha-Geulah* are translated in Leonard B. Gewirtz, *Jewish Spirituality, Hope and Redemption*, Ktav, 1986.
18. Abraham Joshua Heschel, *The Earth is the Lord's*, Meridian Books, 1963. See also Mark Zborowski and Elizabeth Herzog, *Life is With People: The Culture of the Shtetl*, New York: Schocken, 1962.
19. Samuel Heilman calls Berlin a "passive tolerator": Samuel C. Heilman, 'The Many Faces of Orthodoxy, Part II', *Modern Judaism* 2:2 (May 1982), p. 173.
20. Responsa *Meshiv Davar*, I:42.
21. See Eliezer Schweid, 'Two Neo-Orthodox Responses to Secularization, Part II', *Immanuel* 30 (Spring 1986), pp. 107-117; *Ha-Yahadut veha-Tarbut Chilonit*, Kibbutz Hameuchad, 1981, pp. 114-115.

22. Kook frequently refers to this in his writings. For example: "Who impedes me,/Why can't I disclose in writing all my thoughts,/ The most hidden musings of my soul?/Who prevents me,/Who has imprisoned my thought in its shell,/And does not allow it to emerge into the world?", Bokser, p. 385.
23. Agus, *Banner of Jerusalem*, Preface.
24. The argument is contained in his work *Shabbat ha-Aretz*. His underlying motives are highly instructive. "In the matter of *shemittah* we must know that we are duty-bound to endeavour with all our power to so bring it about that eventually the sabbath of the land will be gradually established in all its sanctity on the holy land . . . But how to achieve this holy objective, and with what means, requires careful study . . . I believe that we need to approach our goal little by little." *Iggrot ha-Rayah*, Jerusalem: Mossad Harav Kook, 1962, vol. I, p. 330.
25. *Mishpat Kohen*, Jerusalem: Mossad ha-Rav Kook, 1966; *Da'at Kohen*, Jerusalem: Mossad ha-Rav Kook, 1969.
26. *Eder ha-Yakar*, Jerusalem: Mossad ha-Rav Kook, 1967, p. 108.
27. B.T. *Sanhedrin* 98a.
28. *Eder ha-Yakar*, p. 108.
29. Nachmanides, *Commentary* to Leviticus 18:25.
30. *Netzach Yisrael*, ch. 1.
31. 'The Road to Renewal' in Bokser, p. 301.
32. *Orot*, Jerusalem: Mossad ha-Rav Kook, 1975, p. 62. Translation from Hertzberg, *The Zionist Idea*, p. 429.
33. 'Ha-Neshamot shel olam ha-tohu', in *Orot*, p. 121.
34. *Orot*, p. 126. Translation from Bokser, p. 264.
35. *Orot*, p. 122. Translation from Bokser, p. 257.
36. "The renewal of the desire in the people as a whole to return to its land, to its essence, to its spirit and way of life – in truth, there is a light of penitence in all this". *Orot ha-Teshuvah*, Jerusalem, 1966, 17:2; Bokser, pp. 126-7.
37. *Chazon ha-Geulah*, Jerusalem, 1941, p. 72.
38. *Orot*, p. 164.
39. *Olat Rayah*, Jerusalem: Mossad ha-Rav Kook, 1963, vol. 1, p. 388.
40. *Orot ha-Kodesh*, vol. 1, Jerusalem: Mossad ha-Rav Kook, 1948, pp. 120-121.
41. *Orot ha-Kodesh*, vol. 2, Jerusalem: Mossad ha-Rav Kook, 1948, p. 586.
42. *Iggrot ha-Rayah*, vol. 1, Jerusalem: Mossad ha-Rav Kook, 1962, p. 142.
43. See 'Fragments of Light', translated in Bokser, pp. 303-323; Nechama Leibowitz, *Studies in Devarim*, translated by Aryeh Newman, Jerusalem: World Zionist Organization, 1980, pp. 135-140.
44. *Orot ha-Kodesh*, vol. 2, p. 458; translation in Bokser, p. 228.
45. *Orot ha-Kodesh*, vol. 2, p. 555; translation in Bokser, p. 221.
46. *Orot ha-Teshuvah*, ch. 5; translation in Bokser, p. 53.
47. *Iggrot ha-Rayah*, vol. 2, p. 124.
48. Ibid., p. 79.
49. *Eder ha-Yakar*, pp. 128-9.
50. *Iggrot ha-Rayah*, vol. 1, p. 187.

51. Ibid., p. 148.
52. *Orot ha-Kodesh*, vol. 1, p. 17.
53. Ibid., p. 145.
54. Ibid., pp. 147, 1-3.
55. *Chazon ha-Geulah*, pp. 266-273. For Kook's approach to education see Yaron, pp. 199-202; Eliezer Schweid, *Ha-Yahadut veha-Tarbut Chilonit*, pp. 135-142, 'Mad'ei ha-Yahadut be-Michlol Mad'ei ha-Ruach veha-Chevrah', *Newsletter of the World Union of Jewish Studies*, 26 (Winter 1986), pp. 9-20; Norman Lamm, *Faith and Doubt*, pp. 69-81; Jonathan Sacks, 'Perspectives', *L'Eylah* 22 (Rosh Hashanah 5747) pp. 14-20.
56. Agus, *Banner of Jerusalem*, p. 124.
57. Charles Liebman, 'Religion and the Chaos of Modernity', p. 161.
58. Eliezer Schweid, '*Mad'ei ha-Yahadut be-Michlol Mad'ei ha-Ruach veha-Chevrah*'.
59. Eliezer Schweid, *Ha-Yahadut veha-Tarbut Chilonit*, p. 136.
60. *Orot*, pp. 130-131. Translation in Bokser, pp. 272-273.
61. *Arplei Tohar*, Jerusalem, 1983, pp. 6-7.

4
Joseph B. Soloveitchik: Conflict and Creation

"What can a man of faith like myself, living by a doctrine which has no technical potential, by a law which cannot be tested in the laboratory, steadfast in his loyalty to an eschatological vision whose fulfillment cannot be predicted with any degree of probability, let alone certainty . . . what can such a man say to a functional utilitarian society which is *saeculum*-oriented and whose practical reasons of the mind have long ago supplanted the sensitive reasons of the heart?"

With these words, taken from the introduction to 'The Lonely Man of Faith',[1] we find ourselves for the first time in Orthodox thought in the full pathos of the modern situation. While Hirsch energetically believed that the Orthodox Jew could participate in the secular enterprise, and Kook that tradition would eventually absorb it, Soloveitchik sensed that modern consciousness, with its rationality, pragmatism and scientific method had systematically marginalised religious sensibility. 'Modernity' was not something external to the believer – non-Jewish society and culture for Hirsch, Jewish rebels against tradition for Kook – with which he might negotiate a relationship. It was something within, part of the air he breathed, the language he spoke. It had invaded his personality, and therefore it was within the personality of the believer that the battle had to be fought, or if not fought, then brought to consciousness.

The implications are dramatic. In the very next paragraph Soloveitchik writes that he has never been troubled by the conflicts between the Biblical doctrine of creation and the theory of evolution, between the Biblical concept of man and modern psychology, between revelation and empiricist philosophy, or between the belief in 'Torah from heaven' and Biblical criticism.[2] Almost the entire range of issues that had perplexed Jews since their encounter with enlightenment is dismissed in a few sentences and never returned to. Soloveitchik does not tell us how he resolves the conflicts, but we can hazard a guess. Judaism and the scientific mind operate on different cognitive presuppositions. They are parallel but alternative realities which do not intersect. What he *has* told us is that the issue is not the critical one. At an external, intellectual level the man of faith can navigate the currents of modernity. But what if modernity enters the holy of holies, by which he means not the home or the synagogue or the academy, but the very soul of the believer? This unerring instinct for the heart of the dilemma makes Soloveitchik the most focussed and relentless of modern Jewish thinkers.

BRISK AND BERLIN

Not by accident. To a unique degree. Soloveitchik (1903-) is master of two worlds, those of contemporary philosophy, theology and science on the one hand, and Talmudic dialectic on the other. As halakhist, he is heir to one of the greatest of Eastern European dynasties. His greatgrandfather, R. Joseph Baer Soloveitchik (1820-1892), was for a while joint head of the great yeshivah of Volozhyn with Naftali Zvi Yehudah Berlin. His grandfather, R. Chaim Soloveitchik ('The Brisker', 1853-1918),[3] was a legendary figure whose analytic method revolutionised Talmudic study in the East.[4] His father, R. Mosheh Soloveitchik, was head of the Talmud faculty at Yeshiva University, a position in which his son succeeded him in 1941. This provenance, together with the formidable degree to which he inherited and acquired the family traits – vast erudition coupled with incisive analytical acumen – would have guaranteed him a prominence as the natural leader of American Orthodoxy, a position which he has occupied since his early days at Yeshiva University.[5]

That role, however, was both deepened and made more resonant by his prodigious acquaintance with secular culture, ancient and modern. Within the first few pages of his first published work, *Halakhic Man*,[6] we encounter Heraclitus, Hegel, Kierkegaard, Karl Barth, Rudolf Otto, Tertullian, Eduard Spranger, Ferdinand Lasalle, Chaim Nachman Bialik, Bergson, Nietzsche, Spengler and Heidegger. In *The Halakhic Mind*,[7] written at about the same time, we meet a seemingly endless intellectual pantheon: Mach, Avenarius, James, Pierce, Schiller,

Vaihinger, Bradley, Bosanquet, Royce, Husserl, Santayana *et al.* The exposure to secular philosophy came relatively late, when after a traditional education Soloveitchik entered the University of Berlin at the age of twenty-two. In 1931 he completed his doctorate on Hermann Cohen's epistemology and metaphysics, and married Tonya Lewit, who had herself completed a doctorate at the University of Jena. It was to her that he dedicated 'The Lonely Man of Faith', and her illness and death (in 1967) evoked a profound emotional crisis whose effect on his work is occasionally hinted at [8] and often sensed.

Family relationships figure, to an uncanny degree, in his writings. *Halakhic Man* is prefaced by the quotation, "At that moment the image of his father came to him and appeared before him in the window".[9] The reference could not be more pointed. It is to the Talmudic aggadah which describes the moment of Joseph's temptation, left alone in the house with the wife of Potiphar. Joseph, so the passage implies, might not have resisted had not the image of his father appeared before him, saying: "Joseph, your brothers will have their names inscribed on the stones of the ephod and yours among them. Is it your wish to have your name expunged from among theirs and be called an associate of harlots?" The image of the son of the patriarchs, left alone with the strange woman of secularity,[10] caught between the desire for knowledge and the memory of his father's stern commanding voice,[11] is a powerful characterisation both of the conflict between tradition and modernity and of Soloveitchik's own existential situation.

From the biographical information we possess it appears that his entry into the worlds of literature, philosophy and the university were at the prompting of his mother,[12] from whom he seems to have inherited a taste for literature and a romantic temperament which "looks for the image of God not in the mathematical formula or the natural relational law, but in every beam of light, in every bud and blossom, in the morning breeze and the stillness of a starlit evening".[13] This dichotomy between what he learned from his father ("how to comprehend, how to analyze, how to conceptualise, how to classify") and from his mother ("that there is a flavour, a scent and warmth to *mitzvot*" [14]) assumes massive significance in his writings once transposed to epic, archetypal forms. Over against halakhic man, one might almost say, there is aggadic woman.

Again, there is a haunting description in one of his essays of a personality type, whom he calls *Ish Rosh Chodesh* ('the man of the new moon') and who is typified by the Biblical Joseph and by Soloveitchik's own father, who hides a warm and expansive emotionalism under an exterior which is hard, cold and intellectual. "The more holy and intimate the emotion, the more it must be hidden within".[15] The unspoken worlds which even the closest relationship cannot disclose, the paradoxical limits of communication in which "the word brings out not only what is common in two existences but the singularity and uniqueness of each existence as well",[16] these too figure heavily in his work. His most frequently used image, awesome in its starkness, is that of Adam and Eve, alone with God in the cosmos, seeking solace as husband and wife and discovering an uncommunicable residue of private experience, an ontological loneliness.

FROM AUTOBIOGRAPHY TO THEOLOGY

These autobiographical traces in his work are not accidental but constitutive.[17] Soloveitchik writes not of the world or of God but of the human experience of both. Nor does he write normatively and impersonally, prescribing, as it were, from outside. Instead he writes from within, drawing on his own personal experience and on his observation of the great figures of halakhic scholarship he knew from his father's house. The means by which he translates this from autobiography to theology is *typology*, by constructing ideal types or pure forms of existence which are never entirely represented by real people but which nonetheless provide an organising, interpretive scheme through which we may analyse our inner world.[18] These types are themselves presented *phenomenologically*, as modes of experiencing. Indeed at the beginning of 'The Lonely Man of Faith' Soloveitchik eschews theology in the conventional sense. What he has to say "has been derived not from philosophical dialectics, abstract speculations, or detached impersonal reflections, but from actual situations and experiences with which I have been confronted".[19]

The individual does not encounter these types as simple, static alternatives. Sometimes they are ordered hierarchically, so that the human-spiritual progression is from one to another.[20] In his most famous essays, however, they are counterposed dialectically, such that the man of faith or halakhah oscillates ceaselessly between them. His first published words were: "Halakhic man reflects two opposing selves",[21] and much of his work is shot through with the language of conflict and struggle, antithesis and anguish. At one point Soloveitchik makes clear the difference between this kind of dialectic and its more usual philosophical sense: "Judaic dialectic, unlike the Hegelian, is irreconcilable and hence interminable. Judaism accepted a dialectic, consisting only of thesis and antithesis. The third Hegelian stage, that of reconciliation, is missing. The conflict is final, almost absolute." [22] In short, there is no synthesis. The inner world of Soloveitchik could not be more distant from that of Hirsch's ideal co-existence or Kook's integrative harmony.

How is this emotional landscape, unusual to say the least in the geography of the Jewish personality, to be mapped on to the given world of Jewish law and belief? Here Soloveitchik's genius, and his family tradition, are at their most creative. The analytic method of R. Chaim of Brisk often involved postulating conceptual dichotomies to explain otherwise intractable disagreements. Two conflicting interpretations of a text would be rendered mutually intelligible by ascribing each to an alternative conceptuality. Thus, two different interpretations of a law might be explained in terms of one view predicating the law of the object involved (*cheftza*), the other seeing it as relating to the agent (*gavra*). By thus drawing out the conceptual presuppositions of the halakhah, apparently unrelated arguments could be seen as instances of an overall pattern of disagreement.[23] As a hermeneutic tool, it was a powerful method of extracting universal themes from a literature which had hitherto seemed utterly concrete and case-specific, and Soloveitchik was to draw out its metaphysical implications in *Halakhic Man*, a work wholly devoted to this type of study and the personality it generated.

But his most creative contribution lay not in the description of the method, but in its application, which Soloveitchik extended not only to the halakhic literature, but also to rabbinic midrash and to the Biblical text. This allowed him to discover his 'types' – usually in binary opposition – in the classic texts, whether drawn from Biblical narrative or seemingly arcane halakhic discussions. Thus, as we shall shortly see, two apparently conflicting Biblical accounts of the creation of man are transformed by this method into two conceptualities, two men, two 'ideal types' and two phenomenologies, the 'majestic' and the 'covenantal'. With this brilliant extension of the Brisk method Soloveitchik solved the problem of relating his singular and highly contemporary existentialism to the canonical texts of Jewish tradition, and in the process created a new and powerful form of midrash, or exegetical method. Perhaps it is the case that every new form of Jewish philosophy is or involves a new method of textual interpretation.[24] Certainly this is what gives Soloveitchik's thought its particular power: its ability to move from highly individualised experiences to ideal types, and then to discover those types in Biblical narrative, rabbinic homily and halakhic detail.

Does this method create or discover? Does it read its concepts into or out of the text? This is one of the central questions to be asked, and Soloveitchik asks it. But – and once again Soloveitchik's biography is crucial – what might have been otherwise marginalised as a subjective or eccentric reading of the sources in this case held an unavoidable fascination. For here was the scion of one of the most distinguished family traditions of Lithuanian piety and scholarship, encountering and mastering the Western intellectual tradition, and wrestling with it in explicit, even confessional,[25] public discourse. The *drama* was palpable. Without so choosing, he became the emblematic figure of a generation. In a sense, he had been cast as an archetype, and his choice of themes and method turned destiny into philosophy.

THE TWO ADAMS

The essay in which these themes come most strongly to the fore is 'The Lonely Man of Faith'. Soloveitchik begins with an admission that immediately singles out both his approach and situation. "My interpretive gesture is completely subjective and lays no claim to representing a definitive Halakhic philosophy. If my audience will feel that these interpretations are also relevant to their perceptions and emotions, I shall feel amply rewarded. However, I shall not feel hurt if my thoughts will find no response in the hearts of my listeners." [26]

This is no mere diffidence but an expression characteristic of the man of faith in the modern world. He no longer speaks the shared language of society. He can no longer 'prove' or justify his stance by the standards invoked by a secular world: scientific demonstration or practical utility. How then is he to communicate? Simply by speaking out of his inner situation and hoping to find an echoing response in his audience. The man of faith is lonely. How does this loneliness arise?

With a brilliant exegetical stroke, Soloveitchik discovers an inner division in the religious personality mirrored in the two accounts given of the creation of man in the opening chapters of Genesis. In the first chapter Adam is made 'in the image of God'. He is commanded to 'fill the earth and subdue it'. He is created simultaneously with woman. And the name of God used throughout is *E-lohim*. In the second chapter, almost antithetically, he is made 'from the dust of the earth'. He is commanded to 'serve and protect' the garden. He is created alone, and only subsequently does woman appear. And the Tetragrammaton, the four-letter personal name of God, appears.

The reason for the discrepancies between the two accounts is simple: they describe two different Adams, two ideal types. Adam of the first chapter is man in the aspect of creative and conquering being. As a creature endowed with intelligence and creativity he is 'the image of God'. His characteristic is *dignity*, which resides in his ability to control and dominate the environment. "Only when man rises to the heights of freedom of action and creativity of mind does he begin to implement the mandate of dignified responsibility entrusted to him by his Maker." [27] He is a maker of things, and thus becomes the author of the norms within which creativity takes place, scientific, technological, ethical and aesthetic. Soloveitchik calls him *majestic man*.

Adam of the second chapter explores the universe not as a scientist, seeking knowledge and control, but instead as one tantalised by its mystery and elusiveness. "He encounters the universe in all its colourfulness, splendour, and grandeur, and studies it with the naivete, awe and admiration of the child who seeks the unusual and wonderful in every ordinary thing and event." He seeks not dignity, but *redemption*, a state in which the individual "intuits his existence as worthwhile, legitimate and adequate, anchored in something stable and unchangeable".[28] Dignity is achieved through control over the external world. Redemption comes through control over oneself, through the willingness to be confronted, even defeated, by another being. The second Adam begins with an awareness of his insignificance in the universe ('dust of the earth') and with a profound sense of loneliness. He seeks communication and communion. Soloveitchik calls him *covenantal man*.

The difference between the two types can be seen in the kind of communities and relationships they create. Majestic man forms a 'natural' community to undertake joint enterprises and promote shared interests. Individuals need to work together to control their environment. But the relationships within such communities are collaborative and functional, side-by-side rather than face-to-face. The second Adam seeks community for another reason, to break out of his loneliness and find 'existential companionship'. He seeks what Soloveitchik calls the 'covenantal faith community'. He finds it in speech, the gesture of communication. Thus God is met not in the majesty of the cosmos, in which He is simultaneously ever-present and unapproachably remote, but in the word of the covenant. The word has two forms: prophecy, in which God speaks to man, and prayer, in which man speaks to God. Both prayer and prophecy link human beings to one another as well as to God, for both are objectified in the form of a communal-ethical imperative. The prophet receives a message for the community. The man of prayer speaks on behalf of the community and its normative needs. While majestic man forms a community of interests, covenantal man forms a community of commitments. Thus majestic man encounters God as *E-lohim*, the source of the cosmos, and woman simply as a co-creature. Covenantal man meets God as the Tetragrammaton, the God of face-to-face relationship,[29] and finds woman only after sensing his own loneliness, and after the overpowering sleep of despair.

Why the two Adams? Evidently because both are inescapably part of the human condition: "In every one of us abide the two *personae* – the creative majestic Adam the first, and the submissive, humble Adam the second."[30] Both modes of existence are willed and sanctioned by God. He commands man to build, construct, plan and create. He endorses both majestic man and the communities he fashions. At the same time He "also requires of man to forget his functional and bold approach, to stand in humility and dread before the *mysterium magnum* surrounding him".[31] To reject either would be "tantamount to an act of disapproval of the divine scheme of creation".[32] But therein lies the ceaseless dialectic of the life of faith. In either community, the majestic or the covenantal, man might have found repose, since each poses a problem and provides the solution for it, the one through joint activity, the other through redemptive relationship. But man is commanded to move from one to the other, from prayer to conquest and back again. He is thus fully at home in neither. Hence the loneliness of the man of faith.

'RELIGION' AND 'SCIENCE'

At this point in the argument it is worthwhile drawing out the implications thus far. First, Soloveitchik has affirmed the 'secular' enterprise in a more thoroughgoing way even than Hirsch or Kook. The characteristic achievements of post-medieval civilisation – scientific method, technological mastery, aesthetic creativity – are unreservedly welcomed as part of the life of faith itself. They are the fulfilment of the mandate to Adam the first, to have dominion over his environment. And they enhance human dignity as the image of God: "Only the man who builds hospitals, discovers therapeutic techniques and saves lives is blessed with dignity. Man of the 17th and 18th centuries who needed several days to travel from Boston to New York was less dignified than modern man who attempts to conquer space,[33] boards a plane at the New York Airport at midnight and takes several hours later a leisurely walk along the streets of London."[34]

In this analysis there is no room for a religious-nostalgic longing for the naivete, innocence and wholeness of a pre-technological age. Nor is there even the hint of a possibility of a conflict between religion and science, either at the cognitive level, where they occupy separate domains, or at the functional level, where each possesses its own integrity. More significantly, Soloveitchik rules out even the possibility of a psychological-spiritual critique of the aspirations of enlightenment man. The charge that had been levelled against religion – often specifically against Judaism – since Spinoza was that it had been an instrument of oppression, inducing an attitude of servile submissiveness in its followers.[35] This was the *leitmotif* running through the Marxist critique of religion as sanctifying the social hierarchy, Hegel's and Nietzsche's view of Judaism as 'slave morality', and Freud's perception of faith as a neurotic craving for authority.

Against this, Soloveitchik fully ratifies the human pursuit of 'majesty' so long as it is kept in balance by the dialectical realisation that man, too, is dependent and but a handful of dust.[36] This is an important line of thought, for it appropriates and gives a positive interpretation to the insight of Hegel, Max Weber and more recently Peter Berger,[37] that Judaism was from the outset a victory of rationality and 'secularisation' over paganism – a 'disenchantment' of the world – relative to which Christianity was, in Berger's words, a "retrogressive step".[38]

However, and this is Soloveitchik's second point, there *is* a conflict, one made all the more poignant by the fact that it is not external – the man of faith on one side, the man of science on the other – but wholly contained within the life of faith. In some respects, as he argued powerfully elsewhere,[39] the authentic figure of Jewish spirituality is more like the man of science than like the conventional *homo religiosus*. Nevertheless, the conflict is endless,[40] inescapable and internal. Faith moves man like a pendulum between action and passivity, assertion and submission, cognition and rapture, victory and defeat. The man of majesty cannot live wholly within a world he controls and dominates without becoming demonic and overreaching himself, like the builders of the tower of Babel.[41] The man of redemption cannot live wholly within the community of prayer and find peace in escape from the world: "I hardly believe that any responsible man of faith, who is verily interested in the destiny of his community and wants to see it thriving and vibrant, would recommend now the philosophy of *contemptus saeculi*." [42] The war of cultures – 'religion' and 'science' – has been turned from a static antagonism to a dynamic oscillation within the soul of the believer.

But at this point we face a question, and come to the next and culminating point of the argument. Soloveitchik has taken the dilemma of modernity and identified it in the roots of human existence, in the very opening chapters of the Bible. As such, it is a problem of antiquity too, of humanity *per se*. What then did he mean by announcing at the outset of the essay that the "*contemporary* man of faith lives through a particularly difficult and agonising crisis"? [43] His answer is that in pre-modern times the dialectic of faith was "a wholesome and integrating experience".[44] But the balance has been disturbed. The pendulum no longer swings freely. Majestic man has ousted covenantal man.

THE MAN OF FAITH AND MODERN RELIGION

The dilemma of modernity is that majestic man has achieved unparalleled success in his attempts to explain and control nature. He has been intoxicated into *hubris*, the overreaching sin of seeing the creative, assertive side of his being as the entire reality of man. He has expelled covenantal man from his inner psyche, seeing passivity, submissiveness and ontic incompleteness as out of keeping with the stance of victory over a hostile environment. "By rejecting Adam the second, contemporary man, eo ipso, dismisses the covenantal faith community as something superfluous and obsolete." [45]

The argument might at this point have turned into a conventional attack on the pretensions of Nietzscheian triumphalism. But once again Soloveitchik demonstrates his genius for getting to the uncomfortable heart of the problem. For he does not proceed to set up a new dichotomy between religious and secular, belief and unbelief. His target is not "vulgar and illiterate atheism" [46] at all, but something closer to home: the phenomenon of modern religion itself. Just as he had earlier argued that Judaism extends into the secular, scientific domain, now he argues that the secular has subtly entered into the religious domain and appropriated and distorted its institutions and teachings.

Who is the contemporary 'man of religion'? Certainly not the *homo religiosus* of whom he had spoken in *Halakhic Man*, who seeks "cognition for the sake of grasping the eternal riddle, revealing for the sake of concealing, comprehending for the sake of laying bare the incomprehensible in all its glorious mystery and terror".[47] Instead he is a man of the world, a pragmatist engaged in the pursuit of success, who is nevertheless a member of an organised religion and a supporter of its causes. He creates religious communities, but these are not covenantal faith communities, but instead communities of interest and practical action.

Soloveitchik's insight is that secular man does not exclude religion from his universe. He needs an ethical Absolute to give his norms permanence and stability. There are times when he needs the therapeutic power of the act of faith. There are times too when he needs to turn from the mechanical world to the experience of beauty and the sublime. Even the scientific mind occasionally "yearns for its Creator and rebels against the concrete reality that so entirely surrounds it".[48] Thus far, "the message of faith, if translated into cultural categories, fits into the axiologico-philosophical frame of reference of the creative cultural consciousness and is pertinent even to secular man".[49]

However, the translation is only partially successful. It is true that the classic texts of Judaism occasionally speak in pragmatic terms: obedience to the commands lead to worldly happiness and a pleasant life. But there is another, disturbing, irreducible voice in which faith speaks: "There are simply no cognitive categories in which the total commitment of the man of faith could be spelled out . . . The act of faith is aboriginal, exploding with elemental force as an all-consuming and all-pervading eudaemonic-passional experience".[50] It resists every attempt to reduce it to cognitive or functional terms. And it directly challenges those terms in their aspiration to represent the whole of reality.

Soloveitchik's critique of contemporary secularised religion is devastating:

Notwithstanding the fact that Western man is in a

nostalgic mood, he is determined not to accept the dialectical burden of humanity . . . He, of course, comes to a place of worship. He attends lectures on religion and appreciates the ceremonial, yet he is searching not for a faith in all its singularity and otherness, but for religious culture . . . He is desirous of an aesthetic experience rather than a covenantal one, of a social ethos rather than a divine imperative. In a word, he wants to find in faith that which he cannot find in his laboratory, or in the privacy of his luxurious home . . . If he gives of himself to God, he expects reciprocity. He also reaches a covenant with God but this covenant is a mercantile one . . . Therefore, modern man puts up demands that faith adapt itself to the mood and temper of modern times. He does not discriminate between translated religion formulated in cultural categories . . . and the pure faith commitment which is as unchangeable as eternity itself.'[51]

This note has sounded through Soloveitchik's writings from the beginning. He finds the same phenomenon in modern religion's claim to represent tranquillity and peace of mind as against the chaos of the secular world;[52] in the desire for men and women to pray together, which he sees as turning prayer from loneliness to a desire for security and comfort;[53] in the demand that halakhah be 'meaningful' or that it be submitted to historical or intellectual categories;[54] and in the belief that there can be genuinely theological interfaith dialogue, implying that one faith can be translated into the language of another.[55]

These are all symptoms of the appropriation of faith by majestic man. Against them the man of faith must protest that they capture only half of the religious message. But here is the tragedy. For the other half is precisely that which cannot be translated into terms that modern man would understand. It is, to him, a 'foreign' language. What then can the man of faith do? "When the hour of estrangement strikes, the ordeal of the man of faith begins and he starts his withdrawal from society . . . He experiences not only ontological loneliness but also social isolation." [56] The closing pages of 'The Lonely Man of Faith' end on a defiant but elegiac note, with evocations of the prophetic figures – Moses, Elijah, Elisha, Jeremiah –

who endured social loneliness but could not contain the word of faith that burned like fire in their hearts. "Is modern man of faith entitled to a more privileged position and a less exacting and sacrificial role?"[57] Could there be a more tragic analysis of faith and modernity than this?

THE SECULARISATION OF FAITH

As we noted earlier, Soloveitchik embodied to a remarkable degree – in his biographical and personal prominence, in his unsurpassed mastery of both secular and halakhic scholarship – the existential drama of the meeting of two worlds. In him, the Lithuanian yeshivah met contemporary secular thought. No figure, certainly not Hirsch or Kook, had so known modernity face-to-face. Perhaps it was the sheer familiarity with non-Jewish scholarship which he displayed, perhaps the affirmative tone of the first half of 'The Lonely Man of Faith', or perhaps the memory of the more confident earlier essay, *Halakhic Man*, that encouraged his readers to believe that Soloveitchik spoke for a 'modern' Orthodoxy. The impression was mistaken. 'The Lonely Man of Faith' is an expression that falls little short of despair.

Its final prescription precisely echoes a point made several times by Maimonides, namely that there are times when the man of faith must withdraw from the world. "If [virtuous men] saw that due to the corruption of the people of the city they would be corrupted through contact with them and through seeing their deeds, and that social intercourse with them would bring about the corruption of their own moral habits, then they withdrew to desolate places where there are no evil men."[58] Maimonides' analysis of the religious personality is directly relevant. He portrayed two alternative ideals, the *chakham* and the *chassid*, the sage and the saint.[59] The sage, whose personality is marked by moderation, is the normative figure of Jewish tradition. The concept of the sage as ideal is directly related to the social character of Judaism, and to the ideal of halakhah as the legislation which creates a society. The saint, by contrast, is not the Jew as social being, but a figure in search of personal piety, engaged in a struggle with his personality.[60]

Two circumstances, both abnormal, turn the saintly ideal

from an option to a norm: the process of repentance,[61] and the breakdown of society. When the sage finds his religious life systematically undermined by all available social encounters, he has no alternative but to retreat into temporary seclusion and into the behavioural patterns of sainthood. This is precisely the pattern of Soloveitchik's man of faith who might, like Maimonides' sage, have found the balancing of opposites a "wholesome and integrating experience", but instead, like Maimonides' saint, he must turn to "his solitary hiding and to the abode of loneliness".[62] The two analyses concur that this is an aberration imposed by outside circumstance, not a timeless ideal. Modernity has forced faith into exile.

It is clear that Soloveitchik had pessimism thrust upon him. His earliest work bears an altogether different tone. *The Halakhic Mind*, written in 1944, begins with the sentence: "It would be difficult to distinguish any epoch in the history of philosophy more amenable to the mediating *homo religiosus* than that of today." [63] His argument, from which he has not retracted, is that modern developments in science and philosophy opened up a space for an altogether more fruitful presentation of religion, specifically halakhic Judaism, than prevailed in the pre-modern era where the only possibilities were scholasticism, agnosticism and mysticism. With considerable prescience, Soloveitchik sensed a new era of epistemological pluralism [64] in which the halakhic universe could be set forth as a complete self-sufficient world, objective, quantified, neither dethroned by science nor driven to romantic subjectivism. "Out of the sources of Halakhah, a new world view awaits formulation." [65]

It was not secular *knowledge*, encountered in the University of Berlin, that caused Soloveitchik such searing distress, but secular *man*, encountered in suburban-Jewish America. 'The Lonely Man of Faith' is in essence a critique – before the term was coined – of 'civil religion'.[66] Recent sociological studies of both American and Israeli Judaism [67] have identified a powerful return to Jewish values and symbols, but subtly transposed into a language devoid of transcendence. "For the civil religion, Judaism is very much a matter of concern; God is not." [68] Particularly in America, the new mood is associated with philanthropy and activism, and exactly mirrors the portrait of the religion of majestic man which Soloveitchik had so sharply diagnosed. His suspicion that the secular would enter and possess the sanctuary has been vindicated by subsequent events.[69] It is made doubly poignant by the fact that his own thought has been appropriated by younger thinkers and used to legitimate highly secular readings of Judaism.[70]

Soloveitchik's drama, then, is a heroic-tragic one. The man of faith can certainly engage with modern society and its modes of thought, provided that he has the courage for a double encounter with a dual identity.[71] As majestic man he is part of the secular-human enterprise. As covenantal man he is heir to a faith tradition that cannot be translated into contemporary language, and to a set of emotional responses – defeat, helplessness, the heroism of failure – that are no longer common currency. He may be in, but not of, the modern world. Most Jews, he admits, are not prepared for this inner dialectic, and hence the tradition is no longer the religion of most Jews. A synthesis is possible between the two identities, but not within society as presently constituted. Orthodoxy and modernity are both friends and strangers to one another. In this uncomfortable paradox, the man of faith must live.

NOTES

1. Joseph B. Soloveitchik, 'The Lonely Man of Faith', *Tradition* 7:2 (Summer 1965), p. 8. Soloveitchik's other key works include 'Confrontation', *Tradition* 6:2 (Summer 1964), pp. 5-28; 'The Community', 'Majesty and Humility', 'Catharsis', 'Redemption, Prayer, Talmud Torah', 'A Tribute to the Rebbitzen of Talne', *Tradition* 17:2 (Spring 1978), pp. 7-83; *Be-Sod ha-Yachad veha-Yachid* (ed. P. Peli), Jerusalem: Orot, 1976; *Ish ha-Halakhah – Galui ve-Nistar*, Jerusalem: World Zionist Organisation, 1979; *Divrei Hagut ve-Haarakhah*, Jerusalem: World Zionist Organisation, 1981; *Halakhic Man* (translated by Lawrence Kaplan), Jewish Publication Society, 1983; *The Halakhic Mind*, Seth Press, 1986. Summaries or reconstructions of Soloveitchik's public lectures include: Joseph Epstein (ed.), *Shiurei ha-Rav*, New York: Hamevaser, 1974; David Telsner (ed.), *Chamesh Derashot*, Jerusalem: Orot, 1974, translated as *Five Addresses*, Jerusalem: Tal Orot Institute, 1983; P. Peli (ed.), *Al ha-Teshuvah*, Jerusalem: World Zionist Organisation, 1974, translated as *On Repentance*, Jerusalem: Orot, 1980; Abraham R. Besdin (ed.), *Reflections of the Rav*, Jerusalem: World Zionist Organisation, 1979.

For studies of Soloveitchik's thought see: Eugene Borowitz, *Choices in Modern Jewish Thought*, New York: Behrman House, 1983, pp. 218-242; Elliot Dorff, 'Halakhic Man: A Review Essay', *Modern*

Judaism 6:1 (February 1986), pp. 91-98; David Hartman, *Joy and Responsibility*, Jerusalem: Ben-Zvi Posner, 1978, pp. 198-231; *The Breakdown of Tradition and the Quest for Renewal*, Montreal: The Gate Press, 1980; *A Living Covenant*, New York: Free Press, 1985; Lawrence Kaplan, 'The Religious Philosophy of Rabbi Joseph Soloveitchik', *Tradition* 14:2 (Fall 1973), pp. 43-64; 'Degamim shel ha-Adam ha-Dati ha-Idiali be-Hagut ha-Rav Yosef Dov Soloveitchik', *Mechkerei Yerushalayim be-Machshevet Yisrael*, 4:3-4 (1985), 327-339; Aharon Lichtenstein, 'R. Joseph Soloveitchik' in Simon Noveck (ed.), *Great Jewish Thinkers of the Twentieth Century*, B'nai B'rith, 1963, pp. 281-297; Pinchas Peli, 'Repentant Man – A High level in Rabbi Soloveitchik's Typology of Man', *Tradition* 18:2 (Summer 1980), pp. 135-159; Aviezer Ravitzky, 'Rabbi J. B. Soloveitchik on Human Knowledge: Between Maimonidean and neo-Kantian Philosophy', *Modern Judaism* 6:2 (May 1986), pp. 157-188; Jonathan Sacks, 'Alienation and Faith', *Tradition* 13:4-14:1 (Spring-Summer 1973), pp. 137-162; 'Rabbi Joseph B. Soloveitchik: Halakhic Man', *L'Eylah* 19 (Spring 5745), pp. 36-42; David Singer and Moshe Sokol, 'Joseph Soloveitchik: Lonely Man of Faith', *Modern Judaism* 2:3 (October 1982), pp. 227-272; Morris Sosevsky, 'The Lonely Man of Faith Confronts the Ish Ha-Halakhah', *Tradition* 16:2 (Fall 1976), pp. 73-89; and the essays by Zvi Kaplan, Walter Wurzburger, Zvi Zohar, A. Strikowski, M. Rosenak and A. Shauli-Bick in *Sefer ha-Yovel . . . ha-Rav Yosef Dov ha-Levi Soloveitchik*, Jerusalem: Mossad ha-Rav Kook/Yeshiva University, 1984, vol. 1.

2. 'The Lonely Man of Faith', pp. 8-9.
3. On Chaim Soloveitchik, see S. Y. Zevin, *Ishim ve-Shittot*, Jerusalem: Bet Hillel, pp. 39-86.
4. In 'How is Your Beloved Better than Another?' [Hebrew], *Be-Sod ha-Yachad veha-Yachid*, pp. 212-235, Soloveitchik argues that R. Chaim revolutionised the study of Talmud in the same way as did Galileo and Newton the pattern of scientific thought.
5. As honorary president of the Religious Zionists of America since 1946, and chairman of the Halakhah Commission of the Rabbinical Council of America since 1952. See Louis Bernstein, 'The Rav and the Rabbinical Council of America' [Hebrew], *Sefer ha-Yovel . . . ha-Rav Yosef Dov ha-Levi Soloveitchik*, vol. 1, pp. 18-29.
6. Originally published as *Ish ha-Halakhah, Galui ve-Nistar* in *Talpiot* 1:3-4, New York, 1944.
7. *The Halakhic Mind*, published in 1986, was originally written in 1944: author's note at beginning of book.
8. It is referred to directly in 'Majesty and Humility', p. 33. The frightening example in 'The Community', p. 11 seems to be drawn from personal experience, despite the reference to Tolstoy's *The Death of Ivan Ilich*. Much of Soloveitchik's work is related to death – his several published *hespedim*, the lectures *On Repentance* delivered on the *yahrzeit* of his father, and so on. Elsewhere he writes this into the phenomenology of the halakhic personality: "Halakhic man is afraid of death; the dread of dissolution seizes hold of him" (*Halakhic*

Man, p. 36). He conquers it through the distancing effect of halakhic study itself: "When halakhic man fears death, his sole weapon wherewith to fight this terrible dread is the eternal law of the Halakhah. The act of objectification triumphs over the subjective terror of death." (ibid., p. 73). The process of theologising, as he practises it, is explicitly given a cathartic function by Soloveitchik: "All I want is to follow the advice given by Elihu the son of Berachal of old who said, 'I will speak that I may find relief;' for there is a redemptive quality for an agitated mind in the spoken word and a tormented soul finds peace in confessing', 'The Lonely Man of Faith', p. 6.

9. B. T. *Sotah* 36b.
10. The metaphor of strange woman = secular philosophy is used by Maimonides in his letter to R. Jonathan ha-Cohen of Lunel: "She [the Torah] is my loving hind, the bride of my youth, whose love has ravished me since I was a young man. Many strange and foreign women have nevertheless become rival wives to her: Moabites, Edomites, Sidonites, Hittites. The Lord, may he be blessed, knows that I took these other women in the first instance only in order to serve as perfumers, cooks and bakers (I Samuel 8:13) for her [the Torah], and to show the peoples and the princes her beauty, for she is exceeding fair to behold." *Teshuvot ha-Rambam*, ed. J. Blau, 1961, vol. 3, p. 57.
11. "Father's tradition is an intellectual-moral one. That is why it is identified with *mussar*, which is the Biblical term for discipline." 'A Tribute to the Rebbitzen of Talne', p. 76.
12. Lichtenstein, p. 283; Samuel Heilman, 'The Many Faces of Orthodoxy, Part II', *Modern Judaism* 2:2 (May 1982), p. 193.
13. 'The Lonely Man of Faith', p. 17.
14. 'A Tribute to the Rebbitzen of Talne', pp. 76-77.
15. *BeSod ha-Yachad veha-Yachid*, p. 312.
16. 'Confrontation', p. 14.
17. These are explored in David Singer and Moshe Sokol, 'Joseph Soloveitchik: Lonely Man of Faith', *Modern Judaism* 2:3 (October 1982), pp. 227-272.
18. See *Halakhic Man*, note 1, p. 139.
19. 'The Lonely Man of Faith', p. 5.
20. 'Confrontation' and the major essay *Uvikashtem mi-sham*, in *Ish ha-Halakhah – Galui ve-Nistar*, Jerusalem: World Zionist Organisation, 1979, pp. 115-236, are organised hierarchically and chart a spiritual progression.
21. *Halakhic Man*, p. 3.
22. 'Majesty and Humility', p. 25.
23. See Zevin, op. cit.
24. See Gershom Scholem, 'Revelation and Tradition as Religious Categories in Judaism', *The Messianic Idea in Judaism*, New York: Schocken Books, 1972, pp. 282-303; 'Religious Authority and Mysticism', *On the Kabbalah and its Symbolism*, New York: Schocken Books, 1972, pp. 5-31; Simon Rawidowicz, 'On Interpretation',

Studies in Jewish Thought, Jewish Publication Society of America, 1974, pp. 45-80.
25. "A tormented soul finds peace in confessing", 'The Lonely Man of Faith', p. 6. This semi-autobiographical, semi-confessional stance breaks forth from time to time in Soloveitchik's work and gives it its peculiarly dramatic force. Form here mirrors content, for the lonely struggles of the life of faith, seen as essentially isolated and non-communal, are what have replaced the communal faith experience in the modern world. Soloveitchik in no way negates the centrality of the community, and he often stresses the function of halakhah in objectifying inner experience and rescuing it from subjectivity, romanticism and chaos. But the individual has to struggle towards them. It would be difficult to conceive of Soloveitchik's style of writing, or his vantage point, prior to the twentieth century. On the general issue of modern selfhood, see Lionel Trilling, *Sincerity and Authenticity*, Harvard University Press, 1978.
26. 'The Lonely Man of Faith', p. 10.
27. Ibid., p. 14.
28. Ibid., p. 24.
29. Ibid., p. 33. Soloveitchik here follows Judah Halevi's understanding of the distinction between the two names: *Kuzari* 4:1-16. See Jonathan Sacks, 'Buber's Jewishness and Buber's Judaism', *European Judaism* 12:2 (Winter 1978), pp. 14-19.
30. 'The Lonely Man of Faith', p. 54.
31. Ibid., p. 50.
32. Ibid., p. 54.
33. There appears to be an implicit criticism here of the stance adopted by A. J. Heschel (1907-1972), who had argued in *The Sabbath* that Judaism was a religion of time aiming at time's sanctification whereas technical civilization represents man's conquest of space. *Halakhic Man*, too, with its comparison between the halakhist and the modern theoretical mathematician, is set in counterpoint to Heschel's romantic-nostalgic portrayal of Eastern European Jewry in *The Earth is the Lord's* (*The Earth is the Lord's/The Sabbath*, Meridian Books 1963). A detailed contrast between the two men, both leading theologians of the twentieth century, both heirs of famous dynasties (Heschel was a descendant of several outstanding Chassidic leaders: the Maggid of Mezeritch, Levi Yitzchak of Berditchev and Abraham Joshua Heschel – after whom he was named – the Apter Rav), both deeply immersed in the Western philosophical tradition, might yield some fascinating results. The schools that they represent – for Soloveitchik, Lithuanian talmudism, for Heschel, Chassidism – were directly opposed in the nineteenth century, and some of the classic dichotomies persist in their work. Both in Germany, where he worked with Martin Buber in the Frankfurt *Lehrhaus*, and in America, where he taught at the Hebrew Union College and the Jewish Theological Seminary, Heschel belonged outside the institutional framework of Orthodoxy, and his involvement with the civil rights movement and interfaith dialogue were outside

American Orthodoxy's central concerns. But the contrast between the two men lies along a different axis than a simple Orthodox/non-Orthodox rift.
34. 'The Lonely Man of Faith', p. 14.
35. See Don Cupitt, *Crisis of Moral Authority*, SCM Press, 1985, pp. 106-121; David Hartman, *A Living Covenant*, pp. 1-108.
36. 'The Lonely Man of Faith', pp. 48-53.
37. For a modern examination of Weber's thought in relation to Judaism, see Irving M. Zeitlin, *Ancient Judaism*, Polity Press, 1984. Peter Berger's analysis is contained in *The Sacred Canopy*, New York: Doubleday, 1967, especially pp. 105-125.
38. *The Sacred Canopy*, p. 121.
39. In *Halakhic Man*.
40. Soloveitchik does not always speak as if there were no end to the conflict. Thus, "out of the contradictions and antinomies there emerges a radiant, holy personality whose soul has been purified in the furnace of struggle and opposition . . . This spiritual fusion that characterises halakhic man is distinguished by its consummate splendor, for did not the split touch the very depths, the innermost core, of his being?" (*Halakhic Man*, p. 4). This question is discussed by Lawrence Kaplan, 'Degamim shel ha-Adam ha-Dati ha-Idiali be-Hagut ha-Rav Yosef Dov Soloveitchik', and Aviezer Ravitsky, 'Rabbi J. B. Soloveitchik on Human Knowledge'.
41. 'The Lonely Man of Faith', pp. 57, 63. See also Robert Gordis, *Judaic Ethics for a Lawless World*, Jewish Theological Seminary, 1986, pp. 1-58.
42. 'The Lonely Man of Faith', p. 54, footnote.
43. Ibid., p. 8.
44. Ibid., p. 55.
45. Ibid., p. 56.
46. Ibid.
47. *Halakhic Man*, p. 12.
48. Ibid., p. 14.
49. 'The Lonely Man of Faith', p. 59.
50. Ibid., p. 60.
51. Ibid., pp. 63-64.
52. *Halakhic Man*, pp. 139-143.
53. A. R. Besdin, *Reflections of the Rav*, p. 81.
54. Ibid., pp. 139-149; 'Majesty and Humility', 'Catharsis'; *The Halakhic Mind*, pp. 85-99.
55. 'Confrontation'; *Reflections of the Rav*, pp. 169-177.
56. 'The Lonely Man of Faith', p. 65.
57. Ibid., p. 67.
58. Maimonides, *Shemoneh Perakim*, ch. 4. The translation is taken from Raymond L. Weiss and Charles Butterworth (eds.), *Ethical Writings of Maimonides*, New York: Dover, 1975, pp. 69-70. The rule is codified in *Hilkhot De'ot* 6:1, and given practical expression at the end of *The Epistle on Martyrdom* (translated in A. Halkin and D. Hartman, *Crisis and Leadership: Epistles of Maimonides*, Jewish

Publication Society of America, 1985, pp. 31-34).
59. *Hilkhot De'ot* ch. 1; *Shemoneh Perakim* chs. 3-4; see also *Guide of the Perplexed*, III: 53.
60. This emerges clearly from *Shemoneh Perakim* ch. 4.
61. *Hilkhot De'ot* 2:1-2; *Hilkhot Teshuvah* 2:4. The social character of the halakhah is set out in *Guide* II, 39-40; the law's disregard for the individual *per se*, in *Guide* III, 34. The argument of this and the preceding paragraph needs further elaboration, since it takes issue with the analysis of Aharon Lichtenstein, 'Does Jewish Tradition Recognize an Ethic Independent of Halakha?' in Menachem Kellner (ed.), *Contemporary Jewish Ethics*, New York: Sanhedrin, 1978, pp. 102-123. Lichtenstein's analysis, though remarkably suggestive, rests to my mind on a quite unwarranted assertion of discrepancy between *Hilkhot De'ot* and *Shemoneh Perakim*.
62. 'The Lonely Man of Faith', p. 65.
63. *The Halakhic Mind*, p. 3.
64. Ibid., pp. 19-81. For a modern secular exposition of a similar position, see Richard Rorty, *Philosophy and the Mirror of Nature*, Oxford: Blackwell, 1980.
65. *The Halakhic Mind*, p. 102.
66. 'The Lonely Man of Faith' was published in 1965. The term 'civil religion' is usually attributed to Robert Bellah, 'Civil Religion in America', *Daedalus* (Winter 1967), pp. 1-21.
67. Charles Liebman and Eliezer Don-Yehiya, *Civil Religion in Israel: Traditional Judaism and Political Culture in the Jewish State*, University of California Press, 1983; Jonathan S. Woocher, *Sacred Survival: The Civil Religion of American Jews*, Indiana University Press, 1986.
68. Woocher, p. 91.
69. Liebman, Don-Yehiyah and Woocher all attribute the rise of the new civil religion to the processes set in motion by the 1967 Six Day War.
70. See Irving Greenberg, *The Third Great Cycle in Jewish History*, National Jewish Resource Center, 1981; *Towards a Principled Pluralism*, New York: CLAL, 1986; David Hartman, *A Living Covenant*, op. cit. Both Greenberg and Hartman take up the 'modernist' statements within Soloveitchik's work, while ignoring or taking issue with, his anti-modernist dialectic.
71. This is the argument of 'Confrontation' and 'A Stranger and a Resident' (*Reflections of the Rav*, pp. 169-177).

5
Tradition as Resistance

All three thinkers we have considered, Hirsch, Kook and Soloveitchik, were conscious inhabitants of modernity, aware that with emancipation a radical transformation had overtaken Jewish identity. It had become, in Europe at least, a *divided* identity, split between the Jew's participation in a secular culture and his roots in the Jewish religious, national and ethnic tradition.

Hirsch was convinced that this dualism was viable. Once a solid, enduring basis had been laid for Jewish identity by the institutional structures of a Jewish school, the synagogue, and ongoing adult education, the Jew could enter a secular world, contributing to it as a model citizen. He would find it possible to select the elements of the wider culture that were compatible with Judaism and reject the rest.

Rav Kook, coming at the problem more than half a century later, and from an Eastern European perspective, was less sanguine. A Hirschian solution might work for a minority of Jews, but it would not protect the Jewish people as a whole against assimilation. Moreover, even at its best, it preserved an artificially restricted Judaism, a religion and its laws, rather than a total and environing culture such as had existed in the ghetto and *shtetl*. Judaism could only flourish and be creative in the context of a people and its culture. And this could happen only in the land of Israel.

The passage of yet another half century brought an awareness of the still deepening impact of secularisation. Israeli society had not yet undergone the sanctification of the secular in the way envisaged by Rav Kook. Nor, whether in Israel or the diaspora, was the Hirschian synthesis easy to maintain. The religious Jew who participates in a secular society finds, unwittingly and despite his various defences, that his consciousness is moulded no less by the latter than by the former. It is this awareness that pervades the writings of R. Soloveitchik and gives them their conflicted and ambivalent character.

All three, though, began with an optimistic view of

modernity. In none of their works do we find a nostalgia for the ghetto. None sought to deny or resist the transformations taking place in the conditions of Jewish life. Each, in their different ways, saw emancipation as making possible and necessary a reconstruction of Jewish life and thought. Their work has one detail in common, and at first sight it is a strange one. All three were critical of the philosophy of Moses Maimonides, in particular of that section of the *Guide of the Perplexed* in which he had explained the reasons for the commandments.[1] Each argued that Maimonides had translated Judaism into alien categories, approaching it from the perspective of Greek thought.

Against this, each insisted that Judaism was to be understood from within. It is as if all three saw modernity as offering Judaism the chance to be itself. It was no longer surrounded by a unified, dominant Christian or Islamic culture. It could enter the world of modern thought on equal terms, asserting its own autonomy and integrity. Not only Jews, but Judaism also, had been emancipated. The open society posed a threat to Jewish faith, but it delivered a constructive challenge as well, one from which positive religious achievements might emerge.

MODERNITY AND TRADITION

There is, though, another way of viewing modernity, one which from a religious perspective is deeply pessimistic. Most sociologists of the nineteenth century saw secularisation as an inexorable process. Society was becoming industrialised, urbanised and rationalised. Traditional communities were being uprooted. Even the concept of tradition was on the way to being eclipsed.[2]

Prior to the nineteenth century, the word 'modern' bore a generally unfavourable sense. The sources of wisdom lay in the past. The new was generally inferior to the old. It was in the nineteenth century, under the impact of social and intellectual change, that 'modern' began to become a term of praise.[3] Across several disciplines – history, philosophy, anthropology and biology – time began to be reconceived as a current of progress and evolution from the primitive to the increasingly civilised. The past was now not a model for emulation but a burden to be escaped. It no longer possessed authority over the present. In such a culture, the very idea of tradition is under threat.

Jews were 'latecomers' to modernity.[4] Emancipation invited them to join societies in which these processes were already well advanced. Hirsch was well aware of some of the shortcomings of the world Jews were about to enter. Much of the *Nineteen Letters* is devoted to a critique of the situation in which man is the measure of all things and each individual is the creator of his own ethical values.[5] Nonetheless Hirsch believed that it was possible to absorb the best in Western culture and discard those elements that were incompatible with Judaism. This response, as Marion J. Levy has pointed out, is characteristic of the encounter between traditional and non-traditional cultures: 'The members of a relatively non-modernised society see before them many and various results of the process in which they are, or are about to become, involved. These appeal to them in varying degrees, and almost inevitably the popular leaders, the influential persons, or the society's members in general are obsessed with the belief that they can take what they please and leave the rest.'[6]

This, Levy argues, is a mistake. 'The myth of easy independent selectivity from among the social structures of highly modernised societies must be recognised for what it is and has always been – a hybrid of wishful thinking and sentimental piety.' The impact of modernity on tradition is, he argues, pervasive and undermining. It exercises what he calls an 'explosive subversion.' Was there, then, an alternative strategy to that adopted by Hirsch for the preservation of Orthodoxy in the modern age?

RESISTING THE NEW

There was. It was to reject the entire process of emancipation and Enlightenment. Participation in Western society might or might not be materially beneficial to Jews, but it would be disastrous for Judaism. Such, at any rate, was the view of many traditionalists as they saw its impact on Jewish life. They had witnessed the conversions, intermarriages and assimilation that had already begun to affect the more wealthy and acculturated Jews of Germany by the late eighteenth century. In 1817 they saw the birth of Reform Judaism, in the form of the Hamburg temple, with its deletion from the prayer-book of all references to the ingathering of exiles and the return to Zion. Judaism could not accommodate to modernity without a gradual loss of most of its traditional substance. It must therefore develop the opposite stance. It must resist all change.

The first leader clearly to articulate this position was R. Moses Sofer (the Chatam Sofer, 1762-1839).[7] Born in Frankfurt, he had seen some of the early effects of *haskalah*, Jewish enlightenment, at first hand. It was on his move to Hungary as chief rabbi of Pressburg in 1806 that he began his defence of tradition in earnest. He sharply opposed the new educational trends that were then beginning to emerge amongst Jews. Parents were sending children either to new state schools or to Jewish schools where secular studies were being taught alongside Torah on the model advocated by Naftali Herz Wessely (1725-1805), one of the earliest protagonists of *Torah im Derekh Eretz*.

R. Sofer's objection was not so much to secular study in itself, for which he conceded a need, as to the subtle transformation of Jewish studies in the new curriculum. Torah was being taught in translation. Emphasis was being placed on its plain sense at the expense of the rich, many-layered midrashic interpretations. Judaism was portrayed through rational and ethical categories that laid little emphasis on mystery, authority and revelation. He was a tireless critic, too, of Moses Mendelssohn's translation of the Bible into German. Rightly, he suspected that a major intellectual upheaval was under way even if, for the time being, it endorsed traditional conduct.

Although R. Sofer did not formulate his position in these terms, we can best understand it in terms of a novel understanding of the phrase *Torah im Derekh Eretz*. *Derekh eretz*, 'the way of the world', carried a wide spectrum of senses in the rabbinic literature. It meant, variously, a worldly occupation, mores, etiquette, and civilisation.[8] It represented an area of practical wisdom outside of Torah but complementary to it. 'Culture' in its various nuances is probably its nearest equivalent. Often, rules of *derekh eretz* were derived from what was perceived to be admirable behaviour in the non-Jewish world. Table manners, for example, could be learned from the Persians;[9] honouring of parents from the Romans;[10] astronomy from the Greeks.[11] *Derekh eretz*, the virtues and conventions that bound society, preceded Torah.[12] Some of its rules one could infer simply by observing nature. We could have learnt, said the rabbis, modesty from the cat, honesty from the ant, chastity from the dove and good manners from the cock.[13]

Culture, whether understood as ethics or economics, or arts and sciences, was wider than Torah, though it was subject to Torah's endorsement or disapproval. In the middle ages Jews wrote poetry in the Spanish manner and philosophy in the Islamic neo-Aristotelian style. Their vernacular languages, Yiddish and Ladino, were Jewish adaptations of German and Spanish respectively. Jewish cuisine, habits of dress, music and folklore were a series of local borrowings, naturalised and woven into the fabric of Jewish life. *Derekh eretz* in its broadest sense was the field of interaction between Jews and their host societies.

But prior to emancipation, this interaction was limited. To be sure, Jews mixed with gentile society, primarily in the course of business, but their religious, judicial, welfare and educational institutions were automonous. As long, too, as gentile culture was predominantly religious, there was a natural as well as halakhic barrier to Jewish participation. It might contain quasi-idolatrous motifs. Even if it did not, Jews were forbidden to 'walk in the ways' of gentiles. Any mode of non-Jewish behaviour that held religious significance was prohibited to Jews.[14]

Emancipation took place against the backdrop of a secularisation of both state and culture. Increasingly Jews found themselves able on the one hand and required on the other to become involved in the non-Jewish intellectual and moral environment. The scope and substance of *derekh eretz* was transformed. Jews were expected to speak an unaccented standard German, acquire new forms of manners and civility, make themselves masters of a European cultural heritage, and mix socially as well as pragmatically with non-Jewish society.[15] To this development, Samson Raphael Hirsch and the Chatam Sofer gave diametrically opposed reactions. Each was justifiable on the basis of Jewish tradition, for the tradition had not faced quite this possibility before.

CULTURE AND CONTINUITY

Hirsch saw that Torah was distinct from *derekh eretz*. Jewish law was one thing, Jewish culture another. Jews had – whenever they were allowed to do so – interfaced with other civilisations. They had borrowed and they had given back in return. One should not confuse Judaism itself with the culture of the ghetto, which had been only one historical manifestation of Jewish life, and a narrow one at that. It was the task of Judaism to apply its religious values and norms to any milieu in which it found itself. There was, one might say, the body of Judaism, and there were the various clothes it wore. Jewish life could undergo a change of cultural clothing so long as the body – Jewish faith and law – remained intact.

There is no reason to suppose that the Chatam Sofer would have dissented from this analysis. But his perspective was different. To be sure, Jewish *derekh eretz* had evolved differently in different times and places. But what was at stake now, as it was not so long as Jewish law had coercive power, was Jewish continuity. The direction of assimilation was being reversed. Instead of assimilating local customs into Jewish life, Jews were being assimilated into local gentile society. The old barriers between Jew and non-Jew were breaking down. Jewish survival had been, since biblical times, predicated on a code of differentness. Jews were a people apart. Their laws were 'different from all other peoples'. In the middle ages that had been reinforced by the deep differences between Jews and their Christian or Islamic neighbours. Now the removal of Jewish automony and the secularisation of culture meant that the 'fence' behind which Jews had preserved their separate existence had collapsed. A new code of differentness had to be found.

It lay in *derekh eretz* itself, understood as pre-modern Jewish culture. Traditional habits of behaviour and dress, and especially the Yiddish language, were now to be seen as sacrosanct – not because they had been specified by Jewish law or even seen as matters of religious significance but because, in the new social context, they fulfilled two vital functions. They emphasised Jewish continuity with the past, and they vividly embodied the fact that the Jew was different, unintegrated and at a distance from his environment.

It was this that lay behind the Chatam Sofer's most famous principle, an adaptation of a talmudic rule which had originally referred to the consumption of agricultural produce, and which was now applied to all symptoms of modernity: *chadash assur min ha-Torah*, 'the new is biblically forbidden.'[16] For the new, even in its most innocent guises, was a harbinger of Jewish disintegration. *Derekh eretz* could no longer be regarded, as it had been hitherto, as halakhically neutral. In the specific circumstances of the nineteenth century, all change was a carrier of secularisation.

This ultra-conservative position was in fact a radical extension of halakhah. It was especially carried through to the synagogue. Developments for which some halakhic justification might have been given were now seen – not without cause – as accommodations to non-Jewish *mores*. They were symptoms of Reform. Introducing choirs into the service, moving the *bimah* (the raised platform on which the reader stood) from the centre to the east end of the synagogue, conducting weddings in the synagogue instead of in a courtyard or communal hall, and rabbis who wore canonicals and preached in German instead of Yiddish, were all proscribed by Hungarian halakhists who followed in the tradition of the Chatam Sofer.[17]

The underlying logic of this approach to Jewish law was that 'anything which in itself is permitted, but which has become a symbol of religious disintegration, is *ipso facto* turned into something which is forbidden.'[18] If halakhah was to exercise its role as the vehicle of Jewish continuity it must erect new fences to replace those that had broken down. It must preserve the past for the sake of the future, even in respect of details of the past which had not previously been endowed with religious significance.

Behind this strategy lay a view of modernisation that has received, as we have seen, the endorsement of at least some contemporary secular sociologists. Modernity, Marion J. Levy argues, cannot be selectively embraced. Once admitted, even in part, it rapidly undermines the entire structure of tradition. The alternative to accommodation is resistance, and this was the route consciously chosen by R. Moses Sofer. Jews could not participate in secular culture without ultimately placing Judaism at risk. The new *derekh eretz* would endanger Torah. Torah must be surrounded with a culture of its own, one that was as close as possible to the modes of pre-modern times. The terms of emancipation were to be clearly and firmly declined.

THE SOCIAL CONTEXT OF RESISTANCE

If this had been the whole of the Chatam Sofer's response, it might have been a prescient critique of 'modern' Orthodoxy, but no more. The walls of separation between Jewish and gentile culture were crumbling. Mere protest was powerless to arrest the rapid changes in Jewish existence. Religious beliefs, as Peter Berger reminds us, require a 'plausibility structure'. To carry weight they must be mirrored or 'objectified' in the patterns of social life.[19] Resisting modernity was one thing; providing a social setting in which traditional patterns of behaviour and belief could be preserved was another.

One sector of Jewry, though, did have powerful structural defences against the inroads of secularisation. This was the Chassidic movement, which had spread throughout Eastern Europe during the eighteenth century. Organised as it was around a charismatic religious leadership – the figure of the *Tzaddik* or *Rebbe* – it was a populist and pietist movement stressing devotion, joy and prayer against the more traditional value of Torah study. The rich internal culture of the Chassidim, their strong communities and their powerful focus on single figures of authority, created something approaching a self-sufficient and total Jewish environment. The Chassidic group represented, one might say, the first voluntary ghetto of the modern Jewish world.

Throughout the second half of the eighteenth century, opposition to Chassidism, led by R. Elijah b. Solomon Zalman (the Vilna Gaon, 1720-1797), had been intense. R. Moses Sofer belonged to the anti-Chassidic school, the *mitnagdim*. But by the nineteenth century it had become clear that the battle had moved to another front, assimilation and its Jewish manifestations: *haskalah* (Jewish Enlightenment) and Reform. The opponents of Chassidism would be forced, if they were to succeed in halting the disintegration of tradition, to adopt their own equivalent of the Chassidic strategy. They would have to create enclosed communities with their own internal cultures and charismatic leaders. A new institutional base was needed. It came in the form of the yeshivah, the school of talmudic study. R. Moses Sofer founded a yeshivah on his arrival in Pressburg, and it became the largest since the great academies of Babylon.

Other seminal yeshivot, too, were founded at around this time, the most influential being the one created in 1802 by R. Chayyim of Volozhyn. Though the yeshivah had been, since mishnaic times, a vehicle of Jewish education, the new yeshivah differed from its predecessors in a number of respects. It was independent of the local community, supported by funds raised by emissaries who travelled throughout Eastern Europe and occasionally even America for the purpose. Its students were for the most part not local either. They travelled great distances to be able to study at a particular institution or under a famous teacher. As a result the students were separated from their families for most of the year. The yeshivah became a total environment and its head a figure of quasi-parental authority.[20]

The great yeshivot of the nineteenth century, Volozhyn, Mir, Solobdka, Telz and others, were far more than centres of learning. They became the bases of an intense battle to screen tradition from the inroads of secularisation. There was strict supervision to ensure that neither secular studies nor *haskalah* literature penetrated the yeshivah's walls. A decision was taken to let the Volozhyn yeshivah close in 1892 rather than accede to the Russian government's insistence that it include elementary secular tuition in its curriculum. The negative safeguards were not always sufficient, and after initial resistance the devotional and ethical disciplines of *Mussar* – the movement popularised by the disciples of R. Israel Salanter – were introduced into the Lithuanian centres. The yeshivot, R. Sofer's among them, were the training ground of an elite group of students, many of whom became religious leaders in their own right. Traditionalism had created its own equivalent of the Chassidic Rebbe in the person of the *rosh yeshivah*, the yeshivah head. The yeshivah itself became an instrument of socialisation comparable in intensity to the Chassidic circle. Tradition-as-resistance had found its institutional base.

DECLINE

The traditionalist strategy had its successes, particularly in Eastern Europe where the impact of Enlightenment and social change was delayed until the early twentieth century. But it was rooted, as we have seen, in a pessimistic reading of modernity. It tacitly accepted that a sizeable number of Jews, perhaps the majority, would choose the path of acculturation and assimiliation. These, it did not address.[21] Instead it aimed at salvaging a *she'erit ha-peletah*, a saving remnant who would keep the fire of faith alive until there was a more favourable turn in the cultural climate.

In R. Moses Sofer's Hungary the Reform, or Neolog, movement proceeded apace.[22] Thirty years after his death, the Hungarian government convened a General Jewish Congress to determine the basis of Jewish communal organisation. Already the reformers were in a majority, fielding 126 delegates as against the 94 of the Orthodox. The Orthodox insistence that community regulations be in accord with Jewish law was rejected. The Orthodox representatives then left the Congress and petitioned Parliament for the right to be exempt from the regulations, and to form a separate community structure of their own. In 1870 this was granted.

The Hungarian Orthodox secession set a pattern that was increasingly to become the norm governing Orthodox relations with the Jewish community as a whole. In 1876 the Prussian parliament passed a similar law, and Samson Raphael Hirsch waged a fierce and controversial struggle to persuade his own congregation in Frankfurt to secede from the local Jewish community board.[23] In 1912, alarmed at the growing secularist ambitions of the Zionist movement, Orthodox leaders from across Europe joined forces to create Agudat Yisrael, the organisation that marked their formal separation from the official institutions of Zionism.[24] At each point in this sequence there were major sections of Orthodoxy who refused to disengage from the wider community. In Hungary they were known as the status quo communities; in Germany as *Gemeinde* Orthodoxy; in the Zionist movement they were represented primarily by Mizrachi, the religious Zionist movement founded by R. Isaac Reines. But the weight of rabbinic authority lay behind secession, as Orthodoxy throughout Central and Eastern Europe began to see itself as a minority, unable significantly to influence wider communal trends and best engaged in securing its own strongholds.

Throughout the early twentieth century, secularisation took its toll among the communities of the East. It had a less assimilatory, more collectivist cast than in the West, but it was no less destructive of tradition. Socialism, Communism and Zionism, all revolutionary future-oriented rather than traditionalist ideologies, exercised a powerful attraction. The writings of the rabbinic leaders of this period are heavy with laments over the empty houses of study, the rebellious young, the satanic influences of the new modes of schooling, and the loss of the old order. A sense of powerlessness pervades their reflections.[25] A new generation, formed in the crucible of the First World War, was declaring its independence of religious authority. Had there been time, traditionalism might have staged a recovery. A distinctively East European neo-Orthodoxy might have emerged. But the Holocaust intervened, reducing the last remaining fortresses of tradition to ashes.

REBIRTH

By midway through the twentieth century it would have been a reasonable inference to conclude that, as a response to modernity, traditionalism had failed. The momentum of Jewish life lay elsewhere. In Israel it lay in a secular nationalism which, under leaders like David Ben Gurion, had aggressively shaken itself free of both rabbinic Judaism and diaspora history and which sought its Jewish links directly with the Bible. In America it lay with movements of radical accommodation – Conservative and Reform – which had either abandoned or introduced substantive modifications into Jewish law. Orthodoxy, in both communities, was in a minority. The only forms in which it seemed to exist as a compelling alternative were as religious Zionism in Israel and Modern Orthodoxy in America, the forms, that is to say, that had been pioneered by Rav Kook and Samson Raphael Hirsch. Here at least Orthodoxy seemed to be attuned to and in dialogue with the modern world. The terms of contemporary existence – secular culture and participation in the open society – could not be resisted other than in small, self-reinforcing enclaves. These had existed in Eastern Europe in Chassidic circles and the yeshivot. But they had been destroyed in the

Holocaust. A chapter in Orthodoxy seemed to have ended.

The past forty years have, therefore, witnessed one of the most remarkable reversals of recent Jewish history. For it is traditionalism that today represents the most rapidly growing, and in some senses the strongest, section of contemporary Jewry in both Israel and America. In both communities there has been a stunning growth in the number of yeshivot, to a point which already exceeds nineteenth century Eastern European Jewry at its height. It is traditionalism too, rather than religious Zionism or Modern Orthodoxy, that seems to speak most compellingly and directly to the situation of many contemporary Jews.

One of the crucial factors in this transformation was undoubtedly the fact that the Eastern European yeshivah, if it did not exercise a decisive impact on its wider Jewish environment, was nonetheless a unique training-ground for a particular style of leadership, self-sacrificing and single-minded. A handful of yeshivah heads and Chassidic leaders arrived in the United States in the late 1930s and early 1940s, in flight from the destruction of European Jewry. There they consciously set about reconstructing their communities and institutions. American Jewry, by now the largest remaining Jewish population, had never experienced Orthodox leadership of this stature before.

R. Aaron Kotler, a Lithuanian *rosh yeshivah*, arrived in America in 1941 and set about creating a yeshivah on the European model. He sought a location that would isolate the students from distracting interactions with American life and allow complete concentration on talmudic study. He chose a site in Lakewood, New Jersey, and its success turned it into a model for others to emulate. Under the influence of R. Aaron, R. Shraga Mendlowitz and R. Jacob Kamenetsky, a massive programme was undertaken to create Orthodox Jewish day schools. Immediately after the second World War there were only 30 such institutions in the United States. As of the early 1980s the number had risen to 522.[26]

R. Menachem Mendel Schneersohn, leader of Lubavitch Chassidism, turned his own movement into an active organisation of outreach to the unaffiliated, establishing centres throughout the Jewish world and utilising the entire spectrum of modern techniques of communication and influence. R. Joel Teitelbaum, head of the Satmar

Chassidim, arrived in New York as a survivor of the Bergen-Belsen concentration camp. An extreme opponent of Zionism, he established his community in the New York suburb of Williamsburg and by a combination of personal authority, cultural seclusion and the large families and high birth rates of his followers, Satmar rapidly established itself as a community of considerable size.[27]

The seemingly iron law of American acculturation had for the first time been resisted. Hitherto this had yielded a pattern of progressive Americanisation, a movement of Jews from immigrant ghettoes in the inner city toward outer suburbia, a rapid climb up the educational and occupational ladder and, in the process, an attrition of traditional behaviour and belief. Orthodoxy was associated with the first or immigrant generation, Conservative Judaism with the second and Reform with the third, as Jews sought less demanding and separatist forms of religious identification. Now, however, the nexus of the Jewish day school, yeshivah and separatist Orthodox community seemed fully capable of retaining, indeed intensifying, the loyalties of new generations. Why, then, has traditionalism, with its negative view of secular culture and the open society, emerged from its relative failure in the early twentieth century to its contemporary prominence and success?

THE FRAGMENTATION OF CULTURE

Unlike the syntheses of Hirsch, Kook and Soloveitchik, traditionalism was not a new philosophy of Judaism. To the contrary, it reserved its strongest criticism for the enterprise of philosophising and the attempt to marry Orthodoxy with modernity. It was, rather, a social strategy, and it is to social developments that we must turn by way of explanation.

Early nineteenth century Germany, to which Hirsch's writings were a response, confronted Jews with a relatively coherent secular culture, a palpable public morality and a code of civility that governed social interactions. The secular *derekh eretz* of which Hirsch, and before him Wessely, spoke had identifiable content. To claim to be participants in the wider intellectual milieu Jews had to internalise and formulate their responses to such thinkers as Lessing, Kant and Hegel. This dominates a whole chapter of modern Jewish thought, from Moses Mendelssohn in the eighteenth century to Franz Rosenzweig in the early twentieth. The Orthodox rabbi of Frankfurt who so captured Rosenzweig's imagination, Nehemiah Nobel (1871-1922), was so intense a devotee of Goethe that Rosenzweig wrote of him that it was only in his sermons, as opposed to his lectures that 'the Jew in him came to the fore' and only then 'did he believe himself able to manage without loans from the Christian and pagan cultural spheres, and even there one was never sure one wouldn't be handed a quotation from "the master" [Goethe].' [28]

By contrast, the increasing impact of secularisation has, by the late twentieth century, meant that culture itself has become fragmented as coherent systems of meaning have increasingly moved from the public to the private domain. In the most influential recent survey of contemporary American attitudes, the authors invoke a phrase of John Donne to characterise the present state of culture: "tis all in pieces, all coherence gone.' [29] In a pluralised culture of separate specialisations, an integrated vision, whether in science, philosophy or the arts, is a present impossibility. Already in 1944, in *The Halakhic Mind*, R. Soloveitchik had noted that a confrontation between Judaism and science was no longer possible since science itself was no longer a unified framework of thought but instead a loose collection of diverse disciplines, each independent of the others. In his recent jeremiad on the state of American universities, *The Closing of the American Mind*, Allan Bloom concludes that 'the university now offers no distinctive visage to the young person . . . there is no vision, nor is there a set of competing visions, of what an educated human being is . . . There is no organisation of the sciences, no tree of knowledge.' [30]

The Hirschian vision emerged specifically as a way of negotiating between two substantive and coherent identities, the Jew as participant in modern society with its intellectual canons and universalist ethic, and the Jew as citizen of the faith community with its own history and laws. He was *Mensch-Jissroel*, both man-in-the-abstract and Jew. But the former has since disintegrated into a state which is value-neutral, contenting itself for the most part with reconciling competing interests and matching means to ends, and a series of semi-private associations, religious, ethnic or cultural, which have no ambitions to universality. Necessarily, then, Hirsch's synthesis is inapplicable to societies of the late twentieth century which have undergone advanced secularisation.

Rav Kook's programme, too, fails for the same reason. For it was precisely the task he envisaged for Jewish spirituality that it would sanctify all secular specialisations by teaching each its place within a single harmonising vision of the unity of creation. Judaism would be a kind of meta-discipline revealing the interconnectedness of all knowledge. It would thus correct what Rav Kook saw as the besetting sin of all secularisms, their tendency to see themselves in isolation as a self-sufficient way of interpreting reality. It is just this meta-discipline which the contemporary organisation of knowledge and culture renders impossible. The point was well made by the French anthropologist Louis Dumont: 'In the modern world each of our particular viewpoints or specialised pursuits does not know very well – or does not know at all – what it is about and the reason for its existence or distinctness . . . Our rationality manifests itself within each of our neatly distinct compartments but not in their distribution, definition and arrangement.' [31]

No grand cultural synthesis of the kind attempted by Hirsch and Kook is presently available: not because of the state of Jewish thought but because of the state of secular thought. This, as we saw, was already manifest in the work of R. Soloveitchik which consciously disavows any aspiration to public philosophy and focusses instead on the individual and his private experiences. But if this is so, then the integrated world-view of tradition comes to seem, by contrast with secular culture, to have coherence and power. Certainly there is no compelling ideological alternative, as there was when socialism and secular Zionism were exercising their attractions over Eastern European Jewish youth and when Enlightenment liberalism held a similar sway over German Jewry. The dialogue with modernity, which had produced the phenomena of Modern Orthodoxy and religious Zionism, has come to a halt, for modernity itself no longer speaks with a single identifiable voice.

THE REINSTATEMENT OF TRADITION

This development in the intellectual world has consequences for the social world as well. Jews in the nineteenth century, newly emerging into European and American society, found themselves regarded as lacking in the refinements and sensibilities of the middle-class culture to which they aspired. By the 1960s, the deepening impact of liberal individualism was graphically symbolised in the youth cultures of drug-taking, sexual promiscuity and civil disobedience. The moral revolution seemed to many Jews – not only to Orthodox Jews who took their standards from biblical and rabbinic law, but even to acculturated Jews who took their standards from the civil ethos of a generation earlier – to be less an ethical advance than a retreat into neo-paganism. There was a reaction, throughout the 1970s and 1980s, away from liberalism toward the values of authority, restraint, discipline and community. These were the very values represented by traditionalism, which gained in stature as a result.

The liberal ideal of public neutrality and private morality, with its resultant ethical pluralism, represents a crisis, too, for personal identity. 'The pluralistic structures of modern society have made the life of more and more individuals migratory, ever-changing, mobile. In everyday life the modern individual continuously alternates between highly discrepant and often contradictory social contexts. In terms of his biography, the individual migrates through a succession of widely divergent social worlds.' [32] This can come to be experienced as alienation and what sociologists call anomie, the sense of directionlessness that Emile Durkheim identifed as the symptom of a society in which a common moral code was in the process of disintegration. This has had implications for the development of Jewish consciousness since the 1960s.

First it gave rise to a search for roots and a resurgent ethnic consciousness. This was something of a global phenomenon in the 1960s, and Jewishly it meant the end of assimilation as a conscious strategy. Many of the three million Jewish immigrants to the United States between the 1880s and 1920s had arrived with a positive desire to be absorbed in the American melting pot. As late as the mid-1950s Will Herberg, in his classic study of American religious identities, *Protestant-Catholic-Jew*, argued that ethnicity was still declining as a factor in identity. By 1963, however, Nathan Glazer and Daniel Moynihan concluded that 'the point about the melting pot is that it did not happen.'[33] The new ethnic affirmation meant that for the first time in modernity the traditionalists' distinctiveness of dress, manners and language was no longer strange and counter-cultural. It was the Jewish way of doing one's own thing. Particularism – anathema to the Enlightenment – had re-entered secular culture. A major re-evaluation of the roots of identity was under way.

Second, the search for identity led many Jewish students back into a direct experience of tradition, observing Hansen's law that the third generation strives to remember what the second generation laboured to forget. The late 1960s and 1970s saw a significant movement of *teshuvah*, religious return, as alienated American and then Israeli youth turned to traditionalist yeshivot for a sense of meaning and purpose. The early returnees had often been through various stages of the search for the supernatural – drugs, meditation, and some of the many new sects and cults that developed at this period – before finally seeking a traditional Jewish spirituality. There was though, throughout the *teshuvah* movement, a general sense of rejection of the values of middle-class suburban America. Janet Aviad, in her study of returnees,[34] came across repeated references to the 'emptiness of life', 'lack of values', 'illusions', 'looseness of society' and the 'decadence' of secular life. Students found their parents' Jewish lifestyles empty, dishonest, hypocritical, superficial, materialistic and assimilatory. They came to the yeshivot in search of community, absolute values, Jewish authenticity and a framework in which personal identity had clear content and direction. Again traditionalism, with its long-standing rejection of the relativities of modern culture, was the beneficiary.

THE DEMOGRAPHIC IMPERATIVE

These factors served to enhance the prestige of traditionalism in the wider Jewish community: to 'normalise' it, as it were. But there were other factors that had a more direct impact on its inner life. Menachem

Friedman has charted the impact of post-war economic and social change on the *charedi* or traditionalist community.[35] The growth of the modern welfare state has allowed individuals to spend more extended periods in education. This has meant, for traditionalists, that students are able to spend longer in yeshivot, often remaining after marriage in the school for mature students, the *kollel*.

The need for teachers to staff the increasing numbers of Jewish day schools provides an ideal career opportunity for the wives of such students, enabling them to support their husbands during their extended studies. The men themselves often find means of earning a livelihood through the provision of religious services, as teachers, rabbis, kashrut supervisors, suppliers of religious accessories, and in Israel as army chaplains, judges in religious courts, and teachers within the yeshivah system itself. These occupations require a minimum of interaction with the secular world. So too do those branches of international trade – diamonds, for example – which have become dominated by traditionalists. Increased mobility and the post-war concentration of Jewish life in large urban centres have made the strong sense of kinship within particular *charedi* groups a powerful framework for these avenues of trade and international co-operation.

Business success has been an important compensation for the closure of other career routes: the professions, management, scientific research and other roles requiring advanced secular education. The remark of one Williamsburg chassid is characteristic of the new economic situation: 'Many of our *yunge leit*, our young people, make more money than your college graduates.'[36] Contemporary urban life reinforces traditionalist separatism in other ways, too. The modern metropolis reveals secular life at its worst: in the form of drugs, crime, consumerism, hedonism and inter-ethnic tensions. This heightens the sense traditionalists have of alienation from their environment. Residential mobility allows the creation of the ethnic or religious ghetto, in which social interaction with other cultural groups is at a minimum. Here a lifestyle which in a mixed neighbourhood might be conspicuous is supported by a surrounding and homogeneous community. Close residential concentration also allows for strong internal social controls, essential to the maintenance of religious authority.

In the late nineteenth and early twentieth century, traditionalism had survived longest and most successfully in the context of the small Eastern European township, the *shtetl*. The large city had been the locus of cosmopolitanism, *haskalah*, secularisation and the breakdown of religious disciplines. By the late twentieth century, the 'secular city' has paradoxically become the setting of a traditionalist revival. As Friedman notes, it combines 'togetherness and isolation: ideal conditions for *charedi* life'.[37]

Undoubtedly, though, the key factor in the traditionalist revival has been its high birth rates. For Jews, accommodation to the modern world often went hand in hand with diminished fertility and smaller families. Indeed in America Jews had had lower birthrates than either Protestants or Catholics since the beginning of the century. In the 1970s, however, even this low rate declined sharply to an average of 1.2 children per family.[38] This was well below replacement level, and led to a series of pessimistic demographic projections, one of which estimated a reduction in size of the American Jewish community from six million to tens or hundreds of thousands in the year 2075.

The rate has since risen, but recent research by Samuel Heilman and Steven M. Cohen has shown that family size is directly related to religious affiliation.[39] It found that as against the average non-Orthodox family of 2.0 children, the corresponding size for the 'non-observant' Orthodox was 2.1, for the 'centrist' Orthodox 2.9, and for the 'traditional' (= fully practising) the figure was 4.2. Even this understates the situation, for among some Chassidic groups, notably Lubavitch and Satmar, the average is far higher still. More than one estimate has placed the average Satmar family at between eight and nine children. Current figures, for example, show an enrolment of 28,000 students at Satmar educational institutions in New York.[40] Given the total current enrolment in Jewish day schools throughout North America of 130,000,[41] the demographic impact of traditionalism is enormous.

The reasons underlying this trend are simple. Traditionalists place a high value on the family, early marriage and on a home-centred and child-rearing role for women. Birth-control is generally disapproved. Above all, the Chassidic and yeshivah communities acutely felt the ravages of the Holocaust. Religious leaders stressed the need to repopulate decimated communities. Their internal authority and the strong social sanctions within the circle of their followers meant that they were able to influence the behaviour patterns of their followers as few other leaders could in more diffuse religious settings. One distinctive feature of *charedi* religiosity is its high consistency between belief and practice and the willingness of its adherents to place principle over economic progress. Clearly, the decision to have a large family involves considerable sacrifice, and as the figures show, no other group in Jewry has responded similarly. Outside of Orthodoxy, the individualism of contemporary culture has taken its toll of the family in the form of delayed marriages, non- and out-marriage, family planning, and an increasing incidence of divorce.

The high birthrates of traditionalists and their success in resisting assimilatory trends contrast strongly with the small families and high attritions of contemporary non-Orthodox Jewish groups. Although Orthodoxy, for example, is estimated at only some ten per cent of the American Jewish population, eighty-five per cent of all children enrolled at Jewish day schools are Orthodox, and the day school has proved to be a uniquely powerful vehicle of Jewish continuity. Professor Daniel Elazar recently drew attention to the significance of numbers when practice as well as affiliation is taken into account. Noting that though Conservative Judaism is the largest institutional grouping in American Jewry, only a small percentage of its members 'live up to the standards of observance set by the Conservative movement', he calculated that 'at the late 1984 wedding of two scions of the Satmar dynasty, the number of Jews packed into a single Long Island stadium for the nuptials equalled the whole body of authentic Conservative Jews.' [42] It is clear that a major demographic reversal is in progress, one that will transform the religious life of Jewry and become yet more pronounced in the coming decades.

THE PARADOX OF MODERNITY

So we arrive at a stunning and paradoxical conclusion. The section of Orthodoxy which has most successfully negotiated modernity has been the group that took the most negative view of modernity and most strenuously resisted it.

No outcome seemed less likely in the aftermath of the Second World War. The preceding decades had witnessed the breakdown of tradition in its previous strongholds of the Eastern European townships. In 1930, R. Israel Meir ha-Cohen (the Chafetz Chayyim, 1838-1933) could lament: 'The sanctity of the Holy Torah is declining from day to day at a frightening pace. The new generation is growing up without Torah and faith. They are becoming wayward children who deny God and His Torah. And if, God forbid, this situation continues much longer who knows to what condition we will fall.' [43] The faithful who remained were destroyed in the Holocaust. The future of Jewish life lay in an aggressively secular state of Israel and in a rapidly assimilating America, stigmatised by previous rabbinic visitors from Europe as the *treifa medinah*, an unholy land. Modernity, whether benign in emancipation or brutal in the *shoah*, seemed to conspire to eclipse tradition.

Its re-emergence in late modernity is an extraordinary vindication of R. Moses Sofer's strategy, one constructed on the longest of long-term expectations. Throughout nineteenth century thought, Jewish and non-Jewish, we sense the finality with which the door had been closed on the past as a source of wisdom. A new social and intellectual order had emerged and there was no turning back. R. Moses Sofer evidently believed otherwise, that 'this too will pass.' So long as a remnant could be saved, and around it a fence created through which the corrosive acids of secularisation could not pass, eventually it would inherit a world more congenial to its values. It seemed at the time an unlikely scenario, a century later still more so. But a further half century has reversed all expectations. Traditionalism thrives.

But this poses a critical question. What of Modern Orthodoxy? Has it exhausted its function in the century and a half since Samson Raphael Hirsch published his *Nineteen Letters*? Is a dialogue between Orthodoxy and modernity no longer necessary? In the widening abyss between secular and Jewish values is it even possible? Modern Orthodoxy is currently in eclipse. We have seen some of the reasons why this is so. Is that eclipse permanent or desirable? To this question we now turn.

NOTES

1. Samson Raphael Hirsch, *The Nineteen Letters on Judaism*, translated by Bernard Drachman, New York: Feldheim, 1960, 118-121; *Abraham Isaac Kook*, translated by Ben Zion Bokser, London: SPCK, 1979, 303-305; R. Joseph B. Soloveitchik, *The Halakhic Mind*, New York: Free Press, 1986, 91-102.
2. See Edward Shils, *Tradition*, London: Faber and Faber, 1981.
3. Raymond Williams, *Keywords: A Vocabulary of Culture and Society*, London: Flamingo, 1981, 208-9.
4. See John Murray Cuddihy, *The Ordeal of Civility: Freud, Marx, Levi-Strauss and the Jewish Struggle with Modernity*, Boston: Beacon Press, 1987.
5. See Eliezer Schweid, 'Two Neo-Orthodox Approaches to Modernity – Part I: Samson Raphael Hirsch,' *Immanuel* 19 (Winter 1984-5), 107-117.
6. Marion J. Levy, *Modernization and the Structure of Societies*, Princeton: Princeton University Press, 1969, 752, quoted in Cuddihy, op. cit., 180.
7. See Jacob Katz, 'Contribution towards a biography of R. Moses Sofer,' in *Studies in Mysticism and Religion presented to Gershom G. Scholem*, Jerusalem: Magnes Press, 1967, 115-148.
8. See *Encyclopaedia Talmudit*, vol. 7, Jerusalem, 1956, 672-706.
9. B. T. *Berakhot* 46b.
10. B. T. *Kiddushin* 31a.
11. B. T. *Pesachim* 94b.
12. *Leviticus Rabbah* 9:3.
13. B. T. *Eruvin* 100b.
14. M. T. *Avodah Zarah* 11: 1-3.
15. See Cuddihy, op. cit.; George L. Mosse, 'Jewish Emancipation: Between *Bildung* and Respectability,' in *The Jewish Response to German Culture*, edited by Jehuda Reinharz and Walter Schatzberg, University Press of New England, 1985, 1-16.
16. M. *Orlah* 3:9.
17. See, for example, Responsa *Ktav Sofer, Even ha-Ezer* 47; Responsa *Maharam Schick, Orach Chayyim* 71.
18. I owe this way of putting it to R. Zvi Schachter, 'Tze'i Lakh be-Ikvei ha-Tzon,' *Bet Yitzchak* 17 (1985), 133.
19. See Peter Berger, *The Sacred Canopy: Elements of a Sociological Theory of Religion*, New York: Doubleday, 1967; Peter Berger and Thomas Luckmann, *The Social Construction of Reality*, London: Penguin Books, 1971.
20. See Menachem Friedman, 'Life Tradition and Book Tradition in the Development of Ultraorthodox Judaism,' in *Judaism viewed from Within and from Without*, edited by Harvey Goldberg, State University of New York Press, 1987, 235-255.

21. See, for example, R. Israel Meir ha-Cohen (Chafetz Chayyim), *Chizzuk ha-Dat*, ch.1, where the author compares contemporary alienation from tradition to a cholera epidemic. The task is to save those who can still be saved. Those who have already succumbed must be left to perish. The Chafetz Chayyim (1838-1933) was a figure of outstanding saintliness, and this diagnosis is eloquent testimony to the sense of helplessness which many traditionalists felt in the face of secularisation.
22. See Michael Silber, 'The Historical Experience of German Jewry and its Impact on Haskalah and Reform in Hungary,' in *Toward Modernity: The European Jewish Model*, edited by Jacob Katz, New Brunswick: Transaction Books, 1987, 107-158.
23. See Hermann Schwab, *The History of Orthodox Jewry in Germany*, London: Mitre Press, 1950; Robert Liberles, *Religious Conflict in Social Context: The Resurgence of Orthodox Judaism in Frankfurt am Main, 1838-1877*, Westport: Greenwood Press, 1985.
24. Schwab, op. cit., 115-126.
25. A number of these reflections are collected in Bernard Maza, *With Fury Poured Out*, Hoboken: Ktav, 1986.
26. See Reuven Bulka, 'Orthodoxy Today: An Overview of the Achievements and the Problems'; Charles Liebman, 'Orthodoxy in American Jewish Life,' and 'Orthodox Judaism Today,' in *Dimensions of Orthodox Judaism*, edited by Reuven Bulka, New York: Ktav, 1983, 7-120.
27. Valuable information on the contemporary Satmar community is contained in George Gershon Kranzler, 'The Voice of Williamsburg,' *Tradition* 23:3 (Spring 1988), 53-59.
28. Nahum Glatzer, *Franz Rosenzweig: His Life and Thought*, New York: Schocken, 1961, 107.
29. Robert Bellah, Richard Madsen, William M. Sullivan, Ann Swidler and Steven M. Tipton, *Habits of the Heart: Middle America Observed*, London: Hutchinson, 1988, 276-277.
30. Allan Bloom, *The Closing of the American Mind*, London: Penguin Books, 1987, 337.
31. Louis Dumont, *From Mandeville to Marx: The Genesis and Triumph of Economic Ideology*, Chicago: University of Chicago Press, 1977, 20; quoted in *Habits of the Heart*, op. cit., 278.
32. Peter Berger, Brigitte Berger and Hansfried Kellner, *The Homeless Mind*, London: Pelican Books, 1974, 165. See also Peter Berger, *Facing up to Modernity*, London: Penguin Books, 1979, 101-112.
33. Nathan Glazer and Daniel Moynihan, *Beyond the Melting Pot*, Cambridge: Harvard University Press, 1963, quoted in Charles Silberman, *A Certain People*, New York: Summit Books, 1985, 167.
34. Janet Aviad, *Return to Judaism: Religious Renewal in Israel*, Chicago: University of Chicago Press, 1983.
35. Menachem Friedman, 'Charedim Confront the Modern City,' in *Studies in Contemporary Jewry II*, edited by Peter Medding, Bloomington: Indiana University Press, 1986, 74-96.
36. Kranzler, op. cit., 57.

37. 'Charedim Confront the Modern City,' 91.
38. Samuel Heilman, 'The Jewish Family Today: An Overview,' in *Tradition and Transition*, edited by Jonathan Sacks, London: Jews' College Publications, 1986, 179-208.
39. Samuel Heilman and Steven M. Cohen, 'Ritual Variation among Modern Orthodox Jews in the United States,' in *Studies in Contemporary Jewry II*, 164-187.
40. Kranzler, op. cit., 55.
41. Alvin Schiff, 'The Jewish Day School – The Next Half-Century,' *Judaism* 36:2 (Spring 1987), 220-225.
42. Daniel Elazar, 'Who is a Jew and How? The Demographics of Jewish Religious Identification,' *Jerusalem Newsletter*, 24 September 1986. The argument is summarised in Jonathan Sacks, 'Ideas in Circulation,' *L'Eylah* 24 (September 1987), 21-25.
43. Quoted in Maza, op. cit., 51.

6
Dilemmas of Modern Orthodoxy

In 1982 *Tradition*, the journal of the Rabbinical Council of America, published a symposium entitled 'The State of Orthodoxy'.[1] It came at a time of re-assessment. Since the 1920s the demise of Orthodoxy in America had seemed inevitable. The current of acculturation was too strong. Tradition could not adapt itself to suburban accommodations. It was questionable whether any form of Judaism would survive. But it seemed certain that if it could, it would not be a Judaism based on the non-negotiable premises of tradition: belief in revelation and the binding force of Jewish law.

As we saw in the last chapter, that prediction – like many others in Jewish history – proved false. Charles Liebman's judgement in 1965 that 'the only remaining vestige of Jewish passion in America resides in the Orthodox community'[2] had turned out, seventeen years later, to be triumphantly justified. Jewish day schools and yeshivot were flourishing and multiplying. Jewish learning had become a passion. Many communities that had evinced only a sporadic interest in study hitherto now had active groups following the *Daf Yomi* daily Talmud programme. In New York it could be followed by telephone, through the hour-long Dial-a-*Daf* service whose several hundred lines were fully booked throughout the day and night. Orthodoxy in America had developed a prolific literature of books and periodicals, well-organised youth movements, *mikvaot* and an extensive kashrut network.

The *Tradition* symposium reflected this new reality. But the note of exhilaration was muted. Many, perhaps most, of these achievements had been instigated by groups and individuals closer to traditionalism than to the modern Orthodoxy represented by the symposiasts. *Tradition's* editor, Walter Wurzburger, reflected that 'Modern Orthodoxy . . . is ridiculed by the right wing as an illegitimate hybrid issuing from the union between Orthodoxy and a basically incompatible modern culture'.

So deep was the note of self-doubt that he included in the agenda to be addressed by contributors the question: 'Do you regard modern Orthodoxy as a philosophy of compromise or as an authentic version of Judaism?'

The question provoked an extraordinary outburst from David Singer. 'I am (may God have mercy on me)', he wrote, 'a modern Orthodox Jew, and thus a man without a community. Having crossed a bridge into the modern world, I now find myself stranded there together with a handful of Orthodox intellectuals while the Orthodox community as a whole goes marching off in a traditionalist direction.' As an undergraduate at Yeshiva University in the 1960s he had envisaged an altogether different outcome. Modern Orthodoxy was a philosophy whose time had come. 'Who in his right mind would spurn a form of Orthodoxy which held out the promise of a successful integration of Judaism and Western culture, tradition and modernity, Jewish and American living?'

A generation later, he looked back with unmistakable bitterness at the betrayal of a dream:

> What went wrong? Why did the dream of a modern Orthodox utopia turn to ashes? For a time I was convinced that modern Orthodoxy had failed the acid test: it had been tried and had been found wanting. Now I know better: modern Orthodoxy did not fail, it never happened. With few exceptions . . . the spokesmen for the movement had been engaged in an elaborate charade. While they talked bravely about modern Orthodoxy representing the true ideal of Torah . . . they really regarded it as a survival strategy – this was America; in America one had to compromise; and that compromise was secular studies. In their heart of hearts, most modern Orthodox leaders felt guilty about what they were saying and doing. Their model of authentic Jewishness remained that of the East European yeshivah world – a total absorption in Judaism's sacred texts. Hence, when Orthodox traditionalism reared its head, the spokesmen for modern Orthodoxy immediately retreated.[3]

None of the other contributors put it quite this strongly, but most shared Singer's self-doubts. Modern Orthodox

DILEMMAS OF MODERN ORTHODOXY 83

Jews felt 'a sense of uneasiness' in the presence of the 'superior religious devotion' of the traditionalists, according to one. According to another, modern Orthodoxy 'has largely turned into a philosophy of compromise – a way to maintain an institutional affiliation without taking seriously the spiritual and intellectual demands which that affiliation entails'. It has failed, many argued, to produce its own leaders. For some the problem lay at the grass-roots. 'The modern Orthodox produced many Jewish intellectuals, but not primary and secondary school teachers for the day schools to which they send their children.' For others it lay at the top. It 'has almost no indigenous *gedolim* [outstanding authorities], neither in the narrower sphere of halakhah nor in the broad realm of public leadership, and no first-rank creative thinkers or artists'.

PROBLEMS OF LEGITIMATION

These comments came from leading representatives of modern Orthodoxy itself. Nor was this simply self-criticism. It was an inner echo of the increasing tendency on the part of a resurgent traditionalism to delegitimate modern Orthodoxy. The relationship between modern and traditionalist Orthodoxy is asymmetrical. The former recognise the validity of the latter; the latter deny it to the former. The modernists argue for an Orthodox pluralism, while the traditionalists frequently argue that theirs is the only valid interpretation of the rabbinic heritage. Modern Orthodox thinkers are therefore at a psychological disadvantage, since their views are often discredited by authorities whom they respect.

This was evident in the *Tradition* symposium itself. The editor invited traditionalists to take part in the discussion. All refused. Elsewhere, they made their objections to modern Orthodoxy clear. One reported, in the name of his yeshivah teacher, that 'We no longer have to fear Conservatism – that is no longer the danger. Everyone knows that it is *avodah zarah* [idolatry]. What we have to fear is modern Orthodoxy.' [4] Another spoke of the need to wage an ideological war against what he saw as 'a trend of pseudo-Orthodoxy'.[5] The implication was clear. Modern Orthodoxy in attempting to create a synthesis between rabbinic Judaism and contemporary thought was headed toward, if not already at the point of, heresy.

Nor is the problem confined to the higher reaches of faith and intellect. It translates itself into social terms, as a vacillation between discrepant roles and reference groups. In their lifestyles, it has seemed to some, modern Orthodox Jews are trying to combine the incompatible: an easy modernity and a faithful Orthodoxy. This makes for an awkward division of identities. An acute observer, the sociologist Samuel Heilman, concluded his study of American synagogue life with the remark that 'As modern Orthodox Jews, the members stand between two sources of stigmatisation: the contemporary world, which considers their Orthodoxy a stigma, and the traditional Orthodox community which looks upon their modernity with disapproval.' Since they internalise the standards of both, their identity is fraught with ambivalence. They are 'forever trying to engage in "passing" behaviour'. To the traditionalists 'they must appear strictly Orthodox' while 'to their contemporary colleagues' they must 'seem to be completely engaged with the present and with downplaying their Orthodoxy and the anachronism it connotes'. Heilman concludes that 'rapid, and often sudden, shifting' between roles is an 'integral part' of modern Orthodox behaviour. 'Whether these dual foci of identity can continue to coexist without destroying each other remains to be seen.' [6]

Another sociologist, Charles Liebman, has pointed to the problem modern Orthodoxy has in legitimating its positions. 'Modern Orthodoxy was not a left wing movement because it was not a movement; it was to some of its adherents a state of sin, and to the remainder a condition of schizophrenia. It represented an uncritical affirmation of the American experience without evaluating either the quality of the American experience or its relationship to the Jewish tradition.' [7] It had no difficulty in legitimating its stances on the basis of contemporary secular values – democracy, self-fulfilment, the dignity of the individual, liberalism and sexual equality. What it could not do was to derive the same conclusions from the source it took as primary, namely, Jewish law. As a result, modern Orthodoxy could not but seem to be more modern than Orthodox, and it was bound to lack the endorsement of major halakhists. 'One is hard pressed to think of rabbis with any standing in the Orthodox world who seek to legitimate those behaviour patterns that distinguish the modern Orthodox of the left wing from the right.'[8]

These are formidable criticisms. To a considerable degree they represent the particular dilemma of Orthodoxy in America. There Orthodoxy is not the only, or even the major, institutionalised expression of Jewish religiosity. Conservative Judaism, which in the early twentieth century had still been roughly within the parameters of tradition, has since moved radically toward accommodation with secular and non-halakhic norms, from mixed seating in the synagogue to the ordination of women as rabbis. Reform Judaism has moved further still, to the point of accepting homosexuality and mixed marriages *de facto*, and *de jure* counting as Jews the children of a Jewish father and non-Jewish mother, so long as the children choose to identify as Jews.

In nineteenth century Germany, where Reform and Conservative – or as it was then called, 'positive historical' – Judaism originated, the distinction between these movements and Orthodoxy was relatively clear. Orthodoxy necessarily saw Reform as a heretical deviation from Jewish law and faith. Reform, in turn, saw itself as a revolutionary response to radical social change. Contemporary American culture, in contrast, blurs the either/or of tradition or revolution. It sees religious alternatives in terms of pluralism. They are related, that is to say, not in terms of truth and falsity or orthodoxy and heterodoxy but as competing products in the free market-place of affiliation. The concept of an orthodoxy of any kind is almost impossible to translate into this conceptual scheme.[9] In the Jewish context, the various strands in Jewish religious life come to seem simply denominational alternatives, each equally legitimate as an interpretation of tradition. Between them, the choice of affiliation seems personal and subjective, a matter of choice, not truth.

American Jews, as a result, are highly mobile in their institutional allegiances. Recent surveys have repeatedly shown that while first generation Americans tend to be Orthodox, their children switch overwhelmingly to Conservative synagogues as part of their integration into American life.[10] Orthodoxy represents the attachment of a bare five per cent of the American Jewish population, rising to eleven per cent in Miami and thirteen per cent in New York.[11] In such a minority situation the project of modern Orthodoxy – attempting to mediate between tradition and secular culture – is fraught with implausibility. Those who seek an accommodation with American values can find it carried through with greater vigour in the non-Orthodox movements. Those who seek instead to pass on the tradition undiluted to their children will inevitably prefer a non-accommodating Orthodoxy which maintains, ideologically and institutionally, a conscious isolation from the general environment. There seems to be a choice. A consistent modernity leads away from Orthodoxy. A consistent Orthodoxy leads away from modernity. Modern Orthodoxy is the excluded middle. Such is the present American situation.

MODERN ORTHODOXY IN ISRAEL

But not the American situation alone. Israel too, though it lacks American Jewry's denominations and *de facto* religious pluralism, has witnessed a similar phenomenon. 'The most dramatic development in religious life in Israel during the last decade has been the apparent retreat of modern Orthodoxy and the strengthening of neo-religious tendencies.' [12] There have been conspicuous moves on the part of the younger Orthodox generation toward an increasing rigour of halakhic interpretation and practice. Previous standards with respect to kashrut, agricultural laws, mixing or separation of the sexes and modesty in dress have been called into question and replaced by more demanding norms. The impact of yeshivot, nationalist youth movements, and the heightened authority of religious leaders has led to a breakdown of family customs in favour of a more monolithic conception of halakhic behaviour.[13]

There has been a tendency, too, to negate the complex cultural syntheses associated with modern Orthodoxy. Orthodox schools and yeshivot have taken an increasingly negative view of secular studies, especially the humanities. The pragmatic accommodation with secular politics once characteristic of Mizrachi, the religious Zionist movement formed by R. Isaac Reines in the late nineteenth century, has been replaced with a more direct and unyielding application of religious categories to the political arena. There has been a move away from the alternation between roles that Heilman found typical of American modern Orthodoxy toward a more strenuous and zealous search for personal consistency. The Israeli term for the young affected by this mood is *nisrafim*, 'burned'. The word is graphically descriptive of the new style of religious passion as against the more detached and tolerant manner of a generation ago.[14]

The attitudes associated with religious moderation have been in decline. In Israel these involved a positive attitude toward the state, a willingness to work with secular groups, and a conciliatory stance toward non-religious Jews on the one hand and the Arab population on the other. Religious moderates have generally favoured persuasion over legislation, dialogue over confrontation, and the 'ways of peace' over the 'wars of the Lord'.

In the pre- and early state period there had been many distinguished rabbinic authorities – among them Rabbis Kook, Isaac Herzog, Zvi Pesach Frank, Isser Yehudah Unterman, Moshe Avigdor Amiel and Shlomo Yosef Zevin – who took a highly positive view of the religious significance of the land and state of Israel. Recently, however, there has been a marked decline in the influence of religious Zionism as an ideology.[15] This is not always or even predominantly expressed in terms of direct opposition. The majority of yeshivot simply ignore such celebrations as *Yom ha-Atzma'ut*, Israel's Independence Day, and an ever-growing number of students prefer to continue their talmudic studies rather than serve in the army. But in some yeshivot, notably those for *baalei teshuvah*, religious returnees, the anti-Zionist polemic is overt. Janet Aviad, for example, documents one speech by a yeshivah head on the theme of 'Why we should mourn on Independence Day'. 'As a faithful religious Jew', he told his students, 'I am more anti-Zionist than I am anti-Christian.' While non-Jews sought to harm Jews, he argued, Zionism sought to destroy Judaism itself.[16]

Negative or neutral attitudes toward Zionism had been a feature of traditionalist Orthodoxy since the birth of Agudat Yisrael in 1912. But with the growing impact of yeshivot on Israeli religious life, and a general disillusionment with secular Zionism as a solution to Israel's internal and external problems, the mood has spread outward. Modern Orthodoxy, explicitly or implicitly, was generally predicated on monistic concepts that favoured unity and harmony. Traditionalism, by contrast, is more dualistic, viewing the world in terms of oppositional categories and conflict. The growing rift between secular and religious attitudes on the one hand, Israel, the Arab states and international political opinion on the other, has made dualism a more cogent way of explaining immediate realities for many Israelis in the past two decades.

THE FAILURE OF SUCCESS

There have been sporadic attempts to restate the case for religious moderation. In the summer of 1986, following clashes between religious and secular Israelis, a group of Orthodox yeshivah heads and academics published a call for 'a candid dialogue between the religious and secular communities', an end to 'indiscriminate public battles over any and all religious issues', and an emphasis instead on 'basic principles of justice and responsibility, honesty and decency, concern for the unfortunates in our midst'.[17] At around the same time the religious youth movement, Bnei Akiva, declared itself committed to 'the struggle for human dignity' and opposed 'enmity and hatred between Jews and gentiles'.[18] Several political parties, among them *Oz ve-Shalom*, *Netivot Shalom*, and more recently *Meimad*, have asserted the inner connection between religious values and moderation, diplomacy and tolerance. None of these initiatives, though, has generated a significant base of support or a continuing momentum.

There are, in short, deep problems facing the constellation of values implicit in the phrase 'modern Orthodoxy'. They are evident in two communities as dissimilar as American and Israeli Jewry. They cannot therefore be attributed exclusively to processes occurring in the one and not the other. In Israel, religious issues tend to be fought in the public arena and have a political dimension. In America they have more to do with private life, personal religious observance and synagogue affiliation. In both situations, however, the religious voice that has commanded attention has spoken in the accents of confrontation rather than mediation. Orthodoxy has come to be characterised by its opposition to, not its attempt to engage in dialogue with, secular culture, non-religious Jews and the non-Jewish world. Traditionalism rather than modern Orthodoxy has emerged as the authoritative voice of rabbinic Judaism. Why has this happened?

One point should not be underestimated. Modern Orthodoxy has been the victim of its own success. All legitimating ideologies tend to suffer the fate of Wittgenstein's ladder, that of being cast away once the climb has been made. The great paradox of contemporary Orthodoxy is that *Torah im Derekh Eretz* and religious Zionism are systematically in evidence as empirical reality and in eclipse as religious ideology. There are Orthodox Jewish university professors, scientists, doctors, judges, economists and sociologists. Each of these presupposes advanced secular education, and thus the *de facto* reality of *Torah im Derekh Eretz*. Orthodox Jews too have emerged, especially since the 1973 Yom Kippur War, as the most unconditional supporters of the state of Israel. In terms of American *aliyah*, Orthodox Jews are five times more likely than those of other affiliations to make the decision to leave and live in Israel.[19] The reverse also seems to be true, though we lack precise quantification of the numbers involved: secular Israelis are more likely to leave Israel and live elsewhere than their religious counterparts.[20]

Torah im Derekh Eretz and religious Zionism were primarily legitimating ideologies. They sought religious justification for states of affairs that had not yet been realised: cultural integration in the diaspora and a Jewish state in the land of Israel. The direction of religious thought necessarily changes when anticipation is succeeded by achievement. Orthodox Jews no longer need specific justification for their decision to pursue higher secular education or participate in Israeli life. These have become self-evident, taken-for-granted realities. The burden of justification is now reversed. How, having decided to enter the professions or live in a secular state, can one defend the fact of one's Orthodoxy? Necessarily, in this new statement of tradition-in-modernity, secular knowledge and the state of Israel come to be seen as instrumental rather than essential goods. Neither possesses religious significance in itself. Each is merely a condition and context of something else that had intrinsic value. When a new state of affairs is sought, it must be justified *de jure*. When it has been accomplished, it can be accepted *de facto*. The demise of modern Orthodox ideologies is part of the failure of success. Its goals have been achieved. Other values now need to be stressed.

PROGRESSION OR REGRESSION

But this is only part of the story. The word 'modern', as we noted in the last chapter, has carried a specific implication since the early nineteenth century. It has been not only descriptive but evaluative also. It has implied not only that something is new, but that the new is better, more evolved, sophisticated or compelling than the old.

Neither Samson Raphael Hirsch nor Rav Kook described their programmes as modern Orthodoxy. But the phrase accurately captures the mood of their writings. Behind their visions lay different but identifiable optimisms. They welcomed modernity. For Hirsch it promised a new richness of Jewish life in the diaspora, freed from the artificial privations of the ghetto. For Kook it heralded a renaissance of Jewish peoplehood in Israel, a convergence of people, land and language, religion, culture and landscape, in a messianic process of sanctification. Each was heir to that specific post-enlightenment, pre-Holocaust sense of history as progress, time as evolution. The future would be better than the past.

In retrospect we now see that this was by no means the only, or even the primary, interpretation of time and its processes that could be inferred from tradition. An inner history of Judaism could almost be written in terms of its deep dialectic on the subject of time. On the one hand, the very concept of tradition, Jewish or otherwise, presupposes that the past is a source of wisdom. In Judaism, the past, as revelation, is the sole source of religious knowledge and authoritative command. The primary justification of prophecy or rabbinic insight is not that it is new but that it is old. 'Moses received the Torah from Sinai and transmitted to it Joshua; Joshua to the elders; the elders to the prophets; and the prophets transmitted it to the men of the Great Assembly.'[21]

Reception and transmission link the generations, not

innovation and evolution. The new, if true, is merely a disclosure of the old. 'Bible, Mishnah, Talmud and Haggadah, even what a senior disciple is due to teach in the presence of his master, was already stated to Moses at Sinai.'[22] Each new generation marked a further move away from the pristine force of revelation. Time was a process of decline. 'If our predecessors were human beings', said the rabbis, 'then we are as donkeys.' From the perspective of revelation and knowledge the present is inferior to the past.

Against this, and in constant tension with it, is a distinct future orientation. This is implicit in the ideas of the messianic age, the world to come and the resurrection of the dead. Judaism, like other religious systems, faced times in which reality seemed to contradict belief. Individual suffering conflicted with the idea of Divine justice. Jewish degradation conflicted with Jewish chosenness. Persecution seemed to contradict the Divine protection promised in the covenant. But in Judaism, these conflicts are to be resolved not by metaphysics but by history, specifically by the future.

Biblical and rabbinic thought both veer away from abstract or mystical resolutions to theological dilemmas. What ought to be is not what *is*, once the veil of illusion has been removed from the world of the senses. What ought to be is what *will be*, once the future comes to pass. Gershom Scholem has written that 'the Messianic idea has compelled a *life lived in deferment*, in which nothing can be done definitively, nothing can be irrevocably accomplished'.[23] One can agree with this analysis while dissenting from its evaluation. The messianic idea dictates a life lived toward the future, just as the concept of revelation dictates a life lived toward the past. Judaism is defined between the twin poles of memory and anticipation.

For most of the period between the first and nineteenth centuries, between the rise of rabbinic Judaism and the dawn of emancipation, Jewish thought had been strikingly a-historical. Yosef Hayim Yerushalmi has drawn attention to the fact that, given the importance of history to biblical thought and memory to Jewish religious practice, it is 'all the more remarkable that after the close of the biblical canon the Jews virtually stopped writing history . . . It is as though, abruptly, the impulse to historiography had ceased.'[24] The rabbis neither wrote history nor did they devote religious attention to the seminal events of their own time. They tended to subsume new Jewish tragedies to previous archetypes as if the new were a recurring manifestation of the old: 'the acts of the fathers are a portent for their children'.[25] The rabbinic conception of the present is dominated by an undifferentiated *ha-zeman ha-zeh*, 'this time', stretching between the destruction of the second temple and the messianic age.[26]

It is as if, for eighteen centuries of Jewish consciousness, the historical clock had stopped and time was suspended. Jews were poised between a distant past and a remotely imagined future: between revelation and redemption. Their present situation was neither one nor the other. No change held religious significance. Even the most catastrophic event of that period – the Spanish Inquisition and expulsion – produced only a temporary historical consciousness. Its lasting effect was to drive Jewish spirituality further in upon itself and away from external reality, in the form of Safed mysticism. The profound social changes taking place in Jewish existence from emancipation onward called, therefore, for a major new evaluation. Jews and Judaism were being caught up in the processes of history. A-historical stasis no longer described the Jewish situation.

One response – a reaction of qualified pessimism – was readily available within the tradition. The new circumstances were a threat to Jewish continuity, and were therefore to be seen as yet another one of the trials of exile. The classic expression of this view had been given by Maimonides in his *Epistle to Yemen*: 'These trials are designed to test and purify us, so that only the saints and the pious men of the pure and undefiled lineage of Jacob will adhere to our religion and remain within the fold.'[27] On this view, emancipation was a catastrophe that was nonetheless to be seen as providential. Many would defect from Judaism, convert, intermarry or otherwise assimilate, but the few – the 'true Israel' – would survive. This formed the heart of the traditionalist response to modernity.

It was Samson Raphael Hirsch's achievement to see that an alternative and more positive interpretation could be given. Judaism is, on this view, a-historical but is nonetheless enmeshed in the history of other nations. 'Israel', in this sense, 'is a historical phenomenon.'[28] Its function is to serve as a constant counterpoint to the rise and fall of other civilisations by the force of its religious and ethical example. It 'became necessary that one people be introduced into the ranks of the nations which, through its history and life, should declare that God is the only creative cause of existence.' [29] The task of the Jewish people is to show the world 'the sanctity of humanity by the example of its own life'.[30] On this reading, emancipation offered a significant and constructive challenge to Jews, to live their own tradition in closer proximity to the peoples and cultures among whom they had been dispersed. Thereby they would more fully fulfil the religious mission of exile. If 'the dispersed of Israel were to show themselves everywhere on earth as the glorious priests of God and pure humanity ... what a mighty force we would constitute for steering mankind to the final goal of human education.' [31]

Hirsch remained within the a-historical rabbinic tradition. Emancipation had significance in his thought not so much for the inner as for the outer development of Jewish destiny. For Hirsch a, perhaps the, crucial element of the Jewish vocation was its impact on other civilisations and the developing conscience of humanity as a whole. But the rise of European nationalism in the 1840s, the persistence of European antisemitism, and the continuing attritions of assimilation combined to turn later nineteenth century Jewish thought in another direction: religious Zionism. Emancipation, on this view, provided the context and impetus not for a new Jewish role in the diaspora, but for a revival of the Jewish nation in Eretz Israel. Yehudah Alkalai, Zvi Hirsch Kalischer and later Rav Kook were all to see the transformations of modernity in terms of inner Jewish history, as the prompting of Providence to a human response to the messianic challenge. The process of redemption is completed by Heaven, they argued, but begun by man. Emancipation points to the end of exile.

THE ECLIPSE OF OPTIMISM

Behind these two quite different projections lies an optimism about the immediate implications of history. To be sure, neither Hirsch nor Kook were naive meliorists. They were both fully aware that their time had witnessed unprecedented defections from tradition. This fact occupies a major part of their writings. But neither saw modernity as simply a trial, in which all change is necessarily for the worse. In Hirsch we find a powerful idealisation of the diaspora. In Rav Kook we find an equally powerful idealisation of Zionism as the herald of a national-religious rebirth. If the future offered greater dangers than the past, it afforded greater religious opportunities likewise.

Neither of their specific visions is readily available to Jews in the late twentieth century. The Holocaust bars any return to a celebration of diaspora existence as such. Indeed, A. B. Yehoshua has called the Holocaust 'the final decisive proof of the failure of diaspora existence'.[32] 'If anyone', he argues, 'had illusions about our ability to find our place in the world as a people scattered among the nations, the Holocaust provided the final proof of where this form of existence is likely to lead us.'

Not only is this a matter of safety and survival. The Holocaust mocks the idea of the Jewish ethical mission to humanity, which Hirsch shared with many other early nineteenth century Jewish thinkers. It was, we remember, Hitler who remarked that 'conscience is a Jewish invention'. To be sure, the idea of the Jewish ethical mission had not been completely eclipsed. It has been revived by, among others, the secular Jewish writer George Steiner. But there is a dark abyss of difference between Steiner's *In Bluebeard's Castle* and Hirsch's *Nineteen Letters*.

For Steiner, the Holocaust is the culmination of the Enlightenment. In *The Gay Science*, Nietzsche had pronounced the blasphemy that man had murdered God. In the *shoah*, man attempted to murder the people of God.[33] For Steiner, Jews must continue to be the moral critics of humanity, but in return they must expect not admiration but victimisation.[34] This is not to say that Hirsch's theology is refuted; but we will not easily recover the innocent optimism with which he wrote. Jewish thought has, for the time being and the most part, turned inward from universalism to particularism, from 'mission' to survival.

Nor have Rav Kook's hopes for the sanctification of Jewish life in Israel proceeded as he envisioned. In place of the symbiosis between religion and secular culture there has come a widening rift and a deepening tension. An essential part of Rav Kook's imagined future was a vision which anticipated that Israel's national rebirth would lead to greater harmony between Jews and other peoples, Judaism and other faiths. The continued hostility between Israel and her Arab neighbours, the internal issue of the Palestinians, and Israel's growing international isolation have all been movements in the opposite direction.

To be sure, Rav Kook's mysticism has not been the only casualty. Far more deeply affected has been the secular Zionist premiss that Israel would lead to a 'normalisation' of Jewish existence. In any event, optimism has been succeeded by a more sombre interpretation of history, one which sees Jewish-gentile relationships as inherently hostile and in which Israel is destined to be 'a people that dwells alone'.[35]

There has been, in other words, a perceptible shift in Jewish attitudes in both Israel and the diaspora from optimism to pessimism and from a future- to a past-orientation. Tomorrow is unlikely to be better than yesterday. One can almost precisely date the transformation. The turning-point was Israel's 1973 Yom Kippur War. Until then, Israel's high international prestige had seemed to enhance both Hirsch's and Kook's faith in history. Since then, more dismal images have prevailed.

So deep has the mood gone that contemporary Jewish thinkers are now reluctant to use the word 'modern' to describe themselves. One non-Orthodox scholar, for example, writes that 'The period of Jewish history that began in late eighteenth century Germany has ended. We whose identities were formed after 1933, 1945, 1948 and 1967 are no longer modern Jews. After 1933 we no longer believe in the possibility – or attractiveness – of assimilation. In the face of 1945 and the realisation of what had happened in the death camps, we surely no longer worship at the temple of human progress.' [36] 'Modern' Orthodoxy is no longer described as such. Instead its protagonists have recently preferred the time-neutral phrase 'centrist' Orthodoxy.[37]

A guarded neutrality, tinged with suspicion, had been traditionalism's response to modernity all along. Many of its reservations about emancipation, western civilisation and the aspirations of Zionism seem to have been justified by the events of the past half-century. It will take time and much change before the adjective 'modern' regains a positive resonance in the Jewish vocabulary.

AGAINST MODERNITY

Undoubtedly though, the primary reason for the decline in modern Orthodoxy has been sociological rather than historical. Jews and Judaism have been so deeply affected by the Holocaust and the state of Israel that one may be forgiven for seeing these as the primary determinants of Jewish religiosity in the last forty years. The facts, however, suggest otherwise. For the same developments that have been evident in Judaism have occurred elsewhere, in both Christianity and Islam.

In all three cases religious traditions were confronted by the intellectual and social impact of modernisation. This involved, among other things, a historical consciousness which saw religious truths and institutions not as timeless mysteries but as products of their time; a weakening of communal structures of authority in favour of individual liberty and personal choice; and a rejection of traditional hierarchies, in particular a revaluation of the role of women in society. In all three religions an attempt was made to reformulate religious doctrine and practice to accommodate these changes and show that they were not incompatible with traditional teachings.

To some extent, despite their very different inner logics, the three religions adopted similar tactics in embracing modernity. Classic texts were to be understood in new ways that broke with the literalism of the past. Religious behaviour was to be divided into the timeless and essential on the one hand, and accretions and superstitions on the other. Religious thought moved from the metaphysical to the moral. Reason gained primacy over tradition. Values such as tolerance, democracy and individual dignity came to be stressed over truth, authority and religious discipline. Jewish, Christian and Islamic modernism are each composed of a myriad of variations that differ substantially from one another as well as from modernisms in other faiths. But this should not hide the broad patterns that all religious strategies have in common when they seek to translate tradition into a secular modernity.

At some stage, however – and this seems to have been reached in all three religions some two decades ago – a reaction gathers force. Tradition, it is now argued, cannot be stretched this far. Religious liberalism, which had until then been seen in terms of intellectual openness and ethical concern comes to be seen negatively as 'secularisation' in Christianity, 'westernisation' in Islam and 'assimilation' in Judaism. Traditionalism, which had all along opposed the liberal strategy, emerges from its minority status, shakes off the epithets by which it has hitherto been stigmatised – 'dogmatic' and 'obscurantist' – and commands attention as the voice of religious authenticity.

The emphases of the new traditionalism are different in the three religions. In Christianity it focuses on the literal inerrancy of Scripture. In Islam its form is political, sometimes domestic, sometimes international, as a war against the West and its influence on Islamic life. In Judaism it concentrates for the most part on a strict interpretation of halakhah, though in a movement like Gush Emunim it takes political form as well. In all three religions the new mood is described by its opponents as 'fundamentalism'.

The relatedness of these phenomena is too striking to be dismissed. The revival of traditionalism was unpredicted by most theologians and sociologists. Prior to the 1960s it was generally assumed that modernisation was a linear process. A deepening secularisation was inevitable. Religious institutions, if they were to survive at all, would have to make their peace with it. The reverse now seems true. Why has it happened? The situation is too new for there to be any consensus among sociologists. We can only speculate. One point, though, seems certain. What has happened is not a general return to tradition. The evidence, certainly among Western societies, still points to the continuing decline of traditional religious observance and the marginalisation of religion in society. The traditionalist revival is paradoxical. It is a distinctively modern phenomenon. It is a symptom of religious life in a profoundly secular world. How then are we to explain it?

Modernity – that complex of processes that includes industrialisation, urbanisation, Enlightenment thought and the disjunction between individual and state – has produced its own discontents. The citizen of the modern city is surrounded by a bewildering variety of faiths, commitments and lifestyles. The culture he inhabits casts the individual loose from the constraints of birth, ethnicity, class and family tradition. There are few, if any, features of his life which he experiences as *given*. What he is, he is because he has consciously so chosen, out of the midst of many alternatives. At work, in social life, and at home, he may have to play a variety of only loosely connected roles. Technological, economic and even ethical structures seem to be in a state of flux and change. 'A world in which everything is in constant motion is a world in which certainties of any kind are hard to come by.' [38] The felt incoherence of personal meaning is one of the prices exacted by modernity.

The authors of a recent study of American society put the dilemma simply. 'If it is to provide any richness of meaning, the idea of a life course must be set in a larger generational, historical and probably religious context.' The division of most American lives between work, conceived of as self-responsibility, and leisure, conceived of as self-fulfilment, tends to focus on a self without a context, a self-made self. While this has its satisfactions, 'a life composed mainly of work that lacks much intrinsic meaning and leisure devoted to golf and bridge does have limitations. It is hard to find in it the kind of story or narrative, as of pilgrimage or quest, that many cultures have used to link private and public; present, past and future; and the life of the individual to the life of society and the meaning of the cosmos.' [39]

It was just this 'narrative' that was traditionally provided by religion. Here were the ultimate certainties, the eternal truths and directives that rose above the shifting ground of the human situation. But it is just this that is threatened by the entire constellation of values of modernity. At a certain point, therefore, religion cannot accommodate itself to modernity without compromising its most basic character. To the extent that religions 'go through the modern experience' – favouring choice over truth, autonomy over authority and self over society – to that extent they replicate rather than resolve the problems of contemporary individualism.

RELIGION AS DISENGAGEMENT

Added to the crisis of the modern self is a growing scepticism about the social transformations that modernity was to have heralded. Liberal optimism about the end of tyranny has been succeeded by the knowledge that the twentieth century has seen unprecedented examples of political oppression. Enlightenment promised an end to superstition and intolerance; instead it has led to frightening examples of fanaticism and racial hatred. Science and technology, as well as extending and enriching human life, has given man the power to destroy the world. Economic progress has not prevented – indeed it has at times seemed to be dependent on – increasing disparities between rich and poor, individually and nationally. 'Progress, modernity's master idea, seems less compelling when it appears that it may be progress into the abyss.'[40] These are the global equivalents of Jewry's own disillusionment with the twentieth century.

They amount to a situation in which religion, to address the anxieties and discontents of a significant number of individuals in contemporary society, must be counter-cultural. It must seek to restore what modernity threatens to destroy: personal identity, the coherence of a life, generational continuity and an objective moral order. It must allow the individual to break through the prison of the self into a wider framework of meanings. It must restore a sense of kinship with the past to balance the sense of headlong rush into an uncharted future. These are the common factors of traditionalism, and they explain its power in an uncertain world.

They are not secured easily. Traditional*ism* is not the same as tradition. Traditionalism is tradition in an untraditional age. It is acquired at the price of disengagement from contemporary culture, building strong, supportive and enclosed communities and establishing structures of authority which are at odds with the assumptions of liberal individualism. These certainly are the features of *charedi*, or Jewish traditionalist life, and they are not accidental to it. They are built on the perception that contact with secular culture and society undermines the certainties on which religion depends to provide history, the universe and personal life with meaning.

The question is: Is there an alternative? How much of modern consciousness can religion admit without destroying its own certainties? Contemporary individualism is destructive of the idea of community. Pluralism threatens the idea of objective religious truth. A culture of shifting, transitory allegiances endangers key institutions like marriage and the family. Autonomy – the idea that each person is the author of his moral commitments – is hostile to the Jewish idea of halakhah, namely that we are born into obligations. Can a synthesis be created between tradition and a culture so fundamentally at odds with it? The presumption must be that it cannot. If it cannot, then the choice lies between a religious modernism that breaks with tradition, or a religious tradition that disengages from modernity.

The sharpness of this either/or is often underestimated by religious modernists, who tend to see traditionalism – or 'fundamentalism' – as an escape from reality into the refuge of naive certainty. One of the contributors to the *Tradition* symposium, for example, spoke of 'the preference of our generation for black-and-white absolutes rather than grey hybrids admitting doubts, questions and innovations'. Another argued that 'in an insecure world, many crave security and, without a doubt, blind faith provides more security than does the travail of the intellectual'. But such implied criticism ignores the deep undermining of religious certainties by the scope of choice and pace of change of modern societies.

The search for integrity, security, meaning, 'absolutes', authority and community is part of the classic religious quest, and any religious system that does not provide clear signposts is in danger of abdicating its most basic responsibilities. Many theological liberalisms reached a *reductio ad absurdum* in the 1960s in their attempt to give religious endorsement to an opposite cluster of values. Modern Orthodoxy was not immune to the temptation. There were calls for Judaism to adjust to the 'changing American ethic',[41] and to emphasise 'human adequacy' as against the 'psychologically repressed and inhibited' personality type of tradition.[42] There was an emphasis on Judaism's compatibility with, rather than its critique of, the values of an individualistic age. The danger in this strategy, as a Christian scholar has pointed out, is that 'To gain a hearing in our culture, theology has often assumed a voice not its own and found itself merely repeating the culture's platitudes in transparently figurative speech.'[43]

Undoubtedly the search for cultural synthesis was well-motivated. The 1960s was a decade in which old behaviour patterns seemed to be breaking down. There was, particularly among the student population, a search for religious experience that went hand-in-hand with a rejection of conventional behaviour. *Avant garde* religious thinkers felt challenged to push liberalism to its limits. But in so doing they under-emphasised the contrary values within the tradition: certainty as well as doubt, external truth as against inner consciousness, halakhic norm as well as individual fulfilment.

Religious thought has since had to step back from this precipice. The mood within society has changed. The 1960s were succeeded by a decade of disillusionment and came to be seen, in retrospect, as a time of excess. The religious modernism associated with that period has suffered an eclipse and the religious voice now sought is one which speaks in tones of authority, discipline and ethical certainty.

THE FENCE AROUND THE FAMILY

But the changing mood of Orthodoxy cannot be divorced from a final and perhaps the most pressing consideration: the specific threat to Jewish continuity posed by an open society. Judaism is a faith. But it is the faith of a particular people. It is more than a set of truths and commands. It is a people to whom those truths and commands are addressed and in whose lives they are embodied. The future of the covenant depends on the future of the people of the covenant. Theology, in Judaism, is dependent on demography.

It was in the 1960s that a series of social phenomena began to give rise to alarm. The Jewish family, which had hitherto been a model of stability, showed signs of stress. There was a sharp rise in the rates of divorce. In addition it emerged that Jews were increasingly marrying late, or not marrying at all. Those who married were having smaller families. Most significantly, the intermarriage rate, which had hitherto been minimal, began to accelerate. Recent statistical studies have shown that the rates vary significantly from city to city within America, but they converge on the figure of one in three. That figure accords with the experience of other diaspora communities, pre- and post-war, that have undergone advanced acculturation.

These phenomena are directly related to secularisation. A culture that stresses individualism is one in which the institution of marriage is inherently fragile. It is also one in which the instinctive restraints against intermarriage are virtually impossible to sustain. Religion in a secular culture is only one of a series of commitments of private life. The individual is prior to and independent of his or her religious persuasions. The marriage of two people of different faiths comes to seem no more unlikely than the marriage of two people of different economic, class, racial, cultural or educational backgrounds. One of the crucial transitions from traditional to modern societies is the replacement of birth and role by personal compatibility and romantic love as factors determining the choice of marriage partner.

These facts threaten Jewish continuity at its roots. They are not unprecedented, and biblical Judaism contains many safeguards against too close an interaction with non-Jewish society. These were extended by rabbinic law in the behavioural 'fences' constructed by the sages. Explicitly or implicitly they were protective of marriage and set up barriers against intermarriage. They included the powerful group of laws clustered around the concept of *taharat ha-mishpachah*, 'family purity', laws of modesty, restrictions on the social mixing of the sexes, and laws directed against eating and drinking in non-Jewish environments. They amounted to a discipline of self-imposed segregation, and they are among the Jewish laws most at odds with the assumptions of a liberal, open society.

Here too the traditionalist response has been effective, for it has developed its own contemporary equivalents of the classic rabbinic strategy of social engineering. It has created its own 'fences' with which to shelter the institutions of family life. It has developed increasingly strict conventions on modesty of dress, mixed bathing and the separation of the sexes at social gatherings. It has excluded television and other carriers of the secular ethos. It has stressed its segregation from secular society.

Modern Orthodoxy, by contrast, has emphasised its integration within contemporary life. Its approach to the defence of Jewish institutions is quite different from that of traditionalism. In place of 'fences', authority, submission and social sanction, it has travelled the characteristically modern route of personal autonomy: through the educated choices of educated minds. It has used the methods of instruction, explanation and persuasion. Whether these are strong enough to counter the pressures acting against the Jewish family remains to be seen. More than by its philosophical sophistication, modern Orthodoxy will be judged by its capacity to safeguard Jewish continuity which is, in the last analysis, the continuity of the Jewish family.

So the eclipse of modern Orthodoxy has been part of a fundamental transformation of attitudes, both Jewish and universal, that has been evident in the past two decades. To be sure, the two centuries that have passed since the dawn of emancipation have been dialectical rather than linear. There have been pendulum swings before. A shift from modernism to traditionalism took place in Hirsch's own Frankfurt community in the decades after his death. The drift from optimism to pessimism is evident in the development of R. Soloveitchik's work from the 1940s to the 1960s. The phenomenon of *teshuvah*, the religious return of the alienated, that seemed unprecedented in the 1960s, had indeed taken place before in pre-war central Europe and had included such figures as Franz Rosenzweig, Martin Buber, Gershom Scholem and Jiri Langer. It is too early to tell whether the last two decades are one more swing in the ever-moving pendulum or whether they represent the first signs of the end of Enlightenment and the birth of an era of 'post-modernity'.

But the change is deep. In part it has been born of the specific Jewish experience of the Holocaust and the recent fate of Israel. In part it is dictated by fears about the institutions of Jewish continuity, fears which have focused on birthrates, family stability and intermarriage. In part it is symptomatic of a global pessimism about the disintegrative effect of secularisation on culture, community and morality. The future is no longer bright. The past, therefore, has recovered its force. Religiously, this has meant the revival of traditionalist as against modernist forms. What, then, remains of modern Orthodoxy?

NOTES

1. *Tradition* 20:1 (Spring 1982). For a summary and response, see Jonathan Sacks, 'Modern Orthodoxy in Crisis,' *L'Eylah* 2:7 (Spring 1984), 20-26.

2. Charles Liebman, 'Orthodoxy in American Jewish Life,' in *Dimensions of Orthodox Judaism*, edited by Reuven Bulka, New York: Ktav, 1983, 96.
3. *Tradition*, ibid., 69-70.
4. Chaim Dov Keller, 'Modern Orthodoxy: An Analysis and a Response,' in *Dimensions of Orthodox Judaism*, op. cit, 253.
5. Shelomoh Danziger, 'Modern Orthodoxy or Orthodox Modernism?' *The Jewish Observer* (October 1966), 3-9.
6. Samuel C. Heilman, *Synagogue Life: A Study in Symbolic Interaction*, Chicago: University of Chicago Press, 1976, 266-267.
7. Charles Liebman, 'Left and Right in American Orthodoxy,' *Judaism* 15:1 (Winter 1966), 104.
8. Charles Liebman, 'Orthodox Judaism Today,' in *Dimensions of Orthodox Judaism*, op. cit., 111.
9. Peter Berger points out that 'It is instructive to recall that the literal meaning of the word *haeresis* is "choice." In a very real sense, every religious community in the pluralistic situation becomes a "heresy," with all the social and psychological tenuousness that the term suggests.' Peter Berger, *A Rumour of Angels*, London: Allen Lane, 1970, 62.
10. See, for example, Calvin Goldscheider, *Jewish Continuity and Change*, Bloomington: Indiana University Press, 1986, 151-169.
11. Steven M. Cohen, *American Assimilation or Jewish Revival?*, Bloomington: Indiana University Press, 1988, 121.
12. Charles Liebman and Elizer Don-Yehiya, *Religion and Politics in Israel*, Bloomington: Indiana University Press, 1984, 122.
13. See Menachem Friedman, 'Life Tradition and Book Tradition in the Development of Ultraorthodox Judaism,' in *Judaism Viewed from Within and from Without*, edited by Harvey Goldberg, Albany: State University of New York Press, 1987, 235-256.
14. Ibid., 125.
15. See, for example, Aharon Lichtenstein, 'The Relationship to Israel of Jewish Religious Groups: Orthodoxy,' in *Morasha* 1:1 (Fall 1984), 18-26; Bernard Rosenzweig, Walter Wurzburger and David Levinson, 'The Changing Attitudes of Orthodox Jews to Religious Zionism: A Symposium,' *Morasha* 2:2 (Spring-Summer 1986), 15-29; Reuven Bulka, 'Israel and the State of the Religious Mind,' ibid., 30-34.
16. Janet Aviad, *Return to Judaism*, Chicago: University of Chicago Press, 1983, 63-68.
17. The group published its views under the banner of *Hagut*. A review of their platform is contained in my editorial in *L'Eylah* 22 (Autumn 1986) and in Ben Mollov, 'Hagut: An Analysis,' *Morasha* 2:3 (Winter/Spring 1987), 28-30.
18. See Yochanan ben-Yaacov, 'Bnei Akiva Youth and Educational Direction,' *Morasha* 2:3 (Winter/Spring 1987), 20-27.
19. Chaim Waxman, 'American Aliyah: Dream and Reality,' *Morasha* 2:3 (Winter-Spring 1987), 1-7.
20. See Moshe Shokeid, *Children of Circumstances: Israeli Emigrants in New York*, Ithaca: Cornell University Press, 1988.

21. M. *Avot* 1:1.
22. J.T. *Peah* 2:6; see B. T. *Megillah* 19b; *Berakkot* 5a; *Exodus Rabbah* 28:6.
23. Gershom Scholem, *The Messianic Idea in Judaism*, New York: Schocken, 1971, 35.
24. Yosef Hayim Yerushalmi, *Zakhor: Jewish History and Jewish Memory*, Seattle: University of Washington Press, 1982, 16.
25. See, for example, *Genesis Rabbah* 40:6. See also Yitzchak Heinemann, *Darkhei ha-Aggadah*, Jerusalem: Magnes Press, 1970, 32-35. On the use of this exegetical device in the biblical commentary of Nachmanides, see Ezra Zion Melammed, *Meforshei ha-Mikra*, Jerusalem: Magnes Press, 1975, 950-952.
26. See Jacob Katz, *Exclusiveness and Tolerance*, New York: Behrman House, 1961, 26.
27. An English translation is available in Abraham Halkin and David Hartman, *Crisis and Leadership: Epistles of Maimonides*, Philadelphia: Jewish Publication Society of America, 1985, 91-207.
28. Samson Raphael Hirsch, *The Nineteen Letters on Judaism*, translated by Bernard Drachman, New York: Feldheim, 1960, 30.
29. Ibid., 54.
30. Ibid., 60.
31. Ibid., 65.
32. A. B. Yehoshua, *Between Right and Right*, New York: Doubleday, 1981, 12.
33. George Steiner, *In Bluebeard's Castle: Some Notes Towards the Redefinition of Culture*, London: Faber and Faber, 1971, 29-48.
34. Steiner has expressed this view in a number of essays. The fullest statement is contained in his 'Our Homeland, the Text,' *Salmagundi* 66 (Winter/Spring 1985), 4-25.
35. See Charles Liebman and Eliezer Don-Yehiya, *Civil Religion in Israel*, Berkeley: University of California Press, 1983, 123-166.
36. Arthur Green, *Jewish Spirituality from the Sixteenth Century Revival to the Present*, London: Routledge and Kegan Paul, 1987, xv.
37. Norman Lamm, 'Some Comments on Centrist Orthodoxy,' *Tradition* 22:3 (Fall 1986), 1-12.
38. Peter Berger, Brigitte Berger and Hansfried Kellner, *The Homeless Mind*, London: Penguin, 1974, 165.
39. R. Bellah, R. Madsen, W. Sullivan, A. Swidler and S. Tipton, *Habits of the Heart*, London: Hutchinson, 1988, 82-83.
40. Ibid., 277.
41. Irving Greenberg, 'Jewish Values and the Changing American Ethic,' in *Dimensions of Orthodox Judaism*, 284-309.
42. David Hartman, *A Living Covenant*, New York: Free Press, 1985.
43. Jeffrey Stout, 'The Voice of Theology in Contemporary Culture,' in *Religion and America: Spirituality in a Secular Age*, edited by Mary Douglas and Steven Tipton, Boston: Beacon Press, 1983, 249.

7
An Agenda of Future Jewish Thought

The last chapter suggested a pessimistic conclusion: that Orthodoxy and modernity are fundamentally incompatible. Orthodoxy is predicated on revelation and tradition: on the power of the past to command. By contrast, writes Edward Shils, 'The time through which we have just lived has been one in which what was inherited from the past was thought of as an irksome burden to be escaped from as soon as possible.' [1]

The whole thrust of post-Enlightenment thought has been hostile to religious belief in general, classic Jewish values in particular.[2] Few of the concepts in which the Jewish tradition is constituted can be translated into the terminology of contemporary culture. Halakhah – the idea of right conduct as expressed in *law* – cannot be transposed into the language of autonomy – the idea of right conduct as expressed in personal *choice*. The idea that there are significant roles into which we are born – differentiating between Jew and non-Jew, for example, or between men and women – runs contrary to the modern idea that the only significant roles are those which we choose. The very concept of covenant, and with it the idea of the singular destiny of a chosen people, runs counter to the Kantian idea that ethics is essentially universal, a matter of rules that, if they apply *at* all, apply *to* all.

So the conflicts of consciousness between Jewish tradition and secular modernity are many and deep. The conclusion seems inevitable. There is and can be no synthesis between Judaism and modernity. There is instead an either/or choice. *Either* Judaism *or* modernity but not both. Therefore the project of modern Orthodoxy is destined to failure.

The analysis is true, but the conclusion is false. The programmes of Samson Raphael Hirsch, Rav Kook, Rav Soloveitchik and others are as imperative as ever, perhaps more so. Let us summarise those programmes. Essentially they were four-fold. First there was the critical dialogue between Judaism and contemporary secular culture, as expressed in Hirsch's maxim of *Torah im Derekh Eretz* or Yeshiva University's *Torah u-Mada*, 'Torah and science'. Second was the reconstruction of Judaism as the ethic of a nation in its own land, the project of religious Zionism. Third was the affirmation of *knesset Yisrael*, the congregation of Israel, as an indivisible entity. This led figures like R. Seligmann Baer Bamberger and R. Marcus Horowitz to oppose Orthodox secession from the general Jewish community in Frankfurt and R. Isaac Reines, founder of Mizrachi, to oppose a similar secession from the secular Zionist movement. Implicit here was the assumption that an ongoing dialogue must be maintained between Orthodox Jews and others for the sake of the Jewish people as a whole. Fourth was the Hirschian emphasis on what was traditionally known as *kiddush ha-Shem*, the idea of the universal Jewish ethical example. Judaism might be the religion of a particular people, but it carries a wider responsibility. The Jewish people is to serve as an inspiration and model to humanity as a whole.

These values are currently in eclipse. This fact tells us about the mood of the contemporary Jewish world. But it tells us little about whether that mood is justified.

CONTEMPORARY CHALLENGES

It is not. Consider the four programmes in turn. The first was the dialogue between Judaism and secular culture. Recent figures suggest that as many as ninety per cent of young American Jews attend college. Throughout the Jewish world the present generation of Jews is arguably the most secularly educated of all time. The confrontation between Judaism and the contemporary intellectual environment might have been, in Saadia Gaon's and Maimonides' time, imperative for those few only who had ventured into the foreign fields of philosophy and had become disorientated and lost. Today it is applicable to the overwhelming majority of Jews, whose exposure to secular culture is a daily phenomenon, through the media, literature and the arts, and whose knowledge of the classic texts of the Jewish tradition is, by contrast, meagre and sporadic.

Torah im Derekh Eretz in the late twentieth century may be a more critical undertaking than it was a hundred and fifty years ago when Hirsch first proposed it. There may be fewer points of contact and less likelihood of synthesis. In the process Judaism may have less to learn, and by implication, more to teach. But the imperative is all the more urgent, to engage the taken-for-granted assumptions of contemporary scholarship, politics and ethics in critical conversation with the values of Torah. To abandon this undertaking is to imply that Judaism does indeed have nothing of consequence to say about the ways in which contemporary society understands and organises its world. This is not so much pessimism as a lack of faith in the power and relevance of Torah to all environments and cultures.

The second programme was religious Zionism. The state of Israel has been through difficult times since the Yom Kippur War. The continuing hostility of the Arab states, the internal problem of the Palestinians, the *intifada*, and Israel's international isolation have shaken two of the deepest held assumptions of secular Zionism: that the existence of Israel would end anti-semitism – which it saw as a phenomenon of the diaspora – and would lead to the 'normalisation' of 'the Jewish condition'. What is more, socialism, the secular religion of Israel's early statehood, has been a less than convincing ideology in the last decade. *Shelilat hagolah*, 'negation of the diaspora', another premiss on which secular Zionism was built, has also become increasingly untenable. For the diaspora has persisted and has proved to be the source of Israel's most unconditional support.

There has, in short, been a vacuum in secular Zionist thought as to the distinctive character of a Jewish state and its relationship with the diaspora specifically and international opinion generally. This calls out for a fresh statement of religious Zionism. That religious *groups* can flourish in Israeli society as a sub-section of the population has been established. That religious *thought* can yield a society-wide vision of justice, righteousness and compassion on the model of the Book of Deuteronomy has not yet been established. To abandon the project of religious Zionism as the attempt, albeit tentatively, to shape a messianic order would be a dereliction of Jewish destiny in the face of a merely temporary demoralisation.

The third concern of modern Orthodoxy was the idea of

Jewish peoplehood as something that ultimately transcended ideological schisms. Internally, in the twentieth century, Jews have been deeply divided, between Orthodoxy and Reform, religious and secular, and between those who chose to live in Israel and those who chose to remain in the *golah*. Externally, though, Jews have been tragically conscious that hostility makes no such distinctions. The Final Solution took no account of the religious, political or cultural affiliations of Jews. More recently, anti-Zionism has proved as undiscriminating as anti-semitism.

The Jewish fate, recent history has suggested, is indivisible. Jews have sensed the immense power of what R. Soloveitchik called the *brit goral*, the covenant of shared history. The inner and outer realities of Jewish peoplehood have been sharply discrepant, out of step with one another. Inwardly, ideological and spiritual divisions have deepened. Only external crisis has had the power, momentarily, to unite Jews into a community of shared feeling and purpose. Jewish unity has perhaps never before seemed simultaneously so desirable and so inaccessible. Recovering the substantive reality of *knesset Yisrael*, the covenantal congregation, is another transcending imperative of the present.

The fourth element of the programme, Samson Raphael Hirsch's idea of Judaism as a universal ethical example, is no less relevant to the present. Hirsch was surely correct in his understanding of the role of Judaism in an open secular society. The Jewish destiny, he argued, is neither particularist nor universalist but a complex interaction of both. To be a Jew in a predominantly non-Jewish environment is to be partially integrated and partially segregated. It means living by a set of values, some of which are common to humanity as a whole, some of which are specific to Jews. This is not a comfortable or easily negotiated stance. It is not surprising that it has been described by its critics as 'ambivalent' or 'schizophrenic'.

It is, in fact, neither of these things but the classic challenge of Jewish existence. On the one hand Judaism speaks of the Torah as a private covenant with the Jewish people: 'He has revealed His word to Jacob, His laws and decrees to Israel. He has done this for no other nation.' [3] On the other hand, it projects the values of Torah against the backdrop of mankind. 'Observe them carefully', says Moses about the commandments, 'for this is your wisdom and understanding in the eyes of the nations. They will hear all these rules and say: This great nation is surely a wise and understanding people.'[4] A Jewish perspective is both inward and outward, concerned to maintain a critical distance from other cultures while at the same time engaging their attention and ultimately admiration. To be a Jew is to be a witness to the world of the presence of God.

It is a difficult challenge, and there are two quite different ways of abdicating from it. One is assimilation: the way of total integration. The other is withdrawal from society: the way of total segregation. These are opposite but not equal alternatives. Assimilation leads to Jewish extinction. Withdrawal may be a mode of Jewish survival. But the fact that segregation is infinitely preferable to assimilation does not thereby entail that it is an ideal. It is not. For Jews are summoned to something altogether more vast than mere survival. They are called to play a specific part in the development of human civilisation as a whole. That universal vision was never wholly absent from the Jewish imagination, though there were some ages in which it was less relevant than others.

It is extraordinarily relevant today. Western societies generally have moved from monolithic to pluralist cultures. The Jewish voice on ethical issues is sought and given an attentive hearing. The state of Israel is looked to as a model of democracy and civil liberties in the Middle East. That it is sometimes judged by friends and critics alike by a different standard from that applied to its neighbours is a phenomenon that should be seen for what it is: an implicit ethical compliment. Jews today are faced with possibilities for *kiddush ha-Shem* of which Hirsch, a century and a half ago, could only dream. That this ideal should be treated with scepticism, above all in Orthodox circles, is not only religiously tragic. It is in the long term unwise.

For if Judaism, either in Israel or the diaspora, fails to win the admiration of observers, it will fail ultimately to win the emulation of Jews themselves. Jewish survival, that miraculous succession of defiances of probability, depends on more than the pursuit of survival as an end in itself. It depended, classically, on the pursuit of a vision of a holy people whose fidelity would one day lead the world to

God. However difficult that vision is to sustain in a post-Holocaust world, it must be attempted, for it is essential to Jewish self-definition.

ADJECTIVES AND IDEOLOGY

So the mood of pessimism which has settled over Orthodoxy in the last two decades is, from any wider perspective, untenable. The essential hopes of Samson Raphael Hirsch and Rav Kook have been realised. It has proved possible to engage in advanced secular study, participate in the shaping of a plural society and achieve civic prominence while remaining faithful to Jewish teachings.

The state of Israel exists. The general secular environment is more self-questioning, less abrasive, more open to tradition than at any time since the birth of Enlightenment. Jews today stand at the threshold of religious possibilities that were, a century ago, improbable. The time is opportune, therefore, for a re-engagement of Orthodoxy with the problems of modernity.

But on what basis is it to proceed? Along the lines of Hirsch or R. Kook or R. Soloveitchik? Or along some new intellectual-spiritual axis altogether? We would argue that these are the wrong answers and the wrong way of understanding the question. The burden of our case in this chapter is that Jewish thought generally, Orthodox thought specifically, has been limited and distorted by being allocated into adjectives and ideologies. A certain kind of thought has been labelled 'modern' Orthodoxy. Recently the preferred term has been 'centrist' Orthodoxy.[5] Evidently these terms answer to a perception, or they would not have been coined. But they mislead. Adjectives of ideology have no place in the ongoing life of Torah.

The labels 'centrist' and 'modern', along with their counterparts, 'right-wing', 'left-wing' and 'traditionalist' Orthodoxy, misconceive halakhah and aggadah, Jewish law and thought, and their application to changing circumstance. They make it all too easy for certain positions to be delegitimated. A sociologist may identify different groupings within Orthodoxy and may label and categorise them into movements, denominations and tendencies. But there is a vast difference between the detached observation of the sociologist and the internal reasoning that takes place within Judaism itself. And here these labels have no place.

Traditionally Judaism knew of sharp differences of style, custom and intellectual orientation. There were Ashkenazim and Sefardim, Chassidim and Mitnagdim, mystics and rationalists. There were fierce arguments within Volozhyn yeshivah in the nineteenth century, for example, over whether *pilpul* or *peshat*, intellectual ingenuity or fathoming the plain sense, was the proper method with which to approach the talmudic text. There were equally fierce arguments within the Lithuanian yeshivot as to whether *Mussar*, the discipline of ethics, was a proper part of the curriculum. A living tradition contains such divergences and arguments.[6]

What tradition did not know was the projection of these arguments into ideologies and movements with separate organisational bases and no strong lines of communication between them. Instead the question that confronted the Jew was: what does Torah require of me in this time and place? The question was answerable by reference to the texts and interpretations of tradition. The answer might be influenced by a particular orientation, or *shittah*. But it was not to be determined in advance by an ideological position. The importation of adjectives and ideologies into Orthodoxy is a symptom of the breakdown, socially, of the structures of community and intellectually, of the tradition of argument which is the dialogue between Torah and its application to a given age.

IS ORTHODOXY MODERN?

Consider the two adjectives in turn. In what sense can there be a 'modern' Orthodoxy? First, Orthodoxy can be responsive to its time. A modern Orthodoxy in this sense would be one which bore the signs of its specific place in history. But in this sense *all* varieties of contemporary Orthodoxy, from the most avowedly modernist to the most uncompromisingly 'traditional', are modern. We have argued that R. Sofer's rejection of modern social processes was as much a considered response to modernity as Samson Raphael Hirsch's acceptance of them. Descriptively, all Orthodoxies are modern.

Evaluatively they are not. For quite clearly, as we have seen, there were thinkers like Hirsch and R. Kook who were enthusiastic about the possibilities of modernity while R. Sofer saw it as a threat to tradition. In this second sense Hirsch and Kook were 'modernists'. But neither of them was ideologically so. Hirsch was clear about the dangers as well as the challenges of emancipation. R. Kook believed that the upheavals through which he lived were part of the messianic process. But he had specific expectations about the return of secularists to tradition; and those expectations are open to refutation. In short, neither embraced modernity *a priori* and unconditionally. Modernism, for them, was not an ideology and in this sense they were not exponents of a 'modern' Orthodoxy.

There is a third sense of the word. For more recently there have been thinkers who have deliberately sought to integrate 'modern consciousness' within the tradition in a more radical way than any of the figures we have thus far studied.[7] They have argued that at least some values embedded in contemporary secular society – liberalism, personal autonomy, democracy, role equality between the sexes and pluralism – can be accommodated within halakhic Judaism. They have sought a larger role for the individual as against the community, for halakhic change as against stasis, and for the dignity of the self as against structures of authority.

Emanuel Rackman (b.1910), for example, has called for a 'teleological' approach to halakhah which would allow for development within Jewish law according to a broad sense of its underlying purposes rather than a narrow sense of precedent.[8] Eliezer Berkovits (b.1908), similarly, has argued the case for recovering the flexibility of Jewish law understood as 'the Word intended for this hour, for this generation'.[9] More radically, David Hartman (b.1931) has sketched a complete philosophy of Judaism 'in terms of a covenantal anthropology that encourages human initiative and freedom and that is predicated on belief in human adequacy'.[10] More radically still, Irving Greenberg (b.1933) has outlined a post-Holocaust Judaism in which the very terms of the covenant have been rendered 'voluntary'. Greenberg speaks of a 'third era' in Jewish history, marked by religious pluralism and 'holy secularity'.[11] These thinkers are modern in a thoroughgoing sense. For they believe that Judaism is itself transformed in its encounter with modernity. To be sure, they seek to stay within the rabbinic tradition. But they believe that the tradition itself contains resources for change, and that it has in fact changed with each confrontation with a new social and intellectual order. But it is precisely here that the question arises: can Orthodoxy be modern in this sense and still be Orthodox?

For each of these philosophies stresses one side of the rabbinic tradition at the expense of another. There are tensions in Judaism between legal precedent and underlying purpose, halakhah and personal autonomy, religious authority and individual freedom. Indeed some positions – like Greenberg's denominational pluralism – almost certainly lie outside tradition altogether. Admittedly, Rackman, Berkovits and Hartman are aware of contrary tendencies in Judaism. Hartman explicitly describes his approach to rabbinic texts as 'selective'. His concern, he writes, is 'to locate specific tendencies or possibilities within the rabbinic tradition that could be supportive of a covenantal religious anthropology capable of participating adequately in the challenges of modernity'.[12] But is a selective reading of tradition still tradition? Is it not precisely an attempt to tailor tradition to a set of *a priori* ideological assumptions, rather than to let it speak with its own authoritative voice?

IS ORTHODOXY CENTRIST?

So 'modern' as an adjective describing Orthodoxy is redundant in the first sense, misleading in the second and contestable in the third. The same doubts apply to the adjective 'centrist'. What is any kind of Orthodoxy to be centrist between? Between Orthodoxy and heterodoxy or halakhic and non-halakhic Judaisms there is no middle ground within tradition. Centrism, like the words right- and left-wing, is a term transferred to Judaism from the vocabulary of politics. Roger Scruton neatly defines the view espoused by centrists as 'the supposed political position somewhere between the left and right, where political views are either sufficiently indeterminate, or sufficiently imbued with the spirit of compromise, to be thought acceptable to as large a body of citizens as would be capable of accepting anything'.[13] The use of such an adjective in a Jewish context is a significant symptom of the politicisation of religious life: a phenomenon which affects all sectors of contemporary Judaism and which deserves serious consideration in its own right. But even if its legitimacy is granted the same problems apply to religious as to political centrism: confrontational politics tend to favour clear alternatives over the vague attempt to 'capture the middle ground'.

There is, to be sure, something more substantive to the idea of 'centrism' within Orthodoxy. Maimonides spoke of the 'middle way' between extremes as the ideal conduct of the *chakham* or sage.[14] He was speaking of ethical character rather than communal policy, but there are suggestions in his work that the same applies here too: a balance must be struck whenever there is a conflict between two or more Jewish values. Many of the issues that have created controversy in Orthodoxy in the last two centuries have been of this kind. How was one to choose between social integration and segregation, or Torah and secular study, or concern for the position of women as against concern for the stability of traditional roles and institutions? If both sides of the equation are values within Judaism, as we would argue that they are, then a concern for the tradition as a whole dictates a careful balance between them.

But that balance cannot be specified in advance. Consider one example: the strange fate of Hirsch's idea of *Torah im Derekh Eretz*. Samson Raphael Hirsch and R. Moses Sofer, as we saw, held diametrically opposed views on the relationship between Torah and secular culture. Yet within a generation the gap between Frankfurt and Pressburg was dramatically reduced. Hirsch's son-in-law and successor, R. Solomon Breuer (1850-1926), had been a student of R. Moses Sofer's son and successor, Abraham. Breuer, though he had himself studied at German universities, was a fierce traditionalist. He founded the Association of Orthodox Rabbis in Germany which excluded all rabbis who maintained contact with Reform-dominated communal organisations. He was a prime mover of Agudat Yisrael, which brought together East and West European Orthodoxy in opposition to the Zionist movement and which likewise sought to exclude non-secessionist rabbis.

The principle of *Torah im Derekh Eretz* could not long survive. If Orthodox integrity demanded a principled withdrawal from the general Jewish community, the same argument applied with no less force to involvement in secular culture. In 1890, two years after succeeding Hirsch as the rabbi of Frankfurt, Breuer founded a yeshivah on the East European model. A major revision of Hirsch's programme was under way. Hirsch's daughter, Mrs Solomon Breuer, wrote to R. Moses Sofer's grandson, Shimon, that Hirsch had never intended *Torah im Derekh Eretz* as a universal norm.[15] It was specifically limited to his own community and to the circumstances prevailing at the time. Thus began a process of re-interpretation which has continued ever since. Openness to secular culture was, on this view, a *hora'at sha'ah*, a temporary concession not a universal rule. It had been intended to combat the inroads of the Reform movement, or to comply with pressure from the state that all children receive a general education, or as a means to a professional or business career.

Exponents of Hirsch, among them Joseph, Isaac and Mordechai Breuer, R. Yechiel Weinberg, Dayan Grunfeld and Lord Jakobovits,[16] have pointed out that Hirsch unquestionably believed otherwise. As Hirsch himself wrote, 'We maintain that a familiarity with all those elements which lie at the root of present-day civilisation, and a study of all the subjects required for such an acquaintance, is of the highest necessity for the Jewish youth of our day as it was in fact at all times, and should be looked on as a religious duty'.[17] For Hirsch, *Torah im Derekh Eretz* was permanent, not temporary; an obligation, not a concession. Nonetheless, the revisionists were essentially correct. The Hirschian synthesis was a *hora'at sha'ah*. It was a product of its time.

What does not follow, however, is that Torah without *derekh eretz* is a permanent ideal. The reverse is the case. This too is a *hora'at sha'ah*, a response to the times. The argument over whether Torah study is an exclusive pursuit has been waged at every significant point of rabbinic history. It has taken different forms at different times, and the phrase *derekh eretz* has shifted its meaning accordingly. Was a father obligated to teach his child Torah only, or prepare him, in addition, for an occupation? Was the ideal life one which combined Torah with a worldly occupation or one devoted wholly to study? Was the study of secular disciplines forbidden, or necessary only in an emergency – to refute the heretic and guide the perplexed – or part of the religious duty of knowledge of God and His works? The argument can be traced from the mishnaic period to the middle ages. Each side, at each point, had its adherents. The questions had no single authoritative resolution.

This brings us to a fundamental point. There are areas of Jewish law where rabbinic tradition allows a wide latitude of application. The standard rubric in such cases is 'everything depends on the assessment of the halakhic authority' or 'the ruling depends on the place and time'. There are areas of Jewish law where these statements are made explicitly, others where we recognise the implicit operation of such judgements. Restrictive or open policies on conversion, interactions between Jews and non-Jews, the place of women within the religious life and decisions on how to relate to those who break the Jewish law, all come within this category, as does the cluster of issues embraced by the phrase *Torah im Derekh Eretz*. In all these cases we can trace differences of policy between different Jewish communities at different times.

This is not to say that halakhic rulings are subjective or historically conditioned or the result of sociological causes. They are not. The halakhic process is judicial, the application of precedent to specific circumstance. There are areas of halakhah, however, which require for their application a careful evaluation of the present, one which may involve historical and sociological judgement. In the case of Torah and secular culture, the questions to be answered are: Will a given educational policy enhance or endanger Jewish spirituality? Will it resolve or increase the perplexities of a generation? Will it lead to greater or diminished Jewish commitment? Though the sources on which a ruling must be based remain the same, the answers to these questions will differ systematically from place to place and from one culture to another. These are exceptional but important spheres in which *every* ruling is implicitly a *hora'at sha'ah*, local as to its application.

An important conclusion follows. There is no meaningful ideological sense that can be attached to phrases like right-wing, left-wing or centrist, modern or traditional

Orthodoxy. For there is no unitary, permanent ideological or institutional expression of the relationship between Judaism and its contemporary environment. There are instead as many modes as there are communities and generations. Orthodoxy developed in one way in nineteenth century Frankfurt, in another in Pressburg, and in yet other ways in England, France, Italy and Eastern Europe. Policies that were effective in one context were destructive in another. R. Azriel Hildesheimer (1820-1899), a commanding figure of both rabbinic and secular scholarship, was bitterly criticised as rabbi of Halberstadt in Hungary for his plans to create a modern rabbinic seminary. The same project was outstandingly successful in his subsequent home of Berlin. R. Yechiel Weinberg reports a telling episode. R. Israel Salanter, leader of the Mussar movement, visited Germany where he found R. Hildesheimer conducting a class in *Tenakh* and *Shulchan Arukh* for girls. He remarked: If a rabbi in Lithuania were to do likewise in his community he would certainly be removed from his position. And certainly, such is the law. But nonetheless I hope I can share R. Hildesheimer's place in *Gan Eden*, paradise.[18]

CONFLICTS AND CONTEXTS

The point is crucial, for it allows us to recover perspectives that have been obscured in recent times. Their loss has handicapped Orthodox thought and has plagued Orthodoxy itself with fierce internal conflicts that have disfigured the image it presents to the world. Since the image of Orthodoxy is itself a matter of religious concern – at stake are *kiddush ha-Shem* and *chillul ha-Shem*, the sanctification or desecration of God's name – the issue is not a light one. What, then, are the consequences of the idea that there are important areas of Jewish law where rulings depend on the time and place?

First, apparent conflicts may not be real. Let us imagine hypothetically a single halakhic authority in two different situations, first as rabbi of a 'nominally Orthodox' congregation, subsequently as the head of a yeshivah. Some of the rulings he would give – precisely on controversial topics such as the permissibility of secular study, or mixed youth groups, or the place of women in the community – would vary systematically between the two contexts. To be sure, his rulings on other issues – the permissibility of certain kinds of medical operation, for example – would not. Nor does it follow that his halakhic principles will have changed. It may simply be that as a congregational rabbi he was constrained by such principles as 'Just as it is a mitzvah to say that which will be heeded, so it is a mitzvah not to say that which will not be heeded',[19] or 'Better that they sin unwittingly than knowingly'.[20] But there are areas in which a halakhic ruling is specific to a given time, place and circumstance.

Many of the apparent conflicts between 'left-wing', 'right-wing' and 'centrist' Orthodoxy have been of just this kind. For they have different constituencies. The natural constituency of 'centrism' is the synagogue. That of 'right-wing' Orthodoxy is the yeshivah or Chassidic community. The context of 'left-wing' Orthodoxy is usually academic or intellectual: the university or college campus. The challenges of these three kinds of environment are quite different from one another, and what is an appropriate response to one may be inappropriate to the other. Genuine conflict arises when rulings are divorced from their context and asserted as universal norms. The talmudic literature guarded against this by preserving conflicting judgements within the same tradition, as if to say that there are circumstances in which one judgement is germane and others in which another is more apposite. There are times when the Talmud is explicit; this ruling applies to us, that to them;[21] this to Israel, that to Babylon; this to the 'early generations', that to the 'later generations'; this to the 'pious', that to the average person.

There is, then, no 'left-wing', 'right-wing' or 'centrist' Orthodoxy. These phrases, that is to say, are misconceived if they are taken as ideological alternatives to universal questions stated without regard to context. There is instead a single Torah applied to a specific time, place and person. Judgement as to what is appropriate to a given context is part of halakhic 'wisdom' or what is sometimes called *da'at Torah*. The same applies to communities. The parameters of Orthodoxy will vary as between Israel, where it is called on to address issues in the public domain, America, where Orthodoxy is in a minority, and Anglo-Jewry where it represents the affiliation of the majority. This was the basis of R. Yechiel Weinberg's halakhic critique of Eastern European rabbis who sought to apply their conventions to French and German Jewry. Their rulings, he insisted, were not wrong; they were right; but they originated and had their salience somewhere else.

Much conflict and confusion has followed failure to observe this fact. The vast geographical dislocations of Jewry following the Russian pogroms of the 1880s and in the years surrounding the Second World War led to clashes of custom and perception between indigenous rabbis and those newly arrived from Eastern Europe. Many of the tensions in contemporary Orthodoxy flow from the competing claims to authority of the yeshivah head and the congregational rabbi. Both phenomena arose from the transfer of rules which governed one context into another. Perhaps the process was unavoidable. Certainly the resulting clashes enlivened Jewish life and forced each side to sharpen its self-definition. But they would have been less acrimonious and more creative had they been accompanied by a proper mutual respect for the context-specific nature of certain halakhic traditions.

There are other consequences. For example, it is sometimes lamented that 'modern Orthodox' or 'religious Zionist' yeshivot and yeshivah high schools have moved away from their original ideologies toward a more traditionalist disdain for secular education and 'narrow, particularistic, authoritarian' values.[22] But this is inevitable. The natural environment of traditionalism – its *Sitz-im-Leben* – is the enclosed, segregated community. The one leads to the other. 'Modern' Orthodoxy will always have difficulties in creating its own yeshivot, for its place and role lie elsewhere, namely, in congregational life. The real crisis of 'modern' Orthodoxy has been the sharp split between yeshivot and congregations. Few figures today combine – as was once the norm – the roles of yeshivah head and communal rabbi. This leads to a concentration of *poskim*, halakhic authorities, in yeshivot. Relatively few have had experience of congregations. What follows is an inevitable distance between halakhic rulings and the realities and traditions of congregational life. This leads to the 'crisis of legitimacy' experienced by many congregational rabbis.

THE CHALLENGE OF THE NEW

There is another consequence. The closer Orthodoxy comes to the social processes at work in congregations ('centrism') or to the intellectual currents of the academic world ('left-wing' or modern Orthodoxy proper) the more its environment is subject to change. The segregated community of the yeshivah or Chassidic group may aspire to something approximating stasis. Not so Jews who inhabit the secular world. There, values and intellectual fashions change. It follows that those who attempt to speak to such Jews must reckon with a constantly changing context. In a phrase, 'modern' Orthodoxy must continually re-invent itself.

This brings us back to the idea of *Torah im Derekh Eretz*. It is sometimes supposed that the phrase means that there is a definitive synthesis, whether of the kind envisaged by Hirsch or along the lines set out by R. Kook, between Judaism and secular culture. There is, we suggest, no such thing, for there is no stable entity that can be designated as secular culture. Culture is a process, not a state. It is fluid and constantly in motion. It follows that *Torah im Derekh Eretz* is itself a process rather than an achievement. Dayan Grunfeld, himself a follower and translator of Hirsch, defined *Torah im Derekh Eretz* as 'the relationship between Torah and the civilisation of a given epoch'[23] or 'the proclamation of the sovereignty of the Torah within any given civilisation'.[24] This is a far more general idea than that espoused by Hirsch, and leaves open the possibility that there may, at any given moment, be no synthesis available. We believe that this is a more accurate way of describing the relationship between Torah and the ethos of the age.

Torah im Derekh Eretz is the ongoing critical dialogue that must always occur at the interface between Judaism and its environing culture. It is essentially incomplete, ongoing and open-ended. The resolutions of one generation are inadequate to the next. Secular culture has meanwhile moved on. Its positions have shifted. Its contours have subtly changed. A major error of 'modern' Orthodoxy has been its canonisation of Hirsch, R. Kook or R. Soloveitchik as if their work yielded a definitive philosophy of Judaism in modernity. New challenges may yield different inspirations. It may be that other, hitherto neglected figures of the last two centuries, may come into new prominence: R. Chaim Hirschensohn, for example, or R. Isaac Reines or, from the ranks of German Jewry, Rabbis Hildesheimer, Ettlinger, Bamberger and Hoffman.

There are times in which the philosophical orientation of Judah Halevi is more compelling than that of Maimonides. There are ages in which the relationship between Judaism and general culture is one of congruence, at others a sustained critique. There are periods in which a universalist mood answers to Jewish experience; others at which particularism is more appropriate. Ultimately there is no escape from a continual re-engagement with the sources, biblical, talmudic, midrashic and halakhic and the identification, through their categories, of the dangers and possibilities of the new. *Torah im Derekh Eretz* is not an ideological position but a process, and one whose outcome is impossible to predict in advance.

Tradition renews itself through its encounter with the new. It atrophies whenever it declines that encounter through either systematic rejection or systematic accommodation. *Chadash muttar min ha-Torah*, 'the new is permitted', is as far removed from a living tradition as *chadash assur min ha-Torah*, 'the new is forbidden'. Ironically it has been the most traditionalist communities that have been the most innovative in recent decades and the most quick to respond to changing public moods. It was the yeshivah and Chassidic communities that first noted the trend, in the 1960s, toward tradition, ethnicity and the search for 'roots'. They developed outreach networks, sought *baalei teshuvah*, religious returnees, and created for them new styles of yeshivot. They pioneered new modes of informal education: the lunchtime learning session for businessmen, the 'student encounter' and the residential retreat. They were the first to exploit the educational potential of the telephone (Dial-a-*Daf Yomi*) and cable television. ArtScroll, a traditionalist publishing house, applied modern typographical techniques to traditional texts. To be sure, these are instrumental rather than principled uses of modernity. But they demonstrate that traditionalists, no less than Hirsch in his day, are quick to perceive value-neutral possibilities in the contemporary cultural and technological climate.

There are no static traditions, least of all the tradition of modernity. Those who sought to create a liberal tradition out of the work of Hirsch, R. Kook and R. Soloveitchik quickly discovered that all three could be cited on the opposite side of the argument. The Hirsch who wrote the *Nineteen Letters* was also the Hirsch who advocated Orthodox secession and segregation from the general community. As Samuel Heilman has noted, Hirsch became 'a hero of a traditional Orthodoxy no less than he had earlier become the ideal of those drawn to modernity'.[25] The R. Kook who wrote of the inner harmony pulsating through creation became, after the Six Day War, the inspiration of the ultra-nationalist Gush Emunim, and in the 1980s of the *machteret*, the religiously motivated 'underground' group that perpetrated acts of terrorism against Arab targets.[26] The R. Soloveitchik who valued human creativity at the beginning of 'The Lonely Man of Faith' was also the R. Soloveitchik who delivered a crushing assault on secularism at its end.

Every deeply considered Orthodox response to modernity has strands within it that can be taken in both liberal and conservative directions. Those who wish to do in their generation what Hirsch, R. Kook and R. Soloveitchik did in theirs have no option but to begin again at the beginning, in the meeting between contemporary culture and the biblical and rabbinic texts. Neither the dynamic of the new nor the stasis of the old are achieved without constant re-interpretation.

THE RENEWAL OF TORAH IM DEREKH ERETZ

We have argued, then, against a conception of Orthodoxy that sees it as a set of conflicting ideologies. The parcelling of Orthodoxy into right, left and centrist positions, or into an antinomy of modernism against traditionalism, is a symptom of the collapse of overarching structures of community and the fragmentation of Orthodox life into non-communicating organisational enclaves. The cause is social, the effect intellectual, and the loss spiritual. What is lost is the ongoing critical dialogue between Torah in its full authority and a particular context in its full specificity. Instead Torah is allowed to speak only in those accents ideology has determined in advance. And local context is mistaken for a universal situation.

Tradition then speaks in a series of strident voices, each

of which denies the legitimacy of others, instead of in its classic mode: as an open-ended argument between different perspectives. This delegitimation of alternatives within the same tradition is what is sometimes called *fundamentalism*, and it is important to note that there can be a fundamentalism of the left and centre, no less than of the right. In its place we have argued for the recovery of a non-ideological approach to Jewish thought, one that sees its role as the application of a single Torah to a specific time, place and constituency. Such thought will recognise the presence of conflicting voices within the biblical and rabbinic tradition, as well as the existence of other contexts and constituencies that may evoke different judgements. This is not relativism or pluralism. It is what is involved in the application of Torah to changing circumstance.

What, then, are the issues that shape the agenda of future Orthodox thought? They are what they have been since the threshold of Jewish modernity. For we have argued that the four great projects that have engaged the imagination of the great Jewish thinkers of the last two centuries must be addressed anew in every generation. They give rise to processes, not definitive resolutions. No synthesis or antithesis between Torah and its surrounding culture is final. It is at best provisional. The great questions must be taken up again in every age.

Let us restate them. The first is *Torah im Derekh Eretz*, the meeting between Torah and contemporary culture. But here we must divest ourselves of *a priori* expectations as to what that meeting will yield. Hirsch and before him Saadia Gaon believed it would yield a kind of static synthesis, convergence on a single truth from different starting points. R. Kook – as to some extent did Maimonides – anticipated that it would produce a more enveloping synthesis, a unity of the disciplines. R. Soloveitchik – not unlike Judah Halevi – foresaw conflict. There is, for them, no ultimate meeting point between the universalism of secular thought and the particularism of revelation and covenant. The comparisons between these modern thinkers and their medieval predecessors are tentative and analogies could be drawn in different ways. What they have in common, though, is what Quentin Skinner calls a predilection for the 'Grand Theory',[27] a framework of prior expectation, in this case as to the outcome of the encounter between Torah and secular civilisation.

We have argued for a more modest, case by case approach. The strength of *Torah im Derekh Eretz* lies in its detailed application, not its general philosophical stance. We have had, in recent years, impressive beginnings. There have been useful works on Jewish economic and medical ethics and some initial thoughts on the relationship between Judaism and psychiatry, psychology and psychotherapy. But these are only beginnings. There is a tendency to suppose that a book on one of these subjects sets forth *the* Jewish view on the questions under review, and that therefore no more work needs to be done. But it is in fact rare to find a contemporary issue about which one can aspire to present the Jewish view. At most one can argue *a* Jewish view. *The* Jewish view emerges, if it does at all, only after alternative views have been presented and argued and a consensus develops. *Torah im Derekh Eretz* is a process, not a set of conclusions.

Consider a small, or perhaps not so small, example. Sol Roth, in his recent book *Halakhah and Politics: The Jewish Idea of a State*,[28] argues that within limits Judaism is compatible with democracy, individualism and human rights. At the same time Gershon Weiler's *Jewish Theocracy* appeared in English.[29] Weiler, an Israeli secularist, argues that rabbinic Judaism is radically *in*compatible with politics and a liberal, democratic state. Weiler is opposed to Judaism, but the same point has been made in the name of Judaism by Neturei Karta, opponents of the state of Israel on religious grounds, and by religious nationalists like Meir Kahane who has argued that 'there is a potential confrontation between the Zionist Jewish state . . . and modern ideas of democracy and citizenship'.[30]

At stake is one of the deepest issues facing religious Zionism. And a question like this cannot be resolved by polemics on the one hand, apologetics on the other. It requires sustained, close and critical study informed by halakhah and aggadah on the one hand, political theory and history on the other. It requires, too, an extended and reasoned debate between opposing positions. And it requires that the debate be accessible to a wider audience than academics and scholars if it is to become part of public argument within a Jewish state. That argument is part of what Torah *is* in the public domain.

One of the most serious contemporary threats to Judaism as a living tradition is the divorce of Torah from *derekh eretz*. When Jewish political theorists, for example, are insufficiently grounded in Torah, and exponents of Torah insufficiently knowledgeable in political theory, a question like the ideal form of a Jewish state is secularised on both sides into an issue that can only be settled by political confrontation and a war of cultures. *Torah im Derekh Eretz* is a religious imperative not only – as Maimonides and Hirsch saw it – as a means to the perfection of the self, but more basically as a precondition of a mature halakhic response to the many pressing ethical, social and political questions of our time.

TIKKUN OLAM AND RELIGIOUS ZIONISM

Arising immediately out of this is what Maimonides listed as one of the aims of the halakhic system, *tikkun olam*, 'the perfection of the world', or as we might more modestly translate it, 'the establishment of society'.[31] In both biblical and rabbinic thought, Judaism is actively concerned with society as well as self. This is implicit in the very concepts of mitzvah and halakhah – of religious truth as expressed not only or even primarily in terms of personal experience, but also in terms of *law*. Law governs communities. It creates societies. And it is this fact that has become intensely problematic in the modern world.

For secularisation, as we now know, does not result in the eclipse of religion. Instead it transfers it from the public to the private domain. There, it is experienced not as societal norm but as personal commitment: not as *law* but as *choice*.[32] This affects all modes of religious behaviour, from the most liberal to the most conservative. For liberal Judaisms, such as Reform, it results in the substitution of choice for law altogether, so that personal autonomy is seen as the central value of Judaism.[33] Some Reform thinkers still use the word 'halakhah', but the word has been robbed of its traditional sense. The impact on traditionalist Orthodoxy is quite different but no less profound. Orthodoxy comes to be identified with voluntary communities, above all the yeshivah, instead of with the Jewish people as a whole. Instead of being seen as the law of a people, halakhah is experienced as the code of those who volunteer to be bound by it, a choosing elite.

In either case religious thought has effectively abandoned the public domain. But it is precisely this that lies at the heart of two of the great projects of Orthodoxy in modernity: religious Zionism and the role of Judaism in a secular diaspora.

Consider first religious Zionism. One of the great questions confronting it has always been: what impels rabbinic Judaism, embodying as it does a tradition of political quietism and the belief that exile would be ended only by Divine intervention, to seek to reconstitute itself as a state in the land of Israel? There were two classic answers to this question, one given by R. Kook, the other by R. Reines. The first was mystical, the second pragmatic. For R. Kook, the ingathering of Jews to Israel was the start of a messianic process. For R. Reines it was a simple matter of saving lives from persecution. Though both answers remain relevant and profound, neither speaks lucidly to the situation of Israel in the late twentieth century. On the one hand it is beset by too many conflicts, internal and external, to be *obviously* messianic. On the other, Israel is too exposed to danger, and some diaspora communities are too well-established, for Israel to be the only obvious safe haven for Jewish existence. The classic answers may remain ultimately true but they are not immediately self-evident. Hence the current crisis of religious Zionism.

But there was a third strand of religious Zionist thought which remains tantalisingly germane. Until emancipation, in a series of enclosed and semi-autonomous Jewish communities, Jews lived Judaism as part of the public domain. Education, arbitration, civil disputes and community ordinances were informed by Torah. One could speak coherently of a Jewish culture, enriched by a bricolage of borrowings, but integrated nonetheless. It was emancipation and the collapse of the self-governing *kehillah* that drove Judaism inward and secularised the public domain. And it was this that led a number of traditional Jewish thinkers, among them R. Moses Sofer, to seek Jewish revival away from Europe in a settlement of the land of Israel. Indeed until the 1880s the majority of Jewish settlers of the land was intensely and traditionally religious.

Israel is the one place Jews can today seek to construct a Jewish and Judaic public culture. It 'expands the possible range of halakhic involvement' as David Hartman puts it, to include 'the moral quality of the army, social and economic disparities and deprivations, the exercise of power moderated by moral sensitivities, attitudes toward minorities and the stranger, tolerance and freedom of conscience'.[34] It is the sole remaining Judaic context in which society can become the vehicle for – in Aharon Lichtenstein's striking phrase – 'collective beatitude'.[35]

But this presupposes that Judaism, not just Jews, re-enters the public domain. What would it be for a modern macro-economic system to embody halakhic values? Or a contemporary welfare state? Does Judaism indeed favour a welfare state, or does it prefer a minimalist state which leaves major educational and charitable decisions in private hands? What kind of inequalities of wealth and income are compatible with Jewish values? What generally is the place of halakhah in a secular state? Should it be made law by a secular legislature? Should it remain a voluntary and self-imposed code? What are the possible and desirable interactions between Judaism, culture and society?

Yet again these questions have no immediate and definitive answer, for between the authoritative texts and their contemporary application lies the process of interpretation and argument. Torah is constituted more by the conversation than by its conclusion, which in any event is provisional. But again we are struck by the relative poverty of the detailed working-out of responses to these and related questions. Here too there is a predominance of Grand Theory over detailed analysis. But if Jewish thought does not assume this responsibility, the result will almost certainly be its confinement within the 'four cubits' of home, school and synagogue. In which case a Jewish life can be lived as cogently in Boro Park as in Bayit VeGan, in Harvard no less than in Haifa.

TIKKUN OLAM AND JUDAISM IN THE DIASPORA

A similar though more complex set of concerns arises out of the place of Judaism in a pluralist diaspora. Here we face an issue whose existential impact is recent even if it arose theoretically more than a century ago. Emancipating societies were in theory secular; in practice their public cultures remained residually Christian. Jews saw their interests best advanced by a more universalistic order. They became passionate advocates of liberalism, socialism and secularism. Many – devotees, observers and critics alike – came to see these causes as in some way essentially 'Jewish' without any clear sense of why or how this was so, other than that they were promoted by Jews and were sometimes buttressed by vague references to 'the prophetic tradition'.

These identifications are no longer adequate. Politically Jews, whether in Israel, America or England, are no longer overwhelmingly associated with the left. They have become aware, in the last two decades, of some of the political problems of socialism and the cultural problems of liberalism. They have been reminded, too, that there is a religious politics of the right. As mature members of diaspora societies, they are more conscious also that there is a potential conflict between a Judaic voice on ethical and social questions, and the more narrow concerns of Jewish sectional self-interest. In the modern state, composed as it is of a vast variety of ethnic and religious groupings, there is an unprecedented place for a Jewish contribution to the question, as Mary Warnock puts it, 'What kind of society can we praise and admire?'

Warnock's remark arose in the context of the Committee of Inquiry she chaired, at the invitation of the British Government, into human fertilisation and embryology (1982-1984). It raised important issues of medical ethics, but it raised them against the backdrop of a morally diverse society. Her opening observations are significant: 'In our pluralistic society it is not to be expected that any one set of principles can be enunciated to be completely accepted by everyone. This is not to say . . . that there is no shared morality whatever. The law . . . sets out a broad framework for what is morally acceptable within society . . . Within the broad limits of legislation there is room for different, and perhaps much more stringent, moral rules.' [36]

This distinction between a public legal code and a more demanding moral community comes close to the classic Jewish distinction between the *sheva mitzvot bnei noach,* the Noachide commands binding on humanity as such,[37] and the more rigorous demands – 613 commandments – binding specifically on Jews as the people of the covenant. A Jewish ethic that responded to a pluralist society would therefore have to make a rigorous distinction between

'Jewish' and 'Noachide' halakhah. It is just this that the rabbinic tradition is unusually, perhaps uniquely, well poised to do. But here too the quality of Jewish responses has been low, sometimes failing even to make this elementary distinction between the rules that bind Jews, and those that, according to Jewish sources, bind society as such. There is room here for a renewal of a neglected, because not previously urgent, branch of Jewish thought.

The issue is of more than academic concern. Jews in the diaspora are occupied in shaping and building societies. For the most part their involvements and interactions are with non-Jews in contexts governed by neutral rules and roles. The extant halakhic literature has relatively little to say about these interactions, beyond a general concern for *kiddush ha-Shem*, 'sanctification of God's name', *darkhei shalom*, 'the ways of peace', and the avoidance of *eivah*, 'animosity'. Unless there evolves a more nuanced and articulated set of rules or values for these situations, Jews will inevitably live out compartmentalised identities. For there will be no specific way for them to behave Jewishly in these contexts, nor even a detailed sense of what Judaism regards as acting 'humanly'. They will be 'secularists in the street' however deeply religious they are in their private lives. Perhaps this is just what *galut* – exile – is in our time. But this judgement seems at the very least premature.

Which takes us back to one of the key words of 'modern' Orthodoxy: *synthesis*. The word has standardly been applied to education and culture – to the idea that some fusion is possible of Judaism and secular disciplines. We have argued that synthesis in this sense may simply not be available. It depends on the state of secular culture. What is more religiously interesting is the idea of synthesis as applied to an individual life. Here it is a value long recognised in the rabbinic tradition under the rubric of 'let all your deeds be for the sake of Heaven' [38] or, as Maimonides put it, 'directing the powers of the soul toward a single goal'.[39] That tradition recognises such a value makes it clear that compartmentalisation cannot be a religious ideal.

The question then is: what is it to live one's life in accordance with Jewish law and values as a doctor, lawyer, academic, businessman, industrialist, or any of the countless other occupations in which Jews are engaged, when the people with whom one deals are not Jews or if they are, are not bound by halakhah? Orthodox thought has been almost totally silent on this question. It has disattended it, as if to say that only within Jewish contexts can behaviour be coherently Jewish. But this is to withdraw from the challenge of both religious Zionism and of post-emancipation diaspora life: of living in a non-religious society on the one hand and a non-Jewish one on the other. Can it be that the vast literature of Torah has *no* answer to this question, which today encompasses most dilemmas of most Jews most of the time? Against this we must reaffirm the faith of Ben Bag-Bag: 'Study the Torah again and again, for everything is contained in it'.[40]

It was Franz Rosenzweig who was most perceptive about this impoverishment of Orthodoxy. He argued instead that 'Exactly those things generally rendered permissible by Orthodoxy must be given a Jewish form' and insisted that 'the two worlds, the one of the Jewishly forbidden and the one of the "permissible" extra-Jewish, flow into one another'.[41] Rosenzweig's ideal of the Jew was of a person who had 'prepared himself quite simply to have everything that happens to him, inwardly and outwardly, happen to him in a *Jewish way*'.[42] What that means, remains obscure. Once again, the Grand Theory exists; its detailed working out does not.

Here then is the proper sphere of the search for synthesis. It will be created not in the house of study but in a series of existential models: the employer, perhaps, who creates new ways of acting humanely to employees, or the architect who enhances the urban environment, or the industrialist who reinvigorates an area of inner-city depression. There is no way of specifying in advance the way a life can be a model of *kiddush ha-Shem* or *tikkun olam*, of sanctifying God's name or perfecting society. There are potentially as many ways as there are human lives. Something of this lies behind the stunning remark of the sages: 'The Holy One, blessed be He, made every person in the stamp of the first human being, yet not one of them resembles his fellow. Therefore every person is obliged to say: The world was created for my sake.'[43]

Each life presents a unique set of possibilities for sanctification. Yet there is a task for Jewish thought – indeed for a Jewish literature – in identifying which lives are, and which are not, models for emulation. The range of such models has grown extraordinarily narrow in the last century, dominated by stories of yeshivah heads and Chassidic leaders. The Chassidic literature once celebrated the lives of ordinary Jews in ordinary situations – the 'hidden righteous men' – but it is a tradition in eclipse.

RECOVERING FAITH

The last and perhaps the most urgent task of Orthodoxy in modernity is to think a way forward to recovering the substantive reality of *knesset Yisrael*, the Jewish people as a single entity standing before God. On this, I have written extensively elsewhere,[44] as has Michael Wyschogrod in his impressive theological study, *The Body of Faith*.[45] Suffice it to say that there is a deep inner contradiction between an Orthodoxy which acts as if it were one denomination among others in the Jewish world, and which at the same time believes as a matter of deepest principle that there *are* no denominations within Judaism: that Judaism is either Orthodox or it is not Judaism. If Orthodoxy is to act responsibly toward the whole Jewish world and not simply toward its own immediate constituency, there are deep dilemmas to be faced about its relationship with secular and non-Orthodox Jews. It cannot consistently embrace pluralism, the view that a secular or non-halakhic reading of tradition is legitimate. But it cannot withdraw altogether into segregation without abdicating the responsibilities of religious leadership.

There are problems here that have not been seriously confronted by religious thought, so insoluble do they seem. Once again though let us reiterate that the task of Torah is not necessarily to find solutions. In part it is to frame problems and point the way, if necessary an inch at a time, to making them less intractable. The second half of the final book of Maimonides' *Guide of the Perplexed* is dedicated to the proposition that religious ideals cannot be legislated suddenly and immediately in the human situation. There is slow progress from less to more perfect states.[46] Religious leadership for Maimonides – and in this respect it comes closest to *imitatio Dei* – is a matter of the governance of a total society.[47] The challenge of Jewish leadership in the past two centuries has been to exercise that governance over a Jewish people many of whom have become alienated from Jewish law and faith, and in the absence of any coercive powers. That religious leadership has for the most part retreated into enclaves where its authority remains strong has perhaps been inevitable, but it is a measure of the challenge that still lies ahead.

The perspective that emerges from this survey is paradoxical in the extreme. The great visions that drove Samson Raphael Hirsch and R. Avraham Kook have been substantively achieved. Jews have found it possible to be acculturated and integrated in the diaspora without abandoning halakhah or the fundamentals of Jewish faith. They have constructed a state and society in Israel in which religious Jews and Judaism, far from disappearing as secular Zionists believed, have grown in prominence and influence. And yet at precisely this juncture of success, the traditions of Jewish thought they initiated have lost their way. *Torah im Derekh Eretz* and religious Zionism have become suddenly problematic. The reasons for this, we have suggested, have been sociological rather than intellectual or spiritual. In the wake of the Holocaust, anti-Zionism, deepening secularisation and the intractable problems confronting Israel, Jewish thought has given way to a premature despair of the world and turned instead to a narrow survivalism.

This is understandable, but it remains a failure of trust. The sages explained the phrase 'God of faith' to mean 'God who had faith in the world He was about to create'.[48] Something of that faith is needed in the domain of Jewish thought. There are times when faith in God comes easier than faith in the world He created. Yet both are integral to Jewish belief. Neither the biblical nor rabbinic tradition allows a prolonged retreat from the tense, unpredictable, ongoing dialogue with contemporary culture, with society in its Israeli or diaspora dimensions, and with the Jewish people as a whole. Renewing that holy argument is the future task of Jewish thought. For at stake is the fate of Torah whose living commentary is the Jewish people in dialogue with its covenantal calling.

NOTES

1. Edward Shils, *Tradition*, London: Faber and Faber, 1981, 2.
2. See, for example, Leo Strauss, *Philosophy and Law*, Philadelphia: Jewish Publication Society, 1987.
3. Psalm 147: 19-20.
4. Deuteronomy 4:6.
5. Norman Lamm, 'Some Comments on Centrist Orthodoxy', *Tradition* 22:3 (Fall 1986), 1-12.
6. See the fascinating remarks by Alasdair MacIntyre on the relationship between tradition and argument in his *After Virtue: A Study in Moral Theory*, London: Duckworth, 1981, 206-207.
7. See Charles Liebman, 'Religion and the Chaos of Modernity', in *Take Judaism, for Example*, edited by Jacob Neusner, Chicago: University of Chicago Press, 1983, 147-164; David Singer, 'The New Orthodox Theology', *Modern Judaism* (forthcoming).
8. Emanuel Rackman, *One Man's Judaism*, Tel Aviv: Greenfield (undated).
9. See Eliezer Berkovits, *Crisis and Faith*, New York: Sanhedrin Press, 1976; *Not in Heaven*, New York: Ktav, 1983.
10. David Hartman, *A Living Covenant*, New York: Free Press, 1985.
11. Irving Greenberg's analysis is contained in three papers published by the National Jewish Resource Center: *On the Third Era in Jewish History* (1980), *The Third Great Cycle in Jewish History* (1981) and *Voluntary Covenant* (1982).
12. *A Living Covenant*, 13.
13. Roger Scruton, *A Dictionary of Political Thought*, London: Pan, 1983, 57.
14. Maimonides, *Eight Chapters*, ch. 4; M.T. *Deot* 1.
15. See Samuel Heilman, 'The Many Faces of Orthodoxy', *Modern Judaism* 2:1 (February 1982), 23-52.
16. See, for example, I. Grunfeld, *Three Generations*, London: Jewish Post, 1958; Immanuel Jakobovits, 'Torah im Derekh Eretz Today' *L'Eylah* 20 (Autumn 1985), 36-41.
17. Quoted in Grunfeld, 116.
18. Responsa *Seridei Esh*, 2:8.
19. B. T. *Yevamot* 65b.
20. B. T. *Betzah* 30a, *Shabbat* 148b.
21. B. T. *Berakhot* 44a and generally.
22. Lawrence Kaplan, 'Education and Ideology in Religious Zionism Today,' *Forum* (Fall/Winter 1979), 25-34.
23. *Three Generations*, 8.
24. Ibid., 12.
25. 'The Many Faces of Orthodoxy', 50.
26. On the issues involved, see the collection of articles in *Morasha* 1:2 (Winter 1985) and 2:1 (Fall/Winter 1985).
27. *The Return of Grand Theory in the Human Sciences*, edited by Quentin Skinner, Cambridge: Cambridge University Press, 1985.

28. Sol Roth, *Halakhah and Politics: The Jewish Idea of a State*, New York: Ktav, 1988.
29. Gershon Weiler, *Jewish Theocracy*, Leiden: Brill, 1988.
30. Quoted in Yehoshafat Harkabi, *Israel's Fateful Decisions*, London: I. B. Tauris, 1988, 188.
31. M. T. *Mamrim* 1:2.
32. Peter Berger, *The Sacred Canopy*, New York: Doubleday, 1967.
33. See Eugene Borowitz, 'The Autonomous Jewish Self', *Modern Judaism* 4:1 (February 1984), 39-56.
34. David Hartman, 'The Challenge of Modern Israel to Traditional Judaism', *Modern Judaism* 7:3 (October 1987), 229-252.
35. Aharon Lichtenstein, 'Religion and State: The Case for Interaction' in *Arguments and Doctrines*, edited by Arthur A. Cohen, New York: Harper and Row, 1970, 423.
36. Mary Warnock, *A Question of Life*, Oxford: Blackwell, 1985, 2-3.
37. One of the few recent studies of the issue is David Novak, *The Image of the Non-Jew in Judaism: An Historical and Constructive Study of the Noahide Laws*, New York: The Edward Mellen Press, 1983.
38. M. *Avot* 2:15; see also *Avot de-Rabbi Nathan* (2), 30; B. T. *Betzah* 16a.
39. The title of the fifth of the *Eight Chapters*, Maimonides' introduction to his commentary to Mishnah, *Avot*.
40. *Avot* 5:25.
41. Franz Rosenzweig, 'The Builders: Concerning Jewish Law' in *On Jewish Learning*, edited by N. N. Glatzer, New York: Schocken, 1955, 83, 84.
42. Franz Rosenzweig, 'Towards a Renaissance of Jewish Learning,' in Glatzer, op. cit., 66.
43. M. *Sanhedrin* 4:5.
44. In my forthcoming books, *Traditional Alternatives* and *One People? Tradition, Modernity and Jewish Unity*.
45. Michael Wyschogrod, *The Body of Faith*, Minneapolis: Seabury Press, 1983.
46. See especially *Guide of the Perplexed* 3, 32.
47. See *Guide* 1, 54; 2, 40; 3, 54.
48. *Sifrei* to Deuteronomy 32:4.

TOPICS

8
The Holocaust in Jewish Theology[1]

The holocaust is a mystery wrapped in silence. For almost twenty years afterwards, little was said, still less written about it. Like many others of the post-holocaust generation, I was reluctant to presume on so unfathomable a subject. The questions insist on being asked: How could one dare to speak? And how could one dare not to speak? The conflict itself is part of the continuing presence of the holocaust, so it is here that I begin.

First, I and others of my generation are too far away from that time. Which of us who were born after the holocaust, which of us who did not lose family in the holocaust, can speak about the holocaust? The book of Lamentations speaks about the destruction of Jerusalem with the authority of an eyewitness: *Ani ha-gever ra'ah oni:* "I am the man who has seen affliction".[2] The books written, the films made about the destruction of European Jewry speak to us precisely in the measure that they are *edut:* testimony or witness. And the task of the post-holocaust generation has been not to speak but to listen and record.

We are too far away to speak. But secondly, in an important sense we are also too close. Just as we now ask questions about the holocaust, so tradition tells us that we would ask questions about the exodus from Egypt and the events that preceded it. The Haggadah speaks of four questions asked by four children, the *rasha, tam, she'eno yodea lish'ol* and *chakham*, the wicked, the simple, the inarticulate and the wise. If we examine the Bible, we find that three of the four questions – those of the wicked, the simple and the inarticulate – appear clustered together in the book of Exodus,[3] set at the time of the event itself. The fourth question – that of the *chakham*, the wise son – does not appear until the book of Deuteronomy,[4] at a point in time forty years later. We will not go far wrong if we say that the Biblical time-scale applies to the holocaust too: we should expect it to take forty years even to find the right question, let alone expect an answer.

Third: just as we resist looking too long at the sun for fear of being blinded, we resist from looking too long at the blinding darkness of Auschwitz for fear of being driven to despair. Consider. After the destruction of the first Temple, the author of Lamentations was driven to say: *Haya hashem ke-oyev,* "God has become like an enemy". *Bila Yisrael:* "He has swallowed up Israel".[5] After the destruction of the second Temple, the Talmud states that *din hu shenigzor al atzmenu shelo le'echol basar velo lishtot yayin:* "by rights we should decree that no Jew should ever again eat meat or drink wine".[6] There should never again be Jewish rejoicing. Indeed we never forget those tragedies; we ruled that even in the midst of celebration there should be a *zekher le-churban,* a pause to weep for the destruction.[7] What then would it be like fully to integrate into our lives a *zekher le-shoah,* a weeping for the holocaust? Would it not overwhelm us?

The Talmud itself envisages just such a possibility. It gives the following parable of what Jewish history would eventually be like. It is like a man who was travelling on a road and met a wolf and escaped. And he would then tell people of his deliverance from the wolf. But then he met a lion and escaped. And he would then speak of his deliverance from the lion. But then he met a snake and escaped. And so he forgot the wolf and the lion and would speak only of the snake. So with Israel. *Tzarot achronot meshakhot et ha-rishonot:* "the later sufferings eclipse all the earlier ones".[8]

The revelation of evil contained within the holocaust is blinding indeed. Elie Wiesel has insisted that we call it a revelation, a demonic counterpart of Sinai.[9] Which of us can look at it for long? If turning to look on the destruction of the wicked turned Lot's wife into stone, how much more so looking upon the destruction of the innocent and righteous?

These then are the three reasons why I and many others, confronted by the holocaust, respond as did the Israelites at Sinai: *Vayar ha-am vayanu'u vaya'amdu merachok:* "they saw and trembled and stayed at a distance".[10] This feeling will govern what I have to say, but cannot altogether inhibit it. Because theology must perform the dual task, of respecting such sentiment on the one hand and wrestling with it on the other.

To respect it is to admit that we are not yet in sight of the time when the holocaust is intelligible within the classic terms of Jewish history. We are not yet ready to say where it belongs in the drama between God and His people. We will shortly encounter theologies which deny this, which say that it is perfectly clear what the holocaust means. About such theories I will argue that they are not just premature, but false.

But theology must wrestle with these feelings, and for a simple reason. The Bible is full of commands to remember: "Remember that you were a slave in the land of Egypt".[11] "Remember what Amalek did to you".[12] "Beware lest you forget".[13] Yosef Chayyim Yerushalmi, in his recent study of Jewish history and Jewish memory, has written that "Only in Israel and nowhere else is the injunction to remember felt as a religious imperative to an entire people".[14] "Memory", he says, is "crucial to its faith and ultimately to its very existence".[15] The word *zakhor* in its various forms occurs in the Bible no less than 169 times. And the command to remember is directed to Israel specifically of episodes which we had every reason to wish to forget.

Nor are they acts of memory alone in any simple sense. They are also acts of reliving and acts of redemption. We remember the exodus by reliving the exodus, as if we ourselves had been among those to leave.[16] We redeem our slavery in Egypt by never allowing ourselves to be the victims or perpetrators of another enslavement.[17] All these are commands which apply with equal force to the holocaust as well. Not least because this is what was asked of us by the victims themselves.

There is a moment in Claude Lanzmann's film *Shoah* in which one survivor talks of watching his friends go to their deaths in the ovens. They refused to obey the order to undress, and they stood and sang first the Czech national anthem and then the Hatikva. He, who was not scheduled to die, ran in to join them, knowing for certain that having seen what he had seen he could not continue to live. But they thrust him out, telling him: You must live and bear witness to our suffering.

To live and *bear witness* to their suffering, to live and *give meaning* to their suffering is a command by which all post-holocaust Jews stand bound. For we fail in our covenantal duty to the past if we allow the holocaust to be forgotten.

And we fail in our covenantal duty to the future if we allow the holocaust so to haunt the Jewish condition that Hitler's ghost meets us at every turn. How we map a path between these unacceptable alternatives is the task of theology. To this I now turn.

I

One thinker at least was in no doubt as to the meaning of the holocaust. It is important to confront him seriously and not immediately to dismiss his proposition as an outrage. For it belongs to a central tradition.

One of the great moments of Jewish theological self-definition came in the years leading up to the destruction of Jerusalem and the kingdom of Judah by the Babylonians in 587 B.C.E. Throughout the precarious history related in the books of Kings, disaster had often threatened but had always somehow been averted. For the first time, now, no miracle happens. No escape takes place. The kingdom and the Temple are destroyed and the people taken into exile. It could have been interpreted as the defeat of a people and its God. But the prophet Jeremiah took the opposite alternative: it was the defeat of a people *by* its God.[18] It was, in short, a Divine punishment. The Babylonians, though they were the enemies of God, were unwittingly the instruments of God, agents of His retribution. As Jeremiah himself put it: "And when your people say, 'Why has the Lord our God done all these things to us?' you shall say to them, 'As you have forsaken me and served strange gods in your land, so you shall serve strangers in a land that is not yours.'" [19]

This is the Biblical response to catastrophe: to see it in terms of Divine action and Providence, Divine justice and punishment. It should not surprise us therefore to discover that someone saw the holocaust in just these terms. It was a punishment. The Jewish people had sinned. God was present at Auschwitz, and the Third Reich was the instrument of his anger. This was the thesis propounded and argued with prophetic fervour by the late Rabbi Joel Teitelbaum, the Satmarer Rebbe.[20] What was the sin that merited the destruction of one third of the Jewish people? The sin was: Zionism.

Only one sin could have been punished measure for

measure by the near destruction of Diaspora Jewry, and that was the premature attempt by Jewry itself to put an end to Diaspora, to exile. The Jewish people had, according to the Talmud, taken an oath not to rebel against the nations of the world in their dispersion. They had promised not to hasten the end by an attempt to regain possession of the land of Israel. So long as they lived submissively and passively in exile, the nations too were bound by an oath not to oppress Israel excessively.[21]

The Zionist movement, according to the Satmarer, was a rebellion of unprecedented dimensions against God. First it was worse than idolatry. It was an avowedly secular movement which denied Providence and believed that politics and the exercise of power could achieve what the will of God had evidently not yet decreed. Secondly, it was a contagion, luring into its ranks even religious Jews like those of Mizrachi. Thirdly and most importantly, it broke the very terms of Jewish existence in the Diaspora, the tacit agreement between Jews and their host cultures, whereby Jews might negotiate or pray their way to safety but would never become activist, politically organised, or organise public protests. Zionism was the work of Satan. The Jewish people had been tempted and succumbed. And judgement was duly visited upon them.

I should add at this point that the Satmarer Rebbe, though he was an extremist, was also a scholar and intellect of great distinction. Nor was he speaking from a position of comfort: he was himself rescued from Bergen Belsen. And this very disturbing line of argument becomes more disturbing still if I add another voice. Rabbi Teitelbaum's views represent the ideology of *Neturei Karta*, the ultra-Orthodox opponents of the State of Israel. But in 1977, a member of Agudat Yisrael, *not* an opponent of the state, offered an explanation of the holocaust. He was the late Rabbi Yitzchak Hutner, one of the most revered yeshivah leaders in America. His argument went as follows.[22]

We are wrong to think of the holocaust as solely the product of Christian Europe. A major part in the decision to annihilate European Jewry was played by the Grand Mufti of Jerusalem, Haj Amin al-Husseini. The final solution was agreed on in January 1942, a mere two months after the Mufti's arrival in Berlin for talks with von Ribbentrop and Hitler. The Mufti himself was not an avowed enemy of the

Jews until pressure began to be applied for the creation of a Jewish state. Hence Zionism brought about for the first time a collaboration between the Christian West and the Moslem East to destroy the Jewish people. Zionism was the cause of the holocaust. It is reported that this view now prevails in mainstream yeshivah circles in America.

No comment on these views is necessary, because there is another conclusion about the holocaust to be drawn from exactly the same premise, namely that when tragedy strikes the Jewish people it is always a Divine punishment for sin. In 1962 an Orthodox rabbi in Israel, Menachem Immanuel Hartom, asked just this question.[23] What sin could have been so grave? What sin could have evoked, measure for measure, the annihilation of European Jewry?

His answer is this. The quintessence of Biblical Judaism is that the worst punishment that can befall the Jewish people is *Galut*, exile. Throughout the long second exile Jews believed just that: that they were in exile, that this was dislocation, a not-being-at-home; and they longed for a return to their land. Until the Emancipation. Then, with the end of the ghetto and the granting of civil equality, for the first time Jews argued that this was where they belonged, in an emancipated Europe. Assimilated Jews, Reform Jews, even Orthodox Jews, found positive meaning in German, Austrian or French identity. Some abandoned the hope for a return to Israel altogether. Others deferred it to a metaphysical end-of-days. They became Germans of the Jewish persuasion. For the first time in history Jews *ceased* to be Zionists.

And for this they were punished. The retribution was precise. Having wished to make their permanent home in a strange land they were shown that there is no home for Jews in any land but their own. And the country that sought to make the world *Judenrein* was none other than Germany, the country above all others that had been worshipped by its Jews as the epitome of civilisation, the cultural utopia.

This view is shared by most secular Zionists. A.B. Yehoshua, for example, calls the holocaust the final decisive proof of the failure of Diaspora existence.[24] But Rabbi Hartom is not a secular Zionist. He is a religious Jew seeking an explanation of the holocaust in terms of Divine Providence. And his case is stronger than he himself makes it, because – though he does not mention it[25] – there is a precise Biblical prooftext in the twentieth chapter of the book of Ezekiel.

The prophet says: "You say, 'We want to be like the nations, like the peoples of the world . . .' But what you have in mind will never happen. As surely as I live, declares the Sovereign Lord, I will rule over you with a mighty hand and an outstretched arm and with fury poured out. I will bring you from the nations and gather you from the countries where you have been scattered – with a mighty hand and an outstretched arm and with fury poured out".[26] Ezekiel predicts a time when the desire for assimilation will overtake the Jewish people and the return to Zion will be forgotten. At that time there will be a day of judgement, and the Jewish people will be turned into Zionists against their will.

So there is clear and decisive proof for Rabbi Teitelbaum that the holocaust was a punishment for Zionism. And there is clear and decisive proof for Rabbi Hartom that the holocaust was a punishment for anti-Zionism.

But I have to do more than show that this line of thought leads to contradiction. For there was a third group who saw the holocaust in terms of Providence and Divine punishment. We must have the honesty to see clearly where this form of theology leads.

In 1948, a mere three years after the *shoah*, a German Evangelical Conference met at Darmstadt. It proclaimed that Jewish suffering in the holocaust was the work of God. It issued a call to Jews to cease their rejection and ongoing crucifixion of Jesus.[27] Genocide was the punishment for deicide.

Again I make no comment, except to say this. The idea that Jews were killed for their obstinacy in not becoming Christians was not restricted to Christians who were active collaborators with or passive accomplices of the Nazis. It is to be found even among Christians who were opponents of Hitler. Perhaps the greatest Christian theologian of this century, Karl Barth, himself an opponent of the Nazi regime, wrote during the holocaust that the Jews were serving as witnesses of the sheer stark judgement of God. "This," he wrote, "is how Israel punishes itself for its sectarian self-assertion".[28]

One might well conclude that the attempt to find Divine

meaning in the *shoah* leads only to madness. This was precisely the conclusion drawn by the most radical of Jewish theologians, Richard Rubinstein, in his book *After Auschwitz*.[29] His argument is this. Believing in the Jewish God of history entails that we see the holocaust as an act of God and an act of punishment for sin. But no sin could be sufficient to justify the inhuman evil of the holocaust. No *tzidduk ha-din*, no "vindication of the ways of providence", is sufficient to explain the death of the righteous and the innocent, the million and half children slaughtered. Therefore there is no God of history. Traditional Jewish belief has been shattered. Quoting the rabbinic phrase for heresy, he concludes: *leit din ve-leit dayan:*[30] "There is no justice and there is no judge."

I have to add that Rubinstein is both a theologian and a rabbi, although a rabbi of a kind unfamiliar in British Jewry. He is a Reconstructionist and believes that the only kind of Judaism possible after the holocaust is a secular, even pagan one, which recognises God in nature but not in history. History is meaningless, and in his words, "Omnipotent nothingness is Lord of all creation".[31]

II

What do these four approaches have in common? They assumed that a theology of the holocaust must consist in understanding the holocaust from the point of view of Providence. The Jewish view of history, and the Christian view of Jewish history, are that great tragedies are always acts of God, and therefore acts of justice, and therefore acts of punishment. So an anti-Zionist rabbi sees the *shoah* as punishment for Zionism, and a Zionist rabbi sees it as punishment for anti-Zionism. A Christian theologian sees it as punishment for the Jewish rejection of Christianity. And Rubinstein concludes that a God who would punish in such a way cannot exist.

We could dismiss all four as simply cancelling each other out. Or we could say that when they claim to be talking about the holocaust they are really only talking about themselves. We could say, as most of us would, that though we have the faith that somehow, despite the concentration camps, there is Divine justice, we will never be able to understand it: *Ki lo machshevotai machshevotechem*,

"For My thoughts are not your thoughts, nor My ways your ways, saith the Lord".[32]

We have, though, to go further than this. It is a striking fact that though the prophets evince an intense interest in the revelation of Divine purpose in the specificities of Jewish history, the rabbis do not.[33] In contrast to the apocalyptic literature that flourished from 200 B.C.E. to 100 C.E. the Mishnah is remarkable for its "utter silence" on the "tremendous issues of suffering and atonement, catastrophe and apocalypse".[34] History is no longer the primary locus of the Divine act. To some of the sages the Divine Presence had retreated to heaven. "When (the Temple) was burned, the Holy One, blessed be He, said: I no longer have a seat upon earth. I shall remove my *Shekhinah* from there and ascend to My first habitation." [35] To others, the Divine Presence was itself in exile: "Wherever Israel went into exile, the *Shekhinah*, as it were, was exiled with them." [36] But the lucid presence of God in history which is of the essence of the prophetic literature is at an end, to be recovered only in the Messianic future.

A new emphasis enters the rabbinic response to national tragedy. There are indeed places where the rabbis speak of the Roman destruction of the Temple in the classic terminology of sin and punishment.[37] But in a daring stroke they see God as weeping over the fate of his people. He suffers with them. He mourns as they do.[38] The concept of *kiddush ha-shem* (sanctification of the Divine name) is developed to embrace the death, as well as the life, of the righteous. Alongside martyrdom, never allowing it peace as a sufficient explanation, is the countervailing force of the reiterated question: "Is this the Torah and is this its reward?"[39] Job-like arguments with the ways of Providence are revived and audaciously placed in the mouths of the patriarchs, Moses, even the angels.[40] The aggadic literature contains reflections saved only from blasphemy by their searing pathos: "Were it not explicitly stated in Scripture, it would be impossible to say so, but . . . the Holy One, blessed be He, lamented, saying: Woe to the King who succeeded in his youth but failed in His old age".[41] To be sure, these motifs are present in the Bible,[42] but now they begin to dominate.

Why the sudden change? The answer was given in different ways by Judah Halevi,[43] Maimonides[44] and

Nachmanides,[45] but they converge on a common, if understated, conclusion. Divine Providence governs the affairs of Israel when the Jewish people exist as a sovereign people in the land of Israel. Then there is reward and punishment and prophecy. But exile, diaspora, *Galut* precisely means being removed from the mercy of God and placed at the mercy of the nations. It means the withdrawal of Providence, what the Bible calls *hester panim*, the 'hiding of the face' of God; what Maimonides calls, being left to chance.[46]

Levi ben Gershom (Gersonides, 1288-1344) instructs us to distinguish between tragedies, like the destruction of Sodom, which are the *work* of Providence, and tragedies, like the defeat of the Israelites at Jericho, which are the result of the *withdrawal* of Providence.[47] The difference may be slight, but it is all the difference in the world. If God destroys, then He destroys the guilty. If God withdraws, and then man destroys, the innocent suffer as well.[48]

In rabbinic times and throughout the middle ages there were great catastrophes of which Jews were the victims. There were the Hadrianic persecutions, the murder of Jews in the Crusades, the blood libels, the Inquisition, the pogroms. All of them were faithfully recorded in Jewish memory, written down and recited in *kinot*, elegies which we say to this day. In each case the rabbis and poets tried to find religious meaning in tragedy. But rarely if ever did they find that meaning in terms of sin and punishment.[49] Already the opinion had been voiced in the early rabbinic literature that reward and punishment were reserved for the world to come and that "There is no reward for the precepts in this world".[50] The poets of catastrophe during the Crusades related their sufferings to the binding of Isaac,[51] to the tragedy of Job,[52] to the suffering servant of Isaiah:[53] all the cases in the Bible where suffering is *not* related to sin.[54]

Several centuries later, in the wake of the Spanish expulsion, Solomon Ibn Verga asks: "Tell me the reason for the fall of the Jews since ancient times . . . for behold, I have found their fall to be neither in a natural way, nor due to divine punishment. For we have seen and heard of many nations that have transgressed and sinned more than they and were not punished".[55] *Galut* means exile from history in the prophetic sense of the intimate reciprocity of deed and fate. It means risk, exposure, and a faithful waiting.

Understood in this way, the holocaust does not tell us about God but about man. It tells us not about Divine justice but about human injustice. And this is not radical theology but the whole weight of Jewish tradition in relation to *Galut*.[56] Rabbi Teitelbaum and Rabbi Hartom are wrong in what they assert. Richard Rubinstein is wrong in what he rejects. Significantly wrong. For they have mistaken the nature of the Jewish tradition and blasphemed against the memory of the dead. God forbid that we should add to their death the sin of saying that it was justified.[57] And God forbid that we should follow Rubinstein and add to the death of six million Jews the death of the Jewish God.

III

So where do we turn? Two thinkers, Emil Fackenheim[58] and Irving Greenberg,[59] suggest a wholly different approach. For them, the meaning of the holocaust is to be found not in understanding why it happened, but in grasping the implications of the fact *that* it happened. The holocaust has, they argue, radically changed the meaning of the Jewish existence. It was a unique event in Jewish history and in human history. Any approach to the very nature of faith must now be different.

Let us consider Fackenheim's argument in three stages.[60] The first is that the holocaust has no precedent in the history of human evil. Other great evils have been committed in the course of war or for self-interest. But the Nazi programme of genocide actually hindered the war effort. Troop trains were diverted from the Russian front in order to transport Jews to Auschwitz. There have been other persecutions, of Jews and non-Jews, killed because of their faith. But the Jews of the concentration camps were killed not because of their faith but because of the faith of their great-grandparents, whether the victims themselves held the same faith or another faith or no faith. There have been other murders, but never before an attempt to implicate the victims themselves in the murders. Fackenheim reminds us that the Nazis issued work permits in the camps to separate useless from useful Jews: the former to be killed immediately, the latter to be killed eventually but led to think that they would be spared. But customarily when they issued permits to an able-bodied man they issued not one but two: one for himself, the other to be given at his own discretion to his able-bodied mother, father, wife or one child. The Nazis forced their victims into making the choice. Fackenheim says: I search the whole history of human depravity for comparisons. In vain. The holocaust was unique. It was not just evil. It was evil for evil's sake.

His second point. Jewish life after the holocaust is qualitatively different from Jewish life before the holocaust. We now know that our very decision to remain Jewish may put not only our lives in danger – for that was often true in the past – but it may put in danger the lives of our grandchildren as yet unborn. Every Jew, he says, now faces an unprecedented dilemma. Dare we *morally* raise Jewish children, exposing our offspring to a possible second Auschwitz decades or centuries hence? And dare we *religiously not* raise Jewish children? For if we do not, then we grant Hitler a posthumous victory.

The dilemma leads him to his famous formulation. The holocaust has added a 614th command to Jewish life. After Auschwitz we are commanded to carry on being Jewish, for if we do not, then we complete Hitler's work. We become accomplices in the disappearance of Jews from the world.

This, he argues, has changed the nature of the Jewish world. Before the holocaust there were religious Jews and secular Jews. Now, even the most secular of Jews is a religious Jew, because in merely choosing to be Jewish at all he is obeying the 614th commandment.[61] Putting it another way: precisely because Hitler made it a crime simply to exist as a Jew, simply existing as a Jew becomes an act of religious defiance against the force of evil.

This is an important line of thought, because Fackenheim is trying to rescue something positive from the holocaust. After all, Jews *have* gone on living and having children. Above all, they created the state of Israel, driven by the imperative never again to be vulnerable to another holocaust. And Fackenheim is certainly the most eloquent of Jewish theologians to have confronted the *shoah*.

But in the end, as several critics have pointed out, his argument is crucially flawed.[62] There is no 614th commandment. The holocaust did not make Jewish survival a *mitzvah* unless it was already a *mitzvah*. In the holocaust, for example, gypsies too were singled out, but that did not make it a command to be a gypsy. We can imagine a hypothetical Hitler who decreed a final solution against homosexuals, but that would not of itself sanctify homosexuality.[63] Jewish survival has religious significance *after* the holocaust only because it had significance *before* the holocaust.

In fact, just as many Jews have reacted to the holocaust by remaining Jewish, others have reacted by ceasing to be Jewish. The holocaust proved that it was dangerous to be a Jew. But it also proved that it was dangerous to assimilate, and yet that has not stopped Jewish assimilation. Above all Fackenheim has erred in building a Jewish theology on the very foundations of the holocaust. That way, madness lies. There is no way of building Jewish existence on a command to spite Hitler. That is giving too much to Hitler and too little to God. The people Israel did not survive Egypt to spite Pharaoh, nor did it survive Purim so as not to hand Haman a posthumous victory. Fackenheim errs in saying the holocaust gives new meaning to Jewish life. This surely is wrong. We are Jews today despite the holocaust, not because of the holocaust. The holocaust has *not* changed the meaning of Jewish life: and *that is the miracle.*

IV

Which brings us to the final thinker I want to consider, and the one who, to my mind, most accurately embodies an authentic Jewish response; namely, Eliezer Berkovits.[64] Berkovits disputes the central argument of Fackenheim, that the holocaust is unique. It may indeed be unique from some perspectives, but not in a way that is relevant to faith.

The problem of *tzaddik ve-ra lo*, the "righteous who suffers", is one as old as Abraham. *Hashofet kol ha'aretz lo ya'aseh mishpat*: "Shall the judge of all the earth not do justice?" [65] The answer given by tradition applies to the holocaust too. God, in giving man the freedom to choose to be good, at the same time necessarily gives him the freedom to be evil. God teaches us what goodness is. But He does not intervene to force us to be good or to prevent us from being wicked. This is the extraordinary Jewish conception of the power of God. God is powerful not through His interventions in history but through His self-restraint.

Berkovits quotes the extraordinary interpretation of the verse "Who is a Mighty One like You, O Lord?" (Psalm 89:9), given by the Tannaitic teacher Abba Hanan. "Who is like you, mighty in self-restraint? You heard the blasphemy and the insults of that wicked man (Titus), but You kept silent!" In the school of R. Ishmael the verse "Who is like You, O Lord, along the mighty (*elim*)" (Exodus, 15:11) was amended to read, "Who is like You, O Lord, among the silent ones (*illemim*)" – since He sees the suffering of His children and remains mute.[66] The central religious paradox is that God leaves the arena of history to human freedom, and therein lies His greatness.

So when human beings perpetrate evil it is human beings who are to blame, not God. But then the crucial question arises. Where do we witness God in history? Berkovits answers: God reveals His presence in the survival of Israel. Not in His deeds, but in His children.[67] There is no other witness that God is present in history but the history of the Jewish people.

Hence the demonic character of the Nazi project. The final solution, says Berkovits, was an attempt to destroy the only witnesses to the God of history. The ingathering of exiles after the holocaust and the creation of the state of Israel, revealed God's presence at the very moment when we might have despaired of it altogether. The rebirth of the state came at a moment in history when nothing else could have saved Jews from extinction through hopelessness. The miracle that testifies that God exists is that the people of Israel exist. Though they walked through the valley of the shadow of death, *am yisrael chai*, the people Israel lives.

The only meaning to be extracted from the holocaust is that man is capable of limitless evil. The religious meaning of six million deaths is no more and no less than that they, as other Jews had done before them, died *al kiddush ha-shem*, for the sanctification of God's name, suffering, as Isaiah saw the servants of God would always suffer, until the world finds it in its heart not to afflict the children of God. We find meaning not in the holocaust but in the fact that the Jewish people survived the holocaust. The existence of the state of Israel does not explain the *shoah*, but it gives us faith despite the *shoah*.

That is perhaps as near as we will come to a theology of the holocaust. It helps to explain why Orthodox Judaism has been reluctant to create a new fast for *Yom Ha-shoah*,[68] and why thinking about the holocaust has played a less prominent part in Orthodox circles than elsewhere. Not because Orthodoxy has felt it less acutely than others: on the contrary, no other group lost so much as the worlds of the yeshivah and the Chassidim. Rather it was because the traditional Jewish response has been *not* to sanctify suffering but instead to rebuild what was broken. Indeed it was the ultra-Orthodox groups in particular who have tacitly insisted that the one command to come from Auschwitz was: Let there be more Jewish children. Who is to say that this was not the deepest response of all?

One writer about the holocaust records that he met a rabbi who had been through the camps, and who, miraculously, seemed unscarred. He could still laugh. 'How,' he asked him, 'could you see what you saw and still have faith? Did you have no questions?' The rabbi replied: 'Of course I had questions. But I said to myself: If you ever ask those questions, they are such good questions that the Almighty will send you a personal invitation to heaven to give you the answers. And I preferred to be here on earth with the questions than up in heaven with the answers.' This too is a kind of theology.

V

We have not reached the end of thinking about the holocaust, and in a sense we have hardly begun. The proof is that the most compelling writing about the holocaust today is done not by rabbis, philosophers or theologians, but by novelists like Elie Wiesel. A novel is a vehicle for unresolved tension and ambiguity, and is evidence that a problem still disturbs and bewilders us.[69]

Manifestly, we have not yet learned how to integrate the holocaust into Jewish consciousness as we once integrated the exodus or the destruction of the Temples. The reason is clear. The holocaust does not point anywhere but everywhere.[70] We have considered just a few examples. For some it confirms their faith, for others its confirms their lack of faith. For some it has proved that it is impossible to escape from Jewish identity, for others it has made it all the more urgent to do so. For some it has made it imperative to live in Israel, for others it has made it imperative that Jews be scattered everywhere, that a remnant shall always remain. The reason is not to be sought in the holocaust itself but in something that preceded and still survives it. Namely, that since the Emancipation, there is no such thing as a common Jewish consciousness for any Jewish experience to be integrated into. Each of us relates to the holocaust in our own way; but there is no longer a collective way, as there was when *Tisha b'Av* was instituted. We are no less fragmented after Auschwitz than we were before it.

This, it seems to me, is the central issue to be addressed. Rav Soloveitchik has spoken of the two covenants which bind Jews to one another and to God. There is the *brit goral* and the *brit ye'ud*, the covenant of a shared history and the covenant of a shared destiny.[71] The holocaust has immeasurably deepened the *brit goral*, the covenant of shared history. The sentence of death was over each of us in some way that we can understand, whether we are secular or religious, Zionist or diasporist. What has not been deepened is the *brit ye'ud*, the covenant of shared destiny, of a common future.

In a remarkable passage the Talmud says that though the Torah was accepted at Sinai, it was only fully accepted on Purim.[72] It was on Purim that the Jewish people had stood under the decree directed "to destroy, massacre and exterminate all the Jews, young and old, children and women, on a single day",[73] the first warrant for genocide. It was only after Purim, says the Talmud, that *kiyemu ve-kiblu ha-yehudim*, that the covenant made at Sinai was fully entered into. The covenant of shared history was turned into a covenant of shared destiny.

In our day this has not yet happened. Yet the holocaust still asks this question of us: if Jews were condemned to die together, shall we not struggle to find a way to live together? To find a way of bringing the fragmented, splintered, shrinking Jewish world into a common future is the monumental task facing rabbis and theologians today. On their success will hinge the answer to the question: Was the holocaust a tragedy or a turning point for the Jewish people?

NOTES

1. This paper is a revised draft of a lecture delivered under the auspices of the Yad Vashem Committee on 26 November 1986. I have, as far as possible, left the original form intact, hence the frequent signs of an oral presentation.
2. Lamentations 3:1.
3. Exodus 12:26, 13:8, 13:14.
4. Deuteronomy 6:20.
5. Lamentations 2:5.
6. T.B. *Baba Batra* 60b.
7. T.B. *Sotah* 49a, *Baba Batra* 60b; *Mishneh Torah* (Maimonides) *Taaniyot* 5:12-15; *Shulchan Arukh, Orach Chayyim* ch. 560.
8. T.B. *Berakhot* 13a.
9. I owe the reference to Wiesel to Emil Fackenheim, *The Jewish Return into History*, New York: Schocken Books, 1978, p. 53.
10. Exodus 20:15.
11. Deuteronomy 5:15; 15:15; 16:12; 24:18; 24:22.
12. Deuteronomy 25:17.
13. Deuteronomy 6:12; 8:11.
14. Yosef Chayyim Yerushalmi, *Zakhor: Jewish History and Jewish Memory*, Seattle and Washington: University of Washington Press, 1982, p. 9.
15. Ibid.
16. Mishnah, *Pesachim* 10:5.
17. On the role of the exodus in providing reasons for the commandments in the Bible itself, see David Weiss Halivni, *Midrash, Mishnah and Gemara*, Cambridge MA. and London: Harvard University Press, 1986, pp. 9-17.
18. For a provocative treatment of this aspect of Jewish spirituality, see Dan Jacobson, *The Story of the Stories*, London: Secker and Warburg, 1982.
19. Jeremiah 5:19.
20. The thesis is propounded in two books: Joel Teitelbaum, *Vayo'el Mosheh*, New York: Jerusalem Publishing Co., 1959; *Al ha-Ge'ulah ve'al ha-Temurah*, New York: Jerusalem Publishing Co., 1967.
21. T.B. *Ketubot* 111a, according to which there were three oaths: "One, that Israel shall not go up (to the land of Israel all together as if surrounded) by a wall; the second, that whereby the Holy One, blessed be He, adjured Israel that they shall not rebel against the nations of the world; and the third is that whereby the Holy One, blessed be He, adjured the idolaters that they shall not oppress Israel too much."
22. I am indebted, for this presentation, to Lawrence Kaplan, 'Rabbi Isaac Hutner's "Daat Torah Perspective" on the Holocaust: A Critical Perspective'. *Tradition* 18:3 (Fall 1980), pp. 235-248.
23. Menachem Immanuel Hartom, 'Hirhurim al ha-Shoah', *Deot* 18 (Winter 5720/1961), pp. 28-31.
24. A.B. Yehoshua, *Between Right and Right*, translated by Arnold Schwartz, New York: Doubleday, 1981, p. 12.

156 TRADITION IN AN UNTRADITIONAL AGE

25. Since this lecture was delivered a new book has appeared which takes Ezekiel's text as its title: Bernard Maza, *With Fury Poured Out: A Torah Perspective on the Holocaust*, Hoboken: Ktav, 1986. Maza's thesis is that the holocaust was the work of Providence. Torah-true communities were on the wane, suffering from the impact of emancipation, secularisation and Zionism. The holocaust has driven Jews back to their millenial vocation, the study of Torah. "Decades have passed since the Holocaust, and effects of the Holocaust have come into view. We have seen the resurgence of Torah in the east and in the west since the Holocaust. We know that by sacrificing their lives they made it come to be. It may therefore be that it was the will of Hashem that they gave their lives so that the Torah and the Jewish people who live by it shall live" (p. 226). This is a teleological restatement of the holocaust-as-punishment thesis, and is open to the objections raised against such views by Maimonides, *Guide for the Perplexed*, III, 24.
26. Ezekiel 20: 32-34.
27. I owe this reference to Irving Greenberg, 'Cloud of Smoke, Pillar of Fire: Judaism, Christianity and Modernity after the Holocaust', in Eva Fleischner (ed.), *Auschwitz: Beginning of a New Era?*, New York: Ktav, 1977, p. 13, note 10.
28. Karl Barth, 'The Judgement and the Mercy of God' in F.E. Talmage (ed.), *Disputation and Dialogue*, New York: Ktav, 1975, p. 43. See also Richard L. Rubenstein, 'The Dean and the Chosen People' in his *After Auschwitz: Radical Theology and Contemporary Judaism*, Bobbs-Merrill, 1966, pp. 47-58. One Christian theologian to have reflected deeply on the implications of the holocaust for Christianity is A. Roy Eckardt. See his *Elder and Younger Brothers*, New York: Scribner's, 1967; *Long Night's Journey Into Day* (with Alice L. Eckardt), Detroit: Wayne State University Press, 1982; *Jews and Christians: The Contemporary Meeting*, Bloomington: Indiana University Press, 1986.
29. Richard L. Rubinstein, *After Auschwitz: Radical Theology and Contemporary Judaism*, Bobbs-Merrill, 1966, especially pp. 61-81.
30. *Leviticus Rabbah*, 28:1. The statement is attributed to Cain in *Targum Jonathan* to Genesis 4:8.
31. The final words of his contribution to the symposium, 'The State of Jewish Belief', *Commentary*, August 1966, pp. 132-135. See also his *The Religious Imagination: A Study in Psychoanalysis and Jewish Theology*, Bobbs-Merrill, 1968, especially pp. 171-183. Alasdair MacIntyre has distinguished two kinds of atheism. One is "speculative atheism which is concerned to deny that over and above the universe there is something else, an invisible intelligent being who exists apart from the world and rules over it". The other, in the tradition of Feuerbach and Marx, goes further and claims that "Religion is misunderstood if it is construed simply as a set of intellectual errors; it is rather the case that in a profoundly misleading form deep insights, hopes, and fears are being expressed . . . Religion needs to be translated into nonreligious terms and not simply rejected" (Alasdair MacIntyre,

Against the Self-Images of the Age, London: Duckworth, 1971, pp. 12-13). Rubinstein is an atheist in the second sense.
32. Isaiah 55:8.
33. Yerushalmi notes that it is "remarkable that after the close of the biblical canon the Jews virtually stopped writing history . . . It is as though, abruptly, the impulse to historiography had ceased . . . More sobering and important is the fact that the history of the Talmudic period itself cannot be elicited from its own vast literature." (*Zakhor*, pp. 16-18). Jacob Neusner has similarly argued that "The Mishnah's framers' deepest yearning is not for historical change but for ahistorical stasis" (*Judaism: The Evidence of the Mishnah*, Chicago: University of Chicago Press, 1981, p. 27) and "The Talmud contains virtually no reference to the most important events of the age in which it took shape and reached closure" (*Our Sages, God and Israel*, New York: Rossel Books, 1984, p. xix). One significant moment is captured in the displacement of the historical account of the events surrounding the festival of Chanukkah and the exclusion from the canon of the books of Maccabees in favour of the supernatural narrative of the oil that burned for eight days, T.B. *Shabbat* 21b. That the process is incomplete, however, can be seen in the fact that the military victory is retained in the liturgy in the *Al ha-Nissim* prayer, *Singer's Prayer Book*, pp. 53-54.
34. Neusner, *Judaism: The Evidence of the Mishnah*, Chicago and London: University of Chicago Press, 1981, p. 37.
35. *Lamentations Rabbah*, Proem 24. See also T. B. *Rosh Hashanah* 31a.
36. *Mekhilta de-Rabbi Ishmael, Massekhta de-Pisha*, xii. See E.E. Urbach, *The Sages*, Jerusalem: Magnes Press, 1975, pp. 37-65.
37. T.B. *Yoma* 9b, *Shabbat* 119b, *Baba Metzia* 30b.
38. See, e.g., T.B. *Berakhot* 3a, and many examples in *Lamentations Rabbah*.
39. T.B. *Berakhot* 61b, *Menachot* 29b.
40. See, for a striking example, *Lamentations Rabbah*, Proem 24.
41. Ibid.
42. That Divine pathos is at the heart of prophetic consciousness is the argument of A.J. Heschel, *The Prophets*, Philadelphia: Jewish Publication Society, 1962. The argument with God over the ways of Providence is to be found in several key passages. See, e.g., Genesis 18: 17-32, Exodus 5:22, 32:12, 32:32, Jeremiah 12:1, Habakkuk 1:1-4.
43. See, e.g., *Kuzari*, II, 14, 29-44, V, 22-23.
44. See, e.g., M.T. *Ta'aniyot* 1:1-3, *Guide for the Perplexed*, II, 36.
45. See, e.g., Commentary to Leviticus 18:25. And see, on the general subject, Y. Baer, *Galut*, New York: Schocken Books, 1947.
46. See, e.g., Deuteronomy 31:18, Isaiah 8:17, 64:6, Ezekiel 39:23-24. Maimonides, M.T. *Ta'aniyot* 1:3, *Guide for the Perplexed*, III, 36.
47. See *Perush Ralbag* to Joshua 7:1. See also Commentary of Abarbanel ad loc.: "There is a distinction between punishment which comes about by (a Divine) action and punishment which comes about through removal of providence. When God punishes by direct action, He does not punish the person who has not sinned on

account of him who has . . . Not so the punishment which comes about by chance as a result of God's withdrawing His providence. For this befalls the community in its entirety in that, because there are sinners amongst them, God hides His face from them all . . . All of them become exposed to the workings of chance and accident, so that occasionally the person who has not sinned is also smitten when he is exposed to danger, and the sinner, who may not have been there, escapes unharmed."

48. This is also the sense of the Talmudic statement (T.B. *Baba Kamma* 60a) that "Once permission has been granted to the Destroyer, he does not distinguish between the righteous and the wicked."
49. See Yerushalmi, *Zakhor*, pp. 31-52; David G. Roskies, *Against the Apocalypse*, Harvard University Press, 1984, pp. 15-52. Yerushalmi writes: "The catastrophe (at Mainz) simply could not be explained by the stock notion of punishment for sin, for the Ashkenazic communities of the Rhineland were holy communities, as their own response to the crisis had demonstrated" (*Zakhor*, p. 38). Hence the invocation of the binding of Isaac as the dominant explanatory image for Jewish suffering in the Middle Ages.
50. T.B. *Kiddushin* 39b, *Chullin* 142a. And see Urbach, pp. 436-444.
51. See Shalom Spiegel, *The Last Trial*, New York: Behrman House 1979, for a detailed study of the development of the interpretation of the binding of Isaac as an image for Jewish suffering during the Crusades.
52. See, e.g., the *kinah* 'I said: Look away from me', composed by Kalonymous b. Judah of Mayence, dedicated to the victims of the second Crusade (Abraham Rosenfeld, *The Authorised Kinot for the Ninth of Av*, London, 1965, p. 140). This invokes Job's famous affirmation, "Though he slay me, yet I will trust in Him" (Job 13:15).
53. This is invoked by Judah ha-Levi, *Kuzari*, II, 34-41: "Israel amidst the nations is like the heart amidst the organs of the body".
54. There is frequent reference in the *kinot* to the sinlessness of the victims. "My thoughts are dismayed, shuddering and distraughtness take hold of me; (because) of one single (good deed) did Scripture find for King Abijah hope and expectation . . . (Yet) those who were perfect in all their deeds submitted themselves to slaughter out of fear of the (enemy's) army: to them even burial was not granted" (*Kinah* by Kalonymous b. Judah, Rosenfeld, p. 141). Rosenfeld himself continues the tradition in the *kinah* he composed for the victims of the holocaust: "Distinguished scholars sit on the ground in stunned silence. 'What, Oh what, was their guilt?' they ask, And why was the decree issued without mercy?" (Rosenfeld, p. 173).
55. Solomon Ibn Verga, *Shevet Yehudah*, cited in Yerushalmi, p. 55.
56. That we should see the holocaust in terms of the 'hiding of the face' of God has been argued by Rav Soloveitchik, and recently by Norman Lamm. See Abraham Besdin, *Reflections of the Rav*, Jerusalem: Jerusalem Department for Torah Education and Culture, W.Z.O., 1979, p. 37: "The Holocaust . . . was *Hester Panim*. We cannot explain the Holocaust but we can, at least, classify it theologically . . . The

THE HOLOCAUST IN JEWISH THEOLOGY 159

unbounded horrors represented the *tohu va-vohu* anarchy of the pre-*yetzirah* state. This is how the world appears when God's moderating surveillance is suspended." See also, Norman Lamm, *The Face of God: Thoughts on the Holocaust*, Address published by Yeshivah University, New York 1986.

57. Irving Greenberg argues that this would be to "inflict on them the only indignity left", 'Cloud of Smoke, Pillar of Fire', p. 25. The classic statement against 'criticising the Jewish congregation' is to be found in Maimonides' *Epistle on Martyrdom*, translated in A. Halkin and D. Hartman, *Crisis and Leadership: Epistles of Maimonides*, Philadelphia: Jewish Publication Society, 1985, pp. 15-34. See also T.B. *Pesachim* 87a-b.

58. Emil Fackenheim, *The Jewish Return into History: Reflections in the Age of Auschwitz and a New Jerusalem*, New York: Schocken, 1978; and see his later *To Mend the World*, New York: Schocken, 1982.

59. Greenberg's major statement is to be found in 'Cloud of Smoke, Pillar of Fire: Judaism, Christianity and Modernity after the Holocaust', in Eva Fleischner (ed.), *Auschwitz: Beginning of a New Era?*, New York: Ktav, 1977, pp.7-55. Other elaborations are to be found in *Voluntary Covenant* and *The Third Great Cycle of Jewish History* (New York: National Jewish Resource Center), and *On the Holocaust* (New York: The National Jewish Center for Learning and Leadership).

60. The argument here is primarily based on 'The People Israel Lives', in *The Jewish Return into History*, New York: Schocken 1978, pp. 43-57.

61. A point made consistently by Greenberg too. He speaks of three eras in Jewish history: the Biblical, in which God was the dominant partner of the covenant, the Rabbinic, in which man assumed a more equal role, and the post-holocaust condition in which man is the dominant partner. This is the significance of the secular state of Israel as the response to the holocaust: "The revelation of Israel is a call to secularity; the religious enterprise must focus on the mundane" (*The Third Great Cycle*, p. 17).

62. See Michael Wyschogrod's criticism of Fackenheim's earlier work in 'Faith and the Holocaust', *Judaism* 20:3 (Summer 1971), pp. 286-294, and his critique of Greenberg in 'Auschwitz: Beginning of a new Era? Reflections on the Holocaust', *Tradition* 16:5 (Fall 1977), pp. 63-78; Eugene Borowitz, *Choices in Modern Jewish Thought*, New York: Behrman House, 1983, pp. 201-206; Steven T. Katz, *Post-Holocaust Dialogues*, New York University Press, 1985, pp. 205-247.

63. See Wyschogrod, 'Faith and the Holocaust', pp. 288-9.

64. Eliezer Berkovits, *Faith after the Holocaust*, New York: Ktav, 1973. See also his *With God in Hell*, New York: Sanhedrin Press, 1979.

65. Genesis 18:25.

66. *Mekhilta* 42b; T.B. *Gittin* 56b. *Faith after the Holocaust*, p. 94.

67. *Faith after the Holocaust*, pp. 109-127.

68. See, for example, Sir Immanuel Jakobovits, 'More from the Chief Rabbi's Correspondence Files', *L'Eylah*, Spring 5745 (1985), pp. 32-33.

69. See Yerushalmi's perceptive comments on the contemporary divorce of Jewish history from Jewish memory in *Zakhor*, pp. 81-103.
70. See A.B. Yehoshua, *Between Right and Right*, New York: Schocken, pp. 1-21. And see D.J. Silver, 'Choose Life', *Judaism* 35:4 (Fall 1986) pp. 458-466: "The Holocaust cannot and does not provide the kind of vitalizing and informing myth around which American Jews could marshal their energies and construct a vital culture. Martyrs command respect, but a community's sense of sacred purpose must be woven of something more substantial than tears."
71. The distinction is made in the essay *Kol Dodi Dofek*, in J. D. Soloveitchik, *Divrei Hagut ve-Ha'arakhah*, Jerusalem: Department for Torah Education and Culture, W.Z.O., 1981, pp. 7-55.
72. T.B. *Shabbat* 88a.
73. Esther 3:13.

9
Jewish-Christian Dialogue: The Ethical Dimension

Three images from Jewish tradition help us define the importance of, and the expectations we bring to, dialogue between faiths.

The first is a sobering one, drawn from Jewish law. The Bible contains a series of provisions relating to manslaughter. Someone who kills another inadvertently – "he was not an enemy of his and did not seek his harm"[1] – is given shelter in the Cities of Refuge. The rabbis sought a definition. How were we to tell whether the person was or was not an 'enemy' of his victim? What is the relevant criterion? They answered: If, out of animosity, they had not spoken to one another for three days.[2] The mere fact of not speaking together is the clearest symptom of a breakdown of relationship. Conversely, the mere act of speaking together restores relationship.

The second is the great metaphor of human communication contained in the story of the Tower of Babel. Babel represents the overreaching pride, the *hubris*, of humanity. "If, as one people with one language for all, this is how they have begun to act, then nothing that they may propose to do will be out of their reach. Let us then go down and confound their speech there, so that they shall not understand one another's speech."[3] One of the themes of the Mosaic and prophetic literature is that the lost harmonies set out at the beginning of Genesis – between man and nature in Eden, between humanity after the flood – will eventually be recovered. Zephaniah speaks of the time when God "will make the peoples pure of speech".[4] Learning one another's language of faith is one of the ways we reach back to before Babel.

The third, and perhaps the most moving, are the first recorded words between two human beings, Adam's words to Eve: "This is now bone of my bones, flesh of my flesh. She shall be called *ishah* (woman) for from *ish* (man) she was taken".[5] There is a hidden subtlety in the verse that is missed in translation. Until this point, the text has used the word *adam* (man as species) rather than *ish* (man as an individual personality). Thus Adam names his wife before he names himself. He must discover the identity of the other before he discovers his own. In true dialogue, in the I-Thou meeting, we learn as much about ourselves as about the other.[6]

So in the talking-together between faiths, we can hope to lessen long-standing hostilities. We break down some of the Babel-barriers to communication. And we deepen our own sense of individuality.

But when we talk together, of what shall we speak?

THE ETHICAL DIALOGUE

Two influential Jewish thinkers, Joseph B. Soloveitchik and Eliezer Berkovits,[7] have argued that the most fruitful ground of meeting is not at the level of theology but of ethics. Soloveitchik has spoken of the incommunicability of faith: "The word of faith reflects the intimate, the private, the paradoxically inexpressible cravings of the individual for and his linking up with his Maker. It reflects the numinous character and the strangeness of the act of faith of a particular community which is totally incomprehensible to the man of a different faith community." Accordingly, "the confrontation should occur not at a theological level, but at a mundane human level. There, all of us speak the universal language of modern man."[8] Berkovits likewise argues that "It is not interreligious understanding that mankind needs but interhuman understanding – an understanding based on our common humanity and wholly independent of any need for common religious beliefs and theological principles".[9]

Starting from the Jewish-Christian situation, how shall we begin this dialogue with "common humanity" in the "universal language of modern man"? The problems are threefold.

First: can it be taken for granted that even the Jewish and Christian traditions share a common approach to moral questions? A great deal of the literature in both Judaism and Christianity, almost since the beginning of Christianity, has been devoted to showing how Jewish ethics is superior to Christian ethics, or how Christian ethics is superior to Jewish ethics. Each tradition has often felt it necessary to define itself in opposition to the other – in terms of the contrast between love and justice, or Divine grace and human responsibility, or faith and works.[10]

In part, this is the way any tradition which makes absolute claims about the right and the good reacts to others which offer different answers.[11] But in this case it has much to do with the specific and often highly fraught relationship between Judaism and Christianity, to the argument between what A. Roy Eckardt calls 'Elder and Younger Brothers'.[12]

In the nineteenth century, as part of the dynamic of emancipation, there arose the concept of a shared ethical heritage, the so-called Judeao-Christian tradition. How valid a concept this is, I would not presume to ask. But we might note that it is only one way of viewing the relationship between the two faiths, one that goes against the grain of each faith's self-identity as expressed in most of their history.[13]

Do the two faiths, for example, currently share a common approach to human sexuality, or to the relative roles of individual and governmental responsibility in solving social problems?[14] One of the regular discoveries of dialogue is that each faith is itself more internally diverse than it seems to an outsider. Often it is easier to find agreement between religious liberals, or conservatives, across faiths, than it is for the two wings to agree within a single faith community.[15] A single embracing presentation of 'Jewish ethics' or 'Christian ethics' is sufficiently elusive[16] to make us cautious in assuming that a 'Judeao-Christian' ethic can be fleshed out in any detail.

This should not be taken as in any way lessening the importance of dialogue. The value of talking together is not predicated on the expectation that we will discover ourselves to have more in common than we thought. Nor does it rest on the hope that the encounter will set in motion a gradual convergence of initially opposed traditions. Dialogue has value even if we find ourselves radically and immovably different. The problem facing liberal democracies is not so much to evolve a moral consensus[17] as to find a way of allowing different, incompatible ethnic and religious traditions to live together without threatening one another. "Let all peoples walk, each in the name of its god",[18] said the prophet Micah.

That remains, for a central Jewish tradition, the ultimate aim of mutual acceptance.

A COMMON MORAL LANGUAGE?

The second problem lies in this question: To what extent do any of us share moral problems any more? One effect of modernisation on consciousness – as Alasdair MacIntyre[19] and others have pointed out – is that it has wrecked our moral vocabulary and left us in the most profound confusion as to what is and what is not a moral issue. To take the two most conspicuous recent examples. One: do the problems of the inner cities have a moral dimension, or are they merely questions to be confronted at the level of practical policy? Two: does the AIDS epidemic call for any other moral response than compassion for the victims? Does it call for a reinstatement of traditional sexual morality? Does it even represent a rejection – by God or at least by the human body – of homosexuality and promiscuity? Or is the only possible answer, given the society in which we live, to issue an eleventh commandment: Thou shalt play it safe?

Nowadays religious leaders, both Christian and Jewish, tend to be reluctant to issue clear moral pronouncements. And we can hardly deny the significance of the fact that the most ringing moral denunciation of homosexuality came from lay sources, James Anderton on the Christian side, Chaim Bermant on the Jewish.[20] And here we must confront a very sensitive point.

In no century as much as the twentieth has clear moral leadership been so necessary and so impossible. On the Jewish side, at both the popular and intellectual level, we are still scarred by the thinness, almost the invisibility, of Christian protest during the holocaust years;[21] and again when Israel's existence was on the line in the weeks preceding the Six Day War and in the early days of the Yom Kippur War.[22] On the Christian side, we recognise that there must be similar consternation at the apparently uncritical support on the part of the Jewish community of the actions of the State of Israel.[23] We must recognise that there are grievances on both sides. But what those grievances have in common is the sense that, at critical moments, religious leadership is too partisan to be moral leadership.

In the absence of a shared moral language, religious leadership is faced with the alternative of speaking either to its own faithful – in which case it fails to do justice to powerful opposed ethical claims – or to a minimalist moral consensus – in which case its pronouncements appear vapid and without content.[24] Hence the question: Is religious moral leadership possible in a society which is morally diverse and, for the most part, only marginally religious?

THE PLACE OF ETHICS IN CONTEMPORARY RELIGIOUS LIFE

Which brings us to the third point: With whom, as ministers of religion, *do* we share moral problems? Do we share them with society as a whole, or just with other religious people, or just with people of our own religion, or just with people of our own specific denomination, or just with a minority even of our own congregations: with that small minority which is prepared to give religion the deciding vote in a moral dilemma?

On the one hand it has become increasingly clear in recent decades that the sociological prediction has proved false, that secularisation would slowly extinguish religious life from modern societies.[25] In fact almost all forms of religion have proved remarkably tenacious, and some in particular – those which oppose modernity and which are generally called, in Christianity, Judaism and Islam, 'fundamentalist' – have experienced the most remarkable revival.[26]

The modern democratic state provides much for its citizens, but not all. There remain certain needs – for an identity, for community, for an overarching system of meanings – which the state does not answer and which religion does.[27] That is on the one hand. But on the other, it is by no means certain that the need for ethical guidance is one of them. As rabbis, we may have to acknowledge, for example, that though Judaism has the most detailed code of sexual morality, that code seems to have little influence on what the majority of young Jews actually do. Individualism, hedonism, the pursuit of pleasure and material success are more powerful drives than anything the synagogue can deliver from the pulpit. For obvious reasons. They are there, available and seductive, in the cultural air we breathe. And that cultural atmosphere is not of the synagogue's or the church's making.

The problem can be stated more precisely, taking recent Jewish experience as an example. The two most notable movements in patterns of religious behaviour in recent decades have been in opposite directions. One is the search for individual religious experience, evidenced in the *ba'al teshuvah* (religious return) phenomenon. Individuals have sought out the enveloping, pre-modern culture of the *yeshivot* (Talmudic seminaries) in a renunciation of secular society. The cluster of sectarian, neo-traditional Jewish groups has developed immense spiritual power as Judaism's option of 'de-modernizing consciousness'.[28] The other is the growth of a strong secular-ethnic Jewish identity which has appropriated the symbols and language of tradition in building a 'civil religion'.[29] This is the faith of "Jews who seek to be Jewish through identification with the Jewish people as a corporate entity, its history, culture and tradition, but without necessarily accepting the authoritative character of *halacha* (Jewish law) or the centrality of *halacha* in defining their Jewishness".[30]

Neither of these opposed modes of Jewish identity takes the specific Judaic ethical endeavour as central. Sectarianism is a form of retreat from a world witnessed as corrupt. Civil religion represents a legitimation of secular norms and strives, within them, to maintain group cohesion. Neither undertakes the classic task of religion, to socialise its members into coherent, distinctive and comprehensive forms of life.[31] Hence the third question for religious ethical leadership: Even when we are sure of what moral guidance we wish to give, how do we communicate and to whom? What is our constituency? At what point do we begin if we wish to build a more moral society?

THE RELIGIOUS DOMAIN

There are two conventional ways of considering religious ethics, one by asking what particular way of life is enjoined by a faith for its believers, the other by looking at the authority that lies behind that way of life. Neither approach, I believe, will take us to the common foundation we seek. Even if we can talk coherently of *the* Jewish or Christian way of life, it is too *sui generis*, too faith-specific, to command immediate attention by those who lie outside. And if we turn to authority, it is equally evident that the revelations that lie at the heart of the two faiths are in a tense relation to one another and are not directly persuasive to those who define themselves independently of the Biblical drama.

But there is a third alternative, posed by asking which particular *domain* religious ethics occupies. Here I argue from within the Jewish tradition, in the hope that it captures something of wider significance even if other traditions would express it differently.

To put it briefly, Judaism has had relatively little to say about the two poles of human existence, the individual and the state. The individual as individual, as the lonely man of faith,[32] has almost no independent existence in Jewish thought. We recall the classic definition given by Maimonides of *ha-poresh midarkhei ha-tsibbur*, one who separates himself from the community. Maimonides writes: "Even if he does not commit a transgression but merely holds aloof from the congregation of Israel, does not perform the commandments in common with his people, shows himself indifferent when they are in distress . . . but goes his own way as if he were one of the other nations and not of the Jewish people, such a person has no share in the world to come".[33]

At the other extreme, the state too has little independent significance. Abarbanel famously remarked that the command to appoint a king,[34] to establish a governmental system, is the Torah's concession to the evil inclination.[35] Nor was Abarbanel being merely idiosyncratic. Not only is it the only Biblical command specifically couched in terms of a response to the people's request to be like everyone else: "Let me set a king over me like all the nations around me".[36] Not only did the prophet Samuel try to talk the people out of it.[37] Not only did the prophets rail against the corruptions of governmental power. Not only did monarchy prove, with few exceptions, to be a moral and religious disaster. But the entire thrust of Jewish tradition is towards seeing the governmental domain as a practical necessity, rather than as an institution with a distinctive religious contribution to make.[38] Rabbi Hanina, deputy High-Priest at the time of the destruction of the second Temple, summed up perfectly the extent and limits of the

Jewish respect for political structures: "Pray for the welfare of the government, for were it not for the fear of it, men would eat one another alive." [39]

Jewish spirituality, at least since rabbinic times, finds its most significant context at the level neither of the individual nor the state, but in a series of settings midway between them, namely, the family, the *bet ha-midrash* and *bet ha-knesset* – the fellowships of learning and praying – and the *kehillah*, the community. Which is why Judaism has found it difficult to provide an adequate response to two modern phenomena: the religious search for individual salvation, catered for by some Chassidic groups but looked on with suspicion by many others; and the challenges posed by a Jewish state the majority of whose population is not yet ready for theocracy or religious coercion.

THE ETHICAL DOMAIN

This locus of Jewish values, set at an intermediate point between the individual and the state, may provide a significant point of entry into the problems I have outlined.

First, it is just this middle ground which contemporary secular society fails to provide for. The state is more active in the affairs of its citizens than in previous centuries. At the same time individuals have more choices, more freedoms and more scope for self-expression. It is not at either extreme that we experience our moral poverty, but in the middle: in the loss of the sense of community and in the breakdown of the family. Precisely where secular society is weak, Judaism and religions generally are strong.

Secondly, there are signs that at least some Christian thought is moving in this direction. I take as an example the impressive work of the American Christian ethicist, Stanley Hauerwas. Central to his thinking, especially in his recent book *The Peaceable Kingdom*,[40] are the perceptions that ethics belongs firmly within traditions and communities, and that we make our ethical choices as individuals within a specific historical tradition, and within the context of a community in which that tradition is given living substance. Perhaps even more significantly, some leading secular moral philosophers, like Alasdair MacIntyre[41] and Stuart Hampshire,[42] are moving in the same direction. This is nothing short of an intellectual revolution, because it represents a break with the two ethical systems that have most dominated secular thought for over a hundred years, utilitarianism on the one hand and Kantianism on the other, both of which are attempts to eliminate the concept of ethical traditions.

Thirdly, I must add as a personal conviction that I see no alternative route for the future of ethics. Morality does not flourish when planted at the level either of the state or the individual. When predicated of the state it is too ruthless of dissenting minorities to be tolerated. This is the enduring contribution of liberalism, from Mill to H.L.A. Hart. When predicated of the individual it is too rootless to provide the basis of virtue or character. This is the case presented with overwhelming force by MacIntyre and others.[43]

SOME APPLICATIONS

How might this make a substantive difference to the way we think about ethical issues? Again I argue from within a Jewish perspective, hoping that other traditions may recognise something universal within the particular case.

Consider first the breakdown of traditional sexual ethics, brought forcibly to our attention by AIDS. Ever since the 60s, when homosexuality was legalised, we have generally accepted the liberal premiss that legislating sexual morality is not the business of the state.[44] But if the only alternative to the state is the individual, then we move inexorably to the conclusion that sexuality is a form of self-expression, and from there to the further conclusion that there is no such thing as sexual deviance.[45]

The only effective counterargument, to my mind, is one that locates sexuality firmly within the framework of values of the family. The ideals of heterosexuality and above all fidelity, summed up in the concept of marriage, are not merely part of Biblical ethics. They are written into the entire fabric of the Biblical vision, into its view both of creation – Adam and Eve – and of the covenant between God and man, aptly described by Hosea and Jewish tradition as a marriage.[46]

The underlying logic is apparent in the first chapter of Genesis. All of nature shares with God the property of being creative, of bringing new life into being, but only humanity shares with God the *moral choice* of bringing new life into the world. Only for Adam and Eve is the phrase 'Be fruitful and multiply' experienced not just as a blessing but as a command.[47] Bringing children into the world thus presupposes moral responsibility, for one might have chosen otherwise. That responsibility for those one has brought into existence extends to caring for them in their dependency, and to ensuring that they will have a world to inherit. Hence it is in the family that three great ethical concerns arise: *welfare*, or the care of dependents; *education*, or the handing on of accumulated wisdom to a new generation; and *ecology*, or concern with the fate of the world after our own lifetime.

Once the family is seen as the place where the ethical enterprise begins – something the Bible conveys dramatically by making 'Be fruitful and multiply' the first of all the commands – then traditional sexual ethics becomes not one alternative among many in a sexually pluralistic world, but the only persuasive way of life for those who want to engage in the ethical undertaking.

Another example: the inner cities. Here I must testify, along with other Jewish readers, to a perplexity about *Faith in the City*.[48] In an otherwise outstanding report, one omission was striking. Early on in the document[49] there is a statistical table which summarises the responses of the clergy to the relative seriousness of various social problems. The list includes law and order, race relations, welfare provisions and unemployment. But top of the list nationally were problems relating to the family. It was almost top of the list for clergymen working in the inner cities. What was perplexing was that throughout *Faith in the City* the family appears as a problem and not as a solution.[50] None of its sixty-one recommendations directly relates to ways in which the institution of the family might be strengthened by either the church or other religious and social groups.

Against this, the Jewish community has to testify from its own long experience of inner cities, immigrant and minority status and grinding poverty, that above all it was the strength of the Jewish family that allowed it to break the circle of deprivation. This has a number of dimensions. Educational surveys, for example, regularly highlight the fact that the most potent factor affecting academic success in schools is the degree of parental support and involvement in their children's schooling. A potent factor in motivating enterprise is the all-too-human desire to give one's children more than they might otherwise have. Many forms of deviant adolescent behaviour only make sense in the context of family breakdown.

There has been a determined onslaught against the family this century,[51] and we have to admit that the Jewish world was responsible for two of its most powerful formulations, the Freudian attack on the family as an instrument of repression, and the Kibbutz-socialist attack on the family as an instrument of capitalism.[52] That said, the family remains the most durable institutional context of human flourishing yet devised. The impression conveyed by *Faith in the City* is that family failures are a social datum, not to be addressed as an object of religious policy. But this is a tacit moral judgement, not an empirical conclusion. If human flourishing is part of the object of morality[53] and if the family does indeed contribute to flourishing, then strengthening the family is a legitimate part of the moral project.

ETHICAL PARTICULARISM

As soon as we locate morality within ways of life which are neither embodied in the state nor confined to individual choices, we encounter the phenomenon of pluralism. There are, at this level, moralities in the plural, not a single common morality for humanity as a whole. Stuart Hampshire compares moralities with languages: "There exists a multiplicity of coherent ways of life, held together by conventions and imitated habits, for much the same reasons that there is a multiplicity of natural languages, held together by conventions and imitated habits of speech".[54] There is no single overarching morality, as there is no single all-embracing language.

Arising out of this conception is another, the moral *community*, namely those bound together as speakers, as it were, of the same language. The notion of morality as part of a way of life alerts us to the fact that communities, though they may share a sense of mutual obligation, are characteristically bound together by other things as well: religious faith or ethnic origin, for example. The question which now needs to be posed is: Is it legitimate for us to regard such communities as moral entities? Does it make sense to speak of special obligations to the members of one's group?

The drift of secular ethics since the Enlightenment has been towards *universalism*, that is, towards stipulating that ethical responses are just those we are willing to extend to everyone.[55] If we are not willing to extend them to everyone, they are not ethical, but either a kind of self-interest or a kind of tribalism. Crucial to my argument is that there are features of morality which are unaccounted for by this conception. There is a case to be made for *ethical particularism*.

One of the most powerful moral critiques in the work of Charles Dickens, one of the supreme moralists of all time, is of Mrs. Pardiggle and Mrs. Jellyby in Bleak House, ladies of what he calls "rapacious benevolence", who are so taken up with good works on behalf of the Tockahoopo Indians and the Borrioboola Africans that they completely neglect and ultimately destroy their families. "Never", says the husband of one of them to his daughter, "Never have a *Mission*, my dear child." [56]

We have no difficulty in understanding what Dickens means. There is something that offends against Kantian ethics but which nonetheless answers to our deepest moral intuitions, that says: what does it profit a person if he saves the whole world and neglects those closest to him? The rabbis said it unashamedly. The poor of your family take precedence over the poor of another family. The poor of your town take precedence over the poor of the next town.[57]

We were moved by the activation of the world's moral conscience on behalf of the famine victims of Ethiopia. Yet there were few more telling symptoms of the universalism implicit in Western culture than the failure of the world to be moved by Israel's rescue of Ethiopian Jewry. 'Jews rescue their own', was the cynical reaction. To which the Jewish response is instinctively: If we are *not* the kind of people who will rescue our own, are we the kind of people who will ultimately rescue anyone?

Once again, the family proves to be a moral crux. Michael Wyschogrod asks us to consider the following example:

In the devastating 1976 earthquake in Communist China, there was a report of an incident in which a father insisted on rescuing a local Communist officer rather than his child, whose moans he heard but ignored to save the official, whose social value the father judged above that of his son. By the time he returned to the wreckage in which his son was buried, he found him dead. The Chinese Communist press pointed to this incident as an example of proper Chinese behaviour.[58]

The example forces us to clarify our intuitive moral responses. It presents us with a picture of a coherent way of life, but one which we might intelligibly reject for ourselves. Once we admit parenthood as a moral, not simply as a biological, category then we allow that there may be special obligations which are not universalisable.

We must be very careful at this point. It has been one of the most painful accusations of antisemites that Jews use different ethical standards when dealing with themselves than when dealing with others. Books have been written to refute the charge;[59] it should not be necessary to repeat the arguments here. *Some* moral obligations are surely universal, but they do not exhaust the entire scope of morality. To quote Hampshire again: "human nature, conceived in terms of common human needs and capacities, always underdetermines a way of life".[60] It makes sense to speak of *some* moral obligations which are generated within a specific moral community and which are bounded by that community. This has been historically a deeply controversial proposition. My argument is that it is a corollary of ethical pluralism.

Thus, for example, in the context of ethnic minorities there are two opposed poles of approach. One is to encourage them to develop adequate networks of self-help, welfare, educational and economic. Another is for outside agencies to assume direct responsibility. The former strategy is often assumed to be *obviously* less moral than the latter. Yet the latter is fraught with its own problems, predicated as it is on a paternalistic model which may be resented as threatening ethnic integrity and self-respect. I have tried to show that there *is* a moral case to be made for the first approach. I have argued the rationale of encouraging the vitality of middle-range institutions, from the family to the faith or ethnic community. It is here that moral action is at its least problematic. For it is here that morality begins.

LIMITS

Begins but not ends. Jewish ethics is an instructive instance of the two ways in which ethical particularism must be supplemented to be an adequate conception of morality. One is the growth of empathy. The other is the notion of moral limits. Both are necessary. For there is the signal danger in the kind of ethical thinking here advocated, that morality may indeed become in-group or purely tribal, where the only people we care about are those who share our commitments.

Against this possibility the Jewish ethical tradition provides dynamic models of the ways moral obligation extends outwards from the family. By the book of Exodus the covenantal family of Abraham and his children has become a nation. But obligations to other members of one's people are still often couched in terms of the word 'brother'.[61] Duties are extended beyond the nation by the word 'stranger' together with the rider, "You know the heart of the stranger, for you yourselves were strangers in the land of Egypt".[62] The development of moral character, on this conception, is along the axis of the widening range of imaginative identifications. I owe special duties to those with whom I most strongly identify; but the ethical imagination continually finds unexpected identifications.[63] The moral family, in other words, has an inbuilt tendency to become an extended family.

There is a second rider, different in kind and all the more crucial. Any morality whose context is a less-than-universal community must contain a limiting-case set of obligations for those who lie outside the community. There must be a morality for the outsider; in the case of religions, a morality for the unredeemed. If there is nothing I may not do to one whose soul is not saved, if there is nothing I may not do in order to save a soul, then my morality is so fatally flawed as no longer to be worthy of the name. This surely is the enduring truth of ethical universalism, that there are some elements of morality which apply to humanity as such without qualification. There are duties I owe to those with whom I identify, but there are others I owe precisely to those with whom I do not identify, for whom I have no sympathy, with whom I have nothing in common. If the long, tragic chronicles of religious persecution and attempted genocide are not instances of immorality, we may rightly ask: What is?

Rabbinic tradition records a dialogue[64] between two teachers of the Mishnaic age. Each was asked to provide a statement of the 'great principle' which underlay the Torah. Rabbi Akiva answered by citing the verse, "You shall love your neighbour as yourself".[65] Ben Azzai replied that there is a more fundamental principle: "When God created man, He made him in the likeness of God".[66] In the terms we have been using, Akiva takes as his moral ultimate the complete extension of empathy involved in loving one's neighbour as oneself. Ben Azzai rightly notes that though this may be the end of morality, it is nonetheless not its most basic proposition. Morality has boundaries, and they are set by the recognition that there are certain things one may not do to any human being, whether one loves him or hates him. In the Bible this is grounded in the ontological sanctity of humanity as the image of God. To which ancient rabbinic wisdom added the following comment: "When human beings create things in a single image, they are all alike. God makes humanity in a single image, yet each of them is unique." [67]

On this point, the ethical dialogue between faiths imposes a limit on theological dialogue, and one that needs to be clearly articulated. Three theological positions are usually distinguished.[68] The exclusivist maintains that only his faith is in possession of the truth. The inclusivist maintains that his faith alone is true, but that others unwittingly or partially share it. The pluralist maintains that each faith is its own reflection of the same underlying truth.

If these positions are confined to theology alone, to the vocabulary of salvation, redemption, fate in the afterlife and the like, we can reasonably proceed within the categories they set forth. But if they are taken to entail ethical consequences, then all three must be regarded as inadequate. For if I do not have some moral obligations to those I believe to be categorically in error – if I am not prepared to recognise the image of God in the human being as such, independently of his or my theological commitments – then there is at least a possible line from faith to holocaust. The twentieth century has surely taught us this much.

I would urge, therefore, as part of any dialogue between faiths, races or cultures, that it seeks to establish, for each of the partners, a morally adequate theory of 'the other', the one who is in God's image though he is not in our image.

CONCLUSIONS

To summarise what has been a somewhat extended argument:

Jewish thinkers have advocated a form of dialogue in the realm, not of theology, but of ethics, conducted in the "universal language" of "common humanity". I have argued that it is a given feature of modern Western societies that there is no such universal language. We are in an ethical Babel which shows no signs of converging on a single moral vocabulary. But we need not draw from this situation the two most common inferences, that there is a Platonic universal morality underlying the apparent diversity, or that to the contrary there is nothing left to morality than the expression of individual choice.

There is an alternative conclusion to be drawn, sometimes called 'post-liberal pluralism',[69] that there is an open-ended multiplicity of moral ways of life, each set in its own tradition and embodied in its own form of community. It is in the context of such communities, of which the family is the most basic, that the moral enterprise gets under way and is at its most lucid. A central moral task of religions, though not only of religions, lies in building such communities. The sense of anomie which pervades modernity has much to do with the poverty of secular culture at this intermediate point between the individual and the state. This is the primary moral domain.

The religious ethical endeavour would thus lie in creating persuasive examples of moral communities, each living out its distinctive traditions. Religious leadership can no longer speak to society as a whole on the basis of authority, for that authority cannot be presumed to be accepted by all. But it can speak out of its own experience and example. That too confers a kind of authority, perhaps the only kind for which we can hope in the modern situation.

Dialogue is necessary. Each faith community can learn volumes from others by seeing how they, in quite different ways, build caring communities. As Jews, for example, we have learned much from the Christian tradition of pastoral ministry, and we have incorporated it into our religious life. Long ago, to give another example, the rabbis learned from ancient Roman examples what 'honouring thy father and mother' might mean in practice.[70]

Dialogue has a second aim: to establish a clear sense of the limits of ethical particularism. The growth, throughout the world and in all the major faiths, of religious fundamentalism makes this particularly urgent. Ethics sets boundary conditions for theology. If the unredeemed are not, at some level, objects of moral concern, possessing independent integrity and rights, then faith itself becomes morally untenable.

Dialogue need not be grounded in the belief that, *au fond*, we all share the same faith or the same morality. There is something profoundly moving in such a belief. But there is something equally momentous in the opposite conviction: that our worlds of faith are irreducibly plural yet we have been cast into the same planet, faced with the same questions. Can we live together? Can we learn from one another? Within this vision much is possible. Much, too, is necessary.

NOTES

1. Numbers 35:23.
2. Babylonian Talmud, *Sanhedrin* 27b; Maimonides, *Hilkhot Rotzeach* 6:10.
3. Genesis 11:6-7.
4. Zephaniah 3:9.
5. Genesis 2:23.
6. I owe this exegetical insight to my teacher, Rabbi Dr. Nachum Rabinovitch.
7. Their approaches to interfaith dialogue are analysed in my 'Perspectives', *L'Eylah*, No. 21, pp. 41-47.
8. Joseph B. Soloveitchik, 'Confrontation', *Tradition* 6:2 (Spring/Summer 1964), pp. 23-24.
9. Eliezer Berkovits, *Faith after the Holocaust*, New York: Ktav, 1973, p. 47.
10. For three relatively recent examples on the Jewish side, see Leon Simon (ed.) *Philosophica Judaica: Ahad Ha'am*, London, 1946, pp. 127-137; Abba Hillel Silver, *Where Judaism Differed*, Macmillan, 1972; and the essay 'Romantic Religion' in Leo Baeck, *Judaism and Christianity*, New York: Atheneum, 1970.

11. See 'On Grading Religions' in John Hick, *Problems of Religious Pluralism*, Macmillan, 1985, pp. 67-87.
12. A. Roy Eckardt, *Elder and Younger Brothers*, New York: Scribners, 1967.
13. The question raised here is one of long standing. See Elie Benamozegh, *Jewish and Christian Ethics*, San Francisco, 1873; I.M. Blank, 'Is There a Common Judaeo-Christian Ethical Tradition' in D.J. Silver (ed.), *Judaism and Ethics*, New York, 1970, pp. 95-108; Joseph Klausner, 'Jewish and Christian Ethics', *Judaism* 2 (1953), pp. 16-30; Kaufman Kohler, 'Synagogue and Church in their Mutual Relations, Particularly in Reference to the Ethical Teachings', in *Judaism at the World Parliament of Religions*, Cincinnati, 1894; H.F. Rall and Samuel S. Cohon, *Christianity and Judaism Compare Notes*, New York, 1927.
14. In my original presentation I noted that the Anglo-Jewish community had been moving politically to the right in recent years, while the Church, at least in some of its more publicised statements, had been seen to be moving in the opposite direction. Needless to say, advocates of both individual and public responsibility can find ample precedent in the Biblical literature. See my *Wealth and Poverty: A Jewish Analysis*, London: The Social Affairs Unit, 1985.
15. See A. Roy Eckardt, *Jews and Christians: The Contemporary Meeting*, Indiana University Press, 1986, p. 96.
16. See my 'Jewish Ethics in the Twentieth Century', in the *Blackwell Companion to Jewish Culture*, Oxford: Blackwell (forthcoming).
17. See the very instructive comments in the Foreword to the Warnock Report *(A Question of Life: The Warnock Report on Human Fertilisation and Embryology*, Oxford: Blackwell, 1985, pp. 1-3). Warnock's view is that "in our pluralistic society it is not to be expected that any one set of principles can be enunciated to be completely accepted by everyone". Given this, the question to be faced is: "In what sort of society can we live with our conscience clear?"
18. Micah 4:5.
19. Alasdair MacIntyre, *Secularization and Moral Change*, Oxford University Press, 1967; *After Virtue*, Duckworth, 1981.
20. Bermant's article, 'Depravity, not deprivation is the cause of our ills' appeared in the *Jewish Chronicle*, 26 December 1986. It ended with an affirmation of Goethe's remark, "All guilt is punished on earth".
21. This sense dominates much contemporary Jewish theological writing. See for example: Eliezer Berkovits, *Faith After the Holocaust*; Irving Greenberg, 'Cloud of Smoke, Pillar of Fire: Judaism, Christianity and Modernity after the Holocaust' in Eva Fleischner (ed.), *Auschwitz: Beginning of a new Era?* New York: Ktav, 1977, pp. 7-56; Emil Fackenheim, *The Jewish Return into History*, New York: Schocken, 1978, *To Mend the World*, New York: Schocken, 1982.
22. See, for example, the essays by William G. Oxtoby, A. Roy Eckardt and Frank Ephraim Talmage in F.E. Talmage (ed.), *Disputation and Dialogue*, New York: Ktav, 1975, pp. 220-253.

23. This is stressed, for example, in Janet Sternfeld, *Homework for Jews: Preparing for Jewish-Christian Dialogue*, National Conference of Christians and Jews, 1985, pp. 33-39.
24. See MacIntyre, *Secularization and Moral Change*, pp. 66-76; Stanley Hauerwas, *Against the Nations*, Winston, 1985, pp. 1-50.
25. Two classic studies are Bryan Wilson, *Religion in Secular Society*, Pelican Books, 1969; Peter Berger, *The Sacred Canopy*, Doubleday, 1967.
26. See, for example, Charles Liebman and Eliezer Don-Yehiyah, *Religion and Politics in Israel*, Indiana University Press, 1984.
27. See Peter L. Berger, Brigitte Berger and Hansfried Kellner, *The Homeless Mind*, Penguin Books, 1973, pp. 163-191.
28. The phrase is taken from *The Homeless Mind*, ch. 9.
29. The term 'civil religion' is generally attributed to Robert Bellah, 'Civil Religion in America', *Daedalus*, Winter 1967, pp. 1-21. For studies of Jewish civil religion, see Charles Liebman and Eliezer Don-Yehiyah, *Civil Religion in Israel: Traditional Judaism and Political Culture in the Jewish State*, University of California Press, 1983, and Jonathan Woocher, *Sacred Survival: The Civil Religion of American Jews*, Indiana University Press, 1986.
30. Daniel J. Elazar, 'The New Sadducees', *Midstream*, August/September 1978, p. 22.
31. I borrow this formulation from George Lindbeck, *The Nature of Doctrine: Religion and Theology in a Postliberal Age*, Philadelphia: Westminster, 1984, p. 126.
32. The phrase is taken from the title of the famous article by Joseph B. Soloveitchik, 'The Lonely Man of Faith', *Tradition* 7:2 (Summer 1965) pp. 5-67. Much of Soloveitchik's work is devoted to the phenomenology of aspects of the life of faith. Precisely because the individual subject of consciousness is not the locus of traditional spirituality, this gives his work a peculiarly modern tone, and creates a constant sense of tension.
33. Maimonides, *Hilkhot Teshuvah* 3:11.
34. Deuteronomy 17: 14-20.
35. Abarbanel, Commentary to Deuteronomy 17: 15; see also Ibn Ezra ad loc.
36. Deuteronomy 17:14.
37. I Samuel 8: 4-18.
38. For an insightful study of Judaic political theory, see Gerald J. Blidstein, *Political Concepts in Maimonidean Halakha* (Hebrew), Bar Ilan University Press, 1983. For a historical study of how the 'kingship' model has functioned in Jewish political organisation, see Daniel J. Elazar and Stuart A. Cohen, *The Jewish Polity: Jewish political organization from Biblical times to the present*, Indiana University Press, 1985.
39. Mishnah, *Avot*, 3:2.
40. Stanley Hauerwas, *The Peaceable Kingdom: A Primer in Christian Ethics*, SCM Press, 1984.
41. Alasdair MacIntyre, *After Virtue*.

42. Stuart Hampshire, *Morality and Conflict*, Oxford, Blackwell, 1983.
43. See also 'On the Obsolescence of the Concept of Honour' in Berger, Berger and Kellner, *The Homeless Mind*, pp. 78-89; and Michael Oakeshott, 'The Tower of Babel', *Cambridge Journal*, Volume 2, pp. 65-83.
44. H.L.A. Hart, *Law, Liberty and Morality*, Oxford University Press, 1968.
45. Roger Scruton's attempt (*Sexual Desire*, Weidenfeld and Nicolson, 1986) to ground a traditional sexual morality in considerations of interpersonal intentionality – homosexuality thus fails because it lacks complementarity, strangeness and a sense of risk – seems to me to be a significant failure: significant because it demonstrates how tenuous moral argument is in this area when severed from talk about the family.
46. The imagery is central to the act of wearing *tefillin* (phylacteries). As Jews wind the straps round their finger, they recite the verses: "I will betroth you to me for ever . . . I will betroth you in faithfulness, and you will acknowledge the Lord" (Hosea 2:19-20), symbolically re-enacting the marriage between God and His people.
47. To the animals it is a blessing: Genesis 1:22. To humanity it is a command: Genesis 1:28, 9:1.
48. *Faith in the City: The Report of the Archbishop of Canterbury's Commission on Urban Priority Areas*, London: Church House Publishing, 1985.
49. Ibid. pp. 37-38.
50. See, for example, pp. 334-5: "Moreover there are strong social pressures working against the traditional patterns of family life . . . Any appeal to parental authority, and any attempts to strengthen it, must take account of the social realities of family life today . . ." What from one perspective might seem like realism, from another might appear to be defeatism. Religions have traditionally been powerful agencies in sustaining forms of family life. The passage might be read, perhaps unkindly, as a retreat from this role. I would argue strongly for a move in the opposite direction.
51. For a recent survey, see Digby Anderson and Graham Dawson (eds.), *Family Portraits*, London: The Social Affairs Unit, 1986.
52. For a sensitive portrait of kibbutz methods of raising children, see Bruno Bettelheim, *The Children of the Dream*, Paladin, 1973.
53. See, for example, G.J. Warnock, *The Object of Morality*, Methuen, 1971.
54. *Morality and Conflict*, p. 148.
55. See, for an influential example, R.M. Hare, *The Language of Morals*, Oxford, 1964, *Freedom and Reason*, Oxford, 1965, *Moral Thinking*, Oxford, 1981.
56. Mr. Jellyby, *Bleak House*, ch. 30.
57. Babylonian Talmud, *Baba Metzia* 71a.
58. Michael Wyschogrod, *The Body of Faith: Judaism as Corporeal Election*, Seabury Press, 1983, pp. 215-6. Wyschogrod has penetrating things to say about ethical universalism and particularism.
59. A poignant example is Joseph S. Bloch, *Israel and the Nations*, Benjamin Harz Verlag, 1927.

60. *Morality and Conflict*, p. 155.
61. There are many examples in Leviticus ch. 25.
62. Exodus 23:9.
63. One of the more remarkable imaginative leaps in the Bible is: "Do not abhor an Egyptian, because you lived as an alien in his country" (Deuteronomy 23:8).
64. Sifra, *Kedoshim*, 4:12.
65. Leviticus 19:18.
66. Genesis 5:1.
67. Mishnah, *Sanhedrin*, 4:5.
68. John Hick, *Problems of Religious Pluralism*, p. 91.
69. George Lindbeck (*The Nature of Doctrine*, p. 40) characterises post-liberal theology in terms of the assertion that "Adherents of different religions do not diversely thematize the same experience; rather they have different experiences." The seemingly similar virtues and emotions within different traditions "are not diverse modifications of a single fundamental human awareness, emotional attitude, or sentiment, but are radically (i.e., from the root) distinct ways of experiencing and being oriented toward self, neighbor and cosmos." This was the position advocated by Soloveitchik in *Confrontation*. I have merely added the observation that this extends not only to theologies, but to moralities as well, beyond the minimalist threshold.
70. Babylonian Talmud, *Kiddushin*, 31a.

10
Wealth and Poverty: A Jewish Analysis*

How can we guess what an ancient text – the Bible – would have said about modern social issues such as poverty?

The subject to which I shall give a response from the Jewish tradition is poverty, and the related issues of work, wealth creation, and income distribution. Taking the Jewish religious experience as a model: how does, or can, a religious tradition contribute to social, economic and political thought? And equally importantly, how can it contribute to the human realities which are the context of action in these areas?

There is a problem here from the outset: Judaism, like Christianity, represents a tradition. It is validated by an ancient text, the Bible, and in turn seeks to understand, or to justify, its programme in the present by reference back to that text. But how can it do so? The Bible does indeed have a great deal to say about the poor, about work, and about social justice. But it was revealed in an age whose environmental reality was a relatively primitive economy. It thus does not specifically address the issues of high technology, residual unemployment, trade unions, transnational corporations. How then are we to make the interpretive leap to what the Bible would have said, had it been given today?

I am not sure how to answer that question, or even who is best qualified to do so; a literary critic, a historian, a theologian or a prophet. All I can do is to illustrate, by means of examples, what happened when the Jewish tradition was faced with just this problem.

*Deriving practical policies from values –
the cutting edge of rabbinic thought*

A word, then, about the sources I shall be using, and where their interest may lie. Judaism and Christianity have a common background in the Bible, or what Christianity would call the Old Testament. From there on their paths diverge. One route led on into the New Testament and the Church Fathers. The other proceeded through the debates of the rabbis, ultimately to be collected into a vast literature of law, ethics, homily and legend, of which the most influential works are the Mishna, codified in the early third century, and the Babylonian and Jerusalem Talmuds, compiled several centuries later. The first point, therefore, is that what I shall be describing is an *alternative interpretative history* that can be mapped out for the Bible.

The second point: The talmudic literature is not so much a book or collection of books, as the edited record of centuries of sustained argument over every issue which touched the life of the Jew. Argument is of its essence, and decisions were reached only when absolutely necessary to establish a *community of practice*. For this reason – and it was a point which medieval Christian disputants found hard to understand – Judaism evolved very few authoritative stances on matters of dogma, attitude, or value-structure. On value-judgements, therefore, the tradition will range from the broad consensus to radical divergence. On specific rulings, however, where the issue was often a *conflict* of values, the tradition is more definitive. How did one translate values into practical policies – that is, into law – in a world of limited resources and conflicting claims? This is where rabbinic thought has its cutting edge.

The consensus – poverty is an unmitigated evil, worse than fifty plagues

First, then, the values themselves. On *poverty* there is unusual agreement. It is an unmitigated evil. On this the rabbis would have agreed with Aristotle: no-one would call the virtuous man who suffered happy unless he were merely arguing for argument's sake.[1] "Poverty", said the rabbis, "is a kind of death".[2] "Poverty in a man's house is worse than fifty plagues".[3] "Nothing is harder to bear than poverty; for he who is crushed by poverty is like one to whom all the troubles of the world cling and upon whom all the curses in Deuteronomy have descended. If all other troubles were placed on one side and poverty on the other, poverty would outweigh them all."[4] These, and other rabbinic sayings, are the simple perceptions of those who knew deprivation from the inside; who had lived it and knew it had no saving graces.

This was their experience, but it was experience bounded by certain shared assumptions. First: that man as an embodied soul cannot reach stable religious heights without attending to the needs of the body: If there is no meal, they said, there can be no Torah.[5] Second: that the gifts of God are to be found in this world as well as the next, and that the ability to enjoy is itself a religious experience. One of the early talmudic teachers put it sharply: In the world to come a man will have to face judgement for every legitimate pleasure which he denied himself.[6] Third, and perhaps the strongest of their concerns: poverty meant a particular kind of humiliation. Work at anything, they said, rather than be dependent on others.[7]

There is a marked absence in the literature of any tendency to see poverty as a blessed state, or as conducing to any virtue. The many verses in the Bible which picture Divine identification with the poor were restricted to their two primary meanings: God loves the poor in spirit; and God is the spokesman of the poor when they are oppressed. The rabbis found nothing in the Biblical text to suggest that an abandonment of worldly goods is desirable: to the contrary, asceticism was an implicit disavowal of this world, which God created and pronounced to be good. Nor did siding with the poor mean embracing poverty. No poor man was ever helped by knowing that a saint had joined his ranks, or that prayers were offered on his behalf, or that his condition recapitulated the indigence and poverty of the son of God, or that he was being spared the temptations of this transient, corruptible flesh. He was helped only by being given the chance not to be poor.

*Thus no one should impoverish himself
to relieve the poverty of others*

These attitudes found specific expression in Jewish law. Despite the extreme emphasis in Judaism on charity, the transcending virtue, nevertheless no-one may relieve the poverty of others at the cost of impoverishing himself. Jewish law, for instance, considers the case of someone who in an excess of self-denial donates all his property to religious causes. Such an act is declared to be 'not piety but folly'.[8] The rabbis made a rare and special enactment at Usha, that one may not give away more than a fifth of one's possessions.[9] They also forbade the collectors of communal charitable funds to solicit a contribution from someone who is known to be overgenerous.[10]

The best charity is that which helps the poor dispense with charity

In the other direction, one law is worthy of particular attention. The sources discuss the various gradations of charity: from those who give grudgingly, to those who give less than is proper, to those who wait until they are asked, and so on upwards, to the point where the giver does not know to whom he is giving and the recipient does not know from whom he takes – the state of minimum humiliation. There is, though, a higher level; and here I quote from Maimonides' definitive codification: 'The highest degree, exceeded by none, is that of the person who assists the poor by providing him with a gift or a loan by accepting him into a business partnership or by helping him find employment – in a word, by putting him where he can dispense with other people's aid'.[11]

The ruling is remarkable. Charity is adjudged a virtue, presumably, because it is a sacrifice for the good of others; in this case, though, the sacrifice is non-existent – a loan, a partnership, finding him a job. Nothing more clearly defines the place of charity in the system than this: it may be the highest virtue, but better is the world where it is not needed. Charity is not justified by the good it does to the soul of the giver, but by the degree to which it removes the misery of the recipient, physical and more especially psychological. An act which enables him not to need charity is higher than any charity.

Already in setting out these propositions, one aspect of the rabbinic method should be apparent. Specific moral concepts may not be used as prescriptions for action without taking into consideration context and consequence. Charity is right; but it does not follow that the more charity the better. In each case a policy is to be judged by its long-term effects in removing poverty and the conditions associated with it. The fact that the sages had to make a formal enactment prohibiting excessive self-sacrifice shows religious authority in a highly unconventional role. The act discloses that overgenerosity was an actuality – the sages never legislated against a remote possibility.[12] Yet the rabbis ruled against a seeming virtue. For obvious enough reasons. Impoverishing oneself transgresses a prior duty, that one should oneself endeavour not to need it. And it destroys one's wealth-creating possibilities, and so is in the long-run detrimental to the poor. Simple pursuit of a value may defeat the ends which make it a value.

The dangers of generalising from Biblical sources can be illustrated in a more striking way. And here, as a preface, we should remember that the rabbinic sages saw it as their function simply to safeguard the structures of Mosaic law. They were heirs to an unbroken tradition, a covenant whose terms were immutable. The radicalism of the manoeuvre we are about to consider is, therefore, remarkable.

Values such as redistribution to the poor not to be pursued simplistically: an example in which redistribution yields to economic growth

The Bible contains a great many laws whose function is the redistribution of income, set primarily against the background of an agricultural economy. Various portions of the harvest were set aside for the poor – the corner of the field, the forgotten sheaf, and so on (Leviticus 19:9-10; Deuteronomy 24:19-21). On the third and sixth year of the seven-year cycle, they were given a tenth of all produce (Deuteronomy 26:12). And on the seventh year, all outstanding debts were remitted (Deuteronomy 15:1-2). This last provision was clearly open to circumvention; and the Bible proceeds to warn against it:

'Be careful that you do not have a base thought and say to yourself "The seventh year is approaching, and it will be the remission year." You may look unkindly on your impoverished brother, and not give him anything. If he then complains to God about you, you will be guilty of a sin.' (Ibid, 15:9.)

Here then was a periodic redistributive measure,

designed to relieve the poor of accumulated burdens of debt. The danger was that the wealthy would simply not give loans prior to the seventh year; hence the invocation of Divine concern – always an accompaniment of a law which is difficult to enforce. What happened to this law in a more complex economy? The Mishna records one of the most daring of all rabbinic innovations: "When he saw that the people refrained from giving loans to one another and thus transgressed the Biblical warning . . . Hillel enacted the *prosbol*".[13] The *prosbol* was a technical device whereby a loan was transacted through the court, ceased to be an agreement between individuals, and so bypassed the terms of the year of release. Hillel – perhaps the founding father of rabbinic Judaism – had found a solution within the law.

How he had the authority to do so is a technical question which need not concern us. But why he should wish to do so is another matter. In effect, he had abrogated an established right of the less well off. And Hillel was himself a man whose poverty was legendary.[14]

With the transition from an agricultural to a more commercial economy, loans had become less a response to a disastrous harvest than a normal precondition of trading. A moral appeal to cancel debts was accordingly less likely to succeed and less plausible. The Biblical law, whose original intent was explicitly to benefit the poor, was now working to their disfavour; they could not obtain loans in certain years. Clearly forfeiting the redistribution in their favour would be more than compensated by the assistance they would receive in building up their own trade. Here was an instance, drawn from the Second Temple period, of redistribution yielding to economic growth – on moral grounds agreed to be strong enough to justify inverting a Biblical procedure.

Resolving conflicts of values by practical historical experience

A similar process can be seen in the case of work. First the value. To earn a livelihood, especially by manual labour, was something to which the sages attached religious significance. It made man, in their phrase 'partner with the Holy One, blessed be He, in the work of creation'.[15] And it made him independent, equally essential to the religious personality. 'Six days shall you labour,' was no less of an *imitatio dei* than 'On the seventh day shall you rest.' Great is work for it honours the workman.[16] All study of Torah which is not accompanied by work is in the end futile and the cause of sin.[17] These were characteristic maxims.

One of the religious obligations of father to son was to teach him a trade, 'and whoever does not teach his son a trade teaches him to become a robber'.[18] The rabbinic comment on the Biblical phrase, 'therefore choose life', was 'that is to say, a handicraft'.[19]

Work, though, can never be a supreme value in the Jewish tradition, since there are inbuilt limits to its practice. One day in seven was set aside to rest; and the Sabbath cannot be construed as a day of leisure either, in the modern sense of the word. Essentially it was a day of establishing alternative values, and *par excellence* it was the day of continuing education for the community, through the public teaching of Torah.

Since Torah study was a primary religious act, and could not be encompassed in a lifetime, it gave rise to a certain measure of value conflict. Most shared the view of the second century teacher, Rabbi Ishmael, that one should simply strike a balance between work and study; but his contemporary, Rabbi Shimon bar Yochai, took the view that 'If a man ploughs at ploughing time and reaps at reaping time . . . what is to become of his Torah?' Evidently he felt that any time spent on work represented an unacceptable dereliction of duty. This was the kind of argument that was resolved simply enough by historical experience. Two centuries later, Abaye comments: Many tried the way of R. Ishmael and succeeded. Some tried the way of R. Shimon and did not succeed.[20]

Conflict of values: 'rights' of employees not protected because such protection would interfere with their higher right to offer their services as they choose

There is a large body of Jewish law about relations between employer and employee. But here again, we notice the way in which the transition between value and law is not a simple one. For instance, the Bible contains legislation about slavery. It is apparent that these laws are all in one direction: protection of the rights of the slave, against both abuse and a loss of his own sense of freedom. They are, or were certainly understood to be, moves in the direction of its abolition; and slavery had already ceased to be a live institution during the Second Commonwealth.

One of the provisions of that law, to be found in Leviticus, is 'Thou shalt not rule over him with rigour' (Leviticus 25:43). The law, both in context and terminology, is a specific reminder of the experience of the Israelites as slaves in Egypt, where 'all their bondage wherein they made them serve was with rigour' (Exodus 1:14). The interpretation of the early sages is an interesting one, in that they understood rigour to mean, 'that which breaks the spirit', and so read the law as relating to what we might now call job satisfaction. Two things were prohibited under this rubric: asking a slave to do something which the master did not need, but which he demanded merely as an assertion of his authority; and asking a slave to do something which has no specific end-point – the example they gave was 'Hoe under this vine until I return'.[21]

We would naturally expect that such sensitive concern for the psychology of the worker would be transferred in at least equal measure to an employee. In fact, though, a clear distinction was made: One might not make rigorous demands of a slave; but one may of a hired employee.[22] The reason is obvious enough. In the case of the slave, the law was designed to place severe limits on the rights of the master over the person of the slave. In the case of a free labourer, his relationship to an employer is grounded in freely contracted mutual agreement. And since at any stage the labourer could retract his services, no protection was necessary. On the contrary, it would serve as a constraint on his right to offer his services as he chose.

Another case: a Biblical *right to end contract – not to strike*

The right of the labourer to retract is another case in point. The ruling that 'an employee may retract even in the middle of the day',[23] a third century provision, was based on a careful thinking-through of the verse, 'For to Me the children of Israel are servants: they are My servants whom I brought out of the land of Egypt'.[24] To be a servant of God precluded being the servant of anyone else, so that dependence and slavery were fundamentally at odds with the lesson of the Exodus. This meant that no-one can acquire ownership in a human being; no-one could bind himself contractually to an employer in such a way as to preclude the possibility of his opting out at any stage, should he so choose.

This looks like a very early anticipation of the right to strike. But again, it is not so. The right of an employee to retract meant that he could terminate his contract. A strike has precisely opposite aims, to preserve a contract but to change its terms.[25] In fact, the right of labour to organise itself into unions was recognised from the earliest times in Jewish law.[26] And in recent centuries the question of the right to strike arose and was subjected to deliberation. But no-one who considered the question felt that there was any guidance to be gained from the Biblical verse, or from the law of retraction. The similarity disappeared as soon as the two cases were analysed.[27]

The rabbinic definition of poverty: charity to those beneath subsistence level and the relatively poor – not relative to others but their own previous condition

Let me now consider the question of definition as it was approached by the rabbis. What *is* poverty? Well, it depended. Were we talking about value or about law? Here, for instance, is a conversation between four second-century rabbis.

'Who is wealthy? He who has pleasure in his wealth: this is the view of R. Meir. R. Tarfon said: He who possesses a hundred vineyards, a hundred fields, and a hundred servants working in them. R. Akiva said: He who has a wife who is comely in good deeds. R. Jose said: He who has a toilet near his table.' [28]

This was the kind of table-talk in which the rabbis delighted, coming at a subject from all angles, and perhaps not too seriously. R. Meir gives a philosophical answer: wealth is a state of mind, rejoicing in what you have, whether it is much or little. R. Tarfon won't have any of it: wealth is wealth, and let's not evade the issue. R. Akiva tells us frankly that someone who has a good wife is wealthy whatever else he lacks. And R. Jose replies in the spirit of 'If I were a wealthy man'. If only I didn't have to go so far to the toilet, that would be riches indeed.

But this sort of brainstorming definition is clearly distinguished from the careful parameters of practical policy-making. There was, already at the time, a system of organised communal charity collection and distribution, and one needed to know who was poor in such a way as to be entitled to support. Naturally one turned to the Bible for clarification.

The proof text here was the verse: "Thou shalt open thy hand wide to him, and shall surely lend him sufficient for his need, in that which he lacks" (Deuteronomy 15:8). The reference was to a loan, but the logic applied equally to a gift. What then was meant by the two phrases, 'sufficient for his need' and 'that which he lacks?' Here is the ancient unpacking of the verse:

' *"Sufficient for his need"* means, you are commanded to maintain him, but you are not commanded to make him rich. *"That which he lacks"* means even a horse to ride on and a slave to run before him. It is told of Hillel the elder that he bought for a certain poor man of good family a horse to ride on and a slave to run before him. On one occasion he could not find a slave to run before him, so he himself ran before him for three miles.' [29]

There are therefore two elements in the rabbinic definition of poverty: first, an absolute subsistence level, covered by the phrase 'sufficient for his need'. This included food, housing, basic furniture, and if necessary, funds to pay for a wedding.[30] The second, dictated by the phrase, 'that which *he* lacks', introduces the notion of relative poverty, but in a restricted sense – relative not to others, but to his own previous condition, that to which he had become accustomed. This accords with the rabbis' insistence that poverty – in the sense in which the Bible was concerned with it – had psychological as well as physical reference.

Clearly one needed further clarification of what constituted being accustomed. The story of Hillel referred to a 'poor man of good family,' implying that he had been accustomed to a certain lifestyle from birth. Was the law restricted to such cases? Most thought not.[31] But in practical terms a more fundamental question needed to be answered. What was the purpose of the provision? Was it that the loss of what one was used to constituted genuine *need*; or was it rather that it amounted to a *public humiliation* to be seen to be descending the social ladder? It made a difference. Maimonides, for instance, rules that someone who has lost his income but still possesses wealth, need not sell the family Gauguin, and may apply for support, so long as he does so from private benefactors; but he may not apply to the community funds in such a case.[32] The logic seems to be that humiliation is the decisive factor. Public support cannot prevent this, by its very publicity, and is therefore restricted to providing subsistence needs. Not everyone agreed. In one area, however, there was a means test: the agricultural gifts to the poor specified in the Bible were restricted to those who owned less than 200 *zuz*.[33] Here, it seems, scarce resources forced the rabbis into preferring a distribution amongst those in greatest need.

Preserving the self-respect of the poor

The conception of charity in Judaism is distinctive. Although I have used the word, the Hebrew term used by both the Bible and the rabbis – *tzedakah* – belongs to the notion of justice rather than benevolence; and reflects the idea that since all property ultimately belongs to God, it is a sense of equity rather than of generosity that commands giving to others. The giving of charity could therefore be coerced by communal sanction and was formally organised on a community basis. From the earliest rabbinic times there were such institutions as the *tamhui*, which distributed food daily to whoever applied; the *kuppah*, or community chest, which distributed money weekly to the poor of the city, together with specific funds for clothing, raising dowries for poor brides, and providing burial expenses for the poor.[34] Clearly, though, the distribution of charity in certain cases – such as applying the rule of making good a person's previous living standards – called for fine human judgement. Decisions were made by a panel of three scholars, and the responsibility that rested with them was formidable. R. Jose said, and we can sense what he felt, 'May my share of responsibility be among the collectors of the charity fund, and not among its distributors'.[35]

Poverty was therefore given a definition which went beyond a lack of basic necessities, and which called for case-by-case investigation. The entire legislation was governed by fastidious regard for the feelings of the recipient of aid, for his preservation of self-respect. Clearly, though, the definition was itself cause and effect of a particular social structure, community-based and administered by delegates of the community. One can see the sensitive transition from the Biblical to a more trade and money-based economy. But how one would secure these same situational values within a modern political structure is altogether less clear.

Redistribution not the only solution: Judaism as religious democracy, same Law and Sabbath for all

But if we were to ask what a religious tradition can contribute to the problem of poverty, one would have to recognise that direct confrontation is only part of the answer. Judaism, for example, is an all-embracing culture; and so it has many more resources at its disposal than, say, the politician or economist.

Fundamental to the rabbis' conception of Judaism, for instance, was the idea that its practice should never impoverish or be beyond the reach of the poor. It should be a classless religion. This was not a theoretical issue. Judaism did make economic demands, and it is important that these should not be divisive. Hence, for instance, the institutions that burials should be as simple as possible;[36] and that on the special festive days when the girls of Jerusalem danced before the boys and wives were chosen, they would wear borrowed clothes 'so as not to put to shame those who did not have'.[37]

Let me give an example here of the kind of situation that arose from time to time, and of a characteristic response to it. The festival of Passover involves a major upheaval in the running of a household. No leavened bread, nor anything containing a leavened ingredient, may be eaten or even kept in the home. Different utensils must be used for cooking and eating. The third century Babylonian community followed the rulings of their great leader, Rav. But one of his rulings had severe implications. Any earthenware pot that had been used for cooking during the year, and so had absorbed some leaven, must not merely be put away during Passover, but actually broken and disposed of. In effect this meant that families had to buy complete new sets of cooking equipment each year. This created a concentrated seasonal demand for earthenware pots; and in the free market, traders were quick to take advantage and raise their prices. It was the kind of situation of exploitation familiar to us from the prophetic literature.

Rav's contemporary and friend, Samuel, responded immediately. He gathered the merchants together and informed them that unless they held their prices steady, he would pronounce in accordance with the more lenient tradition which held that old pots need not be broken, simply stored away. It worked.[38]

Many, perhaps most, of the innovations of the rabbis had a similar motive. They were guardians of the tradition, but they were also guardians of the unity of the people; and they were aware that nothing could be more destructive of that unity than a Judaism that was identified with a particular economic class.

The most potent of all religious institutions were those which occupied the realm of not working. The first was the Sabbath, and no-one will disagree with Ahad Ha'am's famous judgement that 'More than the Jews kept the Sabbath, the Sabbath kept the Jews'. It created an alternative world in which differentiations based on work, income, or expenditure had no room in which to operate. At all times, even in those many Jewish communities that lived in grinding poverty, one saved to dress and eat well on the seventh day. It was impossible, on the Sabbath, to internalise the pariah image that the outside world seemed to impose. The Sabbath created the coherence of the religious community. It also, perhaps, was decisive in preserving the attitudes which made the Jews so adaptable and socially mobile. It was, if you like, the insertion into the world of an alternative identity, in which the white tablecloth, the silver candlesticks, the leisurely meals, the assembled family, enacted rather than symbolised a freedom from the existing economic and social order.

This, it seems to me, is an important part of the place of religion within the system. Poverty restricts choice, as indeed does wealth: 'the more property, the more anxiety',[39] as Hillel used to say. But how *significant* the choices are that a given economic standing puts beyond one's reach is, by and large, culturally determined; and a religion succeeds or fails to the extent that it shapes that culture. Naturally Judaism could not rest content without its elaborate programme to alleviate poverty. But it was also well aware that, in most times and places, simple redistribution would not solve every problem.

The Talmud, for example, recreates the following imaginary dialogue between King David and his counsellors:

'At dawn, the wise men of Israel came to him and said: Our lord, the king, your people Israel need sustenance. He said: Let them support one another. They replied: A handful cannot satisfy a lion, and you cannot fill a pit by the earth which you dig from it.'[40]

David proposed redistribution; his sages told him that the cake was not big enough, however it was sliced.

It followed that a major religious task was to maximise the range of significant choices available to a person regardless of income. Nor would Judaism ever have contemplated the obvious strategy of deriding this world for the pleasures of the next. The answer had to be substantive. On the Sabbath the poor man was wealthy, and not in any metaphorical sense. And since the sages had, as it were, dignified wealth by institutionalising charity, they also laid it down as a rule that even the person who subsists through charity must give charity, and be given enough to give it.[41] Above all, they created a culture of study and education, which dominated their lives and to which access was universal and lifelong. They were aware of its democratising implications. They said: Israel had three crowns. The crown of kingship belongs to David and his sons. The crown of priesthood belongs to Aaron and his sons. The crown of Torah, which transcends them all, lies before you. Let whoever wishes, come and take possession of it.[42]

This, then, was the second great alternative world. Again, let me illustrate what I mean with a fragment of a talmudic narrative. Shortly after the destruction of the second Temple, there was some opposition to the attempt by Rabban Gamliel, head of the Jewish community, to systematise the religious tradition and restrict the freedom of argument and opposing rulings. He was particularly harsh on his deputy, R. Joshua, when the two disagreed on points of law. The scholars of the academy responded by deposing Gamliel; and in due course he visited R. Joshua to apologise.

The description is graphic. Evidently stuck for a way of opening the conversation, he looked around R. Joshua's house, noticed that the walls were black, and said: 'Judging the walls, I can see that you must be a blacksmith.' R. Joshua replied: 'Alas for the generation of which you are the leader, seeing that you know nothing of the troubles of the scholars and how they have to make a living.' [43]

The story fascinates me, because it is apparent that R. Gamliel and R. Joshua were able to work and debate together day by day in the academy, the one as its head, the other as his deputy, without the wealthy R. Gamliel being aware that Joshua was a poor man. To this day, this rings true as a description of the spirit of the learning community.

Its second implication, no less important, is that ignorance of the real economic difficulties of a people disqualifies a sage from being a leader.

Proper consideration of social issues: impartiality, expertise in facts and values, and tradition, the need to make decisions

Which brings me to my last point: the place of expertise; and the related question of the status and domain of religious judgement.

The ubiquity of Jewish law, its tendency to see each human activity as a potential sanctification, meant that sages required extensive expertise in the realities to which Torah was applied.[44] To this day, leading rabbinic authorities will be asked questions from medical ethics to a mistake in a Torah scroll; from business practice to the determination of the time of nightfall. Nor, given the situational character of much of Jewish law, can these questions be divorced from the specific human context in which they are asked.

This meant, in practice, that the sage had to be a man of the people; and there was always fierce opposition to the professionalisation of the rabbinate. The sage had to earn his living like anyone else; as sage he was unpaid. Many of the early rabbis were manual workers;[45] the medieval authorities were traders, shopkeepers, and often doctors. If they were often poor men, there was also a tradition that the wealthy would try to marry their daughters to scholars. So if the rabbi himself did not know the problems of large business or high finance, his wife or father-in-law did.

To a large measure this was the source of rabbinic authority. Rabbinic Judaism came into being with the collapse of all formal hierarchies of religion: there was no Temple, no active priesthood, the supreme court had little power and was in decline. The sage had the authority only of his personal Torah learning and his practical wisdom; and the situation is essentially unchanged today, despite the apparent and alien intrusions of, say, the Chief Rabbinate in Israel. Informed and informal consent picks out the leading sages of any generation; and those whose judgement carries weight are, more often than not, men with no formal standing in the community.

One incidental consequence is that there has never been, and could not be conceived, an identification of Judaism with any particular political stance. Another is that it was recognised from the earliest stage that there were vital religious questions which could only be answered on the basis of secular expertise. For example, the most sacred institutions like the Sabbath, the Passover and the Day of Atonement, must be set aside for the saving of life. But the diagnosis of a dangerous condition could only be given by a doctor.[46] This was the archetypal situation in which religious and secular experts had to work hand in hand to prescribe a course of conduct. The same is true about the most crucial political question, namely war. Jewish law allows the present State of Israel to wage war only on essential defensive grounds. But a rabbi has no special expertise in military intelligence and strategy. He is bound, on religious grounds, to yield to the judgement of experts, regardless of their religious standing, and more poignantly – always aware that they may just be completely wrong. It is an axiom of Judaism that 'a judge must rule on the basis of the available evidence'.[47] There is neither religious nor secular infallibility; but decisions must nonetheless be made.

The point at which Jewish law takes off, on any issue to which there is not already an agreed ruling, is *the question*.

Someone – a doctor, perhaps, or a social worker, or a businessman – will turn to a rabbi or a scholar in whose judgement he has faith, and formulate a question. In the case, say, of an issue in genetic engineering or business procedure, the onus is clearly on the questioner to supply the relevant facts in his presentation of the problem. He will be aware that, even though the rabbi will often consult independent experts, he is bound to present the issues as objectively as possible; for a slanted question will not elicit a balanced answer; and if the answer is imbalanced, it will not carry weight with the Jewish community. No rabbi would consciously allow himself to be used for the advocacy of a sectional interest or a particular ideological stance.

His role, once the question has been posed, is to analyse it into its component parts and to bring to bear all the resources of two thousand years of recorded debate. Where does this problem have an analogue in the past? What views were then proposed? How did tradition decide between them? Is the problem really comparable, or have changed circumstances altered the moral issue? The authority of the answer lies only in its cogency, and in the fact that it is a response to a question: to someone who wanted to know. The Jewish encounter with the policy issues of an age, in short, occurs when an expert in the facts seeks the guidance of an expert in the values; and there is nothing to compel that seeking, short of a continued demonstration that Judaism is in touch with life.

And impartiality means no bias to the poor. The rabbinic tradition is for all and is not partisan

Space has allowed me only this most sketchy of surveys. Of poverty at least, Judaism has an *embarras de richesse*. The single point I might have made at the beginning but have chosen to leave to the end is that the one thing Judaism rules out *ab initio*, by specific Biblical command, is a bias to the poor. Precisely because its whole moral code is orientated towards compassion, the Bible uniquely found it necessary to command, 'You shall not favour a poor man in his cause' (Exodus 23:3; see Leviticus 19:15). Compassion, the substrate of judgement, must not distort judgement. The preservation of impartiality, the balance of claims, the reciprocity of rights and obligations, the interdependence of apparently opposed interests, are values essential to the Jewish procedure. These are the characteristics that are often summed up by saying that Judaism is a religion of law. I prefer to describe it as the rule that moral passion must yield to moral rationality if it is to achieve its ends.

Judaism has not given specific answers to the economic and social problems of our time: would that it had. What I have tried to show is the way in which a religion can be the effective context of debate, by cultivating open argument and valuing it as such, by seeing the argument itself as the religious experience, rather than the passion or the persuasion. I have described a particular model of the interaction between secular expertise and religious judgement, and the way in which that judgement might have authority. We have seen the range of ways in which a religion might attempt to alleviate poverty; not least of which was the enriching of its cultural possibilities. And I hope we have seen some of the dangers of extrapolating from Biblical sources to changed economic circumstance.

The rabbis saw themselves as heirs to the prophets; but in fact they were more successful than the prophets, in capturing the imagination of all classes of society. This turned them from an opposition party into a kind of informal government, with all that entailed in terms of responsibility, impartiality, and consideration of consequences. The prophetic tone of voice is essentially the voice from the sidelines. If rabbinic Judaism has anything to say across its borders, it lies in how the voice of religion might be authoritative without being authoritarian, unifying without ceasing to be pluralist, and rational without lacking passion.

NOTES

* In this essay, published originally in 1985 by the Social Affairs Unit, I was asked to respond to recent Christian analyses of poverty and economic ethics. It was thus initially addressed to a Christian audience: hence the comparative tone throughout, especially in paragraph 2. It is reprinted here as it originally appeared, with some minor amendments.

1. Nicomachean Ethics, I:5.

2. Babylonian Talmud, *Nedarim* 7b.
3. B.T. *Baba Batra* 116a.
4. *Exodus Rabbah* 31:14.
5. Mishna, *Avot* 3:21.
6. Jerusalem Talmud, *Kiddushin* 4:12.
7. J.T. *Berakhot* 9:2.
8. Maimonides, *Hilkhot Asakhim va-Haramin* 8:13. Maimonides continues: 'For he thereby destroys his own property and becomes dependent on others: compassion is not to be shown toward him.'
9. B.T. *Ketubot* 50a. See also *Arakhin* 28a; J.T. *Peah* 1:1.
10. B.T. *Ta'anit* 24a; Maimonides, *Hilkhot Mattenot Ani'im* 7:11.
11. Maimonides, *Hilkhot Mattenot Ani'im* 10:7-14.
12. B.T. *Eruvin* 63b; *Baba Metzia* 46b.
13. Mishna, *Shevi'it* 10:3.
14. See B.T. *Yoma* 35b.
15. The phrase occurs in B.T. *Shabbat* 10a. Compare *Avot de Rabbi Nathan* XI: 'The Holy One, blessed be He, did not cause his Presence to alight upon Israel until they had done work, as it is said, Let them make Me a sanctuary that I may dwell among them' (Exodus 25:8). The whole passage is an amplification of Shemayah's pointed saying: 'Love work, hate lordship, and seek no intimacy with the ruling power' (M. *Avot* 1:10), and contains many aphorisms on the religious value of work.
16. B.T. *Nedarim* 49b.
17. Mishna, *Avot* 2:2.
18. B.T. *Kiddushin* 29b.
19. J.T. *Peah* 15c.
20. B.T. *Berakhot* 35b.
21. Sifra to Levictus 25:43; Maimonides, *Hilkhot Avadim* 1:6.
22. Sifra, ibid.; Maimonides, *Hilkhot Avadim* 1:7.
23. B.T. *Baba Kamma* 116b.
24. Leviticus 25:55.
25. See S. Warhaftig, *Jewish Labour Law* (Hebrew), Tel Aviv 1969, vol. 2, pp. 974-984.
26. Tosefta, *Baba Metzia* 11:23; B.T. *Baba Batra* 8b.
27. See Warhaftig, loc. cit. for a review of sources.
28. B.T. *Shabbat* 25b.
29. B.T. *Ketubot* 67b.
30. Maimonides, *Hilkhot Mattenot Ani'im* 7:3.
31. For a survey, see N. Bar Ilan, 'The needy person's right to charity' (Hebrew), in *Techumin*, vol. 2 (1981), pp. 459, 465.
32. *Hilkhot Mattenot Ani'im* 9:14.
33. Mishna, *Peah* 8:8; Maimonides, *Hilkhot Mattenot Ani'im* 9:13.
34. The structure is set out in Maimonides, *Hilkhot Mattenot Ani'im*, ch. 9. For a review of social practice, see Isidore Epstein, *Social Legislation in the Talmud*, London (undated), and Leo Jung, *Human Relations in Jewish Law*, New York, 1967, ch 2.
35. B.T. *Shabbat* 118b.
36. B.T. *Moed Katan* 27b; Maimonides, *Hilkhot Avel* 4:1.

37. Mishna, *Ta'anit* 4:8.
38. B.T. *Pesachim* 30a. For a similar strategy in Temple times, see Mishna, *Keritot* 1:7. For more recent examples, see Leo Jung, op. cit. pp. 106, 113.
39. Mishna, *Avot* 2:8.
40. B.T. *Berakhot* 3b; see comments of Tosafot ad loc.
41. B.T. *Gittin* 7b; Maimonides, *Hilkhot Mattenot Ani'im* 7:5.
42. Maimonides, *Hilkhot Talmud Torah* 3:1, based on M. *Avot* 4:12; Sifrei, *Korach* 119, B.T. *Yoma* 72b.
43. B.T. *Berakhot* 28a; compare J.T. *Berakhot* 4:1.
44. A judge was required to have expertise not only in Jewish law, but in the other disciplines which might be involved in cases on which he had to pass judgement – medicine, astronomy and so on: Maimonides, *Hilkhot Sanhedrin* 2:1.
45. Thus, Hillel was a wood-chopper (B.T. *Yoma* 35b in the text available to Maimonides), R. Huna a water-drawer (*Ketubot* 105a), R. Joshua a charcoal-burner (Berkahot 28a), R. Jose b. Halafta a leather-worker (*Shabbat* 49b), and so on. For Maimonides, earning an independent living by means of a trade was essential to being a Torah authority. See his passionate onslaught against a professional rabbinate supported by communal funds: Commentary to the Mishna, *Avot* 4:7; *Hilkhot Talmud Torah* 3:10, 11. In a letter to his disciple, Joseph ibn Aknin, Maimonides advises him that 'it is far better for you to earn a single drachma as a weaver, tailor or carpenter' than to accept payment for being a rabbi or religious teacher.
46. See Mishna, *Yoma* 8:5, 6; B.T. *Yoma* 83a. A review of the detailed provisions of the law is given in Sir I. Jakobovits, *Jewish Medical Ethics*, Bloch, New York, 1975, ch. 4.
47. B.T. *Baba Batra* 131a; *Sanhedrin* 6b.

11
The Word 'Now'
Reflections on the Psychology of Teshuva

With stunning insight, the sages found truth in a single word.

In a famous verse, Moses asks: "Now O Israel, what does God your Lord ask of you?" The sages added a cryptic comment: "The word 'now' means nothing other than *teshuva*." [1]

Normally we have some clue, in the verse itself or the semantics of the word, as to the logic of the interpretation. Here, though, the evidence is slim. True, the verse could be construed as a call to repentance: it follows Moses' reminder of the golden calf, Divine forgiveness, and the second set of tablets – given on Yom Kippur, the great symbol of reconciliation. But where is the connection between the word 'now' and *teshuva*? What have they to do with one another?

I found illumination from a most unusual source. My father once told me how he gave up smoking, the habit of a lifetime. He said: there is only one way. You take your cigarettes and your pipe and you throw them in the dustbin. You have to decide here and now to make the irrevocable gesture.

It's an experience I have since heard recounted many times by many people. They say, in effect, that to break any longstanding habit or dependency, there has to be a decisive 'Now'. Tomorrow is the enemy of *teshuva*.

Of all *mitzvot*, indeed of all ideas in Judaism, *teshuva* brings us most unremittingly to the bedrock psychological truth: that we are precisely what at any given moment we will ourselves to be. No historian whose concern is to explain the past, no scientist whose business is to predict the future, can deliver this particular truth, which belongs to the radical present. *Teshuva* insists that we can liberate ourselves from our past, defy predictions of our future, by a single act of turning . . . as long as we do it now.

A history of *teshuva* would contain some momentous 'now's. The moment when Akiva[2] decided to give up his life as a herdsman in favour of study, perhaps, or when Shimon ben Lakish[3] turned his back on a career as a gladiator. We know little of the inner and outer realities of these moments, but we do know that both Akiva and Resh Lakish were among the most lyrical spokesmen of the power of *teshuva*,[4] and it is hard to believe that they were not speaking from deep personal experience.

Wherever we are, we can change. This is surely *hakatuv hashlishi*, the third and reconciling verse between the two clashing axioms of Judaism: that God has no image, and that man is made in the image of God. The conclusion, as inevitable as it is powerful, is that man, too, has no image. Unlike all else in creation, he has no pregiven essence, no fated and ordained character. He is only what he chooses to be; and if he so chooses, he can change.

The Freedom to be like Moses

I sometimes wonder whether this was not the very point underlying another quite bewildering comment that the sages made in connection with the same verse: "Now O Israel, what does God your Lord ask of you *but to fear God your Lord* . . .?"

The Talmud records the following question and answer: "Is, then, the fear of God a small thing? Indeed yes: for Moses it was a small thing." [5]

What a powerful question. Moses speaks as if he were making an almost trivial demand. 'What does God ask of you but . . .?' Yet what he asks, the fear of heaven, is the greatest, not the least, of spiritual achievements.

And what a disconcerting reply. Perhaps for Moses, greatest of all men, it was a small thing. But this is not an answer at all, rather a restatement of the problem. If Moses was speaking not to himself but *to us*, how could he imply that what came easily to him might come equally easy to anyone?

However, in the same talmudic passage and from the same verse the sages derived one of their most fundamental propositions. "R. Hanina said: Everything is in the hands of heaven except the fear of heaven, as it is said, 'What does God your Lord ask of you but to fear God your Lord?' " [6]

Meaning: there is one respect in which each of us has precisely the same strength as Moses. Namely, *the strength to choose*. There is no hand of heaven – no physiological, genetic, psychological or Providential compulsion – that forces us to act one way rather than another. The fear of heaven is not in the hands of heaven; therefore the fear of heaven is as live an option to us as it was to Moses. Here is indeed a thing which, if it is small for Moses is small for us.[7]

Or as Maimonides writes in *Hilkhot Teshuva*: "Do not believe what the fools among the nations and the senseless of Israel say: that the Holy One, blessed be He, decrees whether a person will be righteous or wicked at the moment of his creation. It is not so. *Every person may become righteous like Moses our teacher*, or wicked like Jeroboam."[8]

Resolution Precedes Remorse

A small thing, yet a large challenge to our imagination.

No-one who has ever attempted to change others can have failed to sense the power of resistance which is set against *teshuva*. 'I'm too old'. 'I'm not ready yet'. 'You are asking too much'. And the rabbi who is driven to despair does well to remember the words of R. Chayyim of Zans: "In my youth, I thought I would convert the whole world to God. I did not succeed. Instead I discovered that it would be enough to convert the people who lived in my town. I did not succeed. Instead I discovered that it would be enough to convert my family; but I did not succeed. Then I discovered that it would be enough to convert myself. I am still trying."

One half of *teshuva*, as defined by Maimonides, is always easy; the other half painfully difficult. The easy half is to regret the past. The difficult half is genuinely to resolve to act differently in future. On Yom Kippur, the *viddui* comes fluently to our lips: *ashamnu, bagadnu,* with every letter of the aleph-bet we have sinned. But our resolutions are hesitant. There is no note, in the liturgy for Yom Kippur, of confidence in our ability to change.

There is therefore something striking in the way Maimonides constructs his definition of *teshuva*: "What is *teshuva*? It is this: that the sinner abandons his sin, removes it from his thoughts and resolves in his heart never to repeat it . . . Also he should regret the past, as it is said: 'After I returned, I regretted'."[9] The order is precise: first the resolution, and only then the remorse.[10] For without a determination to change, regretting the past is mere self-pity; not yet a part of *teshuva*.

Believing That We Cannot Change

Commentators have often been puzzled by the structure of Maimonides' Laws of *Teshuva*. In the opening four chapters he outlines the nature and procedures of repentance. In chapter seven he takes up his theme where he left it at the end of chapter four. In between, striking the eye as an apparent digression, are two chapters on freewill. Maimonides calls freewill "a cardinal principle, the pillar of Torah and the commandments".[11] Yet many have asked: why expound it here, at this seemingly random point?

Brilliant speculations have been offered.[12] There might, though, be a more modest and straightforward solution.

In the fourth chapter Maimonides outlines 'twenty-four things which impede *teshuva*'.[13] In some cases it is a matter of the gravity of the sin, in others because the sin is such as to drive a person from the environment of *teshuva*. Some are sins between man and man where it is difficult to make amends; others are offences which can seem too slight to merit repentance; and yet others are wrongs which are habit-forming.

There is a sequence here, from the objective to the subjective – from impediments which lie in the nature of the offence to those which lie in its effects on the mind. *Teshuva* can sometimes be formidably difficult. In two different ways. It can be difficult to put things right. Or it can be difficult to *summon the will* to put things right. Psychological barriers are no less real for being subjective.

Maimonides intended his two chapters on freewill to stand as a direct continuation of chapter four. There he considered the *specific* barriers to *teshuva*. Now he turns to the systematic and *general* barrier: the belief that, after all, we cannot change. We are what we were destined to be. We cannot be otherwise.

This is, he says, not merely a belief held by 'fools of the nations' but also by 'most of the senseless folk of Israel'.[14] The belief takes different forms at different times. In

Maimonides' day it came from theology and astrology. Divine providence or the influence of the stars determined the kind of person we were. In our times it comes from the social and behavioural sciences: we are the products of environmental conditioning or genetic programming.

Why does this theory have such a perennial appeal? At all times, its intellectual force is less significant than its psychological appeal. It provides us with a retreat from responsibility; in Erich Fromm's phrase, an escape from freedom.

Against Excuses

The function of determinism in all its forms is to *provide us with excuses*. All excuses are ways of seeing ourselves, helpless in a mesh of forces that are beyond our control. Though we may bitterly regret what has happened in our life, the responsibility lay elsewhere. We say: we did what we could, but other people, or society, or force of circumstance, defeated us. The kind of talk, in other words, to be heard at all times from politicians. Politics is the art of making convincing excuses; because politics makes the mistake Chayyim of Zans warns us about – trying to change the world without changing the individuals who compose the social world. Judaism in its classic forms does not have much to say about politics: but it does regularly deliver the prophetic message that politics is secondary to morality which is dependant on a sense of responsibility which is predicated on a deep sense of human freedom.

All significant change in human behaviour takes place at the microcosmic, not the macrocosmic level. It belongs not to social forces or trends, but to the here-and-now of single individuals. This is the model *teshuva* places before us. And it is borne out by any survey of halakhic priorities.

The laws clustered under the heading of *darkhei shalom* (the ways of peace), for example, are not global, visionary, and political, but have to do with the tiniest fragments of human behaviour: whether a Cohen may forgo his right to be called up first to the Sefer Torah,[15] for instance, or whether while visiting the sick we should attend non-Jews as well as Jews.[16] Peace, at once the highest and most elusive of all Torah values, is to be pursued at the most seemingly trivial level, because this is the only level at which it *can* be pursued. Only in the here-and-now of single human interactions do changes take place that are more than short-lived or illusory. *Teshuva* in particular, and the halakhic system in general, are a discipline of shifting the focus of our attention from the large to the small, the macrocosm to the microcosm. It is here that we change; it is here that freewill belongs.

Maimonides asks a pointed question.[17] Long before the exile in Egypt, God told Abraham that his descendants would be strangers in a land not their own; there they would be enslaved and oppressed. How then, asks Maimonides, was it justice for the Egyptians to be punished for mistreating the Israelites, when they were in fact only fulfilling the Divine decree, acting out a plan that had already been determined, foreseen?

His answer is fundamental. There can be, he says, successful predictions of how large social groupings will behave. Determinism is indeed true at this macrocosmic level. Freedom is not an attribute of nations or masses, but of single individuals. "Each individual Egyptian who oppressed and maltreated the Israelites could have refrained had he so chosen. *For God did not make a decree concerning any specific individual, but only informed Abraham that his descendants would be subjected to servitude in a land not theirs.*" [18] It was predictable that the Egyptians *as a nation* would act as they eventually did. But it was not predictable of any *individual* Egyptian that he would conform to the pattern.

For those who wish to build a barrier against the challenge of freedom, excuses are therefore always to hand. It is always open to us to see ourselves as an insignificant prisoner of wider forces, a speck in the macrocosm which is not in fact free. *Teshuva*, by contrast, is a mental discipline in which we narrow down the focus of our attention until all that is present before us is the *individual* and the *present*, the 'I' and the 'now'.

The Elisha ben Abuya Complex

Maimonides had to confront freewill because, despite the fact that at some level we all acknowledge its existence, there is a constant temptation to deny it. That temptation begins the moment we confront our own failures. The good we do, we are willing to take credit for; but the bad we do is *not our fault*.[19] This denial of freewill – the protection we seek in the making of excuses – is the great and systematic barrier against *teshuva*.

If Freud had given a name to this mental process he might have called it the *Elisha ben Abuya complex*.

Elisha ben Abuya was, by all accounts, one of the outstanding minds of the Mishnaic age, a colleague of R. Akiva and the teacher, no less, of R. Meir. He became, though, a rebel against tradition: an apostate. There are conflicting traditions as to the cause of his apostasy.[20] But on one point the various narratives are clear, and indeed highly moving: R. Meir, his disciple, continued to be attached to this man his colleagues had shunned. Elisha was beyond the pale; so much so that frequently he is not referred to by name, but called instead *Acher*, 'the other one', the one who has forfeited his name. But Meir remained loyal to the man who had once been his master; sought out his company and still believed that he would, must, one day repent.

Against this background is set one of the most poignant scenes in the whole of the rabbinic literature.[21] It is Shabbat, and Elisha ben Abuya is publicly flouting the day by riding on a horse. Nevertheless, as the focus widens we see R. Meir walking assiduously behind him. Not, we are stunned to discover, to reprimand him but . . . "to learn Torah at his mouth".

Heretic teacher and faithful disciple pass along the road, and the narrative suddenly plunges into a quite new dimension of irony. Meir, the guardian of tradition, has become so immersed in the conversation that he has not noticed that they have passed beyond the outskirts of the town and are nearing the limits of the *techum*, the boundary beyond which one may not walk on Shabbat. Acher, the apostate, has seen this; and the following interchange takes place:

Acher: Meir, turn back. I have measured the distance we have walked by the paces of my horse, and we have reached the Shabbat limit.

Meir: You, too, turn back.

The invisible *techum*, the boundary beyond which one may not walk, has become an immediate symbol of the line between worlds, faith and heresy, Judaism and alienation.[22]

Elisha ben Abuya, momentarily more sensitive than his disciple to the fateful character of their journey, tells Meir that he must turn back. Meir, instantly seizing on the fact that his teacher has just disclosed that tradition and conscience have not yet deserted him, invites Elisha to turn back with him: to repent.

Elisha hears the double-entendre, and replies with a staggering confession of his personal tragedy:

Acher: Have I not already told you? I heard a voice from behind the veil[23] say: " 'Return ye backsliding children' – all except Acher."

Heaven has decreed. The gates of *teshuva* are open to everyone – except Elisha ben Abuya. I, says Elisha, cannot repent.

Are we meant to believe that Elisha is telling the truth, that in fact he *has* received the heavenly No? In a sense, the question is massively irrelevant. For even if he were telling a sort of truth, this is the kind of prophetic message one is duty-bound not to believe. Elsewhere the Talmud portrays an encounter between King Hezekiah and the prophet Isaiah. Isaiah tells the king that he is going to die and have no share in the world to come. Hezekiah asks the prophet to help him repent. Isaiah replies: 'The doom has already been decreed.' Hezekiah tells him: 'Son of Amoz, finish your prophecy and go. For I have this tradition from the house of my ancestor (David): Even if the sword is already sharpened and resting on your neck, do not stop praying.' [24] There are some counsels of despair that are not to be heeded, even if they come from a prophet at the behest of heaven.

Elisha ben Abuya and Inauthenticity

True or false, Elisha ben Abuya is saying what he wants to believe: that he is helpless, that he cannot turn for the gates have been locked against him. This is a classic paradox of wish fulfilment, a self-justifying prophecy.[25] If we believe that we cannot change, then we never will. We will be proved correct. *But it was not true.*

What gives the story its mythic power is that there is something of Elisha ben Abuya in all of us. We acknowledge that, in some abstract sense, people can change. The last decade and a half has given us ample examples, in what has already come to be known as the *Teshuva* Generation. Yeshivot in Israel – Or Sameach, Esh HaTorah, Har Zion – are full of individuals who have made more radical changes in lifestyle than any in recent Jewish history. Behind the beards are people who, not long before, were drop-outs, shut-outs or left-outs.[26] But that, for us, always turns out to be someone else: I am not like that. I cannot change. This is the Elisha ben Abuya complex: the voice which says that the gates are open, but not for us.

I remember my first private audience with R. Menahem Mendel Schneersohn, the Rebbe Sh'lita of Lubavitch. In the course of a long conversation I used the phrase – a classic in the vocabulary of excuse-making – "In the situation in which I find myself . . ." The Rebbe allowed the sentence to get no further. "No-one ever *finds* himself in a situation," he said. "He *places* himself in a situation. And if he placed himself in this situation, he can place himself in another situation."

It was a moment of penetrating truth: I was never again able to make that excuse to myself and believe it. The excuse is overwhelmingly tempting. We all make it on Kol Nidrei night. It is written into the liturgy, in the prayer *Kein anachnu beyadakha*: "Like clay in the hand of the potter, like stone in the hand of the mason, so are we in Your hand." [27] The theme of the prayer is simple. The wrong we do is forgivable, because the *yetser* (the inclination which prompts us to wrong) has been planted in us by God Himself and we should therefore be excused for the havoc it plays with our lives. "Remember the covenant; do not look upon the *yetser*", we pray. But this is a speech from counsel for the defence. It is the kind of thing we may say to God; not the kind of thing we can say to ourselves.[28]

The power to turn back is never taken away from us. In our own defence we may say prayers that suggest otherwise. Like Elisha ben Abuya we may even enlist a voice from heaven to support our claim that for us the way is closed. But it never is. These are barriers of the mind; barriers that Maimonides was relentless in tearing down. "Since we have freewill, and whatever wrong we do, we do of our own accord, it is fitting that we turn in *teshuva* ... since we have the power *now* to do so."[29]

The Ishmael Syndrome

The story of Elisha ben Abuya is of a man who felt that he could not liberate himself from his past. Equally powerful is the feeling we can have, in moments of despair, that we cannot liberate ourselves from our future.

A life may have been mapped out for us – by parental expectations, a particular kind of education, a choice of career that now seems irrevocable. Someone was always writing our future, anticipating a course that we would tread. This too is a barrier to *teshuva*, particularly when those expectations are too low.

The extreme case – and it concerns a drama central to the reading of the first day of Rosh Hashana – is *the Ishmael syndrome*.

I first came across a full sense of the Ishmael syndrome, and its relation to rabbinic remarks about the law of the 'stubborn and rebellious son' some years back, when a congregant asked me the following question. Throughout the month of Ellul and the days of *teshuva*, we read Psalm 27: *Le-David Hashem Ori Ve-yishi*. The Psalm contains a strange line: "Though my father and mother reject me, the Lord will receive me." [30] This line had always puzzled him. Which Jewish parent had ever rejected his or her own son? And why did we say this verse at this time of the year?

I reminded him of Ishmael. Born to Abram and Hagar, Ishmael was the fruit of Sarai's despair at being unable to have a child of her own. Even before he was born, he was caught in a web of antagonisms. Sarai drives Hagar, pregnant, away. An angel sends Hagar back, but not without telling her that conflict will be the ongoing fate of her son: "His hand will be against everyone, and everyone's hand against him".[31]

Ishmael is born. Abraham is attached to him. But his existence seems like a reproach to Sarah, and when she gives birth to Isaac she asks Abraham to send him away. Reluctantly, he does so.

The scene we read on Rosh Hashana unfolds. Hagar and her child are in the desert. Their water is gone. She hides Ishmael under a bush, too pained to watch him die. And at the penultimate point, "God heard the boy weeping. God's angel called Hagar from heaven and said to her: What is the matter, Hagar? Do not be afraid. God has heard the boy's voice *there where he is*. Lift the boy up and take him by the hand, for I will make him into a great nation." [32]

The voice breaks in on an almost unbearable moment. Ishmael has been rejected, in turn, by Sarah, then Abraham, then Hagar. He was born, as it were, to the wrong parents. He has no share in the destiny mapped out for the seed of Abraham. His tears on the point of death, though they are tears of a child, belong almost to *objective despair*. There is no place for him in the story.

The angel represents, therefore, a mercy as radical as it is total. "Though my father reject me, the Lord will receive me." *There is no rejection which includes God's rejection.*

The Wayward and Rebellious Son

The episode is no mere isolated story. It has halakhic reverberations. The Torah does not flinch from examining the circumstances in which the seemingly impossible might happen again: in which Jewish parents might deliberately reject a child. It describes a procedure to be followed in the case of a 'wayward and rebellious son', a delinquent whose parents confess, 'He does not listen to us' and whose prescribed penalty is death.[33]

What conceivable logic, what *justice*, could attach to this law? The child envisaged by the Torah is 'a glutton and a drunkard'. Clearly he has few saving graces. But is this sufficient to warrant the ultimate rejection of the death sentence? R. Jose ha-Gelili thought it was. "Did the Torah decree that the rebellious son be brought before the Bet Din and stoned merely because he ate a *tartemar* of meat and drank a *log* of Italian wine? Rather, *the Torah foresaw his ultimate destiny*. For in the end, after dissipating his father's wealth, he would still seek to satisfy his accustomed wants, but being unable to do so, he would go forth to the crossroads and rob. Therefore the Torah said: Let him die while yet innocent and let him not die guilty." [34]

The wayward and rebellious son is punished not as an *actual* but as a *potential* criminal. It is not what he is, but what he will become. If he begins like this, how will he end? "The Torah foresaw his ultimate destiny".

This is logic of a kind: the logic of pre-emption and deterrence. However, not all of the sages shared this view. R. Shimon bar Yochai firmly declared: There never was and never will be a 'wayward and rebellious son'.³⁵

What was at stake between R. Shimon and R. Jose? A Midrash records a conversation between God and the angels when the young Ishmael was crying at the point of death:

> The ministering angels rose to accuse [Ishmael]. They said, 'Lord of the Universe, here is someone who will one day slay Your children with thirst. Will you now provide him with a well?'
> He said to them, 'What is he *now*, righteous or wicked?'
> They said, 'Righteous'.
> He said to them, 'I judge man *only as he is at the moment.*' ³⁶

Ishmael was rescued *ba-asher hu sham*, 'there, where he is'. Meaning: for what he is *now*, an innocent child; not for what he might *predictably become*.

In this exchange, the angels argue the case of R. Jose ha-Gelili: Let the Torah foresee his ultimate destiny and act accordingly. God rejects the argument. Man is judged only for what he is, not for what he might become. So Ishmael is saved. And so too, though the law of the 'wayward and rebellious son' represents Divine justice, it always encounters the existential reality of Divine mercy. And on that basis R. Shimon bar Yochai rests his faith that the law never was or will be put into effect.

For at the heart of *teshuva* is the faith in human freewill which makes *no destiny inevitable*. The judge, and even the parent, may see in the delinquent child a potential criminal, and reject him accordingly. But this rejection – along with *all* rejection – discounts human freedom and the perpetual possibility of turning. Neither aggadah nor halakhah allow this rejection to stand: "If a completely wicked man says, 'Behold you are betrothed to me on condition that I am righteous,' she is betrothed: he may have contemplated *teshuva*." ³⁷

Neither the angels nor R. Jose ha-Gelili were guilty of some monumental heartlessness. We do judge people on the basis of certain expectations of character and continuity. We do condemn and reject them on the basis of a predicted future. It is simply that *teshuva* cuts across this entire frame of reference. No future is inevitable, for where we will be is dependent on *ba-asher hu sham*: the direction we *now* choose to face.

If Elisha ben Abuya was haunted by his past, Ishmael was haunted by his future, which seemed on all reasonable expectations to be non-existent. This too is a universal of certain moods of despair. "Though my father and mother reject me, the Lord will receive me." The verse answers a persistent nightmare with the most radical assurance. The 'now' of *teshuva* is stronger than any human rejection, any pre-scripted future.

Moments of Freedom

"Seek the Lord while He may be found; call on Him while He is near" – Rabbah b. Abbuha said, these are the ten days between Rosh Hashana and Yom Kippur.[38] Did Rabbah mean that there were some days when God was near and others when He was distant? Surely *"Teshuva* and prayer are *always* good"?[39]

The Ten Days of *teshuva* bring us close because they induce a mood that is difficult, perhaps impossible, to sustain thoughout the year. Our careers, relationships, lifestyles, and self-images are predicated upon a past and an anticipated future. This is what gives human character its stability.

The Jewish calendar gives us, though, the charmed moment – the *eit ratzon* – when the past no longer seems compelling and the mapped future no longer unavoidable. For ten days we inhabit the 'now' which means nothing other than *teshuva*. This is what gives human character its monumental freedom – this, and the Divine faith that we will use it to return.

NOTES

1. Deut. 10:12; *Bereishith Rabbah* 21:6. On the 'now'ness of *teshuva*, see Maimonides, Commentary to M. *Avot* 1:13; M.T. *Teshuva*, 2:1, 3:4, 7:2.
2. On Akiva's metamorphosis: B.T. *Ketubot* 62b, *Nedarim* 50a.
3. On Resh Lakish's early life: J.T. *Gittin* 4:9, *Terumot* 8:5; B.T. *Baba Metzia* 84a, *Gittin* 47a.
4. See M. *Yoma* 8:9 for Akiva's response to *teshuva* after the destruction of the Temple (beautifully commented upon in Soloveitchik, *Al Ha Teshuva*, pp. 19-20); B.T. *Chagigah* 15a. And see B.T. *Yoma* 86b: "Resh Lakish said: Great is *teshuva* for through it deliberate sins are accounted as merits". However in J.T. *Peah* 1:1 and *Bamidbar Rabbah* 10:1, this view is attributed to his mentor, R. Johanan.

5. B.T. *Berakhot* 33b, *Megillah* 25a.
6. B.T. *Berakhot* 33b, *Niddah* 16b.
7. See the interesting comment of R. Josiah Pinto (1565-1648) to *Ein Yaakov, Berakhot* ad loc. Different resolutions are given by Maharsha and *Anaf Yosef,* ad loc; R. Barukh Epstein, *Torah Temimah* to Deuteronomy, 10:12.
8. M.T. *Teshuva* 5:2.
9. M.T. *Teshuva* 2:2; the proof-text is from Jeremiah 31:18, part of the *haftarah* for the second day of Rosh Hashana.
10. Maimonides also includes the resolution to change in his formulation of the *viddui* in M.T. *Teshuva* 1:1; "How does one confess? By saying: I beseech you, O God, I have sinned, I have acted perversely, I have transgressed before you and have done such and such. I am contrite and ashamed of my deeds and I will never do this again." (On the difficulties raised against this formulation by R. Menahem Krakovski, *Avodat HaMelekh* ad loc, see the enlightening comments of R. Nahum Rabinovitch, *Yad Peshuta, Teshuva* 1:1, 2:8.)

    Note that Maimonides changes the order in the two rulings: in his text of the confession, remorse precedes resolution; in his definition of *teshuva,* resolution precedes remorse. In characteristic style, R. Soloveitchik maintains that Maimonides is talking about two different kinds of *teshuva*: in the first chapter he speaks of *emotional* repentance, which begins with remorse, a sense of mourning or sickness or spiritual malaise. In the second chapter he speaks of *intellectual* repentance, less spontaneous than the former, which begins with the knowledge that one has acted wrongly and only later proceeds to take on the emotional coloration of remorse (*Al HaTeshuva,* pp. 101-145).

    Alternatively and more simply one might note that Maimonides is always careful to distinguish repentance itself from confession, which is its verbal expression. Though he insists that they share the same elements, they do not necessarily do so in the same order: the sequence of a mental process is not necessarily the same as its articulation (cf, *Moreh Nevukhim* III, 21).

11. M.T. *Teshuva,* 5:3; see *Shemoneh Perakim,* ch. 8; *Moreh Nevukhim* III, 36.
12. R. Soloveitchik suggests, again, that Maimonides is speaking about two different kinds of *teshuva.* In the first four chapters he expounds the 'repentance of expiation' which concerns putting right particular wrongs, and which is triggered not by freedom but by a series of natural responses to sin. In the seventh chapter he treats of 'repentance of redemption' which involves the radical restructuring of the personality, and so presupposes human freedom in its deepest sense (*Al HaTeshuva,* pp. 191-235).

    This distinction is also brilliantly treated by R. Abraham Isaac Kook in *Orot HaTeshuva.* R. Kook, however, does not read it into Maimonides' text.

    R. Nahum Rabinovitch (*Yad Peshuta,* Teshuva, introduction)

suggests that Maimonides was confronting what seems to be a *contradiction* between *teshuva* and freewill. Freewill implies that a mental act of choice is a cause but never an effect of other causes. This presupposes that time is irreversible; for were time to be reversed, what is now a cause would become an effect. However, *teshuva* does change the past – it 'turns past sins into merits' and hence reverses the flow of time. Maimonides was therefore forced to confront and resolve the tension between the two ideas.

13. The list is taken from Alfassi (Rif, *Yoma* 982). See Maimonides, *Responsa* (Blau) p. 216.
14. M.T. *Teshuva* 5:2. In the *Mishne Torah*, Maimonides has no hesitation in using strong language to deride those who hold false philosophical positions: see *Avodah Zarah* 11:16, *Teshuva* 8:6. There is, however, no fallacy to which he devotes so much space to its refutation as the denial of freewill.
15. B.T. *Gittin* 59b. The sages instituted that on a Shabbat or festival, when the synagogue is crowded, a Cohen may not forego his right to be called first. For if he were to do so, there would be arguments, each person claiming that he should be called first; or that the Cohen had showed undue favouritism in allowing X to take his place instead of Y (Rashi ad loc; Ramban to M. *Gittin* 5:8).
16. B.T. *Gittin* 61a.
17. M.T. *Teshuva* 6:5. *Shemoneh Perakim*, ch. 8.
18. M.T. *Teshuva* 6:5.
19. Compare the dream in which R. Ashi interrogates King Manasseh. R. Ashi: 'If you were so wise, why did you serve idols?' Manasseh: 'If you had been there, you would have caught up the skirt of your cloak and run after me.' (B.T. *Sanhedrin* 102b). In another age Manasseh would have made a first-rate sociologist.
20. See B.T. *Kiddushin* 39b, *Chagigah* 14b, 15b, Y.T. *Chagigah* 2:1, *Kohelet Rabbah* 7:8.
21. B.T. *Chagigah* 15a. Compare Y.T. *Chagigah* 2:1, *Kohelet Rabbah* 7:8.
22. The figure of Elisha ben Abuya became a literary archetype for the tensions experienced by Haskalah Jews breaking away from Judaism. See Isaac Deutscher, *The Non-Jewish Jew*, and Milton Steinberg, *As a Driven Leaf*.
23. An expression for something overheard in heaven. See B.T. *Berakhot* 18b; *Yoma* 77a; *Baba Metzia* 59a.
24. B.T. *Berakhot* 10a.
25. Another touching example of heavenly vision as wish-fulfilment is given in B.T. *Berakhot* 28a. Rabban Gamliel had ruled that no student 'whose inside was not as his outside' should enter the Bet HaMidrash. When he was deposed as Nasi, the doors at the Bet HaMidrash were opened, and many hundreds of benches added, "Rabban Gamliel was distressed. He thought, 'Perhaps, God forbid, I have withheld Torah from Israel.' He was granted a dream, in which he saw white casks full of ashes (i.e. the new disciples were not, in fact, worthy of admission). But it was not so. He was only shown the dream to set his mind at rest."

Some of the sages recognized wish-fulfilment as a major component in dreams. "R. Jonathan said: A person is shown in a dream only what is suggested by his own thoughts" (B.T. *Berakhot* 55b).

In particular, this interpretation was given to the second Divine communication to Balaam, where he is told he may travel to Balak, having been told at first that he may not. "The Holy One, blessed be He, said to him: Villain, I do not desire the destruction of the wicked. But since you are bent on going to your own destruction, rise up and go." (*Bamidbar Rabbah* 20:11). The sages based on this incident the axiom: "Man is led down the path he wishes to pursue" (B.T. *Makkot* 10b).

26. For a detached account of the phenomenon, see Janet Aviad, *Return to Judaism: Religious Renewal in Israel*, University of Chicago Press, 1983.
27. Routledge *Machzor*, p. 39. The prayer is built on the phrase in Jeremiah 18:6. See also Isaiah 29:16, 45:9, 64:7; Job 10:1-9.
28. Note how Rashi treats the idea: "The fear of heaven is entrusted to man that he should be the one to prepare his heart for it, even though it lies within God's power to direct our hearts to Him, as is written, 'Behold, as the clay is in the potter's hand, so are you in My hand, O house of Israel'" (Rashi to *Megillah* 25a). The verse in Jeremiah does not therefore refer to actuality, but to possibility. Compare Maimonides, *Guide*, III, 32: "I do not say this because I believe that it is difficult for God to change the nature of every individual person. On the contrary, it is possible, and it is in His power, according to the principles taught in Scripture. But it has never been His will to do it, and it never will be."

The use of the idea, in seeking forgiveness, that we are 'clay in the potter's hand' belongs to the general logic of *melammed zechut*, or of finding a *pitchon peh*. See B.T. *Berakhot* 32a, *Sukkah*, 52b, where Jeremiah's verse is counted among the three texts without which Israel would have been left defenceless.
29. M.T. *Teshuva* 5:2.
30. Psalm 27:10.
31. Genesis 16:12.
32. Genesis 21:17-18.
33. Deuteronomy 21:18-21.
34. B.T. *Sanhedrin* 72a. See M. Sanhedrin, 8:5.
35. B.T. *Sanhedrin* 71a. However, R. Jonathan dissents: There was such a case, 'I saw him and sat on his grave'. See also Y.T. *Sanhedrin* 8:1, where any attempt to rationalise the command is rejected.
36. *Bereishith Rabbah* 53:14; see B.T. *Rosh Hashana* 16b; Y.T. *Rosh Hashana* 1:3.
37. B.T. *Kiddushin* 49b: M.T. *Ishut*, 8:5.
38. Isaiah 55:6; B.T. *Rosh Hashana* 18a.
39. M.T. *Teshuva* 2:6.

12
Alienation and Faith
INTRODUCTION

Of all the phenomena, spiritual and social, that characterize contemporary existence, centrality of significance belongs to alienation. The distance at which the individual stands from an easy, immediate and innocent identification with nation, society, his physical environment, and other people is a distinguishing mark of the age; and one which has its obvious spiritual reflection. For the relationship between man and God is not independent of that between man and the world. When man is prised off the surface of the world by his technical mastery of natural forces; when this succeeds to self-conciousness and reflection; and this gives way in turn to loneliness and despair of innocence regained, then, in parallel, we can trace a widening gap between man and God, from the Thou of revelation, to the He of the Halakhah, to the It of the philosophers, and to the hidden and unreachable God of the crisis theologians, who begin, in His absence, to turn to other consolations.

We must distinguish the ontological condition of loneliness, from the occasional mood of estrangement that comes on men even in the heart of a period of direct relationship. For ours is not the loneliness of the Psalmist: "I am[1] become a stranger to my brothers and alien to my mother's children," for he can still speak the Thou and expect an answer: "For the Lord hearkens to the needy." [2] Nor do we face the God of Isaiah: "In truth you are the God who hides Himself." [3] Intentional concealment is concealment for a purpose, part of the dialectic of revelation, a gesture understood by the lover of God. The Zohar speaks of this in the famous allegory of the maiden in the castle:

> The Torah lets out a word and emerges for a little from its concealment, and then hides herself again. But this she does only for those who understand and obey her.[4]

Our isolation, in contrast, belongs to our times, a time

when, it would seem, even the hiddenness is hidden. A story about the Baal Shem Tov explains the nature of double concealment. It is said that one day on a journey he met a child who was crying, and when he asked him why, the child said: I was playing with my friends, and I was to hide. But I have hidden myself so well that they cannot find me. This, it is said in the name of the Baal Shem Tov, is God's situation. To hide one's face is to seek to be found; but when one is so hidden that even the fact that one exists in hiding, is hidden,[5] then the separation is of a tragic order.

Together with a separation of man from God and the world goes an estrangement of man from himself. If, as Buber says, "All real living is meeting," then the absence of real meeting means the absence of life, in its wholeness and integrity. Identity is given in relation; a man whose meetings are distant encounters does not even possess himself.

This, of course, is a universal phenomenon and a central datum of our political and social philosophy, psychology and theology. The question I want to pose in this essay is: what place does it have in the inner history of Judaism? Must we as Jews participate in this movement of the soul? Is the attempt to stand aside from it an act of bad faith; a misinterpretation of our proper stance towards our location in time; or simply one which, however intentioned, is bound to fail? Do we have a refuge from alienation, or must a *Baal Teshuvah* expect to inhabit the same locus of existential doubt as he did before his return?

I

Obviously our answer to these questions will help to define Judaism's relevance to one of the secular crises of the day. But there is a preliminary point to be made about this constant demand made of Judaism that it be *relevant*. And that is that there are two modes of relevance: one might label them the empathetic or concessive, and the redemptive. One can relate to someone else's problems by entering into his situation, seeing it with his eyes; or by addressing his problems from one's own unchanged perspective. By the first method one wins the advantage of fully understanding his problem, at the risk of losing all that might have enabled one to solve it, even at the risk of being infected with the same problem oneself. Because one's situation is now the same as his, it now afflicts both. The second preserves a way of escape, the possibility of new and unforeseen perspectives, but at the cost of an unmediated distance between the one who asks and the one who answers. Both forms of relevance embody a paradox. But what must be remembered is that neither has an intrinsic priority over the other. And that the possibility that Judaism might stand diametrically opposed to a contemporary movement of consciousness does not, *eo ipso* entail its irrelevance to, or its independence from, its context in secular time.

II

Rabbi J. B. Soloveitchik, in his justly famous article, 'The Lonely Man of Faith',[7] belongs in effect if not in intention to the stance of empathetic relevance. For the Jew, as he conceives him, is (in the paradox of sacrifice) doomed to and at the same time blessed by an existence which is divided, alienated and lonely. This is not to say that for him, Jewish experience is a paradigm of the modern consciousness in its mood of existential despair. In at least three ways the experience he depicts differs from the secular condition:

(i) The alienation of the man of faith is not a consequence of a sense of meaninglessness, but rather the opposition of two sharply sensed and incompatible meanings. His self is not so much distanced from the world as divided within itself. A sense of two realities prevents each aspect of the Jew from making its home in any one of them.
(ii) Whereas the secular man's alienation is born of a sense of being left alone without a God, the alienation of the Jew is God-given, for it arises out of the tension between two fundamental Divine commands. Indeed to feel alienated is to have succeeded rather than to be forlorn; it is to have demonstrated the fidelity of one's response.
(iii) Lastly this religious alienation is not a phenomenon conditioned by time. Rabbi Soloveitchik finds its source in the two aspects of Adam; and it was a tension felt by

the prophets. Modern secularism may make it more acute, but it is part of the permanent condition of the Jew.

Rabbi Soloveitchik is not writing for the unbeliever, to provide him with a mode of re-entry into commitment; nor does he write detachedly, making comparisons. He speaks subjectively, seeking response. But here is a point in time where a defining mood of Judaism finds an echo in the prevalent mood of the secular world, a time when the two might share a vocabulary of the emotions.

I want, in contrast rather than disagreement, to describe an alternative phenomenology of the Jewish self, one which arises equally naturally from the traditional sources, and one in which the divided self occupies a different and impermanent place. There is a sense, strongly present in the account of Adam's creation, persisting through the Torah, explicit in the Psalms, and analysed often enough in Kabbalistic and Chassidic sources, that alienation and loneliness are defective states, the consequence of sin, and that the religious man of any age transcends divisions, subsumes contrasts into harmonious emotion, and exists in unmediated closeness to God, the world and other Jews. In short, I want to argue that Judaism stands to contemporary alienation in a redemptive rather than an empathetic relation.

III

Rabbi Soloveitchik's analysis is too well known to require more than a brief recapitulation here. It is that the two kinds of command given to Adam in the two versions of his creation (Genesis I and II) define two typological responses. There is Majestic man, formed "in the image of God" and commanded to "subdue" the world; and Redemptive or Covenantal man, made "from the dust of the earth" and charged to "guard and keep" the creation. Majestic man is creative, technological, functional, dignified in his mastery over nature and existing in the realm of victorious activity. Redemptive man, on the other hand, is non-functional, receptive, loyal, submissive, separated from nature not by his *de facto* dominion but by the covenant by which he is entrusted to redeem the world by bringing his actions under the will of God. Majestic man lives in the assertion of the will; redemptive man in its extinction. But both live in uneasy co-existence within each Jew, for he has been given both commands. On the one hand he has to master the world, and on the other, he has to offer it in humble dedication to God.

Not only is the Jew an intrinsically divided self, but also ineluctably, a lonely one. For each unquiescent element of his being defeats the attempted consummation of the other. Majestic man, that figure of will and conquest, is vulnerable not to loneliness but to being alone. For "dignity" – his mode of being – is a social category, presupposing recognition by others; and practical power – his objective – requires the co-operation of others. In "natural communities" (functional combinations rather than empathetic unions) he finds his completion. Redemptive man, however, is open to loneliness, for his existence lies neither in the co-operation nor the recognition of others but in his relation, *qua* solitary being, with God. He can transcend this only in the "covenantal community," one forged not by identity of interests but by identity of relationship towards God – a triadic encounter, whose paradigms are prayer and prophecy. Each might find community but for the insistent claims of the other. Majestic man is wrenched from his functional involvement by a sudden awareness of personal encounter with a God who transcends nature; and the Redemptive man is forced at times to relinquish his community of faith by the exigencies of practical labour, and the cognitive categories in which this must be conducted. Neither can be reduced to the other, and thus neutralized. Majesty requires the redemptive vision to give its creative enterprises ultimate validation; and the content of this vision cannot be completely translated into functional concepts. This internal rift is given added poignancy in our time which is an age primarily of technological achievement. Faced with a community of Majestic men the man of faith is bound either to betray himself or be misunderstood; and all that faces him is a retreat into solitude.

This typology, reminiscent in many ways of Hegel's Master/Slave dichotomy, defines a tension which many Jews undoubtedly experience in their oscillation between secular and Jewish involvements, and throws a critical light on the easy assumptions of synthesis and compatibility made, for example, by S. R. Hirsch. But it is clearly of great importance to know whether this is a contingent or a necessary phenomenon – whether Judaism contains within itself the means of transcending this dichotomy without on the one hand retreating from the creative endeavours of Majestic man; and on the other, of excluding all but the atypically righteous (the Patriarchs and Moses according to R. Soloveitchik's concession) from this transcendence.

What makes one suppose that there *is* such a transcendence, accessible as the *natural* consequence of a righteous life, is the constant reiteration of just this claim, particularly in the Psalms. If we take as an example Psalm 1, it is immediately striking that R. Soloveitchik's picture of the restless, wandering, unquiet soul is exactly that of the *unrighteous* man of the Psalm, who is "like the chaff which is blown by the wind" – one is tempted to continue in T. S. Eliot's extension of the metaphor: "driven this way and that, and finding no place of lodgement and germination." [8] The righteous, in contrast, flourish in two dimensions. They are *rooted*, "like a tree planted by streams of water"; and they are possessed of *progress*, for "the Lord regards the way of the righteous" while the movement of the wicked is stultified (graphically conveyed by the order of verbs in v.1. from "walking" to "standing" to "sitting"). Rootedness and progress stand as opposites to alienation on the one hand and nihilism and anomie on the other. These dimensions can be correlated with R. Soloveitchik's typology, for the tree is the image of covenantal man, flourishing in passive receptivity to the source of its life, the "streams of water" being a familiar image for Torah; while progress, "the way", is the symbol of independent and mobile activity.

The significant word in this context is *Ashrei* – the state of the righteous man. Though this is normally translated as happiness, it is neither *eudaemonia* nor *hedone*; it embodies precisely those two aspects mentioned in the development of the Psalm. For its linguistic affinities are with:

(i) the verb *Ashar*, meaning to go straight or to advance (as in Proverbs 96: *Ve-ishru be-derekh binah*, "and go straight on in the way of understanding");

and (ii) the *Asherah* (mentioned in Deuteronomy 16:21),

the "sacred grove" of Canaanitic worship, a tree which flourished under the benign influence of a deity and which was therefore an object of pagan rites. Asher, the son of Jacob and Zilpah (Genesis 30:13) is clearly so-called because of the connotation of fertility implicit in the word.

So that, in the dense poetic logic of the Psalm, the first word contains in association, the two themes which it proceeds to develop – the image of the tree and of the way. And, significantly, these majestic and covenantal aspects are fused in a single unified felicific state.

If we doubted this, we need only remember the connection between *Ashrei* and that other predicate of the righteous, *Temimut;* as in Psalm 119:1 – *Ashrei temimei derekh*. The cluster of meanings gathered round *Tamim* stand in polar opposition to the divided self: complete/finished/entire/innocent/simple/possessing integrity. The concept is clearly related to the subsequent verse (119:10) "With my *whole heart* (*bekol libi*) I have sought thee."

In Psalm 8 the paradox of the two aspects is stated explicitly: "What is man that you are mindful of him?" yet, "You have made him little lower than the angels" – this is clearly the "dust of the earth" become "image of God." But the tone is one of thanksgiving rather than tension, and this is the normal expression of the paradox in Judaism: wonder that a transcendent God should seek a *Dirah betachtonim*, a dwelling in the lowest sphere of existence, and should entrust a physical being with His redemptive work. Of particular interest is the verb used to denote this charge, *Tamshilehu* (v. 7). This is neither the "subdual" commanded to Majestic man, nor the "serving and guarding" of Redemptive man, but a clear synthesis of the two. *Mashal* – to have dominion over – is something which is both *entrusted* to one (its first occurrence in Genesis is in 1:16 where the sun and moon are entrusted with dominion over the heavens) and a position which involves dominance and supremacy. The sense that dominion is something held in trust, or by covenant, is enforced by the linguistic association of the verb *Mashal*, a word which also means, "to represent, or be like" as in an apposite verse from Job (41:25): *Eyn al-afar mashlo*, "There is none on the dust of the earth like him"; and so by extension *Mashal* comes to mean a parable or example, something which reproduces the form of that which initiated it. Significantly, the word "represent" embodies the same ambiguity: to be entrusted as a delegate; and to picture or resemble.

In the light of this, when we turn to the accounts of Adam's creation in Genesis I and II, the natural reading (and that taken by Rashi, for example) is to regard the second as a qualification or explication of the first, rather than to see them as essentially opposed. Cassutto[9] explains it in this way: "As for the repetition of the story of man's creation, it should be noted that such repetitions are not at all incongruous to the Semitic way of thinking. When the Torah described man's creation (twice) the one in brief general outline as an account of the making of one of the *creatures* of the material world and the second at length and in detail, as the story of the creation of the *central being* of the moral world, it had no reason to refrain from duplicating the theme, since such a repetition was consonant with the stylistic principle of presenting first a general statement and thereafter the detailed elaboration . . ." This is itself an echo of Rashi's explanation: "Should you say that the Torah has already stated (in Genesis 1:27) 'And He created the man . . .' etc. then (I say that) I have seen the *Beraita* of Rabbi Eliezer . . . dealing with the thirty-two interpretative rules by which the Torah can be interpreted, and the following is one of them: when a general statement (of an action) is followed by a detailed account (of it) the latter is a particularization of the former . . . He who hears (the second account) might think that it is a different account entirely, whereas it is nothing but the details of the former general statement." [10]

This account still leaves unanswered the question, how are we to resolve the apparent contradiction (or at least contrast of emphasis) between man as "dust of the earth" and as "image of God"; between "serving and guarding" and "subduing"; and between a narrative which invokes the Tetragrammaton and one which does not?

The contrast between the Tetragrammaton and E-lohim as names of God is usually seen in the context of metaphysical categories – transcendence as against immanence, mercy as against justice – but even at the level of grammar we can see, as Cassutto[11] points out, an immediate difference. The Tetragrammaton is a proper name, denoting an individual – the God of Israel; while E-lohim, as its plural form suggests, is the name of a class, the totality of all gods. As a consequence it is used to refer even to heathen deities ("You shall have no other E-lohim besides me"),[12] and can be extended to mean "judges" or "angels." The appearance of synonymy between the two is explicable in terms of the fact that in Jewish belief the class of gods has only one member, so that E-lohim often appears to be a proper name. Cassutto's conclusion is that wherever E-lohim is used, the context is one where what is spoken of is in some sense *universal* (for example, the Wisdom literature), whereas the use of the Tetragrammaton indicates that a *particular* relation between God and Israel is being presupposed (as in the halakhic passages).

Having made this distinction, we can use it to understand the different perspectives from which Adam's creation is seen in the two accounts. The first, using the name E-lohim alone, is a *universal* description not only in the sense of being less detailed, more *general* than the second, but in the important sense of being intelligible (and addressed) to all men irrespective of the value-systems in which they stand. (This could in any case be inferred from Rashi's comment on Genesis 1:1, that the Torah begins with an account of the creation of the world so that Israel should be able to justify their inhabiting the land of Canaan to the "nations of the world" when the latter complained that they had no territorial right to it. This clearly supposes that Genesis 1 was addressed to "the nations of the world" and not to Israel alone). But the second, invoking the four-lettered name of the God of Israel, describes the special relationship between man and God, the relationship that can only exist between man and the *unique* God. In other words, the first articulates the nature of *homo sapiens;* the second *homo religiosus.*

The first version tells us that man was created "in the image of God," and Rashi interprets this to mean, "in understanding and intellectual power." This is *homo sapiens*, man *qua* rational being. And this is his distinguishing feature as a *biological* phenomenon, that which divides man "sharply and importantly from all other known species." [13] But in the second passage we are told that man was formed "of the dust of the earth" and that there was "breathed into his nostrils the breath of life; and man became a living soul," on which Rashi comments, "He made him of both lower (material) and higher (spiritual) elements, a body from the lower and a soul from the higher." Man as an embodied soul is specifically a religious conception, one which cannot be explicated in naturalistic terms. And so this perspective could not be admitted into the earlier account, speaking, as it does, to all "the nations of the world". "In the image of God" – this is a *state;* "He breathed into his nostrils" – this is a relation. The state is independent of the religious life; the relation is its very essence.

A parallel distinction is apparent in the different commands reported in the first and second narrations. In the first, the commands to "be fruitful and multiply and fill the earth" are addressed to man as part of the natural order, mirroring verbatim the blessing given to all other creatures (p. 22). The only difference is that to man it is given as both blessing and *command*, in recognition of man's capacity as rational being to receive and act on imperatives. The two other commands, "And subdue it (the world) and have supremacy" over the other creatures, belong to the realm of description rather than *Mitzvah* – a word which can only be imperfectly translated as "the command which brings relation." *Ya-yetzav* ("and He instructed as a *Mitzvah*") occurs only in the second version (2:16); the first restricts itself to *Va-yomer* ("and He said"). "Subdue" and "have supremacy" are stated as activities in which the *telos* – the purpose in the context of Divine-human relation – is unstated. *Kavash*, to subdue, has in Hebrew the connotation of suppressing or treading down, and has a Biblical extension in the word *Kivshan*, which means a furnace, in which the form of that which is placed in it is beaten down and made pliable. *U-redu*, and have supremacy, similarly means to subject, with the connotation of autocratic disregard for the object over which it is exercised. Rashi notes its affinities with the verb *Rud*, to bring low; its meaning is that the rest of creation is brought low with respect to man. Neither verb has the dimension that we noticed in the word used in the Psalms to mean "dominion" – *Mashal* – that of being given in trust as part of a covenant. The Genesis I account is a neutral description of man's biological relation with the animal kingdom. The religious dimension appears only in the next chapter, supplying the previously missing *telos*, rather than (as it would appear from R. Soloveitchik's account) propounding an opposing one.

The verbs used in Genesis 2 reverberate in associations with the Divine teleology. *Le-ovdah* – "to serve" the creation: this is the paradigmatic act of the Jew in relation to God. Moses is called the *Eved* of the Lord as the highest term of praise (Numbers 12:7). And Kimchi explains the concept in the following terms (commentary to Joshua 1:1): "Anyone who directs all his powers, intentions and concentration to the Lord (i.e., to that aspect denoted by the Tetragrammaton) *so that even his involvement with the secular world* (literally, 'affairs of the world') is directed to the service of God, is called an *Eved* of the Lord." In other words, the *Eved* is precisely the man for whom the conflict between Majesty and Covenant is not transcended but rather *not perceived* at all (*all* his concentration belongs to the Master). We cannot speak in this context of a *dichotomy* of involvements, nor even of a *synthesis* of two separate elements, but only of a *single* task which involves two relationships: man as servant of God, aligning all his actions to the Divine will; and as servant towards the world as well, meaning that he redeems it in a way that it could not redeem itself. This is not incompatible with "subduing" it: it is merely subduing it with a purpose, or re-directing it. It will be said that only a few attain the rank of *Eved* (Kimchi mentions Abraham, Moses, David and the prophets); and while this is true it does not follow that all other Jews are condemned to spiritual tension. For the children of Israel as a whole are called "My servants" by God. The contradiction is resolved by distinguishing between a role and a state; or a task and its achievement. Even though not all have achieved a transcendence it is still their role and their entitlement. To be a man of divided attentions is not an ontological destiny but an imperfection. The actions of a man of faith are comprehended under the concept of *Avodah* – a word in which man's dual aspect as part of nature and as a soul is fused in the idea of an act which *sanctifies* nature by bringing it under the scheme of Divine will. The Jew in the process of *Avodah* is a unity; outside of it, he is a divided being.

Adam's other command was *le-shamrah*: to "guard" the creation. This is a specifically covenantal mode, and one cannot miss the verbal allusion in: "And the childen of Israel shall guard the Shabbat . . . *as an everlasting covenant*" (Exodus 31:16-17). *Shamor* is an act of withdrawal from majesty and creation; not as an act of separation but as a rededication. The word *Shamor* occurs in relation to *Shabbat* only in the second version of the Decalogue, where it is linked with the remembrance that "You were a servant (*Eved*) in the land of Egypt," [15] a memory unmentioned in the first account. So that it is clear that *Shamor* is contrasted with a service undertaken in secular terms, under purely human aegis: "You are *my* servants, not the servants of other servants."[16] Guarding is a qualification of serving, not an alternative to it. It is a part of that inner and harmonious dialectic by which the man of faith gathers the inward strength to dedicate his outward works to the task of redemption. The *Shabbat* command begins: "Six days shall you labour," stating at the outset that the *Shabbat* is not a separate realm but part of a continuum which includes creation and withdrawal, in which man is not simply creative but is "a *partner* in creation." And as the Adam narration reminds us, the act of withdrawal, though it has its own special sanctuary in time, is in fact an ongoing process simultaneous with the act of creation.

To conclude: there is a natural reading of Genesis 1 and 2, enforced by the more explicit testimony of the Psalms, and supported by the traditional commentators, according to which the two accounts of creation do not give rise to a dualistic typology of the man of faith. Instead they describe a state in which an apparent tension is brought within a single harmonious mode of activity whose consequence is at the polar opposite from alienation and internal discord. Admittedly, this belongs to the second narration, but the first is not a contrast but a neutral description, addressed in a wider context, to those who are not themselves men of faith.

IV

There are two difficulties in assessing a typological metaphysic such as R. Soloveitchik proposes. One is in the significance of the qualification that such a schema is "subjective." The other is that its evolution from its textual sources seems to be of a Midrashic order. "Subjectivity" as

ALIENATION AND FAITH 231

a predicate of philosophy done in the Kierkegaardian manner can denote either "inwardness" or "non-provability." It can, as it were, either speak *to* the individual in his inner being, or be spoken *by* an individual as the untestable record of his private impressions. Although these may go together (as in poetry), neither entails the other. As long as the distinction between the two is inexplicit, the border between autobiography and philosophy remains blurred, and this is what makes much existential analysis of religious experience so problematic. As far as establishing a criterion for the deducing of a metaphysic from a Biblical text is concerned, this is too large a subject to be mentioned here: all I have tried to do is to show that an alternative reading can be derived from the same textual details, relying on only grammatical and semantic considerations.

Not knowing how much counterargument is rendered otiose by the qualification of "subjectivity," it is worth considering briefly whether the two aspects of the *involvement* of the man of faith in the world, necessarily generate a bifurcation in his *character*. If not, then the way is clear for an alternative phenomenology of Jewish consciousness; for we would have severed the typology of character from its roots in the Divine command.

When we speak of a pull between a Jew's secular and religious involvements, we are apt to become confused, because there is not one but many things that might be denoted by that contrast. There are at least the following:

(i) the realm of the secular and the realm of the holy;
(ii) a universal concern for human welfare and a particularistic concern for Jewish interests;
(iii) identity *qua* man as such, and identity as a Jew;
(iv) a secular *attitude* towards the world and a sanctifying attitude.

These may be related, but they occupy different dimensions. Identity, concern and attitude belong to distinguishable psychological strata. Each contrast deserves extensive treatment, but in this context we are only interested to know (a) does each of these *have* to be internalized by a Jew, are they contingent, or integral, to his destiny? and (b) is each a *genuine* conflict?

(i) is certainly a pseudo-conflict: the secular and the holy are not objectively distinct realms. There is nothing (in the domain of the halakhically permitted) that cannot be redeemed or made holy by a sanctifying use. This is a familiar theme. Less familiar is the *ex post facto* sanctification of the forbidden when in an act of "repentance from great love" the intentional sins of the penitent are added to his merit.[17] Even if we discount this, for it cannot be directly intended (which would amount to the Sabbatian heresy of redemption through sin), the realm of the forbidden is not the proper territory of the Jew and so does not constitute a distinct area of his involvement.

(ii) is not a conflict at all. Concern for human welfare as such is part of Jewish law, if not an entirely unproblematic one. The welfare of fellow Jews, in order of the proximity of their claims ("The poor who are neighbours before all others; the poor of one's family before the poor of one's city; the poor of one's city before the poor of another city"), is simply part of this general concern; prior but not separate.

(iii) is a spurious opposition. What is to be a man *as such*? A man's identity is given in relation and in the context of some community. Each community has its own culture and vocabulary which gives it its distinctive way of allowing its members to see themselves as men. The idea of universal moral truths, not in the sense of those believed by an individual to *apply to* all men, but in the sense of truths *believed by* all men, is a fiction. There are no cross-cultural moral constants, and the search for them has been criticized in much contemporary work in anthropology and philosophy[18] (Chomsky and Lévi-Strauss notwithstanding). The man of faith *qua* Jew *is* a moral man as such, and no more could intelligibly be demanded of him without this being a tacit insistence on his cultural assimilation. Indeed the *cultural* tensions of the American- or Anglo-Jew are contingencies not merely of their spatio-temporal location but of the particular socio-political attitude prevailing within the non-Jewish society as to the proper cultural stance of its minorities. As a tension, it may be real, but it is not part of the essential God-given directive to the Jew. This is not to argue for separatism, for there are ways of entering into a secular society's common concerns without compromising one's religious integrity, and these have been outlined by R. Soloveitchik in his statement on Interfaith Relationships.[19]

(iv) Only here do we approach something in the nature of a real conflict. The Jew has his part to play in the building of a technology designed to ameliorate the human situation, and this necessitates the adoption of "cognitive-technological" concepts and frames of reference. The causal-deterministic framework, the detached subject-object mode of cognition, the mind ever open to the refutation of its hypotheses, are all necessary to a science whose aim is prediction and manipulation. It is not merely that these have their linear contrasts in the religious mind: a non-deterministic schema with place for responsibility and choice, empathetic I-Thou relation with the objects of experience, and a mind unshakably convinced of its moral truths; for these are contrasts between the scientific and the *moral*, and can be reconciled in purely secular terms. What is irreducible in the *religious* vision is the defining sense of relation with the Transcendent; and this seems to rule out all reconciliation.

We must remember here that what is at stake is not a clash of *empirical claims* between science and religion. How we are to resolve these is a matter of some choice (between qualifying the *Peshat* of the Torah and limiting the epistemological status of scientific extrapolation, for example), and anyway calls for case-by-case analysis. But we are in a position now, in the aftermath of the Victorian chauvinism of science, to regard the clash as essentially resolvable. Instead, what is supposed to remain intractable is the *opposition of attitudes* of the Jew as scientist and as sanctifier of the world. How can a person moving in the nexus of a world-view restricted to the discovery of empirical causes fail at times to lose sight of the God who transcends the observable, the God whom he addresses when he removes himself to prayer, by His four-lettered name?

This, I think, rests on a confusion. Karl Popper[20] has distinguished between what he calls the *essentialist* and the *instrumentalist* views of scientific truth. For the essentialist, scientific laws state simple truths about the world, so that in his view Einstein and Newton are strictly incompatible. Whereas the instrumentalist sees them not as truths at all, in the ordinary sense of the word, but rather as *tools for prediction;* so that Einstein's invention of an instrument which has more extensive predictive application does not *falsify* but instead *restricts the relative usefulness* of Newton's laws. Popper gives a number of reasons for preferring to work under the instrumentalist conception. And if we as Jews adopt it, it becomes clear that the use of scientific hypothesis does not represent the adoption of any alternative world view, any more than does the use of any other instrument, say, the picking up of a hammer to fix a *mezuzah.* Majestic man is simply covenantal man at work, in perfecting the tools by which he is to gain control over the natural world for the sake of enlarging the range of his halakhic activitities, supporting a growing population, removing poverty and disease, and preserving the environment. Only under an essentialist construction of the scientist's search for the truth could we maintain the semblance of an incompatibility between the task of creation and the work of redemption.

V

What, then, is the place of alienation and loneliness in the Jewish analysis of the emotions? Of course, there is no single analysis, but we can detect two recurring tendencies of thought, the one in line with R. Soloveitchik, the other which I wish to present here. A classic source for the alternative phenomenology is the famous chapter 32 of the *Tanya* of Rabbi Shneour Zalman of Liadi:

> Through the fulfilment of (the previously mentioned act of repentance in which the transgressions of the body are distinguished in one's mind from the soul which remains ever in its undisturbed relation with God) . . . by which one's (errant) body is viewed with scorn and contempt, and one's joy is in the soul alone, through this one finds a direct and simple way to fulfil the commandment "And you shall love your neighbour as yourself" (a love which is to be shown) to every Jewish soul, great or small.

> For although one's body is despised and loathed, who can know the greatness and depth of the soul and the spirit in their source and origin in the living God? And

since all (of the souls of Israel) are related, and all emanate from one Father, all Israel are literally called "brothers": in that the source of their souls is in the One God, and they are divided only by virtue of their bodies. Therefore those who give priority to their body over their soul, find it impossible to share true love and brotherhood except that which is conditional on some benefit (and hence ephemeral).

This is what Hillel the Elder meant when he said about this commandment (the love of Israel): "This is the whole Torah; and the rest is commentary." For the foundation and source of all Torah is to elevate and give ascendancy to the soul over the body . . .

Although this passage is written in the context of the practical question of how to achieve the love of one's fellow man, and the theosophical repercussions that an achieved unity has in terms of Divine blessing, it contains a clear statement of the phenomenology of a community of faith.

(1) *Ahavat Yisroel* – the mutual relation of the faith community – is a specifically religious emotion, a distinguishing feature of the men of faith. For it presupposes a metaphysic (man as an embodied soul; the unity of all souls at their source) which is implicit only in the second account of Adam's creation.

How does it differ from other forms of human collectivity? It is not the community of experience adumbrated by Hobbes, a contract founded on mutual self-interest; nor is it the functional community, joined in collective enterprise, to which man belongs in his role as creative or technological being. It is not even the I-Thou encounter with another in which he is known in his full strangeness and otherness. It belongs to the perception of a real unity, a breaking down of the walls between self and otherness. It is unconditional and untempered by time. It does not lie at the surface of the soul's awareness, but hidden in its deepest reaches. It is gained only by the strictest spiritual self-discipline. If we have a model of it in ordinary life, it is in the mutual bond between parent and child. A metaphorical similarity can be found in Jung's concept of the collective unconscious.

What do we mean by saying that it cannot exist at the level of bodily existence, but only "when the body is despised?" Clearly the *Tanya* is not advocating asceticism and body-denial. The contrast which is being indicated here is between two *modes of identity*. How are we aware of our individuality? Man as part of nature individuates himself from his environment by the perception that he is *bodily distinct* from others. He feels pain when his body is injured, but not when it happens to another body. This is the genesis of his opposition self/not-self. And this too is the origin of his sense of existential loneliness; he cannot enter into another mind since it is inseparably linked to another body. Natural man is prey to the anguish of solipsism – in which Descartes, for example, is imprisoned until he brings God into his class of certain knowledge. His experiences are bounded by the concepts of opposition/identity/selfhood/loneliness.

The man who is defined by his relation with God is only dialectically aware of himself as a distinct entity. He was made by God, indeed he can reach God by an inward journey to the depths of his soul. He is joined with God in love and separated from Him in awe. But even the separation is full of the consciousness of God. So his embodiment in the physical world is not his only or his primary reality: he views it teleologically. He is placed here for a purpose, and he can discover this by analyzing his capacities and his environment – this I can effect, this I cannot. His identity is given by his distinctive role in relation to the world, his covenantal mission. But in being himself – in performing his role – he is placing himself in harmonious fusion with the rest of the world, for his role has meaning only in the light of all others. It is said: there are 600,000 letters in the Torah and 600,000 Jewish souls. Each soul is like a letter of the Torah. Each is distinct but meaningful only in the context of the whole. And though they have no independent reality, each is supremely important for if a single letter is missing or malformed, the whole *Sefer Torah* is unfit for use. So for the man of faith individuality belongs to the not-self and to a redemptive function which is of transcendental origin and which embraces the world. Its *reality* is in community, so that the faith community is different in kind from all others: it is not a coming together of initially separate existences, for it is the only air its members can breathe.

This is the typology which relates the "life of the body" to loneliness and the "life of the soul" to communion. It is not as if the man of faith, being an embodied soul, must oscillate between them. For his identity is at the level of soul; body is merely the medium through which he does his redemptive work.

(2) How, on this account, does loneliness enter the life of the Jew? It belongs to the triadic process: sin, separation from God, and loneliness amongst men. And it comes about in this way: he who sins opposes his will to the will of God. And the person in whom this self-assertion is the motivating force, cannot tolerate other selves, for they are potential obstacles to his self-realization. So his only mode of relation is conditional and self-interested, and this is not fully to concede the separate reality of others. He is caught in the prison of the self.

In this way we can understand that strange verse: "And the Lord God said, it is not good for man to be alone. I will make him a help-meet opposite him (*ezer ke-negdo*)." [21] Rabbi Soloveitchik[22] sees in this the permanent paradoxical condition of human relationship; friendship (*ezer*) and otherness (*ke-negdo*) are inseparable. But Rashi has another reading. "If he is worthy, she shall be a help (*ezer*) to him; if he is unworthy, she shall be opposed to him (*ke-negdo*) to fight him." The man who lives his life in the Torah finds union; he who separates himself from it, separates himself from other men, even those closest to him. Loneliness is the condition of sin.

Indeed, this is demonstrated in the very next chapter, in the narration of the first sin. "And the eyes of both of them were opened, and they knew that they were naked." [23] The consequence of sin was self-consciousness, which is the progenitor of loneliness. And what they noticed, significantly, was their bodily state; what they perceived was its tragic significance for those who make it their reality. Immediately their thinking became embedded in physical space; "And the man and his wife hid themselves from the face of the Lord God, amidst the trees of the garden," [24] as if relation and hiddenness were spatial categories.

If we needed further proof of the relation between hubris and alienation we could not find a more graphic illustration than in the episode of the Tower of Babel (Genesis 11). "And the whole earth was of one language and few words." Language is the medium of communication, yet paradoxically those closest to each other are least in need of words, "One language" – the world was a single community; "of few words" – their community was an empathetic union. But the bond was a false one, belonging to the level of material expediency. "And they said to one another, Come, let us make bricks . . . and build ourselves a city and a tower with its top in the heaven, and let us make a name for ourselves." They wanted, true to Aristotle's analysis of the creative urge, to make themselves permanent by externalizing themselves in a physical object. Their reality belonged to the material world. In it they saw permanence and in it they thought they could embody themselves in the work of creation. The result was fitting and inevitable; "And the Lord said . . . come let us go down and confuse their language so that they may not understand one another's speech." This is real ontological loneliness, the severing of the lines of communication.

Alienation, then, has its place in the inner life of the Jew: as the corollary of sin. The Jew who returns, the *Baal Teshuvah*, finds refuge and relation restored to him.

(3) Might we nonetheless be mistaken in thinking that *Ahavat Yisroel* and its corresponding community of faith, constituted the central relational mode of the Jew? If we are, then how are we to account for Hillel's dictum, "This is the whole Torah, the rest is commentary." The answer lies deeper than in the idea that the love of the faith community is triadic, that Jew is bound to Jew in the identity of their relation to God, so that only in the context of a whole life of Torah and *mitzvot* does *Ahavat Yisroel* appear. It belongs instead to the explication of the opaque remark of the Zohar: "Israel, the Torah and God are all one." [25] This is not an ethical but an ontological statement, meaning that our very concept of separate existences lies at the level of religious estrangement; and that through a life not merely lived but *seen* through Torah, God's immanent presence, His will (as embodied in the Torah) and the collectivity of Jewish souls are a real (in the Platonic sense) unity. The very idea of *relation* implies that there are two or more distinct things related. What the Zohar is suggesting is

that the way of experience in Judaism demands a profound revision in our ontological categories; a move similar in kind though opposite in intention to Spinoza's radicalism about "substance". To put it more mildly, as we have shown, *Ahavat Yisroel* contains its own specific notion of personal identity; this can be acquired only in the life of Torah; so that the life of Torah and the precondition of the faith community are identical. Hillel's dictum is therefore precisely correct; and his existence in the community of faith is the *whole* life of the Jew.

VI

The distance between the phenomenology of the Jew and that of secular man is what allows Judaism to hold out what I earlier called redemptive relevance to the crises with which the Jew is faced when he is alienated from his faith. We can make this clearer by a brief account of the relation between love and the self as they are related within and outside of Judaism.

1. "A love which is conditional, ceases when the condition is unfulfilled" (*Avot* 5:19). There are many loves whose nature is tacitly conditional on the satisfaction of the desires of the one who loves. The child loves his teacher because he is dependent on him. The disciple loves his master because he exemplifies the virtues. Because there is an intentional object of desire, when the loved one ceases to satisfy the implicit requirements of that object it ceases to arouse that love. This is a love which is not blind to faults; and also one in which there is a *Yesh mi she-ohev*, "a self that loves." The Jew who loves God as the creator of the material world and its pleasures, is not yet God-intoxicated; nor is he if his love is one which is in love with itself – which lives on satisfactions of prayer, learning or *mitzvot*. For his desires (and so his self) are still intact. His love lives in the tension between self and otherness.

2. "The love which is unconditional will not pass away for ever" (*ibid.*). Here, he who loves is conscious only of that which is loved. Being oblivious of self, it is unconditional: it is the emotional corollary of the ontological condition of the not-self. This is the love of "Nullify your will to His will" (*Avot* 2:4) and is the distinctive quality of the man of faith. But we must distinguish between the unconditional love

which requires a stimulus and that which does not. The Jewish moralists have all been aware that this love is not a passion but a mode of recognition (that all human existence is continually dependent on God). Meditation and prayer are the necessary preliminaries. But not for all. There are those rare spirits for whom this recognition is an immediate and dominating awareness. So that we should not be led into the mistake of thinking that the difference between the exceptional and the normal Jew is one between unconditional and conditional love, which would be to concede that the normal condition is one of paradox and tension. Rather it lies between immediacy and active arousal, or the achievement and the task, both within the single dimension of the unconditional.

This is the emotional geography of the secular and the religious mind. It is not a paradox to say that the Jew abandons selfhood. Conditional love is potentially promiscuous, it can take many objects. It could not be the love of which a monotheistic religion speaks when it talks of the love of God. And this transcendence of *Yeshut*, "*être pour-soi*", is what removes divisions and ends the loneliness of the man of faith.

VII

I spoke earlier about two tendencies in Jewish thought, the one outlined above and the other in which R. Soloveitchik's analysis is foreshadowed. We can trace this back to a disagreement between Nachmanides and Ibn Ezra on the interpretation of the verse (Deuteronomy 11:22), "And you shall love the Lord, to walk in all His ways and to cleave (*le-davka*) to Him." Is it possible that man should be in intimate relation with God at all times? Or must Majesty sometimes interfere with Covenant?

Ibn Ezra comments, "To cleave to Him: at the end, for it is a great mystery," implying perhaps that it is a communion reached only at death. Whereas the Ramban says: "It is, in fact, the meaning of 'cleaving' that one should remember God and His love at all times, and not be separated in thought from Him 'when you go on your way and when you lie down and rise up'. At such a stage, one may be talking with other people but one's heart is not with (i.e., confined to) them, since one is in the presence of

God." The suffusion of man's social existence with his covenantal intimacy with God is for Nachmanides a this-worldly possibility.

But for whom is it possible? Here again the ways divide. One path is taken by Maimonides.[26] By philosophy and meditation a man may reach the rank of prophecy, and this is the highest natural perfection. But it is still the realm of the divided self. "When you have succeeded in properly performing these acts of Divine service, and you have your thought during their performance entirely abstracted from worldly affairs, then take care that your thoughts be not disturbed by thinking of your wants or of superfluous things. In short, think of worldy matters when you eat, drink, bathe, talk with your wife, and little children, or when you converse with other people." *Devekut*, cleaving, is an act of seclusion and prayer is its sanctuary. Emerging into the mundane, one relinquishes that union. Only at the highest level of prophecy, where Moses and the Patriarchs stand, does this partition dissolve. "When we therefore find them (these few exalted men) also engaged in ruling others, in increasing their property, and endeavouring to obtain possession of wealth and honour, we see in this fact a proof that when they were occupied in these things, only their bodily limbs were at work, whilst their heart and mind never moved away from the name of God." This is a level not to be attained through training. It is a specific act of grace. It cannot be the aim of any spiritual journey: it must always be unexpected.

Strangely enough, we find Maimonides' ideas mirrored in the Kabbalistic tradition. Accepting that *Devekut* was for the ordinary man the product of seclusion, the Kabbalah pursued this to its logical conclusion. He who makes *Devekut* his aim must sever his contacts with the world and practise a meditative retreat.

It is only in Chassidism[27] that we find, as it were, a democratization of Maimonides. Cleaving to God in all His ways is removed from Ibn Ezra's category of "mystery" where it had lain even in the Kabbalah. Once the implication of the unity of God is perceived – that nothing exists except in Him – then one can preserve the state of communion and the not-self even when immersed in the world, for by carrying out the Divine imperative one not only realizes but also enters into the reality of God's will. To be sure, there is a distinction to be preserved between normality and grace (Maimonides' lower and higher prophecy), but this is to be conceived, as we have already explained, in terms of the *Devekut* which needs arousal and that which is immediate and ever-present. The normal man of faith still preserves the distinction between *le-ovdah* (practical action) and *le-shamrah* (rededicative withdrawal and arousal) but this is not the opposition of Majesty and Redemptiveness; but the realized and preparatory stages of Redemptiveness itself.

VIII

In summary, not one but two readings of the inner possibilities of the Jew are implicit in tradition; and with them go two interpretations of man's creation, of his stance towards the world and God, and of the nature of his relation to other men. And at a time when loneliness is the condition of the estranged Jew, one reading offers empathy, the other, healing. To state this contrast is not to formulate an opposition; simply to open another gate.

When Moses sent men to spy out the land of Canaan, after their years in the wilderness, they returned with divided reports (Numbers 13). Ten said, "We came to the land where you sent us, and truly it flows with milk and honey . . . (but) it is a land which consumes its inhabitants." But Caleb said, "We should surely go up and possess it, for we are well able to do so." What is at first sight unintelligible is how the ten could have uttered a counsel of despair. They were not ordinary men, but were chosen on God's command from the princes of the tribes. They had already been promised (Exodus 3:17) that God would bring them "up out of the affliction of Egypt . . . to a land flowing with milk and honey." They had seen God revealed on Mt. Sinai. They had been delivered victorious in the battle with Amalek.

There is a Chassidic explanation. In the wilderness, the Israelites had no creative or constructive work to do. Their food and water were provided by God; He guided them; His presence dwelt amongst them in the Tabernacle. They were at the height of covenantal withdrawal, the Divine hand surrounded them like a protective wall. Canaan meant emergence, practical responsibility, the work of building up a nation; and the ten feared immersion in the secular and the hiding of the face of God from sight. "It is a land which consumes its inhabitants." They saw Covenant and Majesty, distinct and opposed, and they trembled and held back. Caleb did not see it. He knew that sanctuary is mere preparation and that redemption was its fulfilment, a work which saw no reality in the secular except as the yet-unredeemed. The ten spoke and the people were unsettled: a divided vision confronted them. Caleb spoke and the people were stilled. All the spies were men of faith (they had seen God with their own eyes); not all of them were lonely men.

NOTES

1. Psalm 69:9.
2. Ibid, v. 34.
3. Isaiah 45:14.
4. Zohar II, 94b.
5. The Baal Shem Tov's remark is based on the verse (Deuteronomy 31:18) "And I will surely hide *(haster astir)* My face." The repetition of the verb is taken to refer to a double concealment, that is, when the hiddenness itself is hidden. See *Toledot Yaakov Yoseph, parshat Bereshit.*
6. Martin Buber, *I and Thou* (translated by R. Gregor Smith), 2nd ed., p. 11.
7. In *Tradition*, 1965.
8. T.S. Eliot, Choruses from *The Rock*, VII.
9. U. Cassutto, *From Adam to Noah*, p. 91.
10. Rashi to Genesis 2:8.
11. U. Cassutto, *The Documentary Hypothesis*, ch. 2.
12. Exodus 20 v. 3: Deuteronomy 5, v. 7.
13. Jonathan Bennett, *Rationality*, p. 5. The whole book is an attempt to characterize the difference in kind between man and the animals without recourse to metaphysical theorizing; simply in terms of the possession of a language with certain logical properties.
14. Leviticus 25:55. See also Rashi's comment on Exodus 21:6.
15. Deuteronomy 5:15.
16. Rashi to Exodus 21:6.
17. *Yoma* 86b. See on this for example the present Lubavitcher Rebbe, Shlita, *Likutei Sichot* (5730) on *parshat Vayikra*, for a remarkable account of the unifying power of the *Baal Teshuva*.
18. See, as a notable example, Peter Winch, *The Idea of a Social Science*.
19. *Rabbinical Council Record*, Feb. 1966. Reprinted in *A Treasury of Tradition*, p. 78.
20. In *Conjectures and Refutations*.

21. Genesis 2:18.
22. See 'Confrontation', *Tradition* 1964 (Vol. 6, no. 2).
23. Genesis 3:7.
24. Ibid., v. 8.
25. *Zohar Chadash* I 24a; II 60a; III 93a.
26. *Guide to the Perplexed* III, ch. 51.
27. See, for a study of this transformation, '*Devekut*, or Communion with God' in Gershom Scholem, *The Messianic Idea in Judaism*.

THINKERS

13
Buber's Jewishness and Buber's Judaism

Why do we ask the question of Buber's Jewishness? His greatest preoccupation was the classic Jewish one: the encounter between man and God in the concrete human situation. The sources of his inspiration were the Bible and the literature of the Chassidim. To say that we ask because his influence has been more noticeable amongst non-Jewish than amongst Jewish thinkers itself forces us again to ask: why should this have been so?

In a brief article, we must give the simple and simplifying answer. In this case, at least there is a mitigating factor. We owe Buber the response that he consistently demanded and gave: the response of relationship, of subjectivity. And my own answer must be: that we fail to find in Buber what must be the heart of any Jewish writing that is to enter and animate the lived actuality of Jewish life – the Torah as law, the halakhah.

Gershom Scholem called Buber, a 'religious anarchist'. And it was to this that he attributed the distance between Buber's vision of Chassidism and the reality of Chassidic life: "His doctrine is religious anarchism, which does not acknowledge any teaching about *what* should be done but puts the whole emphasis on intensity, on *how* whatever one does is done. Therefore, references to the Torah and the Commandments, which to the Chassidim meant everything, become extremely nebulous in Buber's presentation." [1]

It is a simplistic and yet perhaps enlightening comparison, to contrast the first and last great thinkers of post-emancipation German Jewry: Mendelssohn and Buber. For Mendelssohn, the content of revelation was *law*. Law constituted the particularity of Judaism. This proposition served for him as the decisive liberation of the Jewish mind from dogma, from the idea of revealed *truth*. It was less the apotheosis of the halakhah than the freeing of the speculative process from constraints of 'orthodoxy' that motivated his formulation. But still: it stands. At the distance of a universe from Buber, for whom revelation hovers above and beyond the laws in which it was expressed, and the historical moment at which it took place. "Revelation is nothing else than the relation between giving and receiving." [2] "The law is not thrust upon man; it rests deep within him, to waken when the call comes." [3] Revelation has no content. It is a dimension. "My own belief in revelation . . . does not mean that I believe that finished statements about God were handed down from heaven to earth. Rather, it means that human substance is melted by the spiritual fire which visits it, and there now breaks forth from it a word, a statement, which is human in its meaning and form, human conception and human speech, and yet witness to Him who stimulated it and His will." [4]

In a famous dialogue, Rosenzweig challenged him to reassess his view of the law, and at the same time gave a penetrating diagnosis of the source of Buber's reaction against it:

> "Is it really Jewish law with which you try to come to terms? and, not succeeding, on which you turn your back? . . . Is that really Jewish law, the law of millennia, studied and lived, analysed and rhapsodised, the law of the everyday and of the day of death, petty and yet sublime, sober and yet woven with legend . . .? Is the Law you speak of not rather the Law of the Western orthodoxy of the past century?" [5]

How – one is tempted to ask – could Buber seriously claim to be an interpreter of 'Judaism' given the extremity of his stance? At what point does the *Jewishness* of his concern with the personal encounter between man and God, touch the *Judaism* of Mosaic Law?

In attempting an answer, this article takes three approaches: firstly, to set his thought against the background of his distant precursors; secondly, to explore the area of halakhic Judaism which is closest to Buber; and thirdly to see whether at this point of proximity there remains still an unbridgeable gap between them. It deliberately avoids the more familiar portraiture of Buber's relationship with Chassidism, and chooses instead the seemingly incongruous backdrop of medieval Jewish philosophy, and what he himself once called, 'that vexatious Talmud.'[6]

Judah Halevi: Thou and I

Perhaps the most obvious progenitor of Buber's thinking is not Chassidic thought, whose theoretical foundations he consistently derided as 'gnosis', but rather Judah Halevi. Time and again in the *Kuzari* we encounter formulations which, allowing for the cultural chasm between the twelfth and the twentieth centuries, bear an uncanny resemblance to Buber. For I-It and I-Thou, we must read the god of Aristotle and the God of Abraham.[7] The one is reached by speculation and cognition, the other by love and faith. Even the two names of God stand, for Halevi, for this dichotomy, one to denote God as the collectivity of forces, the cause of causes, knowable but unknowing, incapable of relationship with man; the other, specifically the proper name of God, belonging to the vocabulary of dialogue and disclosure.[8] The God of Judaism, known by name, is He who speaks to man, and He to whom man speaks.

Because relationship is central to Halevi, he cannot accept any explanation of the *mitzvot* in terms of means to an end, causes productive to effects. At least to this extent he would have assented to Buber's remark that "I and Thou freely confront one another in mutual effect that is neither connected with nor coloured by any causality." The law, at any rate in its specifically religious parts, is not to be understood in terms external to itself. Each religious act is an encounter with God. This and no other is its Divine meaning. In keeping the Sabbath: "You see what He has conferred on you, as if you had been invited to His table to enjoy His hospitality. You thank Him inwardly and outwardly, and if this joy carries you into singing and dancing, this too is worship and union with the Divine."[9]

It is not as if, after Buber, we can reread Halevi and cast him in the role of religious existentialist. It is rather that the distinctions and emphases that Buber was to make his own are already fully there, explicit and central, in the *Kuzari*.

But it is precisely here, in the analysis of the religious act, that the two dramatically part company. For Halevi did not regard the Divine-human encounter as a possibility that had no boundaries. To the contrary, he felt that it could occur only given specific pre-conditions: a particular people, a particular land, and a particular law. He is perhaps the least universalist of all the medieval thinkers. The Jewish people, the land of Israel, and the law of Moses – these were the three co-ordinates of the Divine presence. And we can understand why he should have thought as he did. For him, the essential religious facts were the actual meetings of God and man in time and space. Theology is religious history. And therefore its focus must be Israel and the Jewish people: the stage and the actors of the Biblical and messianic historical drama.

Correspondingly, Halevi attached greater significance than most other medieval Jewish philosophers to the precise details of the commands. Since they were not to be understood in human terms but as part of the Divine mystery every facet of the religious act had its immutable meaning. God in His wisdom knows exactly what to prescribe for man, to create in the individual, the community and the land, a balance between conflicting forces.[10] No act shaped by human judgement could reach out beyond the human. The paradigm of the religious act for Halevi – and it still takes us by surprise when we read it – is the offering of sacrifices.[11] Here, all the elements of his vision converge: the minutely ordered, unfathomable procedure, performed on behalf of the community, in the appointed place, with its consequence of "I will dwell in their midst".

There is nothing gnostic or magical in his conception. It is simply that in the I-Thou of man's religious life, Halevi takes the Thou more seriously than the I. Contrary to Buber's idea that the law "is not thrust upon man; it rests deep within him, to waken when the call comes", he writes about Moses that "his words were not creations of his own mind . . . prophecy did not (as philosophers assume) burst forth in a pure soul, become united with the Active Intellect . . . and then be inspired." [12] In the religious dialogue, there is an asymmetry. It is true that "Divine Providence only gives man as much as he is prepared to receive".[13] But man prepares; God speaks. In Halevi – in Judaism – God speaks and man answers. In Buber: "they speak the Thou and then they hear." [14]

This difference in order is not slight or insignificant. It is the source of what I am tempted to call Buber's *moral pantheism*, the idea that God is immanent in every human act. If man initiates the dialogue, then he does indeed choose its context, the acts in which he is to discover meaning, relation, Thou. But if God is He who speaks, then the place of meeting is precisely defined by His commands.

In this stark contrast we can locate Buber's point of departure from Judaism. He and Halevi share the same conception of the distinctive form of Jewish religious experience. But from it they derive antithetical conclusions. For Buber, it is an affirmation of the entire human situation in all its particularity; for Halevi, a celebration of the whole Divine Law, in its variegated uniqueness.

In All Thy Ways

How did Buber come to take this step? It may be, as Rosenzweig suggested, that he found the particular forms of nineteenth century German orthodoxy uninviting. But he was after all steeped in, and to some extent influenced by Chassidism, and it seems impossible to suppose that he can have closed his eyes to the rejoicing in the life of the law that was so crucial to it. There is a passage in his writings that is highly revealing:

> The Holy strives to include within itself the whole of life. The Law differentiates between the holy and the profane, but the Law desires to lead the way toward the messianic removal of the differentiation to the all-sanctification.[13]

Did Buber, a master of ambiguity, choose this equivocation as the grounds for parting from Judaism while not seeming to – an axiom in one sense true, in another, Buber's sense, false?

If we must focus on a point, this would be it. In one sense it is true that Judaism recognises itself as coextensive with the whole of life. The proposition which Buber places in the mouth of Chassidism is in fact far too ancient and universally accepted to be called 'Chassidic' at all:

> Everything physical, all drives and urges and desires, everything creaturely, is material for sanctification. From

the very same passionate powers which, undirected, give rise to evil, when they are turned toward God, the good arises.[16]

This is a doctrine recorded in the Mishna, elaborated in the Talmud and Midrashim, and most notably associated with the names of Hillel and R. Akiva:

> "You shall love the Lord with all your heart" – this means, with your two impulses, the evil as well as the good.[17] What short text is there on which all the essential principles of the Torah depend? "Know him in all thy ways . . ."[18]

Both the whole man and the whole circumstances of his existence are to be brought into the religious life.

On the other hand, the reference to the "messianic removal of the differentiation" between holy and profane is, in the sense in which the whole of Buber's work leads us to understand it, no less than Pauline. In the ideal of a messianic transcending of the law and its differentiations, we hear the unmistakable echo of Paul's:

> After that faith is come, we are no longer under a schoolmaster . . . There is neither Jew nor Greek, there is neither bond nor free, there is neither male nor female . . .[19]

Buber rejects Paul on many grounds; but not on this. After all, did not Paul introduce a new dichotomy, between spirit and flesh, rejected by Judaism and certainly by Buber? Nonetheless, the drawing of Pauline conclusions from 'Chassidic' premises is ingenious, incongruous, and ultimately fallacious.

Heschel pursued the logic of his Chassidic starting-point further:

> Judaism calls upon us to listen *not only* to the voice of the conscience but also to the norms of the heteronomous law. The good is not an abstract idea but a commandment, and the ultimate meaning of its fulfilment is in its being *an answer* to God.[20]

This is the territory of the I-Thou meeting for the Jew; Buber found it too narrow a gate to enter. It was the

Pauline rejection of the Law that marked the parting of Christianity from Judaism. Buber parts company at the same point. That he does so without saying so is due to two devices: the first, a piece of linguistic legerdemain, the second and more important, a theological misconception.

The first is his ability to speak at all of the 'messianic removal of the differentiation', the 'all-sanctification'. Certainly there is in the Jewish mystical tradition an idea that the world is divided into the holy and the not-yet-holy; that each religious act liberates a spark of holiness hitherto buried in the shells of the material, God-concealing world; and that in the utopian fulfilment, all will be holy. Certainly this created a tension between the 'Torah of the Exile' and the 'Torah of Redemption' discernible in parts of the Zohar.[21] For what was to be the function of the Law in a fully redeemed world? "In a world in which the power of evil has been broken, all those differentiations also disappear which had been derived from it." [22] But what is significant is that precisely this idea, dangerously anarchic in its messianic conception, is used to provide a new urgency and cosmic depth to *halakhic action* in this pre-messianic world. Lurianic mysticism, on which Chassidism is built, is a mysticism of the halakhic act.[23] Not any act can unlock holiness from its prison. Halakhah is the key, which the right act turns. If there are parts of the mystical literature which express an ambivalence to the Torah of the messianic age, there are none – except in the heresies surrounding and succeeding Shabbetai Zevi – which translate that ambivalence to the here-and-now. On the contrary, they elevate the halakhic act to a prominence which more rationalist expositions of Judaism had tended, perhaps, to subdue. Buber's ambiguity at this point is fatal.

The second is a misconception which Buber may or may not have held, but which it is more charitable to suppose that he did. There is an open-ended element in the religious life – the element of 'Know Him in all thy ways' – which is intrinsically ungeneralisable, irreducible to halakhic codification, because it is concerned with the particularity, the 'Thou', of the situation.

Might there be, then, in Judaism an area of religious significance *beyond the scope of the halakhah*: and might this be the area for which Buber could legitimately stand as theologian?

The answer must be a definite if delicate No. This area of Jewish values calls for careful analysis, and here is not the place for it.[24] However, reference to a few of the more notable sources should be sufficient for our purposes.

Nachmanides, in a famous passage, says this of the Biblical command "And thou shalt do that which is right and good in the sight of the Lord":

> Our rabbis said, 'This refers to compromise and *lifnim mishurat ha-din* (within or beyond the letter of the law). The intent of this is that, initially, He had said that you should observe the laws and statutes which He had commanded you. Now He says that, with respect to what He has not commanded, you should likewise take heed to do the good and the right in His eyes . . . For it is impossible to mention in the Torah all of a person's actions towards his neighbours and acquaintances, all of his commercial activity, and all social and political institutions.[25]

The Bible in commanding the 'right and the good' according to Nachmanides, lays down a general obligation to respond to the particularities of concrete human encounter in the spirit of the law, even or precisely where the law cannot offer precise guidelines. *Lifnim mishurat ha-din* does not here mean simply *within* the letter of the law (that is, forgoing one's legal rights) or *beyond* it (giving the other more than his due), but rather applying the law with sensitivity to the particular human situation. It is not as if Nachmanides contemplated two distinct domains, the legal (*din*) and the extra-legal (*lifnim mishurat ha-din*). Instead he envisages two ways of applying the law, one legalistic, taking no account of the uniqueness of the particular case; the other, compassionate and situational, guided but not fully determined by universal halakhic norms. The latter does not transcend the law, and is indeed part of its essential functioning. We might go so far as to call it the I-Thou dimension of the law. The point is reinforced by one of Maimonides' halakhic commentators:

> Our perfect Torah sets forth general principles for the cultivation of human virtue and for ethical behaviour in the world, in the statement, 'Ye shall be holy', meaning,

as the rabbis said, 'Sanctify yourself with respect to that which is permitted to you' . . . Similarly the Torah says: 'You shall do that which is right and good', meaning that one should deal well and uprightly with men. It was not appropriate in all this to command details, for the commandments of the Torah are obligatory for every period and all time and in every circumstance, whereas man's characteristics and his behaviour vary, depending on the time and the individual.[26]

The point made here is that the law, specifically Biblical law, constitutes the universal framework within which an ethic of situations must take place. Biblical law is self-limiting to this extent, that it does not legislate the unlegislatable cases. But this dimension does not exist in a void. It is framed and informed by the halakhah.

It is a fallacy to argue that because the halakhah does not uniquely determine a course of action in a particular situation, that it is inapplicable to that situation. It is a long way from such partial truths as "It is not as though any definite act of man could draw grace down from heaven" or "It is not as though man has to do this or that 'to hasten' the redemption"[27] to such unacceptable conclusions as "Man receives, and he receives not a specific 'content' but a Presence".[28]

Our hopes, then, of finding a limited area of Judaism beyond the scope of the halakhah where we could wholeheartedly apply Buber's perceptions, must remain unfulfilled.

Two Kinds of Dialogue

With genuine sadness, and a full measure of respect for Buber's outstanding gifts as theologian, poet, interpreter of the Bible, and communicator – albeit transmuter – of Chassidic literature, we must set Buber in another tradition than that of Judaism. He bears the legacy of Kant as well as of the existentialists; a deep reluctance to come to terms with the possibility of authentic inwardness within the framework of a heteronomous law. The most we could claim for him, and it may be the most he would claim for himself, would be that he was the theologian of Jewish secularism.

There is a danger in attempting to express the phenomenology of Judaism without the beliefs which give rise to it, the context in which it is set. In Buber's own terms: it is through the 'content' that we arrive at the 'Presence'; not otherwise.

Buber was a man of dialogue. It is right, then, that he should be remembered by and have significance for those to whom he spoke, rather than those from amongst whom he spoke.

Perhaps ultimately he, who elevated the dialogue to such heights, forgot that there are two kinds of dialogue. The dialogue with the Other creates in its aftermath the dialogue with oneself; the dialogue with other faiths creates its own echo with one's own. In the first phase of dialogue, in the attempt to bridge the chasm between two languages and cultures, it is sufficient to inspire, to give a glimpse of an alternative world. It is no criticism to say that the truths that cross the chasm are partial, fragmentary. But in the second phase of dialogue – the dialogue with oneself and one's own religion – the truth must be complete, authentic, or it is nothing.

A midrash, famous for other reasons, embodies this perception precisely. A Roman challenged Rabban Yochanan ben Zakkai with the claim that the ritual of the Red Heifer was meaningless magic. Yochanan answered him, translating it into an act – an act of exorcism – that was perfectly comprehensible to the Roman in his own terms. The first phase of dialogue was successfully achieved. But when the Roman had left, Rabban Yochanan's students turned to him with that deeper question which dialogue creates: 'Master, what will you answer us?' [29]

It was this second phase of dialogue to which Rosenzweig challenged him, and whose pressure we still feel. Buber has spoken to the world. But what will he answer us?

NOTES

1. Gershom Scholem, 'Martin Buber's Hasidism: A Critique', in Judah Goldin (ed.), *The Jewish Expression*, New York: Bantam Books, 1970, p. 412.

2. 'The Faith of Judaism' in Martin Buber, *Israel and the World: Essays in a Time of Crisis*, New York: Schocken Books, 1965, p. 27.
3. 'Teaching and Deed', in *Israel and the World*, p. 142.
4. 'Reply to C.G. Jung' in Martin Buber, *Eclipse of God*, New York: Harper and Row, 1957, p. 135.
5. Nahum N. Glatzer, *Franz Rosenzweig: His Life and Thought*, New York: Schocken Books, 1970, pp. 237-8.
6. *Israel and the World*, op.cit., p. 23.
7. Judah Halevi, *Kuzari*, 4:16.
8. Ibid, 4:1-3, 16.
9. Ibid, 2:50.
10. Ibid, 2:50, 3:5, 7, 11, 17.
11. Ibid, 1:99.
12. Ibid, 1:87.
13. Ibid, 2:24.
14. Martin Buber, *I and Thou*, Edinburgh: T. and T. Clark, 1966, p. 83.
15. 'The Two Foci of the Jewish Soul', in *Israel and the World*, p. 34.
16. Ibid, p. 34.
17. M. *Berakhot* 9:5.
18. B.T. *Berakhot* 63a. See also M. *Avot* 2:12, *Avot de-Rabbi Nathan* 17:13, *Leviticus Rabbah* 43:3, B.T. *Betzah* 16a, *Kiddushin* 81b-82a, *Pesachim* 8b, *Nazir* 23 a-b.
19. Galatians 3:25, 28. See also Romans 10:12, I Corinthians ch. 12.
20. 'Religion and Law' in Fritz A. Rothschild (ed.), *Between God and Man: An Interpretation of Judaism*, New York: The Free Press, 1965, p. 158.
21. See, e.g., Gershom Scholem, *The Messianic Idea in Judaism*, New York: Schocken Books, 1972, especially pp. 21-24.
22. Ibid, p. 23.
23. Ibid, pp. 37-48.
24. For an excellent introduction to the subject, see Aharon Lichtenstein, 'Does Jewish Tradition Recognise an Ethic Independent of Halakhah?' in Marvin Fox (ed.), *Modern Jewish Ethics*, Columbus: Ohio State, 1975, pp. 62-88.
25. Nachmanides, *Commentary* to Deuteronomy 6:18.
26. *Maggid Mishneh* to Maimonides, M.T. *Shekhenim* 14:5.
27. *Israel and the World*, 37.
28. *I and Thou*, p. 110.
29. *Pesikta de-Rav Kahana*, (ed. Mandelkern), *Parah*, p. 44.

14
The Path of Return: A Preface to the Reading of Rosenzweig

It is nearly two years since William Hallo's translation of the *Star of Redemption* appeared, and Rosenzweig became accessible to us in more than brief glimpses and vicarious memories. Until then we felt we knew the life but not the thought. And this in itself seemed sufficient. For any thinker who took his stand on the irreducibly personal, as Rosenzweig did in opposition to the German idealist tradition, must stand as a living verification or refutation of his words. Or if sincerity can never be a final criterion of the value of any philosopher, at least we knew that Rosenzweig in life stood his own challenge, that philosophy must lead 'into life'. And indeed his life seemed almost like a modern equivalent of that lonely bearer of the burden of the personal – Abraham – with its exile (his near conversion to Christianity), its return (his subsequent working back to the sources of Judaism), its great trials (the progressive paralysis of the last eight years of his life) and its fulfilment in the death which is a judgement on life (Rosenzweig's 'point of all points', Abraham's 'full with his years'). His life was a paradigm in the traditional Jewish sense – it microcosmically recapitulated the history of the race. And now that the thought, too, has been opened to us, and we can see the light of the Star direct and not reflected, it is time to ask, what path has Rosenzweig opened up for us? Is it a path that many can follow, or only the lonely few? Is it a new vision of Judaism or a new path to the old? Will Rosenzweig, like Abraham, become 'a father of many'?

Rosenzweig's was, as we know, the path of return, a 'guide of reversioners' in Steven Schwartzchild's phrase. But it was not *teshuva* in the traditional sense. For orthodoxy had, on the one hand, seen *teshuva* as, at least in part, repentance – a relinquishing of one's past.[1] Whereas Rosenzweig, although he knew his past must be transcended, also knew that it must not be severed or denied: 'in being Jews, we must not give up anything, not renounce anything, but lead everything back to Judaism . . . This is a new sort of learning. A learning for which – in these days – he is the most apt who brings with him the maximum of what is alien'.[2] And on the other hand, orthodoxy had seen in 'return' a stage *in* life rather than a programme *for* life – a first moment only. As a great talmudist once expressed it, '*Teshuva* is needed when the mechanism of Judaism is out of order. It is not part of the mechanism itself'.[2a] But Rosenzweig explicitly saw it as process rather than moment, and rejected the traditional view, both in the name of the personal and in the name of Judaism itself: "What advantage has he who has gone the way, over him who right at the outset ventured the leap, which must come in the end in any case? A very small advantage . . . which we believe justifies the utmost trouble: for only this laborious and aimless detour through knowable Judaism gives us the certainty that the ultimate leap, from that which we know to that which we need to know at any price, the leap to the teachings, leads to *Jewish* teachings".[3]

These two facts about Rosenzweig's thought are of central interest when we come to 'place' him in the conventional schema of religious commitment. For we find at once that we cannot do so – and it is not simply that he cuts across the traditional distinctions between Orthodox and Progressive, but that his thought lies along a completely different axis. Distinctions imply the existence of fixed points of opposition; whereas Rosenzweig is concerned to outline the form of a process or a series of transitions, and to share with us some of the perceptions that one who travels along his path will have. This leaves him with only one fixed point of reference – the self – which is not conceived of as the bearer of convictions but as the subject of experiences, and whose crucial predicates are those not of orthodoxy and obedience but of openness and courage. And this is what leads us to look for a correspondence between the thought and the life, and to read his philosophy as a kind of paradigmatic autobiography.

Another consequence is that we will find no simple answer to the question: what was Rosenzweig's attitude to his native German culture? The Orthodox responses ranged from cultural separatism to the Hirschian coexistence of compartmentalised Jewishness and Germanness. And in general, the Reform reaction was to accept Kantian ethical universalism as the high-point of the human spirit and sift Judaism for whatever was compatible with it, or at most to deny the existence of a cultural gap at all, *in ultima*, as Hermann Cohen did in his patriotic tract of 1915, *The Spirit of Germany and the Spirit of Judaism*. But for Rosenzweig there was no answer short of continual internal dialogue. And for this reason, perhaps the key terms in understanding him are 'conversation' and 'translation'. The German Jew, whose German structures of thought occupy the surface of his mind, and whose atavistic Jewish responses are buried in the deepest recesses of his being, must strive to reach the latter through the channels opened up by the former. And in this process both will be transformed in what he, in another context, calls 'A Holy Wedding'. This is why he uses the metaphor of 'conversation' to describe the working of his philosophy: 'In the new thinking, the method of speech replaces the method of thinking maintained in all earlier philosophies. Thinking is timeless and wants to be timeless . . . Speech is bound to time and nourished by time, and it neither can nor wants to abandon this element. It does not know in advance just where it will end. It takes its cues from others. In fact, it lives by virtue of another's life . . .'.[4]

And this is also why the work of translation is so important for Rosenzweig. It is not just the intrinsic significance of his work on the poems of Judah Halevi and, with Buber, on the Bible; but the centrality for his thought of his methodological self-consciousness about the problems of translating Hebrew thought into German. For no other Jewish philosopher, with the possible exception of Buber himself, could we place the work of translation so near to the heart of his concern. And this is, even in the narrowest understanding of translation, a problem not of language alone but of the patterns of life in which these languages are set. When we read Rosenzweig's comments on translation as an interpretive key to his whole thinking, we see in sudden relief exactly where his concerns lay: "Whoever has something to say must say it in a new way. He will create his language, and when he has said his say, the face of the language will have changed. The translator makes himself a mouthpiece for the alien voice and transmits it across the chasm of space or time. If this alien voice has something to communicate, the language will be different from what it was before".[5] And since we must understand Rosenzweig as both translator and the audience of his own translations (which were part of the personal heuristics of his return to Judaism) we can read the following as a personal statement of the prior condition for making the cultural transition: "the time . . . for such a Holy Wedding (of two languages) is not ripe until a receptive people reaches out toward the wing-beat of an alien masterpiece with its own yearning and its own utterance, and when its receptiveness . . . has become an integral part of the people's historical development".[6] His whole writing on the nature of translation reads like a commentary to that phrase about the path of return: "in being Jews, we must not give up anything . . . but lead everything back to Judaism".

If we were to characterise Rosenzweig in a single phrase, it would not be 'the *Ba'al Teshuva*' (he who has returned) but 'the Translator', with all the wealth of meaning that he himself gave to the word. And it is precisely here that his originality lies. For Rosenzweig was acutely conscious of the theological problems of the meaning of exile for Judaism. A Jewish theology must come to terms with its historical situation, since it is above all a religion which reads Divine significance into the vicissitudes of its people in time and space. One solution – and that taken by the traditional prayer-book in the *Musaph* service for the festivals – is that exile is an act of retribution, calling for a response of atonement ('because of our sins we were exiled from our land'). Another and more positive reading, emphasised most overtly in the mystical tradition, is that exile is a way of sanctifying not only the local dimensions of the Holy Land, but the whole secular world. The picture here is one of 'releasing the buried sparks of holiness' that lie scattered in the realm of the secular, or in another image, that of 'shaking the spice-box so that its sweet smell spreads to all the corners of the room'. But both solutions involve a denial of the independent value of the exile environment. The first sees it as a temptation to be overcome; the second, as the mere physical location of sanctificatory acts which are essentially untouched by their context. They both inherit the linguistic directive of a Hebrew in which 'holy' (*kadosh*) also means 'separate'.

But Rosenzweig, that exiled Jew, affirmed every dimension of his situation. He saw, in exile, revelation. For revelation has a history and is not confined to, even if it was prefigured in, Sinai. And to say that its history (from the 'face-to-face' encounter of Moses, to the voices and visions of the prophets, to the law-maker of the Tannaim and Amoraim, to the remote and only ecstatically accessible 'infinite nothing' of the mystics) is intelligible only in the light of the social conditions of its recipients, is not necessarily to take up the detached perspective of a Max Weber. It might also be the starting point of a theology of Jewish history. And accordingly one might then reason that the positive function of a situation of exile is to open up a whole series of channels of revelation which derive from the new eyes that an alien culture bestows. And what is exciting about this new interpretation of exile is not only that it is the most affirmative (and this of itself would be a religious advance, to be able to discern the positive intention in the seeming withdrawal of Divine involvement in history) but that it explicates the *necessity* of the 'I-here-now' which must underlie any religious response to the individual moment in its full uniqueness.

This explains why Rosenzweig the translator is also the philosopher of exile. Only the translator, with his full grasp of the potentialities of the two cultures, the one timeless, the other mediating it in time, can bring about the 'Holy Wedding'. Only now it is not (as in the traditional image) the reunion between God and His people, but the wedding of the exiled Jew (in full affirmation of his exile) and his Jewishness. And this is the key to the series of brilliantly original observations which fill the *Star of Redemption*. Rosenzweig writes with the perceptiveness of the outsider, seeing new patterns precisely because, understanding other cultures as well as he understands Judaism, he can set them against it and see the divergences – things which would not be consciously articulated by the Jew who had always lived inside the walls of Torah, not so much because they eluded his attention but because his hierarchy of significances was unresponsive to time.

To say this, however, is not enough. For it might sound

as if Rosenzweig had triumphantly solved the paradox of exile. This is not so, and his position is a precarious one, at least from a traditional perspective. To understand this we might begin with his metaphor of 'conversation'. One thing is particularly striking about the accession to the threshold of prophecy (for Maimonides,[7] the legitimate aim of every Jewish life), and that is that it is accompanied by a sudden realisation of the inadequacy of human speech to the Divine Word – Moses' 'I am not a man of words', Isaiah's 'I am a man of impure lips', Jeremiah's 'I cannot speak, for I am a child'. Their message is ultimately not theirs, they become transparent, their self becomes a medium and not an independent reality. And for this reason, any philosophy which sees a real distinction between the subjective and the objective can only be a *preface* to Judaism and cannot speak with an authentically Jewish voice. Rosenzweig saw this and made his subjectivism a starting-point only: "to achieve being objective, the thinker must proceed boldly from his own subjective situation".[8] But if so then the whole of the *Star of Redemption* is a starting-point, leading 'into life' but transcended in life, in the same way as Wittgenstein described his *Tractatus Logico-Philosophicus*, "he (the reader) must, so to speak, throw away the ladder after he has climbed up it. He must transcend these propositions, and then he will see the world aright".[9]

As an illustration of the distance between starting-point and destination, we might, with the added poignancy that Rosenzweig's personal fate lends it, take his analysis of death. This must be the starting-point for subjectivism, for only in the fear of death does the individual realise his ontological loneliness: "All knowledge of the whole has its source in death, in the fear of death". "Only the singular can die, and everything mortal is solitary".[10] But death in Judaism has no ultimate reality, for Judaism knows no ultimate loneliness. Death is, as Rosenzweig notes, the gate through which the 'I' cannot pass.[11] But because the Jewish soul is more than the 'I', because in its alignment with the Divine will it encompasses the Whole, death is not its boundary. Much of the meaning of this is open to Rosenzweig, who sees for example the connection between marriage and death as twin symbols of union of the mortal and the Divine. But in his comments on the Day of

Atonement [12] – the day he held back from Christianity and began his lonely path back to Judaism – he still sees the 'solitary individual' confronted by the fact of death. Whereas, traditionally, it is the day par excellence when the community stands together in absolute collectivity ('*Our* father, *our* king', 'For the sins *we* have committed'); and the shroud (*kittel*) that the worshipper wears is not a symbol of death but of the angelic orders, of eternity, of self-effacement.

This is why Rosenzweig will stand as the Translator and not as the *Ba'al Teshuva*. For as he himself wrote, "to translate is to serve two masters",[13] and while one's perceptions of Judaism are still mediated by the forms of a previous non-Jewish vision, they are not yet visions from *within*. This does not mean that they must be 'renounced', but they must be transformed by taking their place in a different context. And ultimately the 'speech' will be stilled to the silence that knows that it has arrived at its place of destination, and needs and can have no other voice than the infinite resonances of the Divine word. Had he reached that far, we would not remember him as Franz Rosenzweig (that bearer of 'the first name and surname – the *personal* in the strictest sense of the word' [14] as he said of Kierkegaard), but as some set of initials – as Rashi, Rambam, Ravad – in the striking effacement of identity by which tradition hides its individual talents in permutations of the holy letters: another column of commentary clustering round the text of Jewish history.

Rosenzweig is indispensable to us. We needed to be shown the religious meaning of exile in a way that did not blind us to the call of the moment and of the place. He has given new meaning to the old maxim that everyone who sees something new in Judaism is as if he were standing in the immediacy of Sinai; and he has opened this possibility not only for himself but for each of us. But if his words show us the path and lead us to the gate, they do not take us through to the other side. And yet in his last utterance, that great affirmation of death ('now it comes, the point of all points, which the Lord has truly revealed to me in my sleep') he himself transcended his thought, and finally passed 'into life'.

NOTES

1. Maimonides, M.T. *Teshuvah* ch.2.

2. 'On Jewish Learning' in Nahum Glatzer, *Franz Rosenzweig: His Life and Thought*, New York: Schocken Books, 1970, p. 231.
2a. This was expressed to me by the late Dayan Yechezkel Abramsky.
3. Glatzer, p. 241.
4. 'The New Thinking', in Glatzer, p. 199.
5. Glatzer, p. 253.
6. Ibid, p. 257.
7. See Maimonides, M.T. *Yesodei ha-Torah* ch. 7, *Guide of the Perplexed*, II: 35-48, III:51.
8. *Briefe*, p. 597; Glatzer, p. 179.
9. Ludwig Wittgenstein, *Tractatus Logico-Philosophicus* 6.54.
10. Franz Rosenzweig, *The Star of Redemption*, translated by William Hallo, London: Routledge and Kegan Paul, 1971, pp. 3-4.
11. Ibid, p. 273.
12. Ibid, pp. 326-7.
13. Glatzer, p. 254.
14. *The Star of Redemption*, p. 7.

15
Rabbi Joseph B. Soloveitchik: Halakhic Man

Judaism and Philosophy, never natural friends, seemed since the Middle Ages to have suffered an almost total estrangement. There had been, to be sure, Jewish thinkers of distinction in the modern age – men like Hermann Cohen, Leo Baeck, Mordecai Kaplan, Franz Rosenzweig and Martin Buber. But each stood some way from the mainstream of rabbinic tradition, of *halakhic* and *aggadic* Judaism. Their works mapped out new forms of Jewish consciousness instead of translating the old forms into a new language. To confront modernity, it appeared, one had to move away from Orthodoxy. To remain Orthodox, one had to resist the confrontation.

We might have concluded that just as there was an age of prophecy, so there was an age of philosophy – in this case that remarkable five hundred year flowering between Saadia Gaon's *Emunot VeDeot* and Joseph Albo's *Ikkarim*. Maimonides had been its Isaiah, Albo its Malachi, and philosophy had then fallen silent. Perhaps the expulsion of the Jews from Spain in 1492 was as decisive a watershed for the possibility of philosophy as had been the destruction of the Second Temple for the possibility of prophecy.

If so, we would have been wrong. Post-war American Orthodoxy, by some happy combination of circumstance, discovered that the *bat kol* of Jewish philosophy could be heard once more. 'Modern Orthodoxy' was the label under which were grouped such diverse thinkers as Norman Lamm, Emanuel Rackman and Eliezer Berkovits, Walter Wurzburger and Michael Wyschogrod, and a younger generation which contained the subtle and elegant Aharon Lichtenstein as well as radicals like Irving Greenberg and David Hartman.[1]

Here was a group which despite its label had no common programme or stance. It was not a movement or a school of thought. Yet it had a rough-and-ready kind of unity. It had an institutional focus in Yeshiva University. It had a medium of expression in the journal *Tradition*. And above all it had a prophet: Rabbi Joseph B. Soloveitchik, known to an entire section of American Jewry as simply 'The Rav'.

The last few years have seen a flurry of activity in making Soloveitchik's work more accessible. Volumes of his hitherto unpublished or uncollected writings have appeared. Lectures have been transcribed and translated.[2] Recently a massive two-volume *festschrift* appeared, occasioned by his eightieth birthday and an impressive tribute to the range and depth of his influence.[3]

English readers will be particularly grateful that this literary harvest now includes a translation of the classic essay *Ish ha-Halakhah*,[4] which had for many years been the single written expression of Soloveitchik's philosophy. Published as an article in 1944 in the journal *Talpiot*, it had lain like a buried treasure: difficult to track down, hard to read, and imposing formidable intellectual demands on the reader. It subsequently appeared, in 1976 and 1979, in two Hebrew volumes of the Rav's essays, and has now been issued on its own as *Halakhic Man* in a translation by Lawrence Kaplan, himself a student of the master.

What emerges from the book? What or who is Halakhic man? What is distinctive about the way he approaches the world? And how – surely the key question – has R. Soloveitchik entered into the confrontation with modernity which others before him had declined.

Halakhah and the Search for Authenticity

First, though, a personal reminiscence. I met the Rav in the summer of 1967. I was then a student with one year of philosophy behind me. American Jewry seemed at the time to be populated by theological giants who spoke a language of such richness and creativity that a pilgrimage seemed a necessary part of an education. (It was probably the last such moment. Nowadays, even to meet the best of the Americans, one would have to travel to Israel.)

Commentary magazine had recently taken soundings from most of the leading thinkers and had published the results in a volume entitled *The Condition of Jewish Belief*. With this book in one hand and a Greyhound bus ticket in the other I set out to meet as many as possible of the figures in its pages. It soon became clear that a major landmark in this densely populated region was Rabbi Joseph Soloveitchik.

Everyone pointed in his direction. For the non-Orthodox perhaps even more than within his own world, he was the object of awe and surprise. Here was a representative of the world of *mitnaged* yeshivot, a member of a famous halakhic dynasty whose grandfather – R. Chayyim Soloveitchik of Brisk – had been one of the shaping geniuses of the analytical school of talmudic study. Yet this figure from an apparently closed world had studied philosophy at the University of Berlin, written a doctorate on Hermann Cohen, and was steeped in the literature of existentialism. He delivered discourses on the phenomenology of faith illustrating his argument with arcane sections of Jewish law one moment, rapturous quotations from the Song of Songs the next – all in a fluent and highly rhetorical Yiddish!

He was the culturally impossible made real. A Renaissance man who compassed the intellectual world within four cubits of the halakhah. He was a living embodiment of Hamlet's paradox: 'I could be bounded in a nut-shell, and count myself king of infinite space'. What could he be like in the flesh? After several fruitless attempts to track him down, I eventually encountered him at the beginning of the new year in his Talmud *shiur* at Yeshiva University. He was a strangely forbidding figure, slight, gaunt, dressed in a conventional business suit, with cold abstracted eyes turned in upon some private vision. It was his custom, he told me, to sit with his students in silence for an hour or two before the class preparing the passage they would study that morning. If I cared to come the next morning, he would sit outside the class and talk to me.

Next morning I was there, and we sat together on a bench in the corridor. Instantly the austerity was gone. In the unique kinship that is *lernen*, he put his hand on my shoulder and started to sway backwards and forwards expounding his philosophical thesis as if it were a difficult Tosafot. His question was fundamental: What is authentic, autonomous – what is *Jewish* – about Jewish philosophy?

Judaism, he maintained, had one unique heritage from which every authentic expression must flow and in reference to which every proposition must be validated: the halakhah. A philosophy not rooted in the halakhah would fail to capture what it sought to describe.

For instance, he said – in a reference to A.J. Heschel – it was possible to construct a philosophy of Shabbat as a 'sanctuary in time'. This might be a beautiful idea; but it was a misleading one. Shabbat for the halakhah was the thirty-nine *avot melakhot* (parent-categories of forbidden work) and their derivatives. Any philosophising must begin and end with this point.

A philosophy of the individual, his freedom and grandeur, must take as its starting point some concrete halakhic application. This was to be found in the Laws of Repentance in Maimonides' Code. He was, he said, expounding just such a philosophy in his lectures on *Teshuvah* (they have since been transcribed and published by the late Pinhas Peli and constitute the best point of entry into his method and tone of voice).

Although halakhah seemed an inauspicious reservoir of ideas – it was, on the face of it, no more than a system of concrete laws for particular applications, lacking wider reference to the mysteries of existence – those ideas could be found by patient uncovering of the conceptual world they presupposed. Halakhah was the visible surface of a philosophy: the only philosophy that could lay legitimate claim to being Jewish.

That still seems in retrospect the best summary of his work.[5]

Text and Life

But the idea that halakhah is the basis of Jewish philosophising has a double sense. For halakhah might mean either of two things: a *process* or a *product*, the process of studying Jewish law or the product of that study, the law itself.

In Rabbi Soloveitchik's later work – the lectures on *Teshuvah*, for example – the latter comes into play. A piece of halakhah, a paragraph in Maimonides' Code perhaps, becomes the starting point for ever widening philosophical meditation. Not always is it a legal text that sets the discourse in motion: in the two major articles he wrote in the 1960s, *Confrontation* [6] and *The Lonely Man of Faith*,[7] the text in question is a Biblical one, in both cases the creation of man in the book of Bereishit.

In this vein R. Soloveitchik represents a classic tradition of *derashah*, wide-ranging exegesis which moves from a text to the complex world behind the text, a style used in the *Akedat Yitzhak* of Isaac Arama, the *Derashot* of Rabbenu Nissim of Gerondi, and in the Chassidic work which has frequently influenced R. Soloveitchik, *Likutei Torah* of R. Shneour Zalman of Liadi.

But in *Halakhic Man* we are in different territory. Here the subject is halakhah as process – the act, the life, of studying halakhah. We are not invited to reflect on any particular text; rather we are introduced to the kind of person who devotes himself to talmudic study.

Is there, though, just one kind of Talmud student? Clearly not. A point needs to be made here if we are to understand what *Halakhic Man* is about. It is one thing to ask: What kind of person becomes a talmudist? And quite another to ask: What kind of person does a talmudist become? There are many different motives for studying Talmud; but the process changes the person, as he becomes increasingly involved, enveloped and shaped by the activity. So we can talk of an ideal type – the person in whom this process is complete – and still say something of great relevance. Few readers of *Halakhic Man* will recognise themselves in its pages, but they will learn something of what they might become.

Ideal and Real Worlds

Who then is the man of halakhah? R. Soloveitchik begins by telling us who he is not. He is neither the man of science (cognitive man) nor is he the conventional man of religion (*homo religiosus*). The man of science seeks to *dispel* the mystery of existence by uncovering the laws that govern the universe. The man of religion *seeks out* the mystery of the universe by reaching to the unfathomable beyond the laws.

Halakhic man is neither, or rather he is something of both; he 'reflects two opposing selves'.[8] He is not like the empirical scientist trying to understand the laws that operate within things we can observe. Instead he is like the mathematician who constructs models or abstract systems which may or may not correspond to the world. The essence of the Halakhah, which was received from God, consists in creating an ideal world and cognizing the relationship between that ideal world and our concrete environment'.[9]

This view of halakhist as mathematician yields a strange but characteristic vision. When the halakhist witnesses a dazzling sunrise, he is no poet seized by its beauty or uniqueness. He relates it to his ideal system; here is an event which triggers off certain obligations with regard to prayer, *tefillin* and so on. He encounters a mountain and asks: is this a private domain within the laws of Shabbat? He sees a spring of water and it becomes for him a *mikveh*-equivalent, satisfying the requirements of a place for immersion and purification.[10]

Like the mathematician, theory pleases him more than practice: 'the pillar of halakhic thought is not the practical ruling but the determination of the theoretical Halakhah. Therefore, many of the greatest halakhic men avoided and still avoid serving in rabbinical posts.'[11] He would like reality to correspond to his system, but 'as long as this desire cannot be implemented, halakhic man does not despair . . . He goes his own way'.[12]

In many ways, therefore, he is quite unlike the conventional type of the religious man. He does not long for transcendence and escape from the narrow imperfections of the real world.[13] Nor does he have a morbid fascination with death and the afterlife. The entire halakhic system cherishes life in the here-and-now, and sees death as defiling. The afterlife is a place of religious reward, but 'the receiving of a reward is not a religious act; therefore halakhic man prefers the real world to a transcendent existence because here, in this world, man is given the opportunity to create, act, accomplish'.[14]

Torah is law for the human situation: that is why it was given to man, not the ministering angels. When the sages of the Talmud pictured God and the heavenly hosts, they saw them assembled as a *yeshivah* disputing points of concrete halakhah: laws concerning leprosy, the red heifer, and so on. R. Soloveitchik puts this epigrammatically. In conventional religion 'the lower yearns for the higher'. In halakhah, 'the higher longs and pines for the lower'.[15]

Certainly halakhic man has a place for eternity. Does he not say, in his blessing over the Torah, 'And everlasting life has He planted in our midst'? It is simply that he reverses the usual direction of such feelings. Eternity is not a refuge into which he wants to escape. It is something he wants to incorporate into the world: he 'longs to bring transcendence down into this valley of the shadow of death . . . and transform it into a land of the living'.[16]

This endows Judaism with a special kind of spirituality. First, there is no escape from the problem of suffering. Halakhic man cannot say, beholding injustice, that there is a world beyond this in which all wrongs are righted. 'There is nothing so physically and spiritually destructive as diverting one's attention from this world'.[17] Hence the powerful definition given by R. Chayyim of Brisk of the role of the rabbi: 'To redress the grievances of those who are abandoned and alone, to protect the dignity of the poor, and to save the oppressed from the hands of his oppressor'.[18]

Second, halakhah sees holiness always as embodied in the concrete, the finite. When Solomon completed the Temple he stood aghast at the impossibility of the project he had been commanded: 'Behold, heaven and the heaven of heavens cannot contain Thee; how much less this house that I have built?' (I Kings 8:27). In Jewish mysticism this unanswered question becomes a cosmic paradox. But halakhic man does not sense the problem. He has an obsession with the precisely quantifiable. Each holy act and object has its exact dimensions. It is here – in the measurable world of the senses – that the religious life becomes *objective*. 'The fundamental tendency of the Halakhah is to translate the qualitative features of religious subjectivity . . . into firm and established quantities.'[19]

The thrust of Halakhah is against the private and the subjective. Its practitioners do not experience the mystic dread or love of self-abnegation when standing before God; nor do they fear death. R. Soloveitchik relates of his grandfather, R. Chayyim, that when fear of death seized him he would immerse himself in study of the laws of corpse defilement, and became calm. 'The act of objectification triumphs over the subjective terror'.[20]

At this stage the anecdotes quoted with admiration may strike the casual reader as unearthly, even callous. Take, for instance, the case of R. Elijah Pruzna whose daughter was on the brink of death. The rabbi, dressed in *tallit* and *tefillin*, was engaged in prayer. He came to his daughter's room, asked the doctor how long she had to live, returned to remove his Rashi's *tefillin* and put on those of Rabbenu Tam, so that he could complete the command before being present at her death.[21]

An episode like this is a crux for our understanding of the halakhic personality. Only in a culture which utterly cherished both life and children could it be other than heartless. But because we *know* that the rabbi was at a juncture of distress no less than Job's, we stand in awe at the power of a religion which sets him outside of himself and his grief. 'There is a time for everything and a season for every activity under heaven' (Ecclesiastes 3:1). The wisdom of *Kohelet* here becomes a total emotional discipline.

Self-Creation

It would be wrong, though, to conclude that the halakhic system aims at effacing personality by a regimen of controlled emotions. Indeed the latter half of *Halakhic Man* is devoted to showing how far individual creativity is encouraged. This looks like a contradiction; but the picture R. Soloveitchik draws can be summed up this way. Halakhic individuality belongs to the mind, not to the heart. We are unique not in what we feel but in what we think. The halakhic hero is not a man of emotion, but a man of intellect.

The Talmud, in a series of dramatic vignettes, describes how the Almighty willingly yielded His authority to the sages when it came to interpreting Jewish law. 'Even the Holy One, blessed be He, has, as it were, handed over His imprimatur, His official seal in Torah matters, to man; it is as if the Creator of the world Himself abides by man's decision and instruction.' [22]

This endows the halakhist with extraordinary dignity under the eye of heaven. As interpreter of the tradition, he shapes the rules to which even the Almighty conforms. R. Soloveitchik cites with approval the remarkable dictum of R. Chayyim of Volozhin. In Ethics of the Fathers, R. Judah ha-Nasi had said, 'Know that which is higher than you (*mimkha*)'.[23] R. Chayyim read this as: 'Know that what is higher *proceeds from you*'.[24] Man, says R. Soloveitchik, 'constructs the worlds which are above him'.[25] He is, with God, co-creator of the ideal world which is Halakhah.

Halakhic man is neither modest nor humble. His most essential character is strength of mind.[26] He is not unemotional, but his feelings are dictated by his thoughts. This is the meaning of that strange passage in *Avot* which says, 'He who walks by the way and studies and breaks off his study and says, "How beautiful is this tree", is reckoned by Scripture to have committed a mortal sin.' [27] This does not mean that we should be indifferent to the beauties of nature, but it means that 'cognition should precede rapture'.[28] Accordingly the man of Halakhah loves truth above all things. He cannot be a poet: nor can he be a politician. Truth does not yield to public pressure or expediency. His words may offend, but halakhic man is unmoved.

How then does this individuality arise? For this is no mere rhetoric. It is here that Halakhah takes its stand at the point most opposed to conventional religion. It refuses to value the merging of the individual with the universal. 'The most fundamental principle of all is that man must create himself'.[29] It happens in three stages.

The first is represented by the idea of *teshuvah*. This should not be confused with repentance. Repentance means atonement, regret, seeking to put things right with the Almighty by mourning the past. Not so *teshuvah*, which has to do with the active reconstruction of personality. In *teshuvah* the individual creates for himself a new identity, forges a new future; and in so doing rewrites his own past. *Teshuvah* is essentially creative. Through it we create ourselves.[30]

The second stage belongs to the idea, as set out by Maimonides, of Divine Providence and human choice.[31] We belong, all of us, to the species 'man'. If we were passive, responding only to our drives and biological instincts, we would be no more than members of a species. We would live and die having experienced pleasure and pain, but having contributed nothing that was uniquely our own. But Judaism confronts us at every moment with a choice: to be active, creative, and thus to be an individual. To the degree that we exercise this choice, we experience Divine Providence as a personal encounter. We create; therefore we meet the Creator.[32]

The third and highest stage is that of the prophet. Again R. Soloveitchik follows Maimonides,[33] this time in regarding prophecy as a permanent religious possibility and not just a passing moment in the history of Israel. The prophet has so remade his personality, through *teshuvah* and the constant exercise of choice, that he has made the complete transition from man, the member of a biological species to man, the partner and voice of God.[34]

Ideal Teacher

Such, then, is Halakhic man. An intellectual aristocrat who carries a world within his head, a world of which he is co-author with the Almighty. Study is his primary religious act: study understood as a dialectic between the received tradition and individual creativity; study magnified to epic proportions as the crucible in which a new selfhood is forged; study seen as a unique, almost mystical, encounter. God is met through the mind.

R. Soloveitchik has little to say about God and much about man. But his vision of God is recognisably that of the talmudic sages, who saw Him as the Ideal Teacher. He provides his students, the children of Israel, with Torah as the constitution of an ideal world. He listens to their arguments, their discoveries, with acquiescence and delight. He longs to speak with them as intellectual equals. Above all: He *leaves them work to do*, whether it be in perfecting the universe or adding a new interpretation to a text. Divine grandeur belongs supremely to Divine self-restraint – 'Wherever you find God's greatness there you find His humility'.[35] It is the self-restraint of the teacher who wishes his disciples to grow.

R. Soloveitchik's *Halakhic Man* is an astonishing tour-de-force. Readers will be spell-bound by the flow of erudite reference. In its pages and footnotes they will meet Kierkegaard and Nietzsche, Heidegger and Niebuhr, Kant and Hegel, rubbing shoulders with Rashi and Tosafot, Maimonides and Nachmanides, the Gaon of Vilna and the Maggid of Mezeritch. One wonders whether such company has ever before been assembled in a single mind.

As well as being a complex and subtle work it is also a simple one: for it is in essence a homage to his grandfather, R. Chayyim of Brisk, and to the kind of personality he represented. And despite the range of philosophical influence that lies behind it, the key figures in this universe are not Aristotle and Kant, nor yet Maimonides, but two eighteenth century theoreticians of the halakhah, R. Chayyim of Volozhin (1749-1821) and R. Shneour Zalman of Liadi (1745-1813). Though they stood on opposite sides of the great *Mitnaged* – *Chassid* divide, they shared a powerful sense of the mystical quality of Talmudic study through which the mind of man encompassed and was encompassed by the Divine will.[36]

Nor was this sentiment new in the eighteenth century. A midrash reports that 'Ben Azzai was sitting expounding Torah and fire blazed around him . . . He explained: I thread words of Torah onto the Prophets and words of the Prophets onto the Hagiographa, and the words of Torah are as joyful as when they were given at Sinai when they were given in fire'.[37] 'Oh how I love Thy law,' says the Psalmist, 'It is my meditation all the day'.[38] Torah as the object of study, devotion, rhapsody is as old as Torah itself. What then is modern about *Halakhic Man?* What made a generation feel that R. Soloveitchik had broken the philosophical silence and spoken to his age?

The Divided Self

For there is no mistaking the fact. Despite its classical lineage, *Halakhic Man* is a distinctively modern work, in three ways a document of its time.

First its religious hero, the archetypal man of Halakhah, is a personality riven by conflict. This is, in fact, his singular glory, a cause for celebration: 'Out of the contradictions and antimonies there emerges a radiant, holy personality whose soul has been purified in the furnace of struggle and opposition and redeemed in the fires of the torments of spiritual disharmony.[39]

This theme, a relatively minor one in *Halakhic Man*, was to become a *leitmotif* of the Rav. The conflicts are many: between the cognitive and religious sensibilities, between man as member of a species and man of God, between Majestic Man who creates and takes responsibility for the world, and Covenantal Man who is receptive, reflective and searches for communion.[40] The man of faith is not at peace – not with himself, not with the world. In community he finds loneliness; in intimacy, distance; in speech, silence.

In part we recognise this thinking-in-oppositions as a heritage of the Brisk method of talmudic analysis, translated here into a psychological, existential plane. But it also takes its place in a wider dislocation of the religious personality since the eighteenth century. Not for nothing did Arthur Green call his study of the Chassidic Rebbe Nachman of Bratslav, *Tormented Master*, or Elie Weisel entitle one of his volumes, *Four Hasidic Masters and their Struggle against Melancholy*. A.J. Heschel's last book was a study of the Rebbe of Kotzk and his face-to-face encounter with despair.[41] These are the modern heroes of Judaism, men who stood at the edge of the abyss, conscious that beneath the thin surface of our interpreted world is the *tohu va vohu* of disorder and destruction.[42] 'Chaos and void lie in wait in the dark alleyways of reality and seek to undermine the absolute being, to profane the lustrous image of creation'.[43] Perhaps R. Soloveitchik's greatest contribution is to have brought this dark emotional world into the halakhic arena, making him the first non-Chassidic Rebbe. A sense of loneliness permeates his work, whether or not he is talking explicitly about it. There is little in *Halakhic Man*, where there could have been so much, about the delights of intellectual companionship, *chevrutah*. This is in strange contrast to Talmudic Judaism itself, which has nothing positive to say about isolation. 'There is either companionship or death', said the rabbis;[44] 'A sword is upon those who sit alone and study Torah'.[45]

Modern halakhic man has friends: but they are people of the mind. He 'embraces the entire company of the sages of the *masorah* . . . He walks alongside Maimonides, listens to R. Akiva, senses the presence of Abaye and Rava'.[46] But his peers are of the past; the present offers him little. The people around him are impatient, secular. 'When the hour of estrangement strikes, the ordeal of the man of faith begins and he starts his withdrawal from society . . . He returns, like Moses of old, to his solitary hiding and to the abode of loneliness'.[47]

Nothing in the classic literature of rabbinic Judaism dwells in this land of anguish, conflict, isolation, divided self.[48] When R. Soloveitchik seeks a precedent he finds it in the prophets, or the voice of the lover in the Song of Songs, or in the image of Adam and Eve alone in the universe. His modernity consists in this, that his hero – so often reminiscent of Kierkegaard – lives in a world in which faith is uncommon: an act of choice made against the stream of his culture.[49]

Argument and Autobiography

Not only in content do we sense this alienation, but in form as well. R. Soloveitchik's writings are normally cast in the stylistic and intellectual medium of phenomenology and typology. Here is a kind of personality, he seems to say; let me show you from the inside what his mental world is like. It is a kind of rarified, idealised autobiography – a common enough genre outside of Judaism, but unusual within it. And here lies his second mark of modernity.

Eugene Borowitz has pointed out the shortcoming of this philosophical method: 'What remains missing in Rabbi Soloveitchik's thinking is the way by which searching, critical moderns might come to such faith.' *Halakhic Man* shows us the inner workings of the rabbinic personality. But why should we want to become such a personality, if not because we were independently persuaded of the truth of its axioms – revelation, covenant, the historicity of Sinai? 'Most Jews do not begin with his faith but might be open to argument seeking to demonstrate its reasonableness'.[50] Yet argument of this conventional kind is precisely what is absent from the writings of the Rav. Nowhere does he adopt the stance of 'Let me convince you of the truth of my faith'. Instead he invites us to enter his world, leaving it to us to decide – by conviction or commitment – whether we will finally care to share it with him.

Occasionally he touches upon these questions, only to dismiss them out of hand. He tells us that 'I have never been seriously troubled by the problem of the Biblical doctrine of creation vis-a-vis the scientific story of evolution . . . I have not been perplexed by the impossibility of fitting the mystery of revelation into the framework of historical empiricism . . . I have not even been troubled by the theories of Biblical criticism which contradict the very foundations upon which the sanctity and integrity of the Scriptures rest'.[51] It is not that he has easy answers, but that he knows that there are no answers, nor could there be. 'Covenantal commitment eludes cognitive analysis by the *logos* and hence does not lend itself completely to the act of cultural translation. There are simply no cognitive categories in which the total commitment of the man of faith could be spelled out'.[52]

This is the post-Kantian heritage, the end of an optimistic friendship between revelation and reason of which many of the medieval Jewish philosophers dreamed. We would be wrong to overdramatise the breakdown. On the one hand Maimonides himself was acutely conscious of the limits of human language in speaking about God; on the other R. Soloveitchik remains committed to the role of intellect in the religious life. What is modern is the feeling which keeps breaking through of the impossibility of communication at the level of faith. We cannot speak to the secularist; we cannot have meaningful dialogue with other faith communities;[53] as soon as we approach the 'faith gesture', conversation falters and lapses into misunderstanding and silence.

The most the modern halakhic Jew can say is: Here I stand. This is my vision. Perhaps that is all he could ever say. But never before were we so conscious of the limits of argument, the privacy of faith.[54]

Tragedy and Kaddish

The third mark of the modernity of *Halakhic Man* is to be found in what it does not say. The kabbalists spoke of a time when the empty spaces between the letters of the Torah would be as lucid as the letters themselves.[55] R. Soloveitchik's empty spaces are eloquent.

Ish ha-Halakhah originally appeared in 1944. The date reverberates with tragedy. The world of the Lithuanian yeshivot, to which it is a tribute, was at that moment being reduced to ashes. In retrospect the work is a *hesped*, a funeral oration; or more precisely a mourner's *kaddish* to a shattered universe.

R. Soloveitchik has defined the saying of *kaddish* as 'courageous and heroic mourning' in which grief is transcended and we affirm that 'However terrifying the grave is, however nonsensical and absurd everything appears . . . we declare and profess publicly and solemnly that we are not giving up, that we are not surrendering, that we will carry on the work of our ancestors as if nothing had happened, that we will not be satisfied with less than the full realization of the ultimate goal'.⁵⁶

Kaddish is a response to death but it does not mention death. *Halakhic Man* does not mention the events that were occurring as it was being written. But it reads as a response to them, even in – precisely in – its silence.

How so? It is as if, by constructing in the mind the ideal world of the halakhic system, a world peopled with architects – Hillel, Akiva, Rav, Shmuel, Rashi, Maimonides, R. Chayyim of Brisk – who never die, the real world and death itself can be defied. Halakhah in a moment of crisis takes on the role of therapy and consolation. Here are letters of fire that cannot be destroyed by fire. Here is a Torah untouched by holocaust.

One contemporary scholar has suggested that the formation of the Mishnah in the wake of the destruction of the Temple follows the same psychological course. There were two responses – apocalypse and Gnosticism – which took that historical event to be of cosmic significance. But there was a third, chosen by the rabbis of the Mishnah, which responded to history by retreating from history. The rabbis' 'deepest yearning is not for historical change but for ahistorical stasis'.⁵⁷ Jerusalem lay in ruins, but survives in the Mishnah as 'a city of the mind, a particular place, framed in all due locative dimensions and requisite spatial descriptions, which, in fact, existed nowhere but in the mind, which by nature is utopian'.⁵⁸ The resemblance between this and R. Soloveitchik's characterisation of the halakhic universe is uncanny.

Certainly there were to be both apocalyptic and gnostic responses to the holocaust amongst the Jewish thinkers of the modern age. In their company R. Soloveitchik emerges as a contemporary Yochanan ben Zakkai, not dwelling on tragedy but concentrating on the quiet task of reconstruction, of reaffirming that which endures, of raising up disciples. In the seclusion of Yavneh not the public drama of Massada, in the 'four cubits of the halakhah' not the arena of history, lay the strength to survive.

Philosophy or Midrash?

Where, finally, does *Halakhic Man* belong in the context

of R. Soloveitchik's work as a whole, in what is now the rich mosaic of his available writings? In that corpus it is the most austerely philosophical of his statements, and in time it may come to be seen as the least influential of his contributions to the development of Orthodoxy. Two other directions already seem more decisive: first his restoration of the crown of pure halakhic study to its original glory, and second his recovery of an authentic voice of twentieth century *midrash*, accessible to us in his published lectures – astonishing in their beauty, scope and dramatic intensity.

It may be that, after all, philosophising does not bring out the best in the Jew. To adopt the philosopher's stance, to stand back and reflect on one's place in nature and history, cannot be comfortable to a member of *Am Yisrael*. That place, for us, is never secure. The unknowability of God and the threat of history make any philosophy of Judaism veer betwen the tragic and the ironic. *Halakhic Man* is no exception.

Our happiest moments come not in abstraction from life but in application to texts. R. Soloveitchik's *midrash* is perceptibly more resilient, less etched with despair, than his purer moments of philosophising. It is as if the parts of Judaism were more than the whole; as if the individual verses were more than the book; as if specific moments came to more than the religious life as a whole. In the detail of Judaism is joy; in the totality is pain.

But that is not to deny the enduring value of the book. A sober analyst of the history of Jewish philosophy may conclude that its practitioners solved no ultimate problems; rather, they allowed certain personality types and mental frameworks to take their place in Judaism. The rationalist feels at home because of Maimonides; the anti-rationalist, because of Judah ha-Levi. R. Soloveitchik, in his philosophical writings, has answered no questions, but he has done what a great Jewish thinker should. He has given a home to the previously unhoused: to the Jew in the modern world who experiences conflict, loneliness and the sharp unease of faith.

NOTES

1. A recent anthology of Modern Orthodoxy is Reuven Bulka's *Dimensions of Orthodox Judaism*, Ktav, New York, 1983.

2. The major collections are *Shiurei Ha Rav* (ed. Joseph Epstein), Hamevaser, New York, 1974; *Hamesh Derashot*, Jerusalem, 1974; *Al ha-Teshuvah* (edited P. Peli), Jerusalem, 1975, translated as *On Repentance – in the thought and oral discourses of Rabbi Joseph B. Soloveitchic*, Pinchas Peli, Orot, Jerusalem 1980; *Be-Sod ha-Yahid ve ha-Yahad* (ed. P. Peli), Orot, Jerusalem, 1976; *Ish ha-Halakhah, Galui ve Nistar*, Jerusalem, 1979; *Divrei Hagut ve Ha'arakhah*, Jerusalem, 1981; see also *Reflections of the Rav* (adapted by Abraham Besdin), Jerusalem, 1979.
3. *Sefer Yovel* (edited by S. Israeli, N. Lamm and Y. Raphael), Mossad HaRav Kook/Yeshiva University, Jerusalem, 1984.
4. *Halakhic Man*, translated by Lawrence Kaplan, Jewish Publication Society of America, Philadelphia, 1983.
5. Discussion in the thought of Rabbi J.B. Soloveitchik can be found in the following: A. Lichtenstein, 'R. Joseph Soloveitchik', *Great Jewish Thinkers*, Bnai Brith, New York, 1963, pp. 281-297; Lawrence Kaplan, 'The Religious Philosophy of Rabbi Joseph Soloveitchik', *Tradition*, 14:2 (Fall 1973) pp. 43-64; Jonathan Sacks, 'Alienation and Faith', *Tradition*, 13:4-14:1 (Spring-Summer 1973), pp. 137-162; Morris Sosevsky, 'The Lonely Man of Faith Confronts the Ish Ha-Halakhah', *Tradition*, 16:2 (Fall 1976), pp. 73-89; Pinchas Peli, 'Repentant Man – A High Level in Rabbi Soloveitchik's Typology of Man', *Tradition*, 18:2 (Summer 1980), pp. 135-159; David Hartman, 'Soloveitchik's Response to Modernity' in his *Joy and Responsibility*, Jerusalem 1978, pp. 198-231; Eugene Borowitz, *Choices in Modern Jewish Thought*, Behrman House, New York, 1983, pp. 218-242.
6. *Tradition*, 6:2 (Spring-Summer 1964), pp. 5-29.
7. *Tradition*, 7:2 (Summer 1965), pp. 5-67.
8. *Halakhic Man*, p. 3. References are to the English edition.
9. Ibid, p. 19. Some suggestive remarks on this model building characteristic of halakhic thought are contained in Adin Steinsaltz, *The Essential Talmud*, New York, Bantam Books, 1977, pp. 229-240; and in the same author's 'The Imagery Concept in Jewish Thought', *Shefa Quarterly* 1 (1979), pp. 56-62.
10. Ibid, pp. 20-21.
11. Ibid, p. 24.
12. Ibid, p. 29.
13. Ibid, p. 30.
14. Ibid, p. 32.
15. Ibid, p. 39.
16. Ibid, p. 40.
17. Ibid, p. 41.
18. Ibid, p. 91.
19. Ibid, p. 57.
20. Ibid, p. 73.
21. Ibid, p. 77.
22. Ibid, p. 80.
23. M. *Avot* 2:1.
24. R. Chayyim of Volozhin, *Nefesh Ha-Hayyim*, 1:4, note.

25. *Halakhic Man*, p. 82.
26. Ibid, p. 79.
27. M. *Avot* 3:8.
28. *Halakhic Man*, p. 85.
29. Ibid, p. 109.
30. Ibid, pp. 110-117.
31. *Guide of the Perplexed*, III, 17.
32. *Halakhic Man*, pp. 123-128.
33. M.T. *Hilkhot Yesodei Ha-Torah* ch. 7; *Guide*, II, 32.
34. *Halakhic Man*, pp. 128-131.
35. B.T. *Megillah* 31a.
36. See R. Chayyim of Volozhin, *Nefesh ha-Hayyim*, and R. Shneur Zalman of Liady, *Likkutei Amarim (Tanya)*, especially part 1, ch. 5. For an introduction to the work of R. Chayyim, see Norman Lamm, *Scholarship and Piety*, in *Faith and Doubt*, Ktav 1971, pp. 212-246.
37. *Leviticus Rabbah* 16:4.
38. Psalm 119:97.
39. *Halakhic Man*, p. 4.
40. See *The Lonely Man of Faith*, op. cit.
41. Arthur Green, *Tormented Master, A Life of Rabbi Nachman of Bratslav*, Schocken, New York, 1981; Elie Wiesel, *Four Hasidic Masters and their Struggle against Melancholy*, Notre Dame Press, 1978; A.J. Heschel, *A Passion for Truth*, Secker and Warburg, London, 1974.
42. See Heschel, op. cit., pp. 228-9.
43. *Halakhic Man*, p. 103.
44. B.T. *Ta'anit* 23a; see B.T. *Baba Batra* 16b.
45. B.T. *Berakhot* 63b; *Ta'anit* 7a; *Makkot* 10a.
46. *Halakhic Man*, p. 120.
47. *The Lonely Man of Faith*, p. 65.
48. Not only in the talmudic literature. Compare the essentially harmonious conception of the ideal personality in Saadia Gaon, *Emunot ve Deot* Book 10; Judah ha-Levi, *Kuzari*, II, 50; Maimonides, *Hilkhot Deot* ch. 1. Being caught in the grip of powerful and conflicting emotions is a barrier to prophecy: Maimonides, *Shemoneh Perakim*, ch. 7.
49. See, for further analysis, J. Sacks, 'Alienation and Faith', op. cit.
50. E. Borowitz, *Choices in Modern Jewish Thought*, p. 241.
51. *The Lonely Man of Faith*, pp. 8-9.
52. Ibid, p. 60.
53. *Confrontation*, op. cit., pp. 18-21. R. Soloveitchik does not in fact rule out the possibility of dialogue but insists that it should be a confrontation which establishes 'our otherness as a metaphysical covenantal community'.
54. Privacy as distinct from subjectivity. The key concepts of the halakhic system – revelation, tradition, law, intellect, and *mitzvah* as objectification-through-action – all militate against religious subjectivity. It is just that the public language of a secular culture is unsympathetic to the aspirations of the man of faith and sees them

as 'absurd', 'insane', 'mad', 'unpardonable' and 'foolish' (*Lonely Man of Faith*, pp. 61-2).
55. A statement attributed to R. Levi Yitzchak of Berditchev. See Gershom Scholem, *On the Kabbalah and its Symbolism*, Schocken, New York, 1972, pp. 81-2.
56. 'A Eulogy for the Talner Rebbe' in *Shiurei Ha Rav*, op. cit., p. 20.
57. Jacob Neusner, *Judaism: the Evidence of the Mishnah*, University of Chicago Press, 1981, p. 27.
58. Ibid, p. 47.

16
Rabbi Joseph B. Soloveitchik's Early Epistemology

In 1941, Rabbi Joseph B. Soloveitchik succeeded his late father as professor of Talmud at the Rabbi Isaac Elchanan Theological Seminary. In 1944, he published the now famous essay *Ish Ha-Halakhah*[1], an epic phenomenological study of the halakhic personality. From then on, for twenty years, almost nothing appeared until 'Confrontation'[2] – which argued the impossibility of theological interfaith dialogue – laid the ground for 'The Lonely Man of Faith'[3] a year later. This article, at one level an analysis of the perennial conflicts of the *homo religiosus*, at another a prescient critique of what has subsequently come to be known as 'civil religion'[4], firmly established Rabbi Soloveitchik as the outstanding Orthodox philosopher of the age.

To the initiated, however, he had held that position long before. Already by 1963 he was included as one of the three Americans in Simon Noveck's collection of *Great Jewish Thinkers of the Twentieth Century*[5], and Aharon Lichtenstein's essay in that volume did much to project his thought to a wider audience. Those who were familiar with his philosophical positions at that stage knew them as *Torah shebe'al peh*, through the spoken medium of lectures, *derashot* and *shiurim*. Lichtenstein explained that this was not to be taken as a distaste for the act of writing, but rather as a perfectionist's reluctance to publish. "The fact is, that although R. Soloveitchik has published very little, he has written a great deal."[6] Eugene Borowitz wrote that "I have been present when he has lectured by utilizing a portion of a sizable manuscript, but no book by him has appeared."[7] There was an air of mystery about this submerged iceberg of the unpublished corpus, added to by such tantalising hints, thrown out by Soloveitchik himself, as "The role of the multi-valued logic in Halakhah will be discussed by me, God willing, in a forthcoming paper".[8] This has now been at least somewhat dispelled by the publication of *The Halakhic Mind*.[9]

This, the author notes, "was written in 1944 and is being published for the first time, without any revisions or additions". It is a remarkable work, different in kind from his other writings: a sustained exposition of epistemology and the philosophy of science, quite devoid of the dialectical tension, rhapsodic prose,[10] anecdotal digression and exegetical innovation that so animate the rest of his *oeuvre*. The most technical of his writings to appear thus far, it displays a yet more awesome command of the philosophical literature than that which astounded readers of *Ish Ha-Halakhah*. Most interesting, perhaps, is the reference in the footnote[11] to the essay *U-vikashetem Mi-Sham*, first published in 1978,[12] which contains some of Soloveitchik's most profound theological reflections. It is now clear that a draft of this essay existed in the early forties[13], and thus a much more complete picture of those years is beginning to emerge.

Epistemological Foundations

The long period between 1944 and 1964 during which no major writings of Soloveitchik were published led to a conception of his thought, based solely on *Ish Ha-Halakhah*, which had to be radically revised on the appearance of 'The Lonely Man of Faith'. Here, and even more so in the essays published thirteen years later in *Tradition*,[14] was an existentialism of divided selfhood and ceaseless conflict. The man of faith, wrote Soloveitchik, was condemned to move between the 'majestic' and 'convenantal' communities, "commanded to move on before he manages to strike roots in either", an eternally wandering Aramean.[15] Or as he was subsequently to write, yet more dramatically, "Man is a dialectical being; an inner schism runs through his personality at every level . . . Judaic dialectic, unlike the Hegelian, is irreconcilable and hence interminable. Judaism accepted a dialectic, consisting only of thesis and antithesis. The third Hegelian stage, that of reconciliation, is missing." [16]

This was not what readers of *Ish Ha-Halakhah* had expected. As Eugene Borowitz notes in reference to the earlier essay, "Most readers thought that Rabbi

Soloveitchik had restated the *mitnagdic*, anti-Chassidic, tradition of Eastern Europe and wanted intellect, as utilized in *halakhic* reasoning and living, to be the central feature of modern Jewish life. When his later papers appeared . . . it became clear that the early impression was wrong. While an overarching intellectuality is manifest in these later publications, they are concerned with facing the conflicted human situation depicted by modern existentialism, not arguing for a latter-day rationalism."[17]

The discrepancies perplexed a number of commentators.[18] Was the life of faith consummated in a serene equilibrium, or destined to remain torn and divided? Was the man of faith essentially creative (Halakhic Man) or submissive (the Lonely Man of Faith)? Was there, or was there not, a higher synthesis between the messages of creation and revelation? Some suggested that in *Halakhic Man*, Soloveitchik was drawing an ideal type while in the 'Lonely Man' he was projecting his personal spiritual dilemmas.[19] Others argued that Halakhic Man was only the first typological stage in the religious life, and that his full development was closer to the Lonely Man of Faith.[20] A third possibility was that the differences could be traced to the languages in which the various essays were published and the audiences to which they were addressed. In his English essays, Soloveitchik warned of the dangers implicit in secular culture and argued that it must be counterbalanced by a different set of values. In his Hebrew essays, speaking to members of the halakhic community, he could afford to be less critical and more harmonising.[21]

Nor did these exhaust the possibilities. A recent study suggests that the difference lies between the *religious* personality as a general phenomenon – man as such, facing God, the world and his fellow man – and the *halakhic* personality as a specifically Jewish mode of resolving the tensions of the former.[22] Borowitz himself supplied the simplest solution. Soloveitchik had simply changed his mind: "We cannot now know if there have been major shifts in his thought over these four decades or whether the progress of his thought has come about by slow evolution." [23]

The hermeneutic problem may remain. On this, I will say more below. But the publication of *The Halakhic Mind* allows us to see a full outline of the early philosophical structure.

Aviezer Ravitsky has pointed out that *Halakhic Man* and *U-vikashtem Mi-sham* are complementary studies.[24] The former is an *analytical* treatment of the halakhic personality, splitting it into its component parts (cognitive man and *homo religiosus*). The latter is a *synthetic* treatment of the same personality, moving in Hegelian dialectic through freedom (active speculation and the search for religious experience) and submission (to the revealed Divine command) to the ultimate union of the Divine and human will. *Halakhic Man* describes human types; *U-vikashtem Mi-sham* describes cognitive stages.

The programme of *The Halakhic Mind* is essentially prior to both these enterprises. In it, Soloveitchik sets out his claim for the cognitive status of religion, for the methodological autonomy of the philosophy of religion, and for the primacy of halakhah as the basic datum on which a philosophy of Judaism should be based. This looks very much like the epistemological prologue to the two other works. And if *U-vikashtem Mi-sham* was indeed extant at least in outline at the time, it would seem that by 1944 Soloveitchik had already formulated an impressively complete philosophical system along three disciplinary axes: methodology, analysis and synthesis.

Cognitive Pluralism

The central argument of *The Halakhic Mind* is that religion constitutes an *autonomous cognitive domain*. Soloveitchik has no taste for apologetics, for the justification of religion in terms drawn from outside itself. He notes "the passionate desire of every philosopher of religion to legitimate the cognitive validity and truthfulness of religious propositions. Yet the problem of evidence in religion will never be solved. The believer does not miss philosophic legitimation; the skeptic will never be satisfied with any cognitive demonstration." [25]

In the past, rationalisation had distorted the presentation of Judaism. Soloveitchik singles out for criticism – in terms highly reminiscent of Samson Raphael Hirsch[26] and Rav Abraham Isaac Kook[27] – Maimonides' treatment, in the *Guide of the Perplexed*, of the reasons of the commandments. "In rationalising the commandments genetically, Maimonides developed a religious 'instrumentalism'.

Casuality reverted to teleology . . . and Jewish religion was converted into technical wisdom."[28] He had subjected them to interpretation in terms foreign to themselves. He had sought the 'why' instead of the 'what', a failing he avoided in the *Mishneh Torah*.[29]

The avoidance of rationalisation does not mean the suspension of the rational. Soloveitchik is equally critical of religious irrationalism of the *credo quia absurdum est* kind, and of mysticism and subjectivity, of which he accuses much of late nineteenth and early twentieth century philosophy. What, then, is the alternative? Normally there would be none. But the starting point of the book is that the twentieth century has opened up a gap between science and philosophy, and in the void thus created there is room – perhaps for the first time – for a fully autonomous religious epistemology.

The first and last sentences of *The Halakhic Mind* define the challenge: "It would be difficult to distinguish any epoch in the history of philosophy more amenable to the mediating *homo religiosus* than that of today . . . Out of the sources of Halakhah, a new world view awaits formulation."[30] The argument between is devoted to two questions: How has this happened? And what would be the shape of a religious philosophy that took advantage of it?

The answer to the first is that traditionally, philosophy and science have been allies. The result was that "the only realm of reality to which the philosopher had access was . . . the scientifically charted universe".[31] This placed religion on the defensive, having either to conform to scientific criteria of knowledge (rationalisation) or be driven into escapist postures (agnosticism, mysticism). However, the Galilean-Newtonian physics on which philosophy from Descartes to the neo-Kantians is premised, has been supplanted by the counter-intuitive phenomena of modern science: relativity, quantum mechanics and non-Euclidian geometry. This posed a crisis for philosophy which Bergsen was the first to diagnose. The result has been the emergence of *epistemological pluralism*.

It arose from the fact that concepts in the new sciences neither mirrored ordinary experience nor remained constant between disciplines. Thus 'space' might mean one thing to the mathematician, another to the physicist, and a third in ordinary experience. Philosophy could not postulate a unified conceptual world and at the same time embrace modern science. But therein lies the great liberation, for "as long as general philosophy explored a quantitatively constructed universe, the philosophy of religion could not progress".[32] Now there opens up an alternative to the scientific description of reality, namely one which focuses on the *qualitative* aspects of experience. This is where religious experience belongs, in the "concrete world full of color and sound".[33]

Soloveitchik insists that the 'non-scientific' character of religion does not signify that it is non-cognitive. To the contrary: "The *homo religiosus* must regain his position in the cognitive realm."[34] Against several modern philosophies of religion, Soloveitchik argues that the believer is concerned not with the transcendental domain, but with the here-and-now viewed from a religious perspective; not with interpreting God in terms of the world but the world under the aspect of God. The task of a new philosophy of religion would be to uncover its distinctive conceptuality, probing what 'time', 'space', 'casuality' and so on mean within its world. Hence the conclusion of the first half of the argument, that for the first time in the history of thought religion can be presented autonomously, as a cognitive system independent of but parallel to science.

From Objective to Subjective

The question now arises: how should such a philosophy proceed? Soloveitchik proposes two criteria. The first is practical, or more strictly, ethical. "Epistemology would do well to cast aside such canonized concepts as objectivity and ethical neutrality and survey philosophical doctrines from a subjective, normative standpoint."[35] Such considerations militate against irrationalism, subjectivism and mysticism for these lead in the end to moral corruption. "It is no mere coincidence that the most celebrated philosophers of the third Reich were outstanding disciples of Husserl."[36]

The second is theoretical. The philosophy of religion should imitate the method of modern science, namely 'reconstruction' or sensing the whole within the parts. "The structural designs of religion cannot be intuited through any sympathetic fusion with an eternal essence, but must be reconstructed out of objective religious data and central realities."[37] Religion may proceed, like art, from subjective experience to objectified forms, but it must be explored in the reverse direction. One may try to gain an insight into the inner world of the artist by examining his works, but the reverse is impossible: from a precise description of his inner state one could not infer the art he will produce. So too in religion. The subjective can only be reconstructed from the objective, the actual forms in which it is concretised in specific traditions. Of these forms, the 'cult' is to be preferred to the 'ethos' as being more indicative of the unique character of a particular religion.

Soloveitchik thus has a series of objections against religious subjectivism which he summarises as follows. First, it fails to satisfy *homo religiosus*, who seeks more than inward experience. He wants ethical guidance and a religious community. Second, subjective religion has no defences against barbarism, to which it frequently descends. Third, it renders religion esoteric and non-democratic. "Aristocracy in the religious realm is identical with the decadence of religion."[38] Religious liberalism errs by proceeding in the wrong direction, from subjectivity to objectivity. But in reality there is no pristine religious subjectivity: "If one seeks primordeal subjectivity he would find an evanescent flux, neither religious nor mundane, but, similar to Aristotelian matter, unregulated and chaotic."[39]

The only valid procedure is to travel inwards from the objectified forms of religion, beginning with the received text of revelation. "The canonized Scripture serves as the most reliable standard of reference for objectivity."[40] The halakhic tradition is perfectly suited to this role. "Objectification reaches its highest expression in the Halakhah. Halakhah is the act of seizing the subjective flow and converting it into enduring and tangible magnitudes . . . In short, Halakhah is the objectifying instrument of our religious consciousness, the form-principle of the transcendental act, the matrix in which the amorphous religious hylo is cast."[41]

The Halakhic Mind ends by dissociating itself from medieval Jewish philosophy. Firstly, it had never succeeded in shaping the experience of the majority of the Jewish community. Secondly, it is rooted in non-indigenous sources, ancient Greek and medieval Arabic. Thirdly, it cannot meet the requirement of living continuity, since its concepts are by now outmoded. An autonomous Jewish philosophy is now possible and necessary, and it can only be constructed on the basis of halakhah.

Halakhic Mind and Halakhic Man

Such, then, is the argument of the book. What impressions does it leave? First, it is obviously close in spirit to the work undertaken in *Ish Ha-Halakhah*. The two books share an admiration for modern mathematics and theoretical physics as cognitive paradigms, and seek to establish their kinship with a philosophy based on halakhah. There are differences. The *homo religiosus* of *The Halakhic Mind* is not that of *Ish Ha-Halakhah*, but this is a matter of terminology rather than substance. The project of the two books is altogether different. *Ish Ha-Halakhah* describes halakhic man from the inside, *The Halakhic Mind* establishes the philosophical significance of such a description. It belongs, in other words, to the world of the footnotes of the early part of *Ish Ha-Halakhah* and constitutes a kind of systematic introduction to it. The two books differ in style and tone too. *The Halakhic Mind* is a sober philosophical work, and the persuasive, evocative style of *Ish Ha-Halakhah* would have been irrelevant to its purpose. But the setting is the same in both cases: a sense that romantic religion and philosophical subjectivism have failed, and that the need is for a presentation of religion as a form of cognitive, disciplined perception.

Second, *The Halakhic Mind* is not a prologue to *Ish Ha-Halakhah* alone but to an entire programme, a new kind of Jewish philosophy. This would undertake to gather the entire corpus of objectified Jewish spirituality – Biblical text, halakhic literature, liturgy, mysticism and so on – and seek its subjective correlative. "Out of this enormous mass of objectified constructs, the underlying subjective aspects could gradually be reconstructed." [42] In the light of this, both early works, together with *U-vikashtem Mi-sham*, are merely introductory. A good example of the detailed work one would expect, having read *The Halakhic Mind*, would be the lectures gathered in *Al Ha-Teshuvah*, where a particular body of halakhah is treated to 'subjective reconstruction'. There is thus every reason to suppose that Soloveitchik has been faithful to the call he issued in those early years, and that his 'philosophy' is to be found as much in his analysis of texts as in his more overtly philosophical statements.

Third, there is a surprising but unmistakable echo of Samson Raphael Hirsch in the book's closing pages. There is the same attack on Maimonides and others (Mendelssohn for Hirsch, Hermann Cohen for Soloveitchik) for interpreting Judaism through non-Jewish concepts. There is the same call "to know Judaism out of itself".[43] Hirsch writes that "the Bible . . . should be studied as the foundation of a new science. Nature should be contemplated with the spirit of David".[44] For 'Bible' read 'halakhah' and we have the programme of *The Halakhic Mind*. Soloveitchik's critique of religious liberalism is mounted on the same foundation as Hirsch's critique of the Science of Judaism,[45] namely that any philosophical study of Judaism must live in the details of the text and command and be built bit by bit through an extended effort of exegesis.

Indeed, even the weaknesses of *The Halakhic Mind* mirror those of Hirsch. There is the same equivocation between a penetrating methodological critique of reform and a quite disparate ethical denunciation. Both see humanism as prone to corruption, religious liberalism as arbitrary; both attack the elitism of rarified theologies. Though the temperaments of the two men could not be more different, they share the same movement from emancipation to self-emancipation. The epistemological pluralism with which *The Halakhic Mind* begins is a kind of metaphysical equivalent to the social processes experienced by Hirsch in mid-nineteenth century Germany. Both create space for Judaism to be itself.

Fourth, inevitably, the book has a somewhat dated feel about it. For those raised in the atmosphere of Wittgenstein's *Philosophical Investigations*, philosophical pluralism is not the Copernican revolution it may have seemed forty years ago. Nor is science, after T.S. Kuhn's *The Structure of Scientific Revolutions* (1962), the pristine paradigm of knowledge it once was. Indeed, the 'scientific' outlook – cognition, control, creation – came to seem, to Soloveitchik of 'The Lonely Man of Faith', a more threatening force than the subjective religiosity he attacked in *The Halakhic Mind* and *Ish Ha-Halakhah*. Had Hans Georg Gadamer's *Truth and Method* (1960) been available two decades earlier, one of the central arguments of *The Halakhic Mind* (the opposition between physics and modern humanistic sciences[46]) might not have been necessary. None of this is to say that Soloveitchik's case has been rendered obsolete. To the contrary, it has been reinforced to the point where it may have been rendered redundant. But the book will remain invaluable as his most explicit methodological statement, his point of departure, the external justification he gave for his long journey inward to a disciplined Jewish subjectivity.

Liberation and Privation

The Halakhic Mind is a deeply impressive work, furnishing new evidence of Rabbi Soloveitchik's unrivalled mastery of secular sources and disclosing a tone of voice we had not heard before, the Dr. Soloveitchik of Berlin rather than the Rav of Yeshiva University. It will raise two questions: Does it succeed in its own terms,[47] in providing a philosophical justification for the cognitive autonomy of religion? And, what light does it shed on Soloveitchik's other works and his intellectual development? Both are beyond the scope of this review and the competence of this reviewer. Some tentative speculations, though, seem inescapable.

First, Soloveitchik insists at critical stages of the argument that the pluralism he is endorsing is nonetheless a form of *realism*. It corresponds to something real in the world. It is not pragmatism. It does not deny the absolute character of Being. "Teleological heterogeneity . . . does not invalidate the cognitive act, for, in the final analysis pluralism is founded on reality itself . . . Pluralism asserts only that the object reveals itself in manifold ways to the subject, and that a certain *telos* corresponds to each of these ontological manifestations."[48]

Yet the very force of the argument suggests that reality can be sliced up and interpreted in infinitely many ways. And if reality corresponds to each of them, is it significant to say that it corresponds to any? This is the conclusion reached by Richard Rorty in his *Philosophy and the Mirror of Nature* (1980), a work which in many ways parallels *The Halakhic Mind*. Rorty's remarks on the implications of twentieth century philosophy are directly relevant and challenging. "It would make for philosophical clarity if we just *gave* the notion of 'cognition' to predictive science, and stopped worrying about 'alternative cognitive methods'. The word *knowledge* would not seem worth fighting over were it not for the Kantian tradition that to be a philosopher is to have a 'theory of knowledge'." [49]

Closely related to this is Soloveitchik's demonstration that religion is indeed cognitive, namely that its mental acts are *intentional* or 'coordinated with an object'. He alludes, in footnotes, to the problematic nature of the demonstration. Brentano denied that intentional acts were cognitive; Scheler disagreed; Soloveitchik declares his indebtedness to Scheler.[50] But this spreads the net of cognition very wide indeed – to all mental acts – and would not justify the conclusion he wants to reach, namely, that some forms of religion are more cognitive than others, halakhic Judaism most of all.

This relates to another ambivalence, here as elsewhere in Soloveitchik's work, between the universal and the particular. Is *The Halakhic Mind* about religion or about Judaism? Is the *homo religiosus* portrayed in its pages, religious man *tout court*, or the Jew? He is "an enthusiastic practitioner of the cognitive act", he is a "social being", he seeks ethical guidance and wants to change the world rather than accept it. In short, he has a predisposition to welcome halakhic Judaism. Soloveitchik seeks to demonstrate the autonomy of religion as cognition, and then to establish Judaism as the supreme example. But he has provided an argument for the autonomy and incommensurability of religions in the plural, so that the success of the first part of the argument must *ipso facto* weaken the second. He testifies to this at one stage by saying that sometimes one must choose one's philosophy "from a subjective, normative viewpoint".[51] There is a straight road from *The Halakhic Mind* to the argument in 'Confrontation' that there is no ultimate dialogue between religions since "the numinous character and the strangeness of the act of faith of a particular community . . .

is totally incomprehensible to the man of a different faith community".⁵²

These are all symptoms of the dual direction of Solveitchik's thought, projecting the autonomy and cognitive integrity of the halakhic system on the one hand, arguing its supremacy over other systems on the other. The former embraces pluralism, the latter rejects it. Which brings us back to our starting-point: the relation between Soloveitchik's early work and his later, more pessimistic and conflicted essays.

The transition from nineteenth century liberalism to twentieth century pluralism – both terms construed in their widest sense – seemed to promise much to religious orthodoxy. Instead of having to justify itself at the bar of an enlightenment universal religion or ethic, it could declare independence without forfeiting rationality. Did not the multiplicity of models of knowledge, of which mathematics and science provided ample examples, show that even within the 'hard' disciplines there was methodological pluralism? The life of faith too had to be understood on its own terms, in its own concepts, rather than be subjected to the disciplines of science, history, anthropology and psychology. This was liberation indeed, and *The Halakhic Mind* bespeaks the mood.

But the pluralism of knowledge was mirrored in society. It had correlatives in the real world. The single universe of pre-modernity – the universe inhabited by Maimonides, in which the God of Abraham and of Aristotle were indeed one; the universe in which science, philosophy and religion competed in a single arena; the universe whose last Jewish inhabitant was Rav Abraham Isaac Kook – was shattered. In its place were not merely pluralities of thought-worlds, but of identities, roles and lifestyles as well. Consider the markers of modernity invoked by one major sociological study: 'plurality of life-worlds', 'dichotomy of public and private spheres' and 'multi-relational synchronization'. Personal identity is 'peculiarly open, differentiated, reflective, individuated'. Modern man is afflicted with a 'permanent identity crisis', and suffers 'from a deepening condition of "homelessness" '.⁵³ This world is instantly recognisable. It is the world of 'The Lonely Man of Faith'.

Soloveitchik makes an important point at the beginning and end of *The Halakhic Mind*. Judaism is timeless and autonomous. But how much of it can be expressed in the language of the world depends on where the world is at a given point of time. The pluralism of contemporary culture, which he was the first to recognise, was both a liberation and a privation. It liberated tradition from having to vindicate itself in alien terms. But it prised tradition from its moorings in the collective order and made it seem as just one system among many, either consciously chosen (the *ba'al teshuvah* phenomenon) or validated by an act of faith which is "aboriginal, exploding with elemental force" [54] and eluding cognitive analysis. Soloveitchik's genius and the poignancy of his intellectual development are both evidenced in this: that he was the first to explore the positive possibilities of the liberation, and the first to chart the tragic dimension of the privation.

NOTES

1. Published in *Talpiot* 1:3-4, New York, 1944.
2. Published in *Tradition* 6:2, (Summer 1964), pp. 5-28.
3. Published in *Tradition* 7:2, (Summer 1965), pp. 5-67.
4. See Charles Liebman and Eliezer Don-Yehiya, *Civil Religion in Israel: Traditional Judaism and Political Culture in the Jewish State*, University of California Press, 1983; Jonathan S. Woocher, *Sacred Survival: The Civil Religion of American Jews*, Indiana University Press, 1986. The description given by Woocher of American Civil Judaism exactly mirrors the religion of majestic man described in the last twelve pages of 'The Lonely Man of Faith'.
5. Simon Noveck (ed.), *Great Jewish Thinkers of the Twentieth Century*, B'nai B'rith, 1963, pp. 281-297.
6. Ibid, p. 287.
7. Eugene Borowitz, *Choices in Modern Jewish Thought*, New York: Behrman House, 1983, p. 222.
8. 'The Lonely Man of Faith', p. 51.
9. Published by Seth Press, distributed by The Free Press, 1986.
10. "[Halakhic man's] affective life is characterized by a fine equilibrium, a stoic tranquility" (*Halakhic Man*, translated by Lawrence Kaplan, Jewish Publication Society of America, 1983, p. 77). One of the more interesting things about *Halakhic Man*, with its passionate rhetoric, is that it could not have been written by halakhic man.
11. Note 98, p. 130.
12. First published in *Ha-Darom* 47 (Tishri 5739), pp. 1-83; subsequently in *Ish ha-Halakhah – Galui ve-Nistar*, Jerusalem: World Zionist Organisation, 1979, pp. 115-235. The section on *shinui* and *chiddush* to which Soloveitchik alludes in *The Halakhic Mind* is to be found in the latter, pp. 204-207.

13. Aviezer Ravitsky notes that an early version of *U-vikashtem Misham*, under the title of *Ish ha-Elokim*, was "already written in the years following the appearance of [*Ish ha-Halakhah*]". Aviezer Ravitzky, 'Rabbi J.B. Soloveitchik on Human Knowledge: Between Maimonidean and neo-Kantian Philosophy', *Modern Judaism* 6:2 (May 1986), pp. 157-188, note 17. The present version was clearly written later, and is perhaps a reworking of several papers.
14. 'The Community', 'Majesty and Humility', 'Catharsis', 'Redemption, Prayer, Talmud Torah', 'A Tribute to the Rebbitzen of Talne', *Tradition* 17:2 (Spring 1978), pp. 1-83.
15. 'The Lonely Man of Faith', p. 55.
16. 'Majesty and Humility', p. 25.
17. *Choices in Modern Jewish Thought*, p. 223.
18. In addition to the articles cited below, see David Hartman, *A Living Covenant*, The Free Press, 1985, pp. 60-88. In his early writings, Hartman argues, Soloveitchik was "struggling to present halakhic man as an attractive model for Orthodox Judaism in the modern era".[71] In his later writings he "senses that if there were a total translation of the halakhic experience into Western rational categories, commitment to halakhah would be weakened" (84-85). For much of the rest of the book, Hartman takes issue with the turn in Soloveitchik's thought.
19. David Singer and Moshe Sokol, 'Joseph Soloveitchik: Lonely Man of Faith', *Modern Judaism* 2:3 (October 1982), pp. 227-272.
20. Lawrence Kaplan, 'The Religious Philosophy of Rabbi Joseph Soloveitchik', *Tradition* 14:2 (Fall 1973), pp. 43-64, on the basis of the essay 'Al Ahavat ha-Torah u-Geulat Nefesh ha-Dor'.
21. Lawrence Kaplan, 'Degamin shel ha-Adam ha-Dati ha-Idiali be-Hagut ha-Rav Yosef Dov Soloveitchik', *Mechkerei Yerushalayim be-Machshevet Yisreal*, 4:3-4 (1985), 327-339.
22. Aviezer Ravitsky, loc. cit.
23. *Choices in Modern Jewish Thought*, p. 223.
24. Aviezer Ravitsky, loc. cit., pp. 159-160.
25. *The Halakhic Mind*, p. 118, note 58.
26. Samson Raphael Hirsch, *The Nineteen Letters*, translated by J. Breuer and B. Drachman, New York: Feldheim, 1960, pp. 117-132.
27. R. Abraham Isaac Ha-Cohen Kook, *Talelei Orot*, translated in Ben Zion Bokser, *Abraham Isaac Kook*, London: SPCK, 1979, pp. 303-305.
28. *The Halakhic Mind*, pp. 91-99.
29. Soloveitchik offers here a fascinating analysis of Maimonides' use of the term *remez* (M.T. *Teshuvah* 3:4; *Mikvaot* 11:12) as signifying 'descriptive hermeneutics'.
30. *The Halakhic Mind*, pp. 3, 102.
31. Ibid, p. 6.
32. Ibid, p. 32.
33. Ibid, p. 40
34. Ibid.
35. Ibid, p. 52.
36. Ibid, p. 53.

37. Ibid, p. 62.
38. Ibid, p. 80.
39. Ibid, p. 90.
40. Ibid, p. 81.
41. Ibid, p. 85.
42. Ibid, p. 91.
43. Samson Raphael Hirsch, *The Nineteen Letters*, p. 127.
44. Ibid.
45. Samson Raphael Hirsch, *Judaism Eternal*, translated by I. Grunfeld, London: Soncino, 1959, vol. 2, pp. 285-286.
46. *The Halakhic Mind*, pp. 30-36.
47. For some other questions, see Steven S. Schwarzschild's review of *The Halakhic Mind* in *Sh'ma*, 1986, pp. 127-8.
48. *The Halakhic Mind*, p. 16.
49. Richard Rorty, *Philosophy and the Mirror of Nature*, Oxford: Blackwell, 1980, p. 356.
50. *The Halakhic Mind*, pp. 41-44, 116 (note 50), 120 (note 62).
51. Ibid, p. 52.
52. 'Confrontation', pp. 23-24.
53. P.L. Berger, B. Berger and H. Kellner, *The Homeless Mind*, London: Penguin Books, 1973, pp. 62-77.
54. 'The Lonely Man of Faith', p. 60.

Index

Abarbanel, 157
  on monarchy, 167
Acculturation, 69
Adler, Nathan Marcus, 7
Aggadah, xxii
Agnosticism, 49
Agudat Yisrael, 66, 87, 116, 143
Agus, Jacob, 32-34
Ahad Ha-Am, 15
AIDS, 164, 169
Akiva, Rabbi, xx, 175, 204, 252
Albo, Joseph, 267
Alienation, 219-244
Aliyah, 89
Alkalai, Yehudah, 20-21, 93
Altmann, Alexander, 14
American Judaism, 85-86
Amiel, Moshe Avigdor, 87
Anarchism, religious, 247
Anderton, James, 164
Anomie, 72
Anti-Zionism, 110
  religious, 87, 141-143
Anti-semitism, 21, 93, 109
Arama, Isaac, 271
Argument, xxii, 134
Aristotle, 184, 249
Arkush, Allan, 14
Artscroll, 123
Asceticism, 185
Assimilation, 59, 62, 93, 111
Auschwitz, 140, 142, 149, 150, 153, 154
Autonomy, 100
Avenarius, 36
Aviad, Janet, 73, 87

Ba'alei Teshuvah, 87, 123, 166
Baal Shem Tov, 220
Babel, 44, 161, 238
Baeck, Leo, 267
Baer, Yitzhak, 31, 157
Bamberger, Rabbi Seligmann Baer, 6, 108, 123

Bar Kochba, xvi
Bar Ilan, N., 201
Barth, Karl, 36, 145
Bellah, Robert, xiv
Ben Azzai, 175
Ben-Yaacov, Yochanan, 104
Ben Gurion, David 67
Benamozegh, Elie, 178
Berdyczewski, Micha, 22
Berger, Peter, 4-5, 44, 54, 64, 104, 179
Bergman, Samuel H., 32
Bergson, Henri, 36, 291
Berkovits, Eliezer, 114-115, 267
  on Holocaust, 151-152
  on Jewish-Christian dialogue, 162
Berlin, Rabbi Naftali Zvi Yehudah, 22-23, 32
  on Orthodox secession, 23
Bermant, Chaim, 164
Bernays, Rabbi Isaac, 6-7
Bernstein, Louis, 51
Bettelheim, Bruno, 180
Bialik, Chayyim Nachman, 15, 22, 36
Biblical criticism, 35
Bing, Rabbi Abraham, 7
Birth rates, 75
Blank, I. M., 178
Blidstein, Gerald, 31, 179
Bloch, Joseph, 180
Bloom, Allan, 70
Bloom, Maurice, 32
Bnei Akiva, 88
Body, needs of, 185
Bokser, Ben Zion, 32, 33
Borowitz, Eugene, 50, 136, 159, 279, 287-289
Bosanquet, 37
Bradley, 37
Brentano, 297
Breuer, Isaac, 16

303

Breuer, Jacob, 14
Breuer, Mordechai, 117
Breuer, Solomon, 16, 116
Buber, Martin, 53, 103, 220, 247-257, 267
  and Jewish law, 247-255
  and Judah Halevi, 249-251
  and moral pantheism, 250-251
  and Paul, 252-253
  and revelation, 248
Bulka, Reuven, 79, 104
Butterworth, Charles, 54

Cassutto, Umberto, 226-227
Catastrophe, biblical responses to, 142
  rabbinic responses to, 147
'Centrist' Orthodoxy, 95, 112, 115-121
Chadash assur min ha-Torah, 63, 123
Charedi Orthodoxy, 74-76, 99
Charity, 185-187
  institutions of, 193
Chassidic group, 122-123
Chassidic literature, 133
Chassidic thought, 241, 247
Chassidic movement, 64
Chayyim of Zans, Rabbi, 205, 207
Chibbat Zion, 23
Choirs, synagogue, 63
Chomsky, Noam, 232
Christianity, 6, 27, 44
  dialogue with Judaism, 161-181
Civil Religion, 49, 166
Cognitive pluralism, xiv, 290-292, 296-297
Cohen, Arthur A., 15, 16
Cohen, Hermann, 37, 261, 267, 269, 295
Cohen, Steven M., 75, 104
Cohen, Stuart, 31
Cohn-Sherbock, Dan, xxiii
Community, 5, 12
  concept of, 223
  in Jewish mysticism, 235-237
  two types of, 42
Compartmentalisation, 19, 131

Concealment, Divine, 219
Conflict, 44
Consciousness, conflicts of, 107
Conservative Judaism, xii, 67, 69, 76, 85
Conversion, 59
Covenant, 101, 154
Covenantal Man, 42, 222-223, 277
Creativity, 41
Crusades, 148
Cuddihy, John Murray, 17
Culture, 60
Cupitt, Don, 54

Da'at Torah, 120
Damascus Affair, 20
Danziger, Shelomoh, 104
Darkhei shalom, 131, 207
Darwin, Charles, xii
De-modernising consciousness, 166
Death, 51, 264-265, 272-273
Dependence, 185
Derashah, 271
Derekh eretz, 60-63, 69
Descartes, 236
Determinism, 207-208
Deutscher, Isaac, 217
Devekut, 240-242
Dialectic, 39, 43
Dialogue, Jewish-Christian, 161-181
  Berkovits on, 162
  Soloveitchik on, 162
  two kinds of, 256
Diaspora, 129-133, 144
Dickens, Charles, 172
Differentness, 62
Divine Presence, 147
Divorce, 101
Don-Yehiya, Eliezer, 55
Dorff, Elliot, 50
Drach, David, 6
Drachman, Bernard, 14
Dualism, 88
Dumont, Louis, 71
Durkheim, Emile, 31, 72

Eckardt, A. Roy, 156, 163

Ecology, 170
Economic growth, 188
Education, Jewish, 5, 60, 68, 81
Eivah, 131
Elazar, Daniel, 31, 76
Elijah, 47
Eliot, T. S., 224
Elisha ben Abuya, 208-212
Elisha, 47
Ellis, Marc, xxiii
Emancipation, xi, xvii, 5-6, 19, 58-61, 92-93, 144
Empathy and ethics, 174
Employer-employee relations, 189-190
Enlightenment, xi, 4, 99, 103, 107
  and ethics, 172
Epistemological pluralism, 49
Epistemology and Jewish thought, 287-301
Epstein, Isidore, 32
Essentialism and Instrumentalism, 233
Ethical pluralism, 72, 171-173
Ethical domain, 168-169
Ethoipian Jewry, 172
Ethnic minorities, 173
Ethnicity, 72
Ettlinger, Rabbi Jacob 6-7, 123
Evil and freewill, 151-152
Evolution, 35
Exclusivism, 175
Exile, xv-xviii, 8, 12, 19, 24-26, 93, 144, 148
Ezekiel, 145

Fackenheim, Emil, 15
  and Holocaust, 149-151
Faith in the City, 170
Family, 101-103, 169-171
  and Jewish ethics, 169-171
  and Freud, 171
  and the kibbutz, 171
  the modern Jewish, 101-103
Fear of Heaven, 204-205
'Fence around the law', 63
Finkelstein, Louis, 31
Formstecher, Solomon, 6
Fox, Marvin, 15

Frank, Zvi Pesach, 87
Freewill, 204-211
Freud, Sigmund, 7, 31, 44, 209
Friedman, Menachem, 74-75, 104
Fromm, Erich, 207
Fundamentalism, 97, 100, 125, 165

Gadamer, Hans Georg, 296
Galileo, 51
Galut, see Exile
Ge'ulah, see Redemption
Geiger, Abraham, 7
Gemeinde Orthodoxy, 66
Gersonides, 148
Gewirtz, Leonard, 32
Glatzer, Nahum, 79, 257
Glazer, Nathan, 73
God, names of, 226-227
Goethe, 70
Goldscheider, Calvin, 104
Gordis, Robert, 54
Graetz, Heinrich, 8
Green, Arthur, 105, 278
Greenberg, Irving, xxi, 55, 105, 114-115, 149, 267
Grunfeld, Dayan I., 14, 117, 122
Gush Emunim, 97, 124

Ha-Cohen, Rabbi Israel Meir, 77
Haggadah, 139
Halakhah, xx-xxii, 47-48, 100, 107, 114-115, 126-127
  and individuality, 274-276
  and local circumstance, 118-121
  and objectivity, 293
  and secular expertise, 197-199
  and society, 19, 129
  and 'subjective reconstruction', 295
  and subjectivity, 273
  economic factors in, 194
  in the thought of Soloveitchik, 270-285
  process and product, 270-271
Halakhic study, 52
Halevi, Judah, xiii, 19, 53, 123, 125, 147, 282

Halevy, Isaac, 16
Halivni, David Weiss, 155
Hallo, William, 259
Hamburg Temple, 60
Hampshire, Stuart, 168, 171, 173
Hansen's Law, 73
Happiness, 224
Hare, R. M., 180
Harkabi, Yehoshafat, 136
Hart, H. L. A., 169
Hartman, David, xiv, xxi, 51, 55, 105, 114-115, 267
  and religious Zionism, 129
Hartom, Menachem, 144, 149
Haskalah, 64-65, 75
Hauerwas, Stanley, 168
Hebrew University, 29
Hegel, xii, 36, 44, 70, 223, 276, 290
Heidegger, Martin, 36, 276
Heilman, Samuel, 6, 32, 52, 75, 84, 87, 124
Heraclitus, 36
Herberg, Will, 72
Hertzberg, Arthur, 32
Herzl, Theodor, 32
Herzog, Isaac, 87
Herzog, Elizabeth, 32
Heschel, A. J., 22, 53, 157, 270, 278
Hess, Moses, 21-22
  and Reform, 21
Hezekiah, 210
Hick, John, 178, 181
Hiding of the face of God, 148, 219
Hildesheimer, Rabbi Azriel, 6, 119, 123
Hillel, xix, 188, 192, 235, 238-239, 252
Hirsch, Rabbi Samson Raphael, xviii, 3-17, 19, 20, 23, 35, 39, 43, 48, 57, 59, 61, 62, 66, 67, 69, 71, 77, 90, 107-109, 112-114, 116, 122-125, 127, 134, 224, 261, 290, 295
  and emancipation, 6-13
  and ethical mission, 94, 110, 111
  and history, 92-93
  and Jewish education, 8-10
  and Jewish nationalism, 12-13
  and modernity, 12
  and secular culture, 9-11
  and Reform, 8, 10
  Nineteen Letters on Judaism, 7-8
Hirsch, Samuel, 6
Hirschensohn, Rabbi Chaim, 123
Historiography, 91
History and theology, 91
Hobbes, 235
Hoffman, Rabbi David Zvi, 6, 16, 123
Hoffman, Lawrence, 31
Holiness and finitude, 273
Holocaust, 67, 94, 103, 134
  and Christian theology, 145
  and Jewish theology, 139-160
Homosexuality, 164, 169
Hora'at sha'ah, 15, 117-118
Horowitz, Rabbi Marcus, 108
Hubris, 45
Husserl, 37
Hutner, Rabbi Yitzchak, 143

Ibn Ezra, 240-241
Ibn Verga, Solomon, 148
Idel, Moshe, 31
Imitatio Dei, 189
Inclusivism, 175
Income redistribution, 187-188, 196
Interfaith dialogue, 47, *see also* Dialogue
Intermarriage, 59, 101-102
Isaac, binding of, 148
Isaiah, 210
Ishmael, 212-215
Islam, 27
Israel and Diaspora, 25-26

Jacobson, Dan, 155
Jakobovits, Lord, 15, 117, 159, 202
James, William, 36
Jeremiah, 47
Jewish day schools, 68, 81
Jewish education, 60
Jewish identity, 3, 57

Jewish peoplehood, 110, 133
Jewish philosophy, xiii-xv, 40, 293
Jewish socialism, xii
Jewish thought, xii-xv, 107-136
Job, 147-148
Joseph, 37-38
Joshua, 90
Judaeo-Christian tradition, 162-163
Judaism, and class, 194-197
  and education, 196
  and philosophy, 267-268, 282
  and politics, xxii, 198-199, 207
  and the public domain, 128-129
  and secular culture, 108, 122-127
  and secular study, 117-119
Jung, C. J., 235
Justice, 213-214, 273
  Divine, 142-149, 151-153

Kabbalah, 23
Kahane, Meir, 126
Kalam, xiii
Kalischer, Rabbi Zvi Hirsch, 20-21, 93
Kamentsky, Rabbi Jacob, 68
Kant, xii, 9, 70, 276
Kaplan, Lawrence, 51, 135, 155, 268
Kaplan, Mordecai, 12, 267
Kaplan, Zvi, 51
Katz, Jacob, 14, 32
Katz, Steven, 159
Kehillah, 19, 168, *see also* Community
Keller, Chaim Dov, 104
Kellner, Menachem, xiv
Kiddush ha-Shem, 108, 111, 119, 131-132, 152
Kierkegaard, xx, 36, 231, 265, 276, 279
Kimchi, Rabbi David, 229
Klausner, Joseph, 178
Knesset Yisrael, 108, 110, 133
Kohler, Kaufman, 178
Kollel, 74

Kook, Rabbi Abraham, xviii, 3, 13, 19-34, 35, 39, 43, 48, 57, 67, 69, 71, 87, 93-95, 107, 112, 114, 122, 124-125, 128, 134, 290, 298
  and evolution, 27
  and messianic age, 24
  and modernity, 29-30
  and Orthodoxy, 28
  and rebels against tradition, 25
  and secular study, 28
  and teshuvah, 27
  and tolerance, 30
  and unity of existence, 24, 26
  and Zionism, 24
Kotler, Rabbi Aaron, 68
Krakovski, Menachem, 216
Kranzler, George, 79
Kuhn, T. S., 295

Ladino, 61
Lakewood Yeshivah, 68
Lamm, Norman, 16, 34, 105, 159, 267
Lanzmann, Claude, 141
Lasalle, Ferdinand, 36
Leadership, religious, 133
Leibowitz, Nechama, 33
Lessing, 70
Lévi-Strauss, 232
Levinson, David, 104
Levy, Marion, 59, 63
Liberal individualism, 72, 99
Liberal Judaism, xii
Liberalism, 130, 169, 298
  religious, 97-100
Liberles, Robert, 14, 32
Lichtenstein, Rabbi Aharon, 51, 52, 54, 257, 267, 287
  and religious zionism, 129
Liebman, Charles, 13, 20, 31, 34, 55, 81, 84, 104
Lifnim mi-shurat ha-din, 254
Lindbeck, George, 179, 181
Loew, Rabbi Judah of Prague, 23, 24
Love and the self, 239-240
Lubavitch Chassidism, 68, 75

Lunel, Rabbi Jonathan ha-Cohen
of, 52
Mach, 36
Machteret, 124
MacIntyre, Alasdair, 135, 156, 164, 168
Maimonides, Moses, xiii, 5, 9, 11, 19, 48, 49, 52, 58, 108, 123, 125, 127, 147, 193, 241, 264, 267, 275, 276, 278, 280, 282, 290
  Epistle to Yemen, viii, 92
  Guide of the Perplexed, v, 58, 133
  on charity, 186
  on freewill, 205-211
  on Middle Way, 116
  on reasons for the commandments, 58
  on separation from the community, 167
  on Teshuvah, 205-206
Majestic Man, 41, 47, 222-223, 277
Man, two accounts of creation of, 222-230
Marcus, J. R., 16
Margolies, Rabbi Moses Zebulun, 16
Marx, Karl, 21, 31, 44
Maza, Bernard, 156
Meimad, 88
Mendelssohn, Moses, 5, 6, 9, 11, 60, 70, 247, 295
Mendlowitz, Rabbi Shraga, 68
Mensch-Jissroel, 12, 20, 70
Messianic Age, 21, 91, 92
Metzger, Alter, 32
Midrash, 40
Mill, John Stuart, 169
Mitnagdim, 64
Mizrachi, 66, 86, 108, 143
Modern Orthodoxy, 48, 64, 67, 71, 77, 81-105, 112-115, 121, 267
  and problems of legitimation, 81-86
  and synthesis, 83-84
  and traditionalism, 83-84
  in America, 85-86
  in Israel, 86-88
Modern consciousness, 114
Modernism, 114
  religious, 96-100
Modernity, xi-xii, 3-4, 35-36, 45-50
  and Eastern European Jewry, 22-23
  and morality, 164-165
  and the secularisation of religion, 45-50
  and tradition, 58-59
  discontents of, 97
Mollov, Ben, 104
Monism, 88
Moral community, 171
Moral revolution, 72
Moses, 3, 47, 90, 147, 203-204
Mosse, George L., 17
Moynihan, Daniel, 73
Mussar, 65, 113
Mysticism, 49

Nachman of Bratslav, xi, xix, 278
Nachmanides, xv, 19, 24, 148, 240, 254, 276
Neo-Orthodoxy, 20
Neo-Platonism, xii
Netivot Shalom, 88
Neturei Karta, 126, 143
Neusner, Jacob, 16, 157
Newton, 51
Niebuhr, H. Reinhold, 276
Nietzsche, xii, 36, 44, 45, 94, 276
Nissim, Rabbenu, 271
Noachide commands, 130-131
Nobel, Rabbi Nehemiah, 70
Normalisation, 95, 109
Novak, David, 136
Noveck, Simon, 287

Oakeshott, Michael, 180
Ontological loneliness, 38, 219
Orthodoxy, xviii, 3, 69, 76
  and ideology, 112-125
  in America, 85-86
  in Germany, 6
Otto, Rudolf, 36
Oz ve-Shalom, 88

Particularism, 73
  ethical, 171-173
Peck, A. J., 16
Peli, Pinchas, 51, 270
Philosophy and science, 290-291
Pierce, 36
Pinsker, Leo, 32
Pinto, Rabbi Josiah, 216
Pittsburgh Platform, 31
Plausibility structure, 64
Pleasure, 185
Pluralism, 100, 125, 129-130, 133, 298
  cognitive, xiv, 290-292, 296-297
  epistemological, 49
  ethical, 72, 171-173
  post-modern, 176
  religious, 175
Politics, and halakhah, 126
  and Jewish attitudes, 129-130
Popper, Karl, 233
Post-modernity, 103
Poverty, 183-202
  definition of, 191-194
Prayer, 42
Progress, 99
Prophecy, 42
Prosbol, 188
Providence, Divine, and Holocaust, 142-149
Purim, 154

Rabbinic dress, 63
Rabinovitch, Rabbi Nachum, 216
Rackman, Rabbi Emanuel, xxi, 114-115, 267
Rashbam, xx
Rashi, 226-227, 237
Ravitzky, Aviezer, 51, 290
Rawidowicz, Simon, 52
Redemption, xvi-xviii, 20, 42, 92, 93
Reform Judaism, xii, xvii-xviii, 6, 19, 60, 63, 65, 67, 69, 85, 127, 161
  and homosexuality, 85
  and mixed marriages, 85
Reines, Rabbi Isaac, 66, 86, 108, 123, 128

Relevance, empathetic or redemptive, 220
Religion, and cognition, 297
  and modernity, 4-5
  and science, 43-45
  and the individual in Judaism, 167
  and the state in Judaism, 167
Religious and secular in Israel, 88
Religious domain, 166-168
Religious moderation, 87-88
Religious pluralism, 85, 114-115
Remembering, and Jewish spirituality, 141
Resh Lakish, 204
Resistance to modernity, 63
Resurrection of the dead, 91
Revelation, 35, 92
Rorty, Richard, 55, 297
Rosenak, Michael, 51
Rosenberg, Shalom, 31
Rosenbloom, Noah, 14
Rosenzweig, Bernard, 104
Rosenzweig, Franz, 70, 103, 132, 248, 251, 256, 259-266, 267
  and death, 264-265
  and exile, 262-265
  and German culture, 261-263
  and Teshuvah, 259-265
  and translation, 261-262
Rosh Yeshivah, 65,
  and congregational rabbi, 121
Rosh Hashanah, 212
Roskies, David, 158
Roth, Sol, 126
Royce, 37
Rubinstein, Richard, 146, 149

Saadia Gaon, xiii, 15, 108, 125, 267
Sabbath, 189, 195
Sacred and secular, 29
Safed mysticism, 92
Sage and saint, 48-49
Salanter, Rabbi Israel, 119
Santayana, 37
Saperstein, Marc, 31
Satmar Chassidim, 68-69, 75, 76
Schachter, Rabbi Zvi, 78

Scheler, 297
Schiff, Alvin, 80
Schiller, 36
Schneersohn, Rabbi Menachem Mendel, 68, 211
Scholasticism, 49
Scholem, Gershom, xviii, 15, 52, 91, 103, 244, 247
Schorsch, Ismar, 13
Schwartzschild, Steven, 259
Schweid, Eliezer, 14, 15, 32, 34
Science of Judaism, 6, 8, 10, 16, 28, 295
Scientific and religious truth, 233-234
Scruton, Roger, 115, 180
Secession, Orthodox, 20, 23, 66, 108, 116, 124
Secular and religious, 231-234
Secular city, 75
Secular culture, 69
Secular study, 60, 86
Secularisation, 4-5, 58, 67, 102-103
Secularism, 130
Segregation, 111, 133
Self, the Jewish, 221-244
the modern, 98
Sexual ethics, 169-170
Shabbetai Zevi, xvi
Shauli-Bick, A., 51
She'erit ha-peletah, 66
Shelilat ha-golah, 109
Sheppard, David, xxii
Shils, Edward, 78, 107
Shneour Zalman, Rabbi, of Liadi, 234, 271, 277
Shokeid, Moshe, 104
Shtetl, 75
Silber, Michael, 79
Silver, Abba Hillel, 177
Silver, D. J., 160
Sin and alienation, 237-238
Singer, David, 51, 82
Singer, Michael, 31
Skinner, Quentin, 125
Slavery, 190
Socialism, 109, 130

Sofer, Rabbi Abraham, 116
Sofer, Rabbi Moses, xviii, xxi, 3, 60-66, 113-114, 116, 128
Sofer, Rabbi Shimon, 117
Sokol, Moshe, 51
Soloveitchik, Rabbi Chaim, 36, 39, 269, 273
Soloveitchik, Rabbi Joseph, xiv, xviii-xxi, 3, 31, 35-55, 57, 69, 103, 107, 112, 122, 124-125, 215-216, 221-244, 267-301
and conflict, 277-279, 288-289
and dialogue, 162
autobiography and theology, 36-39
Halakhic Man, xx, 36-37, 39, 46, 48, 267-285, 287-290, 294
The Halakhic Mind, xii, 36, 70, 287-301
The Lonely Man of Faith, xix-xx, 35, 38, 40-50, 124, 221-244, 298
on *brit goral*, 110, 154
on philosophy and halakhah, 269-271
on religion and science, 43-45
Soloveitchik, Rabbi Joseph Baer, 36
Soloveitchik, Rabbi Mosheh, 36
Sosevsky, Morris, 51
Spanish inquisition, 92
Speech, 42
Spiegel, Shalom, 158
Spinoza, xi, 21, 44, 239
Spranger, Eduard, 36
Status quo communities, 66
Steinberg, Milton, 217
Steiner, George, 94
Steinheim, Salomon, 6
Steinsaltz, Adin, 283
Stout, Jeffrey, 105
Strike, right to, 190-191
Strikowski, A., 51
Subjectivism, 292-293
Subjectivity, 230-231
Suffering, 140
Synagogue customs, 63
Synagogue, and rabbinate, 120-121

Synthesis, 10-11, 39, 71, 86, 100-101, 107, 109, 122, 131-133
  in the thought of R. Kook, 28-29

Taharat ha-mishpachah, 102
Tanya, 234
Teitelbaum, Rabbi Joel, 68
  and Holocaust, 142-143, 149
Tertullian, 36
Teshuvah, 73, 203-218
  in the thought of Rosenzweig, 259-265
  in the thought of Soloveitchik, 275-276
Theology, liberal, 100
Tikkun olam, 127-133
Time, Jewish attitudes to, 90-93
Tolstoy, 51
Torah study, and work, 189
Torah im derekh eretz, xix, 10-11, 60-64, 89, 108, 116-118, 122-127, 134
  as temporary concession, 117-118
Trade Unions, 191
Tradition and secularisation, 58-64
Traditionalism, 95, 97, 99, 121
Trilling, Lionel, 53
Tzaddik, 64

Universalism, 111, 130, 172, 174-175
Unterman, Rabbi Isser Yehudah, 87

Vaihinger, 37
Vilna Gaon, 64, 276
Volozhyn, 22, 23
  yeshivah, 65, 113
  Rabbi Chayyim of, 274, 277

Warhaftig, S., 201
Warnock, G. J., 180
Warnock, Mary, 130
Waxman, Chaim, 104
'Ways of the Gentiles', 61
Wealth and poverty, 183-202
Weber, Max, 263
Weiler, Gershon, 126

Weinberg, Rabbi Yechiel, 117, 119, 121
Weiss, Raymond, 54
Welfare, 170
Wellhausen, xii
Wessely, Naftali Hartwig, 10, 60
Wiesel, Elie, 153, 278
Williams, Raymond, 78
Wilson, Bryan, 179
Wittgenstein, 89, 264, 295
Woocher, Jonathan, 55
Work, 188-189
World to come, 91
Wurzburger, Walter, 51, 104
Wyschogrod, Michael, xiv, 133, 159, 172, 267

Yaron, Zvi, 32
Yehoshua, A. B., 94, 144
Yerushalmi, Yosef Hayyim, 91, 141
Yeshiva University, 16, 82, 269, 296
Yeshivah, 65, 68, 74, 81, 121-123, 127, 166, 211
Yetser, 211
Yiddish culturalism, xii
Yiddish language, 61, 62
Yom Ha-Atzmaut, 87
Yom Ha-Shoah, 153
Yom Kippur, 203, 205
Yom Kippur War, 89, 95, 109

Zborowski, Mark, 32
Zeitlin, Irving, 54
Zevin, Rabbi Shlomo Yosef, 51, 87
Zionism, and holocaust, 142-145
Zionism, religious, xix, 20-22, 67, 71, 87, 93, 108, 109, 126-129, 132, 134
  and R. Kook, 24-26
  current crisis, 128
Zionism, secular, xii, xvii-xviii, 21-22, 25, 67, 95, 109
Zohar, 219, 238
Zohar, Zvi, 51